Literature and Transformation

Literature and Transformation
A Narrative Study of Life-Changing Reading Experiences

Thor Magnus Tangerås

ANTHEM PRESS

Anthem Press
An imprint of Wimbledon Publishing Company
www.anthempress.com

This edition first published in UK and USA 2022
by ANTHEM PRESS
75–76 Blackfriars Road, London SE1 8HA, UK
or PO Box 9779, London SW19 7ZG, UK
and
244 Madison Ave #116, New York, NY 10016, USA

First published in the UK and USA by Anthem Press in 2020

Copyright © Thor Magnus Tangerås 2022

The author asserts the moral right to be identified as the author of this work.

All rights reserved. Without limiting the rights under copyright reserved above,
no part of this publication may be reproduced, stored or introduced into
a retrieval system, or transmitted, in any form or by any means
(electronic, mechanical, photocopying, recording or otherwise),
without the prior written permission of both the copyright
owner and the above publisher of this book.

British Library Cataloguing-in-Publication Data
A catalogue record for this book is available from the British Library.

Library of Congress Control Number: 2019955671

ISBN-13: 978-1-83998-539-3 (Pbk)
ISBN-10: 1-83998-539-9 (Pbk)

This title is also available as an e-book.

CONTENTS

Preface   vii

Acknowledgements   xi

Chapter One	Introduction	1
	Transformative Reading Experiences	1
	Presuppositions: Change, Crisis, Being Moved	10
Chapter Two	Intimate Reading: A Narrative Method	17
	The Anteroductive Logic of Inquiry	17
	Reliability and Validity	19
	Research Design Overview	21
	Sampling in Interview-Based Qualitative Research	21
	Recruitment Strategy	22
	Interview Method	25
	Presentation of Narratives	30
	Philology and the Manuscript Matrix	30
	Critical Selection of Narratives for Interpretation	31
	The Construct of Life-changing Fiction Reading Experience	33
	Analysis of Narrative Structure	34
	Idiographic Interpretations of the Narratives	35
Chapter Three	Veronica's Bruise	37
	Listening to the Heart	51
Chapter Four	Nina's Life-Long Friend Flicka	67
	The Nostos of MySpace	83
Chapter Five	Esther's Episode	101
	From Discord to Concord	114

Chapter Six	Jane's Visionary Reading	131
	The Big Bang and the View from Above	145
Chapter Seven	Sue's Buried Life	161
	Re-membering the Body's Song	173
Chapter Eight	Reading by Heart: Lexithymia and Transformative Affective Patterns	191
	Mode of Engagement	192
	Realisation through the Experience of Being Moved	198
	Alloiosis: Qualitative Change from Crisis to Resolution	202
	Complex Affective Configurations	203
	Art for Heart's Sake	207
Bibliography		209
Index		219

PREFACE

A few years ago I came across an article by the science fiction author Nicola Griffith, in which she wrote about the responses she had had from her readers. Her books, it turned out, had changed people's lives, helping them to accept their own identity and situation:

> A woman in Australia, married with two children, read *Ammonite* and wrote me a letter to tell me that my novel had shown her what the empty space inside her meant: she was a lesbian. At a bookstore reading in the South, a man told me *Slow River* had made his job bearable during a truly awful period in his life. A woman in the Midwest approached me at a convention: No, she didn't want to chat, but she thought I ought to know that *Ammonite* had literally saved her life: she had been planning to kill herself but instead, for six months, read the book cover to cover, over and over, endlessly, immersing herself in a world of women until she knew it was okay to be a woman, to stay alive and become herself.[1]

Shortly thereafter, an author I know told me of a reader who had contacted him to say that his novel had given him the courage to go on with his life when everything was black. About this time I also discovered David Shield's intriguingly titled memoir, *How Literature Saved My Life*. The serendipitous confluence of these events impressed themselves upon me. I myself had previously experienced the transformative power of the written word: in my late teens I felt 'like some watcher of the skies, when a new planet swims into his ken' as I discovered the hitherto hidden continent of poetry. Later on, as a literary scholar I would come to feel that there was something missing from, or taken for granted in, literary studies: the question of literature's importance and meaning in our troubled lives. It was as if the wonder and deep engagements with literary works was deemed self-explanatory or, even, an affective fallacy, something to be set aside in order to move onto the 'important' stuff: explication, judgement, criticism.

However, many avid readers find sustenance and meaning in literature, which is why we are drawn to it in the first place. As William Nicholson once said, 'we read to know we are not alone.' And so I decided to find out more about the role of literature in readers' lives. In a time in which there is purportedly a 'crisis in the humanities',[2] a time in which the importance of the classics is dwindling and people read fewer books, I believe it is

---

[1] http://www.lambdaliterary.org/memo/03/31/books-change-lives-sometimes-books-save-lives-queer-books-save-queer-lives/.
[2] For a discussion of this crisis, see Philip Davis, *Reading and the Reader* (Oxford: Oxford University Press, 2013), vii.

incumbent upon literary scholars to address this exigency; to illuminate the vital link between imaginative literature and the soul's needs, not by offering yet another *apologia*, but by empirically investigating the meaning of literature in readers' lives.

The experience of the work of art, argues the influential literary scholar Rita Felski, 'is not just a matter of conveying information, but also of experiencing transformation'.[3] 'If you are listening to what people are saying', proposes Felski, 'they will explain at length how and why they are deeply attached, moved, affected by the works of art which make them feel things'. And then she asks: 'What would it mean to do justice to these responses rather than treating them as naïve, rudimentary or defective?'[4] The purpose of this work is precisely to replace Felski's *if* by *when*, in order to turn her conditional *would* into a definite *does*: in other words, to do justice to people's responses by *listening* to them relating *at length* how they are *moved, affected and changed* by works of literature. I wish to find out how reading imaginative literature may be experienced as life-changing, and what such experiences can tell us about the value of literature and reading. Such a method of inquiry requires careful elaboration. In the chapters that follow, I will first look into what previous research can tell us about transformative reading experiences, as well as psychological studies of narratives of life-change. Thereafter, I will explicate the procedures and justifications of a method that I call Intimate Reading. The method attempts to present a clear rationale for how to approach interviews, how to transcribe and edit narratives, how to critically select narratives for interpretation and how to interpret them. In recent years, narrative methods of qualitative inquiry have flourished.[5] The concept of narrative, however, is elusive, indeterminate and contested. It is 'variously used as an epistemology, a methodological perspective, an antidote to positivist research, a communication mode, a supra-genre, a text-type'.[6] As such, it is necessary to clarify methodological and procedural problems related to such inquiry.

The main body of this book is the presentation in detail of five dialogic narratives of life-changing experiences, and my subsequent interpretations of these. The first narrative presents Veronica's experience of reading D. H. Lawrence's *Lady Chatterley's Lover*. My interpretation addresses four main issues: the nature of Veronica's crisis prior to and during the reading experience, her account of her process of transaction with the novel, her interpretation of the kind of change she has undergone and what role she ascribes to *Lady Chatterley's Lover* in the configuration of her story. I will argue that Veronica's *problem*, that of finding the strength to escape from the entrapment of a confining relationship, only masks a deeper crisis: an emotional bruise that can no longer be held at bay by avoiding contact with her underlying emotions. An essential element of her mode of

---

[3] Rita Felski, 'Context Stinks!', *New Literary History* 42, no. 4 (2011): 573–91: 575.
[4] Ibid., 585.
[5] Represented by, for instance, Barbara Czarniawska, *Narratives in Social Science Research* (London: Sage, 2006); D. Jean Clandinin, *Handbook of Narrative Inquiry: Mapping a Methodology* (London: Sage, 2007); Jaber F. Gubrium and James A. Holstein, *Analysing Narrative Reality* (London: Sage, 2009).
[6] Quoted in Catherine Kohler Riessman, *Narrative Methods for the Human Sciences* (Los Angeles, CA: Sage, 2008), 183.

engagement with the novel is the visceral and a bodily form of knowing. What appears to be a rather straightforward case of deciding to take action, may only be a surface manifestation of a deeper change having taken place: Veronica learns to 'listen to the heart'. The meaning of her story must be understood in relation to her serendipitous discovery of the book, and how the reading experience opens up for another transformative experience many years later, when reading *The Winter's Tale*. The latter enables her to heal her bruise, by metaphorically 'bringing her mother back to life'.

The second narrative is the only one to thematise an accumulative experience of rereading. Nina has returned to Mary O'Hara's novel *My Friend Flicka* time and again in the course of her life. It has been a companion for 40 years, 'making unbearable times bearable'. Central to Nina's life is the 'great struggle' to find her 'own place in the world', and 'the enormous process of turning things around' in order to achieve this. Like Ken's story, 'a coming-of-age story, about arriving at something, about overcoming something', Nina's is a story of a quest: to overcome, by healing the split in her psyche, and to arrive at a point where she can express herself in an authentic and creative manner. In my interpretation I look at the nature of Nina's crisis, showing how it can best be understood as an inner exile, an identity crisis made up of four distinct stages: foreclosure, diffusion, moratorium and achievement. These correspond to the various life-phases she recounts: conversion and apostasy, the 'terribly frightening rootless years', being 'confronted with herself' and subsequently having to withdraw from the world for years, before finally realising that she is a musician. I understand her protracted crisis of diffusion to be due to her experience of poor self-esteem and unattainable ideals for herself. Only by a gradual process of transmuting internalisation, in which the repeated readings of *Flicka* is essential to her self-restoration, does she achieve identity. This deepening attunement to the work through repeated readings I propose to call *palilexia*.

The third narrative is that of Esther's encounter with Norwegian poet Inger Hagerup's *Episode*. Esther's experience of her parents' troubled marriage was severe enough to make her suffer an internal conflict constituting a crisis. I interpret her reading experience in terms of a metamorphosis: just as the visage of the poems' character is transformed, so is her view of her parents. This recognition of the underlying truth about her parents' union is a special kind of *anagnorisis:* it is deeply affective and strikes Esther as a sudden revelation. Through a process of catharsis her confusion and despair is dispelled, allowing her to achieve a sense of inner reconciliation with her parents. The transformative reading experience motivates her quest to learn the language of emotions. This search takes the shape of a 'voyage and return', in which Esther looks for a way of helping people recognise the truth of their relationships. When she eventually discovers it in the form of Emotion-Focused Couples' Therapy, with its focus on the subtext of vulnerability, it also marks the return to *Episode*. The life-long return to, and development of, the transformative affective images and patterns embedded in the poem is reflected in her work as a therapist. The poem and the experience of reading it is still alive and active, lending a profound meaning to Esther's remark that she 'learned the poem by heart'.

The fourth narrative concerns Jane's reading of Doris Lessing's *Shikasta*. Her reading experience begins before she opens the book, and goes on for many years after she closes it. It has 'shaped her life' and is both the centre and the circumference of her redemptive life story. Jane's story fits neatly into McAdams's study of generative adults: those who begin life by being a special child, experience adversity before turning things around and gradually find a way to give of themselves to a larger community. At the right time, in a moment of *kairos*, Jane encounters *Shikasta*. She loves and trusts Lessing, yet she is shocked by the truth the book reveals. I interpret this 'Big Bang' as a special kind of sublime experience. In her deeply affective and contemplative reading of *Shikasta*, Jane seems to enact a *metabolic* mode of engagement, marked by slow digestion and an immediate turn from one framework to another. This brings about a *metanoia*, a change of mind and heart. She spends many years accommodating the Big Bang, before she finally discovers her vocation: Shared Reading.

The final narrative presented is about Sue's discovery of the vitality of poetry through her encounter with Matthew Arnold's *The Buried Life*. In his phenomenological investigation of subjective experience that leads to change, Daniel Stern suggests that conscious present moments be divided into three different kinds. The first kind is the regular, ordinary present moment. Secondly, there is the *now moment*. This is a present moment that 'suddenly pops up and is highly charged with immediately impending consequences'.[7] Thirdly, there is a *moment of meeting* 'in which the two parties achieve an intersubjective meeting and each becomes aware of the other's experiencing. They share a sufficiently similar mental landscape so that a sense of 'specific fittedness' is achieved.'[8] These moments of meeting usually follow immediately upon *now moments*, and, argues Stern, constitute 'the key moments of change in psychotherapy'.[9] My interpretation revolves around several such moments of meeting: Sue and *The Buried Life*; Sue and I in dialogue; my own reading of the poem; and my understanding of her story. I seek to understand the nature of her affective realisation, how being lifted up in the encounter with the poem can effect a re-membering of a forgotten part of the lived body. I argue that Sue's mode of engagement with the poem can be understood as an interaffective attunement that opens up contact with a deep source of vitality.

In the final chapter, I attempt to circle in a specific mode of engagement with literary works manifested in all these experiences, which I call 'reading by heart'. I discuss how the experience of being moved may be a vital part of affective transformation, and the relations between such experiences and the resolution of life-crises.

---

[7] Daniel N. Stern, *The Present Moment in Psychotherapy and Everyday Life* (New York: W.W. Norton, 2004), 151.

[8] Ibid. Stern's basic assumption is that 'change is based on lived experience. In and of itself, verbally understanding, explaining or narrating something is not sufficient to bring about change. There must also be an actual experience, a subjectively lived happening' (xiii). I concur with his view.

[9] Ibid., xi.

ACKNOWLEDGEMENTS

When I first set out to investigate transformative reading experiences, I could not possibly envisage how rewarding this undertaking would prove to be. I am grateful for all that I have learned, and to all those who have helped me along the way. I wish to thank my editor at Anthem Press, Megan Grieving, for having great faith in this project, and the production team led by Kanimozhi Ramamurthy for invaluable help in bringing the book through to its completion. I am greatly indebted to Professor Philip Davis, who has read various versions of this manuscript and kindly encouraged me throughout, ever since inviting me to spend an invaluable six months as a guest researcher at the University of Liverpool. My heartfelt thanks also to Dr Jane Davis, founder and Director of the Reader for warmly welcoming me into the wondrous world of Shared Reading. I thank my wife and family for their unflagging support during the entire journey.

Finally, and above all, I would like to express my deepest gratitude to each and every participant in this inquiry, who generously gave of their time and courageously shared their life-changing experiences. In sharing them, you have also changed me. *Hjertelig takk*.

Chapter One

INTRODUCTION

Transformative Reading Experiences

In her autobiography *Why Be Happy When You Could Be Normal?* Jeanette Winterson writes:

> I had no one to help me, but the T. S. Eliot book helped me. So when people say that poetry is a luxury, or an option, or for the educated middle classes, or that it shouldn't be read at school because it's irrelevant, or any of the strange and stupid things that are said about poetry and its place in our lives, I suspect that the people doing the saying have had things pretty easy. A tough life needs a tough language – and that is what poetry is. That is what literature offers – a language powerful enough to say how it is.[1]

Winterson regards poetry as a medicine for the soul: 'Fiction and poetry are doses, medicines. What they heal is the rupture reality makes on the imagination.'[2] This is of course an ancient idea. In *The Therapy of Desire* the philosopher Martha Nussbaum writes:

> From Homer on we encounter, frequently and prominently, the idea that *logos* is to illnesses of the soul as medical treatment is to illnesses of the body. We also find the claim that *logos* is a powerful and perhaps even a sufficient remedy for these illnesses; frequently it is portrayed as the only available remedy. The diseases in question are frequently diseases of inappropriate or misinformed emotion. […] *logos* is being said to play a real healing role, and to heal through its complicated relationship to the intellect and the emotions.[3]

The interest in *Logos* as the medicine for the soul has seen a great revival in recent years with the emergence of various forms of bibliotherapy. 'Over half of English

---

[1] Jeanette Winterson, *Why Be Happy When You Could Be Normal?* (London: Vintage, 2011), 40. Reading helped her feel belonging, gave her access to new experiences and helped her deal with hardship: 'I felt less isolated. I wasn't floating on my little raft in the present; there were bridges that led over to solid ground […] Literature is common ground.' Rachel Kelly, in her book *Black Rainbow: How Words Healed Me – My Journey through Depression* (London: Yellow Kite Books, 2014), relates how reading poetry helped her conquer two serious episodes of depression: 'It's no exaggeration to say that poetry proved a lifeline.' She drew strength from the ability of Gerard Manley Hopkins to celebrate the healing powers of nature, and George Herbert's *Love*, which functioned as an antidote to the negative stories that dominated her mind at the time.
[2] Winterson, *Why Be Happy When You Could Be Normal?*, 40.
[3] Martha Nussbaum, *The Therapy of Desire: Theory and Practice in Hellenistic Ethics* (Princeton, NJ: Princeton University Press, 1994), 49.

library authorities are operating some form of bibliotherapy intervention,' according to a study cited in the *Guardian*.[4] Bibliotherapy includes not just fiction, however, and some forms have an instrumental rather than aesthetic orientation. And yet there are ways of mediating literature in which it is the very attention to the aesthetic dimension that brings about medicine for the soul. One programme of organised reading of imaginative literature, in which the emphasis is on the shared enjoyment of aesthetic experience and where therapeutic benefits in the form of increased mental well-being come as secondary gains, is the research-based community-intervention programme Shared Reading, a project initiated by the Reader Organisation in cooperation with the University of Liverpool.[5]

The issue of how literature affects our personal lives has often been bypassed in literary studies, which, while tacitly adumbrating the primacy of this deep engagement, remains parasitic upon it. Several of the major philosophers of hermeneutics and aesthetics explicitly assert the potential of literature to change the reader's life or personality, marking it out as the aim of reading and the ontological legitimation of art. In *Truth and Method*, Gadamer writes: 'The work of art is not an object that stands over against a subject for itself. Instead the work of art has its true being in the fact that it becomes *an experience that changes the person* who experiences it.'[6] Transformative reading is what testifies to the truth of art: 'In the experience of art we see a genuine experience induced by the work, *which does not leave him who has it unchanged.*'[7] Paul Ricoeur maintains that fiction is as important for self-understanding as history: 'Self-understanding [is] mediated by the conjoint reception – particularly through reading – of historical and fictional narratives. Knowing oneself is interpreting oneself under the double guidance of historical and fictional narrative.'[8] Self-understanding is achieved via the appropriation of the truth of narratives. Moreover, the transformative power of fiction is what gives it its virtue: 'The figuration of the self through the mediation of the other may be a genuine means of self-discovery [...]. Self-construction might be a way of becoming what one really is [...]. The fictive model has a revelatory virtue only insofar as it has a power of transformation.'[9] Jan Mukarovsky, one of the most influential theorists in establishing Literary studies as a science, also highlights the transformative effects of art:

---

[4] http://www.theguardian.com/books/2008/jan/05/fiction.scienceandnature. Accessed 6 January 2016.
[5] The mission statement of The Reader Organisation reads: 'We bring people and great literature together. Our primary way of doing this is through our shared reading model, bringing people together in weekly groups to listen to poems and stories read aloud. Thoughts and experiences are shared; personal and social connections are made.' http://www.thereader.org.uk/what-we-do-and-why.aspx. As part of the preparations for this dissertation I volunteered for The Reader Organisation and completed their training programme 'Read to Lead'.
[6] Hans Georg Gadamer, *Truth and Method*, 2nd edn, trans. Joel Weinsheimer and Donald G. Marshall (New York: Continuum, 2003), 103. (My emphasis.)
[7] Ibid., 86. (My emphasis.)
[8] Paul Ricoeur, *Philosophical Anthropology*, trans. David Pellauer (Malden, MA: Polity, 2016), 229.
[9] Ibid., 241.

The work becomes capable of being closely connected to the entirely personal experiences, images and feelings of any perceiver – capable of affecting not only his conscious mental life but even of setting into motion forces which govern his subconscious. The perceiver's entire personal relation to reality, whether active or contemplative, will henceforth be changed to a greater or lesser degree by this influence. Hence the work of art has such powerful effect upon man not because it gives him – as the common formula goes – an impression of the author's personality, his experience and so forth, but because it influences the perceiver's personality, his experiences and so forth.[10]

The work, because it is so intimately connected to our personal experience, can affect us so deeply that it changes us by influencing our personality and worldview. What these thinkers reiterate is the *potential* for transformative reading. Yet it is a phenomenon curiously under-researched, even in reader-response studies, although Louise Rosenblatt postulates the occurrence of life-changing reading experiences:

> The reading of a book, it is true, has sometimes changed a person's entire life. When that occurs, the book has undoubtedly come as a culminating experience that crystallises a long, subconscious development. In such cases the book usually opens up a new view of life or a new sense of the potentialities of human nature and thus resolves some profound need or struggle.[11]

Reader-response criticism regards the interaction between reader and text as central, and reading is conceived as a personal event at a certain time in a certain context.[12] Whereas traditional reader-response theory did not address actual readers, but dealt with the concept of the ideal reader (Iser) and the model reader (Eco), Janice Radway underlined that reception studies should look at the experiences of real readers, and their encounters with works of literature. Louise Rosenblatt, one of the most influential proponents of reader-response approaches to literary studies, argued that literature must be understood in its living context. 'Transaction' was the term she chose to designate 'a two-way process involving a reader and a text at a particular time under particular circumstances'.[13] Rosenblatt differentiates between two modes of engagement in reading: the efferent and the aesthetic. In the efferent mode 'attention focuses on what is to be carried away at the end of the reading'. When the aesthetic attitude predominates, 'attention will shift inward, will center on what is actually being created *during* the actual reading. [...] Out

---

[10] Jan Mukarovsky, *Structure, Sign and Function*. Trans. John Burbank and Peter Steiner (New Haven, CT: Yale University Press, 1977), 106–107.
[11] Louise M. Rosenblatt, *Literature as Exploration*, 5th edn (New York: Modern Language Association of America, 1995), 188.
[12] For a discussion of five different types of Reader Response theories, see: Lois Tyson, *Critical Theory Today: A User Friendly Guide* (New York: Routledge, 2006).
[13] Louise M. Rosenblatt, 'The Literary Transaction: Evocation and Response', *Theory into Practice* 21, no. 1 (1982): 268. For a psychoanalytic approach to individual reading experiences, see Norman Holland's well-known study *5 Readers Reading* (New Haven, CT: Yale University Press, 1975).

of these ideas and feelings, a new experience, the story or poem, is shaped and lived through.'[14] The positive transformative effects Rosenblatt enlists as the aim of literary education rest upon the aesthetic mode of engagement. By 'living through' the work, the reader can achieve insight and emotional liberation.

In a seminal work in reception studies, Hans Robert Jauss argues that all aesthetic enjoyment is the result of a meeting between reader and work.[15] Although he uses the term 'interaction' and emphasises the historical horizon of expectation in which the reader is embedded, his concept is similar to Rosenblatt's 'transaction' in that he seeks to differentiate progressive from regressive encounters between reader and work. 'Self-enjoyment in the enjoyment of something other' is the formulation Jauss has chosen to designate the balance needed for the interaction to be progressive. It is a 'pendulum movement in which the self enjoys not only its real object, the aesthetic object, but also its correlate, the equally irrealised subject which has been released from its always already given reality'.[16] He identifies five interaction modes which are predicated upon identification with the hero. In the admiring mode of identification with the perfect hero, the progressive form is characterised by emulation and exemplariness; the negative by entertainment by the extraordinary and a need for escape. In the sympathetic mode of identification with the imperfect hero, the progressive is marked by compassion as the result of moral interest, solidarity and readiness to act, whereas sentimentality (enjoyment of pain) and self-confirmation leads to regression. In the cathartic mode of identification with the suffering hero of tragic works the progressive response takes the form of disinterestedness and free reflection; whereas the progressive response to the beset hero of comedy is marked by sympathetic laughter and free moral judgement. The regressive responses to this mode are marked by bewitched fascination and mockery, respectively. In the ironic mode of identification with the anti-hero, there is either progression in the form of creative response and refinement of perception, or there is regressive boredom and solipsism. Each of these patterns allows for a progressive or a regressive attitude. An important caveat made by Jauss is that 'this model is provisional and has the specific weakness of lacking the foundation that a theory of emotions would give it'.[17] Although several theories of emotion have been developed in the years since Jauss offered his model, I do not know of any attempts to apply such theories to an expansion of his model.

A central idea in the theories of Rosenblatt and Jauss is the reciprocity of text-interpretation and self-interpretation. This reciprocity, however, may be of either a

---

[14] Rosenblatt, 'The Literary Transaction: Evocation and Response', 269.
[15] Hans Robert Jauss, *Aesthetic Experience and Literary Hermeneutics: Theory and History of Literature*, vol. 3, trans. Michael Shaw (Minneapolis: University of Minnesota Press, 1982). Rita Felski has also theorised about different forms of interaction between reader and work: Rita Felski, *Uses of Literature* (Malden, MA: Blackwell, 2009). In this neo-phenomenologically inspired work Felski criticises post-structuralist approaches to literature, seeking to ground reading in experiential terms. She lists four main types of interaction: recognition, knowledge, immersion and shock.
[16] Jauss, *Aesthetic Experience*, 32.
[17] Ibid., 158.

virtuous/progressive/self-modificatory or vicious/regressive/self-absorbed kind. The former marks the potentiality for transformative reading experiences. However, it is necessary to investigate actual occurrences. As David Miall concedes, 'reading is potentially capable of transforming the self, although the extent to which it actually does so will depend upon the concerns that emerge from the reader's prior experience, or [...] the extent to which the reader's imagination is seized by the text'.[18]

Expressive Enactment and Self-Modifying Feelings

In his close, personal, readings of works that have influenced him, Philip Davis embellishes on what is at stake in such progressive modes of reading:

> For despite the undeniable risk that the personal may be the place of utmost falsification, I know that anything I really think and believe is registered most deeply when it is registered at the personal level. Some other levels are safer, but none in the state of present society is more finally testing. I am not suggesting that you read simply in order 'to find your self' – the self, in that sense, is all too often and too consciously an egoistic fabrication. I am talking about taking books personally to such a depth inside, that you no longer have a merely secure idea of self and relevance to self, but a deeper exploratory sense of a reality somehow finding unexpected relations and echoes in you.[19]

Davis's description bears similarities with the empirical findings made by Kuiken et al. in a series of phenomenologically inspired experiments. They identify a mode of engagement they call 'expressive enactment'. Such enactment is marked precisely by a self-modificatory pendulum movement as opposed to a self-absorbed mode of interaction. Their empirical work has the advantage of affording greater analytic precision than the vague term 'identification' allows for. Kuiken et al. aim to 'reawaken interest in the notion of aesthetic experience'[20] and to investigate empirically 'the transformative potential of literary reading'.[21] They argue that other reader-response approaches have failed to take into account how the reader's sense of self influences and is being affected by reading. The basic premise for their approach to empirical reading studies is that literary texts afford a different mode of understanding than that offered by non-literary texts: 'We read literary texts because they enable us to reflect on our feelings and concerns, clarify what they are, and reconfigure them within an altered understanding of our own and other's lives.'[22] Through combining experimental studies and numerically aided

---

[18] David Miall, 'Beyond the Schema Given: Affective Comprehension of Literary Narratives', *Cognition and Emotion* 3, no. 1 (1988): 55–78. Doi: 10.1080/02699938908415236.
[19] Philip Davis, *The Experience of Reading* (London: Routledge, 1992), xvi.
[20] Don Kuiken, David S. Miall and Shelley Sikora, 'Forms of Self-Implication in Literary Reading', *Poetics Today* 25, no. 2 (2004): 198.
[21] Ibid., 173.
[22] Shelley Sikora, Don Kuiken and David S. Miall, 'Expressive Reading: A Phenomenological Study of Readers' Experience of Coleridge's *The Rime of the Ancient Mariner*', *Psychology of Aesthetics, Creativity, and the Arts* 5, no. 3 (2011): 258.

phenomenology, Kuiken et al. have identified what they call 'expressive enactment', 'a form of reading that penetrates and alters a reader's understanding of everyday life' and 'modifies feeling, and reshapes the self'.[23] The think-aloud and self-probed retrospection approach, in which readers mark striking passages when reading and subsequently comment upon them, is designed to 'capture the temporally unfolding *experience* of a text rather than its consummating *interpretation*'.[24] They argue that such 'expressive reading' constitutes a distinct and particular level of feeling in relation to literary reading. These self-modifying feelings 'restructure the reader's understanding of the textual narrative and, simultaneously, the reader's sense of self'.[25] The dynamics of feeling response in this domain is such that 'aesthetic and narrative feelings interact to produce metaphors of personal identification that modify self-understanding'.[26] According to the authors, it is within this fourth domain that 'we can locate what is distinctive to literary response'.[27] In several studies they have attempted to determine the distinctive characteristics of this form of self-implicating reading and the affective response that literary texts invite from readers. Not all readers engage in this form of reading; in fact only a minority do so. They found that nine out of forty readers manifested commentaries that reflected expressive enactment.[28]

They have found two different factors that dispose readers towards expressive enactment. The first factor is a personality trait named 'absorption'.[29] Readers who score highly on this trait are 'more likely to report affective theme variations and self-perceptual shifts'.[30] The second factor, coming to light in an experimental study where expressive enactment occurred frequently among readers who had suffered a significant loss, was the impact of personal crisis.[31] We do not know exactly how these two factors co-operate. However, we may reasonably conjecture that both are necessary if the transformative reading experience is to have lasting effect in the life of the reader and become an integrative part of their self-concept. Kuiken and Miall consider that this approach to reading may be 'more deeply tied to particular life circumstances than theoretical discussions of historically relative and institutionalized reading practices would allow', and raise the following question of utmost relevance to an inquiry into life-changing reading experiences: 'What if, for example, expressive enactment […] occurred with greater regularity among individuals who are psychologically predisposed by experiences

---

[23] Kuiken, et al., 'Forms of Self-Implication in Literary Reading', 172.
[24] David S. Miall and Don Kuiken, 'A Feeling for Fiction: Becoming What We Behold', *Poetics* 30, no. 4 (2002): 239.
[25] Ibid., 223.
[26] Ibid., 221.
[27] Ibid., 223.
[28] Kuiken et al., 'Forms of Self-Implication', 194.
[29] T. Cameron Wild, Don Kuiken and Don Schopflocher, 'The Role of Absorption in Experiential Involvement', *Journal of Personality and Social Psychology* 65, no. 3 (1995): 569–79.
[30] Don Kuiken, Leah Phillips, Michelle Gregus, David S. Miall, Mark Verbitsky and Anna Tonkonogy, 'Locating Self-Modifying Feelings within Literary Reading', *Discourse Processes* 38, no. 2 (2004): 267.
[31] Kuiken et al., 'Forms of Self-Implication', 172.

of loss, death, and bereavement?'[32] Without expanding on other types of possible life crises, Kuiken and Miall stipulate that self-modifying reading may be 'dependent upon the opening – or closing – of experiential windows during such seemingly inevitable life crises'.[33]

Kuiken et al. examine two different forms of self-implication, one that functions like simile and one that functions like metaphor. The former is marked by explicitly recognised similarity between personal memories and aspects of text-world in a comparative gesture; the latter is characterised by metaphors of personal identification in a process during which the reader comes to identify asymmetrically with an instance in the text: I am like the character, but the character is not like me. In their example of readers' engagement with a short story by Katherine Mansfield, when the reader finds that 'I am Mrs Bean' this is not equivalent to her saying 'Mrs Bean is me'.[34] Kuiken et al. posit that it is this metaphoric self-implication that constitutes the distinct mode of engagement termed 'expressive enactment'. Regarding one of the readers who participated in a study in which bereaved persons read this poem, Kuiken et al. uncovered three significant aspects of her account. They found that she spoke 'with the characteristic attunement to feeling'; she used the pronouns 'you' and 'we'; and 'she repeatedly returns to a theme in the poem that, through its successive variations, is gradually woven into the imaginative life that accompanies her grief and into her reflections about the loss of her grandfather and father'.[35] The expressive mode of reading is regarded as a 'hybrid mode of engagement' that is attentive to both narrative and stylistic aspects of the text.

Kuiken et al. have related their phenomenological findings to the two central affective concepts in literary history, catharsis and the sublime. Kuiken and Miall propose that the concept of catharsis constitutes one particular form of the more general pattern of 'hybrid engagement' of aesthetic and narrative feelings. They suggest that when a sequence of affective responses constitute a modification of a first feeling by a second, this may be considered a form of catharsis. This is because in Aristotle's theory, they maintain, catharsis modifies inappropriate emotions, and 'fear in the end appears to be modified by pity'; this 'radical qualification of one emotion by another in our rereading of catharsis suggests that Aristotle's tragic catharsis is a special case of a more general process in literary reading'.[36] A cathartic shift may have occurred in several of the readers that took part in their study, 'as earlier feelings are recontextualised by other more inclusive feelings'.[37] In another study, Kuiken et al. discuss 'apex experiential reading moments' in terms of the sublime. They identify a core process involving apex moments that leads to self-alteration. Building on Gendlin's phenomenological concept of felt sense, they delineate a process through which 'an inexpressible felt sense guides reflective

---

[32] Ibid., 194.
[33] Ibid.
[34] Ibid., 184.
[35] Ibid., 191.
[36] Ibid., 234.
[37] Ibid., 237.

explication of the something "more" that the felt sense prescribes', leading to either of two forms of sublime feeling, sublime enthrallment and sublime disquietude.[38] These are characterised in terms of affective bearing and epistemic tone: 'the expressive depth of sublime enthrallment also has the affective bearing of wonder and the epistemic tone of reverence while the expressive depth of sublime disquietude also has the affective bearing of disquietude and the epistemic tone of discord'.[39]

Studies of expressive enactment have not looked at how it may lead to long-lasting self-change. Raymond Mar et al., in their review of empirical research 'on the dynamic interaction between emotion and literature', conclude that 'studies of reading and of emotion tend to examine short-term outcomes; it is time to begin looking at whether profound and long-lasting changes can occur after engagement with meaningful narrative fiction.'[40] Some such studies have been made already.

Catherine Ross, in the context of studying information-seeking and the role that reading for pleasure may serve, conducted interviews with 194 self-declared avid pleasure-readers. The premise behind the study was that 'since meanings are constructed by readers, we must ask the readers about the uses they make of texts in the context of their lives'.[41] What transpired was that the majority of readers reported serendipitous encounters in which a book had made a significant difference to their life. Among the questions put to all informants was the following: 'Has there ever been a book that has helped you or made a difference to your life in one way or another?'[42] Ross found that 'approximately 60 per cent of the readers in the study provided sufficient detail about one or more particular books that it was possible to discern a significant way in which a book had helped in the context of their lives'.[43] What is not clear from the report is how many of these significant reading experiences involved works of fiction. What the study did show, however, was that 'their key feature is that they tell a story that readers can relate to their own lives', says Ross, with the caveat that 'the resemblances between reader's life and the life represented in the text may be discernible only to the reader'.[44] Moreover, 'sometimes the encounter with the significant book

---

[38] Don Kuiken, Paul Campbell and Paul Sopcak, 'The Experiencing Questionnaire: Locating Exceptional Reading Moments', *Scientific Study of Literature* 2, no. 2 (2012): 264.

[39] Ibid., 265.

[40] Raymond A. Mar, Keith Oatley, Maja Djikic and Justin Mullin, 'Emotion and Narrative Fiction: Interactive Influences before, during and after Reading', *Cognition and Emotion* 25, no. 5 (2011): 819.

[41] Catherine Sheldrick Ross, 'Finding without Seeking: The Information Encounter in the Context of Reading for Pleasure', *Information Processing and Management* 35, no. 6 (1999): 783. A seminal study related to the psychological mechanisms involved in reading for pleasure is Victor Nell, *Lost in a Book: The Psychology of Reading for Pleasure* (New Haven, CT: Yale University Press, 1988). One of his findings is that readers can use fiction for affect regulation, by transforming negative affect to positive: fear is turned into a feeling of control, depressiveness to joy, disquiet to tranquility.

[42] Ross, 'Finding without Seeking', 785.

[43] Ibid., 790.

[44] Ibid.

was accidental', and in all cases 'reading was interwoven into the texture of their lives, not separate from it'.[45] Ross subsequently analysed 15 accounts of significant reading experiences, finding:

> The most commonly occurring claim (in one third of all the cases) was that the book had opened up a new perspective, helped its reader see things differently, or offered an enlarged set of possibilities [...] In about a quarter of all cases, readers said books provided models, examples to follow, rules to live by, and sometimes inspiration. [...] In some cases, reading changed the readers' beliefs, attitudes or pictures of the world, which change in turn altered the way readers chose to live their lives after the book was closed.[46]

Ross concludes that the interviews provide evidence that 'when the right match is made between reader and story, readers use the text to create a story about themselves. They read themselves into the story and then read the story into their lives, which then becomes a part of them.'[47]

The phenomenological psychologist Paul F. Colaizzi made the first inquiry into what he terms 'existential change occasioned by reading'.[48] Colaizzi found that the outcome of the reading experience 'is not so much the creation of a new world as of discovering a new way of living one's own world'.[49] The reading does not provide information about the world, but restructures the way the persons relate to themselves and their lifeworld. According to Colaizzi, the transformative reading experience falls into three temporal phases: before the reading commences ('Readiness'), during the act of reading ('revealing power of the book') and the after-effects of the reading ('consequences'). Other studies corroborate the before-during-after structure identified by Colaizzi. The psychologists Swatton and O'Callaghan investigated the significance of healing reading experiences in the life history of their informants. They identified three main elements which correspond to Colaizzi's categories. First, there is a 'context of struggle' that preceded the healing process. Secondly, there is the unfolding of the healing process itself, which was characterised by a personal process that gave the readers insight into choices and possibilities for liberation 'in an exploration and awakening to the experience of healing'.[50] The third stage they found to be a working through of the effects of the reading, in which the book 'has continued to provide inspiration in the participant's lived experience'.[51]

---

[45] Ibid., 787.
[46] Ibid., 793.
[47] Ibid.
[48] Paul F. Colaizzi, 'Psychological Research as the Phenomenologist Views It', in *Existential-Phenomenological Alternatives for Psychology*, ed. Ronald S. Valle and Mark King (Oxford: Oxford University Press, 1978), 57.
[49] Ibid., 60.
[50] Susan Swatton and Jean O'Callaghan, 'The Experience of 'Healing Stories' in the Life Narrative: A Grounded Theory', *Counselling Psychology Quarterly* 12, no. 4 (1999): 427.
[51] Ibid., 413. See also Laura J. Cohen, 'Phenomenology of Therapeutic Reading with Implications for Research and Practice of Bibliotherapy', *Arts in Psychotherapy* 21, no. 1 (1994): 37–44.

Presuppositions: Change, Crisis, Being Moved

Underneath the majority of studies of transformation, whether conceptualised as redemption, quantum changes or epiphanies,[52] runs a common current: William James's seminal inquiry into ordinary people's accounts of transformative religious experiences. In the lectures that make up *Varieties of Religious Experience*, James progressively passes beyond the surface manifestations of the varieties of religious experience to the underlying essence, the core of the spiritual experience itself. When surveying the history of the different narratives of Christianity, he finds a gradual circling in of one particular experience: the crisis of self-surrender and the idea of an immediate spiritual help, experienced by the individual in his forlornness. 'The crisis of self-surrender is the turning-point in two different senses: The critical point around which James's investigation turns, and the point where the life of the individual is transformed from egocentricity to allocentricity, from forlornness to redemption: 'In such a surrender lies the secret of a holy life.'[53] Crisis-surrender-redemption is at the heart of James's phenomenology of transformation and constitutes his narrative of narratives. In the conclusion to his study, James speaks of formulating the *essence* of religious experience, and indicates that this experience may perhaps better be called *transformation* than *conversion*: 'Our ordinary alterations of character, as we pass from one of our aims to another, are not commonly called transformations, because each of them is so rapidly succeeded by another in the reverse direction; but whenever one aim grows so stable as to expel definitively its previous rivals from the individual's life, we tend to speak of the phenomenon, and perhaps to wonder at it, as a "transformation".'[54] A transformation into a stable alteration and unification of character on a higher level is the result of self-surrender. The preceding crisis cuts across the dichotomy of the Healthy minded and the Sick soul. Only when confronted with the inadequacy of any rational approach, or the problem of holding onto problems, can the crisis be fully faced. And only then can the person surrender to a greater force and be redeemed. But this involves the greatest risk: there is no guarantee that when giving oneself over, one will be received by anyone or anything.

Change

In order to understand how persons and personalities change, it is important to conceptualise the different levels at which change might take place. According to the psychologist

---

[52] See Jon E. Skalski and Sam A. Hardy, 'Disintegration, New Consciousness, and Discontinuous Transformation: A Qualitative Investigation of Quantum Change', *Humanistic Psychologist*, 41 (2013): 159–77; William R. Miller and Janet C'de Baca, *Quantum Change: When Epiphanies and Sudden Insights Transform Ordinary Lives* (New York: Guilford Press, 2001); William L. White, 'Transformational Change: A Historical Review', *Journal of Clinical Psychology: In Session* 60, no. 5 (2004): 461; Matthew G. McDonald, 'The Nature of Epiphanic Experience', *Journal of Humanistic Psychology* 48, no. 1 (January 2008): 89–115.
[53] William James, *The Varieties of Religious Experience: A Study in Human Nature*, ed. Martin E. Marty (London: Penguin, 1982), 175.
[54] Ibid., 153.

McAdams, 'a number of scientifically oriented personality researchers and theorists today agree that human individuality can be captured well with respect to three different layers or levels of personality variables.'[55] However, the first level is that of dispositional traits. This is what McAdams refers to as 'the psychology of the stranger'.[56] These traits are both observable and measurable, and is what any stranger that observed you would be able to tell about you.

In their study 'On Being Moved by Art: How Reading Fiction Transforms the Self', Djikic et al. tested the hypothesis that reading fiction can cause significant changes in the experience of one's own personality traits under laboratory conditions. The results showed that the experimental group experienced significantly greater change in self-reported experience of personality traits and that emotion change mediated the effect. The authors emphasise that 'it may not be the sheer presence, but the quality of art-induced emotions – their complexity, range, and intensity – that potentially facilitate the process of trait change'.[57]

The second level of change is that of motivation, or 'characteristic adaptations', those specific features of psychological individuality that 'speak to what people *want* or *value* in life and how they pursue what they want and avoid what they do not want in particular *situations* and *time periods*, and with respect to particular social roles'.[58] This level is organised in terms of two dimensions: approach/avoidance and self (agency) vs other (communion). The third level, which is the one McAdams has focused on in his research on life stories, is that of *meaning*, which he calls 'integrative life narratives': how people make sense of their lives. This level is only loosely tied to behaviour and action. The only way to gain access to this deepest level of people's self is by listening to their story. It is an 'internalized and evolving life story that reconstructs the past and imagines the future to provide a person's life with identity (unity, purpose, meaning)'.[59] I assume that accounts of life-changing experiences will primarily relate to this level.

Conceptualisations of the change process tend to fall into two categories. On the one hand, change is represented as an incremental process by means of exercising willpower, while on the other, change is viewed as a dramatic and discontinuous spontaneous transformation. Between the Road to Recovery and the Road to Damascus, however, there may lie a network of lanes and alleys of change processes. I believe that Aristotle's concept of *alloiosis,* in which *being moved* and *being changed* are connected, may be appropriated to designate this landscape.

'Sensation consists in being moved and acted upon, for it is held to be a species of qualitative change', says Aristotle in *De Anima* (quoted in Todd, p. 3). Robert Todd has

---

[55] Dan P. McAdams, *The Redemptive Self: Stories Americans Live By* (Oxford: Oxford University Press, 2013), 277. Whether the three levels he delineates should be regarded as aspects of personality or different approaches to studying personality is somewhat unclear.
[56] See Dan P. McAdams, *The Art and Science of Personality Development* (New York: Guildford Press, 2016).
[57] Ibid., 28.
[58] McAdams, *The Redemptive Self*, 281.
[59] Ibid., 286.

analysed the different change concepts in Aristotle's philosophy. The generic term for transformation is *metabole*. There are two main kinds of transformation. The first kind comprises *genesis*, 'coming into being', and *phthora*, 'ceasing to be': something that was not, is; something that was, is no longer. The second kind involves different categories of *kinesis*: apart from changes in quantity and place (locomotion), there is alteration, qualitative change: *alloiosis*.[60] The kinesthetic refers then not just to physical movement in space but also to qualitative visceral internal movement, *being moved*. The subjective experience of being moved leads to a qualitative change, *alloiosis*. I propose *alloiosis* as a concept to encompass the different kinds of qualitative changes that deeply moving reading experiences bring about. Implied in such *alloiosis* is an antecedent state, which we may call a crisis.

Crisis

Gerald Caplan understands the term crisis to cover major life stresses, of some duration, which endanger mental health. Such crises disrupt customary modes of behaviour, altering circumstances, plans, emotions and self-concept, and impose a need for psychological work which takes time and great effort. A crisis thereby constitutes a challenge, as the individual must abandon old assumptions and create new meaning.[61] Moos and Schaefer state that crisis theory is 'concerned with how individuals manage major life transitions and crises',[62] and it must address the fundamental questions of why some individuals 'transcend the most profound life crises, whereas others break down after experiencing seemingly minor stressors'; what the adaptive tasks in 'managing varied life transitions' are; whether there be 'common phases or stages through which individuals progress as they negotiate a life crisis'; and how resources affect the 'ultimate psychosocial outcome of a life crisis'.[63] They argue that previous crisis theories have placed more emphasis on the harmful than on the potentially positive influence of life events, and that crises often provide an essential condition for psychological development. Their understanding of crisis is that it represents a disruption of established patterns of personal and social identity:

> Similar to the requirement for physiological homeostasis, individuals have a need for social and psychological equilibrium. When people encounter an event that upsets their characteristic patterns of thought and behavior, they employ habitual problem-solving strategies until a balance is restored. A crisis is a situation that is so novel or major that habitual responses are insufficient; it leads to a state of turbulence typically accompanied by heightened fear, anger, or guilt. Because a person cannot remain in a state of disequilibrium, a crisis is necessarily

---

[60] Robert T. Todd, 'Introduction', in *Themistius: On Aristotle's Physics 5–8. Ancient Commentators on Aristotle*, trans. Robert T. Todd (Bloomsbury: London, 2008), 3.
[61] Gerald Caplan, *An Approach to Community Mental Health* (London: Tavistock, 1961).
[62] Rudolf H. Moos and Jeanne A. Schaefer, 'Life Transitions and Crises: A Conceptual Overview', in *Coping with Life Crises: An Integrated Approach*, ed. Rudolf H. Moos (New York: Plenum, 1986), 9.
[63] Ibid., 4.

self-limited. Even though it may be temporary, some resolution must be found. The new balance may be a healthy adaptation that promotes personal growth or a maladaptive response that foreshadows psychological problems. Thus, a crisis is a transition or turning point that has profound implications for an individual's adaptation and ability to meet future crises.[64]

Central here is the notion of crisis as a turning point or critical juncture. It is interesting that they formulate the crisis as the turning point. A different conception would be that crisis is the antecedent of the turning point, or even that the turning point precipitates crisis. 'Personal growth and an expanded repertoire of coping skills often follow the successful resolution of a crisis. But failure to manage a situation effectively may foreshadow impaired adjustment and problems in handling future transitions and crises.'[65] Thus, in line with the etymology of the word crisis, we may say that it represents a forking path. A psychological crisis is a life event that an individual perceives as stressful to the extent that normal coping mechanisms are insufficient.[66]

In order to manage a situation, the individual must have an adequate cognitive appraisal of the significance of the crisis, and be able to regulate emotions and preserve self-image. Moos and Schafer make an important point: 'An individual is especially receptive to outside influence in a time of flux.'[67] This ties in with the studies finding that *life-crises increases the likelihood of self-altering reading experiences*. Moos and Schafer divide crises into developmental life transitions (from childhood to death and bereavement) and unusual crises (special family stressors, disasters, violence, terrorism, war and imprisonment). Kneisl and Riley distinguish between two kinds of unexpected crises: situational and cultural.[68] In my view, we may operate with three broad kinds of crises: developmental, situational, and existential (inner conflicts related to things such as life purpose, direction and spirituality). A crisis can sometimes be obvious both to others and to the person, other times it can be less apparent but can still lead to dramatic inner changes.

Being Moved

'To receive deep impressions is the foundation of all true mental power,' writes George Eliot in her letters.[69] My supposition is that any transformative reading experience will

---

[64] Ibid., 9.
[65] Ibid., 23.
[66] Various definitions are all consistent with their view. Gerald Caplan, *Prevention of Mental Health Disorders in Children* (New York: Basic Books, 1961), defines it thus: 'People are in a state of crisis when they face an obstacle to important life goals [that is] insurmountable by the use of customary methods of problem-solving'. Richard K. James and Burl E. Gilliland, *Crisis Intervention Strategies* (Pacific Grove, PA: Brook/Cole, 2001) define crisis as 'a perception of an event or situation as an intolerable difficulty that exceeds the person's current resources and coping mechanisms'.
[67] Moos and Schaefer, 'Life Transitions and Crises', 23.
[68] Carol R. Kneisl and E. Riley, 'Crisis Intervention', in *Psychiatric Nursing*, 5th edn, ed. H. Wilson and Carol R. Kneisl (Menlo Park, CA: Addison and Wesley, 1996), 711–31.
[69] George Eliot, *The George Eliot Letters*, vol. 5, ed. Gordon S. Haight (New Haven, CT: Yale University Press, 1955), 55.

have deeply moved the reader. Cova and Deonna argue that *being moved* is a subject in which 'there has been a conspicuous lack of interest on the part of philosophers and psychologists'.[70] Menninghaus et al. concur, pointing out that *being moved* is not established as a well-defined psychological construct, and believe that further research on aesthetic experiences 'might strongly benefit' from doing so.[71] They propose that it is 'a concept that vicariously stand in for' other visceral terms such as *stirred*, *touched* and *gripped*, and 'hence serves as an umbrella term for what we call *the being-moved group*'.[72] Menninghaus et al. provide the following definition:

> Episodes of being moved are intensely felt responses to scenarios that have a particularly strong bearing on attachment-related issues […]. In all these instances, one's own agency and causation by one's own behavior have relatively little importance for the elicitation of feelings of being moved; rather, an (empathic) observer or witness perspective prevails.[73]

A witness situation prevails, and agency is of little importance. Being moved is marked by viscerality (cf. verbs such as 'moved', 'stirred' and 'touched'), low arousal and high intensity, moist eyes, subjective feelings and a process of meaning-making. Although researchers claim that it is a subspecies of emotion, I maintain that *being moved* must be differentiated from the concept of emotion, in which *interestedness*, a tendency towards action, is a constituent part. I propose that being moved and emotion are two fundamental and complimentary affections, belonging to different experiential realms. Thomas Dixon in his historical account has traced the emergence of the psychological concept of *emotion* in the eighteenth century. He argues that it displaced more differentiated typologies (including affection and passions), and it has consequently hampered attempts to explore the vast range of affective states that fall outside its province.[74] His argument critiques the prevailing view held for instance by Robert Solomon in his influential book about emotions. Solomon argues that there has been a negative view of the emotions because of the split between reason and emotion in the rationalistic conceptions of Western thought.[75] Dixon maintains that such a view fails to differentiate between emotions on the one hand, and passions and affections on the other, and that it was the departure from the older differentiation that lead to the reason-emotion dichotomy.

---

[70] Florian Cova and Julien A. Deonna, 'Being Moved', *Philos Stud* 169 (2013): 448. I will discuss the phenomenon of being moved in my literature review.
[71] Winfried Menninghaus, Valentin Wagner, Julian Hanich, Eugen Wassiliwizky, Milena Kuehnast and Thomas Jacobsen, 'Towards a Psychological Construct of Being Moved', *PLOS One* 10, no. 6 (2015): 25.
[72] Ibid., 3.
[73] Ibid., 12.
[74] Thomas Dixon, *From Passions to Emotions: The Creation of a Secular Psychological Category* (Cambridge: Cambridge University Press, 2009).
[75] Robert C. Solomon, *Passions: Emotions and the Meaning of Life*, 2nd edn (Indianapolis, IN: Hackett, 1993).

In his review of research on the relationship between art and emotions, Silvia argues that 'the psychology of emotions is a good starting point for exploring emotional responses to art'.[76] This sounds reasonable, given the enormous upsurge in research on emotion. Jenefer Robinson, who has explored the role of emotion in both literature and the arts, emphasises that 'we need to have a firm grasp of what emotions are before we go on to tackle more difficult questions about emotion and the arts'.[77] However, one of the problems of starting out from emotion is that there is no unified theory. Difficulties in understanding the nature of emotion translates into difficulties in understanding aesthetic emotions. Scherer, on the one hand, argues that aesthetic emotions are different from ordinary emotions because they lack the appraisals of goal relevance and coping potential.[78] Lazarus, on the other hand, maintains that there are no exclusive or prototypical aesthetic emotions. When it comes to basing research into the aesthetics of literary response on theories of emotion, Miall and Kuiken make a pertinent critical point. They argue that it is not to be expected that such theories can illuminate the role of feeling in literary response; 'the position may rather be the reverse: given the nuance and detail that literary response affords to the study of feeling, the conclusions that we eventually reach about feeling may point psychological investigations in new and more productive directions.'[79]

Through the method of Intimate Reading, described in Chapter Two, this book aims to contribute to our understanding of the relationships between feelings, the experience of being moved and literary responses.

---

[76] Paul J. Silvia, 'Emotional Responses to Art: From Collation and Arousal to Cognition and Emotion', *Review of General Psychology* 9, no. 4 (2005): 357.

[77] Jenefer Robinson, *Deeper Than Reason: Emotion and Its Role in Literature, Music and Art* (Oxford: Clarendon Press, 2005), 2. Robinson argues that 'little has been done on the role of emotion in understanding narrative', 101. However, recent years has seen the advent of Affective Narratology. See for instance Patrick Colm Hogan, *Affective Narratology: The Emotional Structure of Stories* (Lincoln: University of Nebraska Press, 2011).

[78] K. R. Scherer, 'Which Emotions Can Be Induced by Music? What Are the Underlying Mechanisms? And How Can We Measure Them?', *Journal of New Music Research* 33, no. 3 (2004): 239–51.

[79] Miall and Kuiken, 'A Feeling for Fiction: Becoming What We Behold', 222.

Chapter Two

INTIMATE READING: A NARRATIVE METHOD

Crucial to the study of narratives and life histories are orientations to changes and turning points. Narrative psychologists McAdams and Bowman look at transitions and 'changes in the direction or the trajectory of our lives' with the aim of finding out how 'people make meaning out of the transitions in their lives'.[1] A central method for doing so is to study the stories people tell about their lives. McAdams and Bowman have identified a narrative sequence that is 'especially prevalent in accounting for life-transitions or life-narrative turning-points': when an emotionally negative situation is turned into a positive outcome, they label this a 'redemption sequence'.[2]

As such, the assumption and invocation of narrativity appears to be embedded in the research problem of life-changing reading experiences. In light of this, it would seem apposite to choose a narrative inquiry approach to my investigation of life-changing reading experiences. However, I encountered certain methodological problems with narrative inquiries, related to the ontological status of data, problems of selection and presentation, and how to interpret the narrative data. To address these problems, four critical procedures were developed: (1) *subservation*, the mode of attending to the readers' communication of their experience; (2) *text production*, from a manuscript matrix of transcripts and memos a narrative is presented; (3) *critical selection of the narratives*, through a preliminary comparative analysis those narratives that corresponded most closely to the construct of life-changing experience of reading fiction were selected; and (4) *idiographic* interpretations based on the hermeneutic logic of anteroduction.

The Anteroductive Logic of Inquiry

A narrative of a life-changing reading experience implies a series of seven transformations from the act of reading:

1. Remembering this reading experience as life-changing
2. Telling the researcher about this in a dialogic exchange

---

[1] Dan P. McAdams and Philip J. Bowman, 'Narrating Life's Turning Points: Redemption and Contamination', in *Turns in the Road: Narrative Studies of Lives in Transition*, ed. Dan McAdams, Ruthellen Josselson and Amia Lieblich (Washington, DC: American Psychological Association, 2001), xv.
[2] Ibid., 5.

3. Recording the dialogue
4. Transcribing the record of the dialogue and producing a text
5. Critical selection of texts for interpretation
6. Interpreting the texts idiographically
7. Appropriating the meaning of these interpretations

From one stage to the next, there is a transformation of meaning. Not only is the experience changed in remembering it, it is also changed in the dialogue of the telling, changed again in turning the transcript of the record into text and subsequently interpreting it. I am not concerned with what is lost at each point, or with what *really* happened. With each step, something essential is distilled and carried forward to be *realized*, or appropriated. Meaning is carried forward towards a telos: a realization and appropriation of the meaning of the narrative of the experience. This is literally a process of *anteroduction*. The methodology is thus based on an *idealist* ontology. This kind of idealism makes no positive assertions of a 'higher' reality. Nor does it deny that there is a reality or realities. It simply states that the expression, sharing and understanding of experiences are meaningful and worthy of appropriation. In Gadamer's words, an idealist ontology is not to be taken in the sense that one 'denies the existence of the external world, but in the sense of affirming that our understanding is able to grasp the real kernel, and that there is an ultimate identity of the subjective approach and reality, a common rationality in consciousness and being'.[3] Any attempt to equate this process with what is loosely termed a 'hermeneutic-phenomenological approach' falls short of the mark. Ricoeur's hermeneutic arc encompasses processes (5) and (6) predominantly. The transition from the oral transmission of a significant event to an authoritative text via attentive listening, recording and transcribing is the province of *philology*. This has been neglected in qualitative scientific discussions of justificatory processes and criteria. Philology is the study of *reliability* of textual editions. Hermeneutics is the study of the *validity* of inferences drawn from critically selected texts. But what study exists for *transduction*, the overall conclusions drawn from a comparison of these interpretations? I believe this is the true providence of phenomenology, as far as it attempts to describe essences and to see the universal in the individual. Essences are 'the web of ideal possibilities and relationships that constitute a particular domain of experience'.[4] As such, Husserl conceives of phenomenology 'as a realm of a priori ideal meaning structures which provide the necessary structural links between empirical psychological acts on the one hand and the realm of ideal entities […] on the other'.[5]

Ricoeur comes very close to identifying hermeneutics with a distinct logic of inquiry: 'Hermeneutics is the theory of the operations of understanding in their relation to the interpretation of texts.'[6] According to Ricoeur, hermeneutics has always had a

---

[3] Hans-Georg Gadamer, 'The Hermeneutics of Suspicion', *Man and World* 17 (1984): 316.
[4] Dermot Moran, *Introduction to Phenomenology* (London: Routledge, 2000), 108.
[5] Ibid., 109.
[6] Paul Ricoeur, *Hermeneutics and the Human Sciences*, trans. John B. Thompson (Cambridge: Cambridge University Press, 1995), 43.

double filiation: to struggle against misunderstanding and lack of clarity on the one hand, and, following Schleiermacher, to understand the author better than he understands himself, on the other. It is this latter filiation which is changed in contemporary hermeneutics: instead of a psychological transposal into the mind of the author, the focus of attention is turned to the reader. 'The text must be unfolded, no longer towards its author, but towards its immanent sense and towards the world which it opens up and discloses.'[7] This unfolding towards can only be revealed as a carrying forward towards its destination in application or appropriation. Ricoeur uses a spatial metaphor to signify this relation: 'to interpret is to explicate the type of being-in-the-world unfolded *in front of* the text'.[8] It is not something that lies *behind* the text, but is *ahead* of it, towards which we must move. Hence, whereas both Dilthey and the hermeneuticists of suspicion unfold the text back towards its author or its underlying origin, we see that Ricoeur's orientation is anteroductive. Ricoeur upholds the doubleness: interpretation is both the struggle to establish the immanent sense of the text and to appropriate meaning, where 'understanding is not concerned with grasping a fact but with apprehending a possibility of being'.[9]

By regarding sense-making as only a necessary stage on the path towards understanding, it becomes 'possible to situate explanation and interpretation along a unique *hermeneutic arc* and to integrate the opposed attitudes of explanation and understanding within an overall conception of reading as the recovery of meaning'.[10] To interpret is then to follow the path of thought opened up by the text, to place oneself *en route* towards the *orient* of the text. In other words, one asks *whither* does the text lead us. But this appropriation must be postponed until the termination of the process, it is 'the anchorage of the arch in the ground of lived experience'.[11]

This hermeneutic arc takes us through several stages: a preliminary structural analysis of the internal relations of the text in comparison with other texts, an interpretation of the text's meaning and an act of appropriation where the interpreter relates it to his or her horizon. The aim is not to recover the originary experience of the readers with who I enter into dialogue; I do not intend to establish 'what really happened then'. Rather, I seek to realise the meaning of the lived experience through a dialogue with my horizon of understanding.

Reliability and Validity

What is the essence of *reliability?* The notion of replicability is a local interpretation of reliability. Data production is reliable if you have *access to* the same object of interpretation as I do. If only the researcher(s) have access to the data, then the production is not

---

[7] Ibid., 53.
[8] Ibid., 141.
[9] Ibid., 56.
[10] Ibid., 161.
[11] Ibid., 164.

reliable. This does not mean that the raw data must be presented to you, but they must be objectively *re-presented*. Reliability can mean one of two things: I provide you with the means for replication. Then you obtain data under the same set of circumstances by going out there. Or, I show you how I developed the data, and re-present all the data to you. Then you have indirect access to the same data as I do. I must show how I went from having no data to *these* data, that is, how the data are *produced*. 'Pro-duction' means 'to bring forth'. Thus it has a double meaning: developing data (collecting and re-presenting) and bringing them forth for inspection. If the data production is reliable it enables you to re-produce this process; not necessarily in an act of replication, but mentally retracing the steps. So in the context of interviews with participants, reliability means that you are shown a re-presentation of the entire dialogue. This does not mean that you must either be present in the room during the dialogue, nor that you be able to listen to the recording. It does not mean that you are provided with the transcript as such, it means that you are provided with a *text* that re-presents the dialogue. In this text, no utterance has been deleted or added. But the transcript has been modified into written language, that is, turned into sentences with punctuation. But, would not a transcript that represents as much accurate information about speech as possible be the most reliable? No. If you read such a transcript, you will not get a proper characterisation of the person. It weakens the ethos of the speaker. I must endeavour to represent the speaker as ethically as possible. In the context of a narrative approach, to present the transcript in all its minutiae is not an accurate representation. A transcript is suspended communication, frozen between the dynamics of the oral dialogue and the fixed textual representation. In the context of an interview, reliable data does not mean that the person's utterance is an objective recalling of what really happened. Nor does it mean that the researcher's influence can somehow be subtracted to arrive at objectivity. It does not mean that the recording captures everything that passed between the people in the room, nor that every sound on the recording be turned into a sign in the transcript. It does not mean that the text to be interpreted is the transcript itself. What it does mean is this: In presenting the text to you, the entire dialogue is re-presented in written form. So in addition to presenting the text, I must show you how the transcript was transformed into scripture. In doing so, I will have produced consistent and reliable data. As such, these data are *real*, they are here. 'Data' does not mean 'found', as it is taken to mean in a positivist approach. Nor does it mean 'made', as it does in a constructionist approach. 'Data' means given: what is given to us, researcher and reader, for analysis and interpretation.

Hence, the method of Intimate Reading emphasises *two criteria of reliable data production*: that the reader be given sufficient insight into how the data were *developed*, and that the reader is *presented with* all the data from which idiographic interpretations will be made.

What is the essence of *validity?* That any inference, whether inductive, deductive, retroductive or anteroductive, is *well grounded in the data*. Hence, internal validity means that the analysis or interpretation stays as close to the data as possible. In interpreting a text, this amounts to *close reading*. External validity does not necessarily entail generalisation to other situations in time and space. It means that the interpretations are related to an external context, whether that be 'the world out there' or to a set of concepts and ideas, a theory, in a manner which has a demonstrable logic of inquiry.

The justificatory processes may be conceptualised as follows:

1. Ensuring that data production is reliable is the province of philology, the study of establishing authoritative textual editions of orally transmitted significant experiences.
2. Ensuring that the critical selection of texts for interpretation and the interpretive inferences drawn from them are valid is the province of hermeneutics.
3. Ensuring that theorising from the idiographic interpretations meets the criterion of external validity is the province of phenomenology.

It is the procedures related to solving these problems that constitute the method of Intimate Reading. The mapping of my *methodos* – the research design and choices undertaken before, during and after interviews – will be presented in the following.

Research Design Overview

The data collection design was uniform: to recruit 15–20 participants for a single-session in-depth interview in a secluded environment; estimated length was 90–150 minutes. The participants were to be specifically instructed to bring the literary work in question to the interview. Interviewing was chosen as the method of data collection because few documents of transformative reading experiences of general readers exist. A single-session format was chosen due to both practical constraints and theoretical considerations. The theoretical considerations will be discussed in the next section on interview method. This section deals with choices pertaining to recruitment and selection of participants and the ethical considerations of the study.

Sampling in Interview-Based Qualitative Research

The psychologist Oliver C. Robinson has, on the grounds that sampling has not been subjected to thorough methodological discussion in textbooks, developed a clear and useful guide to sampling in interview-based qualitative research. His framework divides the sampling procedure into four components: (1) setting a sample universe by means of definite inclusion and exclusion criteria for potential participation; (2) selecting a sample size; (3) devising a sample strategy; and (4) sample sourcing. He argues that these four concerns must be made explicit for a qualitative study to be trustworthy.[12] There are, in my view, two problems related to the concept and practice of sampling in interview-based studies. Firstly, sampling is tied to the concept of *generalisation*. However, not all qualitative studies aim to generalise. In my view, generalisation is only an aim in inductive

---

[12] Oliver C. Robinson, 'Sampling in Interview-Based Qualitative Research: A Theoretical and Practical Guide', *Qualitative Research in Psychology* 11, no. 1 (2014): 25–41.

research strategies. Secondly, sampling implies that the selection is made from a population in order to determine data *collection*. Hence it deals with *who* one should collect data from/about. It does not encompass the critical dimension of qualification of the data collected. In qualitative studies one ought to distinguish between sourcing participants and critically selecting qualified data. Problems of validity may arise if critical selection is understood to be a one-step procedure related to data collection. Therefore, the concept of sampling is problematic. Using a term from Heidegger, we may say that the concept should be put 'under erasure': it is insufficient, and yet one must use it as it is an integral part of the research nomenclature.[13] I will use 'sampling' to designate the process of recruiting participants. However, I will use 'critical selection' to designate the process of judging which transcribed interviews meet all the inclusion criteria for a Life-Changing Fiction Reading Experience (LCFRE), a construct that can only fully be defined after a preliminary comparative analysis of all interviews. In my view, such construct validity can only be determined a posteriori, as the data collected must be subjected to qualification through a critical selection procedure.

When selecting *sample strategy* there are two main options in qualitative research: convenience sampling or purposive sampling. Convenience sampling is simply finding convenient cases who meet the required criteria of the sampling universe and selecting the first ones until the requisite number of participants is obtained. This means that generalisation is problematic. Purposive sampling seeks to ascertain that particular categories within the universe be represented in the final sample. Purposive sampling may be divided into two kinds, according to Robinson: cell, quota and stratified sampling on the one hand, and theoretical sampling on the other. The latter differs because 'it takes place during the collection and analysis of data, following sampling and provisional analysis of some data'.[14] It is originally associated with Grounded Theory. In case study, *intensity sampling* can be used: 'this aims to locate an *information-rich* case, chosen specifically to be insightful, comprehensive, articulate and/or honest.'[15] For my procedure, this implies that stage one consists of convenience sampling. However, the second stage, of critical selection, is purposive. It may be regarded as intensity selection, selecting those narratives that correspond to the defined construct by satisfying criteria for inclusion. Hence I have used convenience sampling, but theoretical/intensive selection of LCFRE narratives. The first of these two separate stages will be explicated in the following. I will discuss the procedure of critical selection in a subsequent section of this chapter.

Recruitment Strategy

The sourcing strategy I adopted was to use as many different channels of communication as possible.

---

[13] See Martin Heidegger, *The Fundamental Concepts of Metaphysics: World, Finitude, Solitude*, trans. William McNeill and Nicholas Walker (Bloomington: Indiana University Press, 1995).
[14] Robinson, 'Sampling in Interview-Based Qualitative Research', 34.
[15] Ibid., 35.

Participant Name	Age	Author: Book Title[a]
Esther	Late 50s	Inger Hagerup: *Episode* (poem)
Camilla	Late 30s	Marguerite Duras: *The Lover* (novel)
		Goethe: *The Sorrows of Young Werther* (novel)
Veronica	Early 30s	D. H. Lawrence: *Lady Chatterley's Lover* (novel)
Nina	Mid-40s	Mary O'Hara: *My Friend Flicka* (novel)
Jane	Late 50s	Doris Lessing: *Shikasta* (novel)
Sue	Late 40s	Matthew Arnold: *The Buried Life* (poem)
Sonja	Early 20s	Samuel Beckett: *Worstward Ho* (prose)
Katherina	Early 20s	Karine Nyborg: *Ikke rart det kommer kråker* (short stories)
Emma	Mid-20s	Stephen Chbosky: *The Perks of Being a Wallflower* (novel)
Anjali	Late 40s	Camilla Collett: *Amtmannens Døtre* (*The District Governor's Daughters*) (novel)
Marge	Late 50s	Mrs Oliphant: *The Days of My Life* (novel)
Marco	40	James Ellroy: *The Black Dahlia* (novel)
Paula	Late 20s	Enid Blyton: *Adventures of the Wishing-Chair* (novel)
		William Blake: *The Tyger* (poem)
		Sylvia Plath: *The Bell Jar* (novel)
Agnes	Early 50s	Charlotte Perkins Gilman: *Mr Peebles' Heart* (short story)
Eleanor	ca 35	Robert Pirsig: *Lila. An Inquiry into Morals* (novel)
Damian	Late 20s	Alexander Pope: *Essay on Man* (poem)

[a] See Bibliography for which editions of these works were used.

List of strategies and participants sourced

1. Inviting myself into lectures in literary studies to address audience (Sonja, Katherina)
2. Put up poster in libraries (Marco)
3. Contacted person directly after reading about them in the media (Esther, Anjali)
4. Via friends and social media (Emma, Nina)
5. Serendipitous encounters through attending events related to literature and reading (Camilla, Tess, Marge)
6. Via Gatekeeper: Access to the Reader Organisation's network in the United Kingdom (Jane, Sue, Veronica, Eleanor, Paula, Agnes, Damian, Brian)

In total I had contact with 27 readers, of which 23 were female and four were male, who reported transformative reading experiences. Four of these readers, although initially willing to participate, unfortunately 'got off the hook' because of time constraints or hesitation.[16] Five of them I declined to interview in this context, as they did not meet

---

[16] These four readers, two female and two male, had been changed by the following novels: Sigurd Hoel: *Syndere I Sommersol*; Terry Pratchett: *Snuff*; Marcel Proust: *Remembrance of Things Past*; Isabel Allende: *City of the Beasts*.

the principal inclusion criterion: *The life-changing reading experience must have been brought about by a particular work of imaginative literature* (novel, drama, poetry, short story, prose; all subsumed under the category of 'fiction'); they reported works of non-fiction. Hence I interviewed a total of 18 participants, of whom 15 were female and 3 were male. Two of those interviews, although highly fascinating and information-rich, insufficiently met the inclusion criterion to merit transcription; they told me of their general experiences of reading. All interviews were conducted in Norway or the United Kingdom during January–December 2016.

Participants Who Met Inclusion Criteria

Table showing the list of participants' ages and the books they stated had changed them

These 16 interviews were transcribed. The age range of participants was between 21 and 69 years. Most of the transformative experiences happened in late adolescence or early adulthood. There were four exceptions: Beth was in her late 40s when she encountered *Mr Peebles' Heart*. Sue was in her mid-40s when she read Arnold. Nina has read the book at different ages throughout her life, but her transformation happened when she was in her early 40s. Paula's reading experiences took place in childhood, adolescence and young adulthood. This picture, in which transformative reading experiences are concentrated to predominantly two periods, late adolescence or mid-life, accords with the findings of Appleyard, who, in his account of the different developmental stages of readers, states that these are the life-stages in which such changes are most likely to occur.[17] Interestingly, this table reveals the broad range of literature that is conducive to life-changing experiences. There is in this table a mix of old and new, high-brow and middle-brow, prose and poetry, realistic and fantastic representations.

Bracketing Preconceptions

In preparing for the interviews, I intended to reflect on my preconceptions by means of preparing a list of questions. This was not an interview-guide, but simply a guide to my own presuppositions: what I was aware of being curious about. What I attempted to bracket was the notion that I was going to *elicit stories* of life-changing reading experiences. I would endeavour not to be evaluating their experience as we spoke. Thoughts like 'is this really a life-changing experience?' and 'is it detailed enough?' – although these might appear in consciousness at certain junctions – were to be suspended. Such suspension may be understood as 'defusion': In a scientifically based intervention programme called Acceptance and Commitment Therapy, Russ Harris defines defusion as a cognitive strategy involving 'looking *at* thoughts rather than *from* thoughts; noticing thoughts rather than being caught up in thoughts; and letting thoughts come and go rather than

---

[17] J. A. Appleyard, *Becoming a Reader. The Experience of Fiction from Childhood to Adulthood* (Cambridge: Cambridge University Press, 1991).

holding on to them'.[18] My attention would go towards the other's experience and the person's expression of that experience, as fully as possible. I identified two kinds of intrusive judgements that I would attempt to suspend, as they would get in the way of attending to the other's experience: *Am I performing my role well enough?*; *Is the person 'coming up with the goods?'*

Moreover, I reflected on the importance of the context of the interview. I have considerable experience of interviewing people in various contexts, as a journalist and as course instructor responsible for student intake interviews, and I also have ample experience as counsellor and careers advisor. This experience is of course very helpful for conducting research interviews, and yet it is important to be aware of the distinct objectives of a research interview. It must be distinguished on the one hand from therapeutic contexts and on the other hand from interviews in which one is looking for specific answers to questions. As Kvale says, 'Although the research interviewer can learn much from therapeutic interviews, it is important to distinguish between the different forms of human interaction. In therapy the main goal is the change of the patient, in research it is the obtaining of knowledge.'[19] Considering the fact that the interview method diverges from questioning for specific information, I have decided not to regard or refer to the interviewee as 'informant'. Instead, I have chosen the neologism 'intimant'. This term was chosen in accordance with the overall term chosen to designate the method: 'intimate reading'. There are four reasons for this choice: (1) the term is partly synonymous with close reading, and my method involves close interpretation of particular narratives; (2) the term is antonymous with 'distant reading', the approach developed by Franco Moretti for comparing segments of many texts and which may serve as a common denominator for coding-based approaches to data analysis;[20] (3) the persons interviewed reveal intimate experiences; and (4) in communicating an experience which goes deeper than what can be conveyed in words, the expression is an *intimation* of their experience. I will come back to this in my discussion of interview approach.

Interview Method

I have chosen to conceptualise my method of interviewing as *subservation*: inviting the participant to tell me of their experience, and subjecting myself to this telling. The aim of subservation is not to obtain information about something. It is 'paradigm'-neutral, in that it neither asks persons for *descriptions*, nor aims to *elicit* stories from the interviewee. The aim is to facilitate *intimation*.[21] In intimation, the interviewee speaks from

---

[18] Russ Harris, *ACT Made Simple* (Oakland, CA: New Harbinger, 2009), 97.
[19] Steinar Kvale, 'The Psychoanalytic Interview as Qualitative Research', *Qualitative Inquiry* 5, no. 1 (1999): 105.
[20] See Franco Moretti, 'Conjectures on World Literature', *New Left Review* 1 (2000): 54–68.
[21] Cf. https://www.etymonline.com/word/intimation: 'mid-15c., "action of making known", from Middle French *intimation* (14c.), from Late Latin *intimationem* (nominative *intimatio*) "an

an embodied utterance position. Intimation involves more than the interviewee's conscious expression and the interviewer's conscious understanding. By intimation is meant the interviewee's communication of their lived experience, encompassing both telling and reflecting; there may be an *implicit* level of communication not directly expressed in words and perhaps not even fully in the person's awareness, and the response of the interviewer to this expression can only be an approximation to the full meaning of the communication. The interviewee does not have a ready-made story to convey, nor is one 'co-constructed' in the dialogue. The interviewer's main task is *active listening*. What Balint says of listening in the doctor–patient dialogue also holds for intimation in dialogue: 'While discovering in himself an ability to listen to things in his patient that are barely spoken because the patient himself is only dimly aware of them, the doctor will start listening to the same kind of language in himself.'[22] As interviewer, I attempt to reflect my unfolding and evolving empathic understanding back to the intimant, while at the same time facilitating a shared reading of significant passages from the literary work in question. The aim is to enable the intimant to speak *from* and *within* the felt emotional reality, expressing it as their emotional truth. The facilitation of intimation and the authentic responding to its expressions is to *subserve* the intimant; this necessitates that I as interviewer *subject* myself to their experience as it is lived in the interview. I must *respond* to the person's intimation. The 'instrument' of subservation is the interviewer's empathy.

Riessman, in explicating how the research can facilitate storytelling in interviews, singles out three factors that are not technical, but which are all about *empathy*: giving up control, emotional attentiveness and the ability to listen. The interviewer may have a semi-structured approach, but must be willing to deviate from agenda: 'Creating possibilities in research interviews for extended narration requires investigators to give up control, which can generate anxiety. Although we have particular paths we want to cover related to the substantive and theoretical foci of our studies, narrative interviewing necessitates following participants down *their* trails.'[23]

The phenomenologist Claire Petitmengin has elaborated an interview method that enables a person to become conscious of his or her subjective experience of felt meaning and describe it with precision. Our most intimate experience, says Petitmengin, is difficult to access and therefore requires inner effort: 'Not only do we not know what we know, but that we do not know that we do not know.'[24] Her aim is to enable the other to become conscious of his or her present ongoing inner experience, and to increase the

---

announcement", noun of action from past participle stem of Latin *intimare* "make known, announce, impress" (see *intimate* (adj.)). Meaning "action of expressing by suggestion or hint, indirect imparting of information" is from 1530s'.

[22] Michael Balint quoted in Josie Billington, *Is Literature Healthy?* (Oxford: Oxford Univ. Press, 2016), 65.

[23] Riessman, *Narrative Methods for the Human Sciences*, 24. The central importance of empathy is emphasised also by other researchers:

[24] Claire Petitmengin, 'Describing One's Subjective Experience in the Second Person: An Interview Method for the Science of Consciousness', *Phenomenology and the Cognitive Sciences* 5, no. 3–4 (2006): 234.

participant's introspective expertise. That, of course, was not my aim. However, there are certain facets of the technique she elaborates that are of great concern to my method, in as much as she intends to 'enable the interviewee to access an intimate dimension of himself'.[25] Firstly, Petitmengin emphasises the importance of maintaining the interviewee's attention. There must be 'a 'container' for the attention of the interviewee [to] help him to remain within the boundaries of the experience being explored'.[26] Furthermore, the interviewer must enable the interviewee to relax and enter into the experience. Thirdly, when the person digresses, she must be gently led back to refocusing through regular reformulation by the interviewer of what the subject has said. This can also be done through asking a question. Moreover, the interviewer must 'guide the interviewee towards the "re-enactment" of the past experience'.[27] When the person is brought into the 'evocation state', she is in contact with her past experience. Whereas Petitmengin regards the re-enactment as a Proustian experience of vivid recollection of all details, I understand the 'evocation state' merely to involve an affective memory, where the feelings associated with the reading experience are once more re-membered as the person becomes aware of the kinaesthetic and felt sense of her experience. In this state of evocation both the description of memories and the reflections on the experience are deepened. Thus the method is directive in always bringing the other back to the experience, and yet non-inducive in that the interviewer does not know what he is looking for but must remain open to what comes.

Biographic-Narrative Interview Method

I decided to develop an approach that combines elements of Petitmengin's non-inducive direction of embodied utterance with a biographic-narrative interview method (BNIM), and shared reading of significant passages. Social scientist Tom Wengraff has developed a method called *Biographic-Narrative Interview Method*. I was initially drawn to this method because it is inspired partly by Carl Rogers's non-directive dialogue method, as well as focusing on in-depth listening to the person's experience. Wengraff's approach 'restricts interviewer interventions initially to a single (narrative) initial question' and restricts subsequent interventions to a particular type according to a definite narrow procedure.[28] Thus one may say that the two central concepts of his approach are the single question aimed at inducing narrative (SQUIN) and pushing for particular incident narratives (PINs). This interview method relies on dividing the interview into two sessions. In the first session, the only question from the researcher is the SQUIN: 'Please tell me your life story,' or 'Please tell me about your experience of X.' During this session, the interviewer notes down the topics that the interviewee

---

[25] Ibid., 254.
[26] Ibid., 239.
[27] Ibid., 244.
[28] Tom Wengraff, *Qualitative Research Interviewing: Biographic Narrative and Semi-structured Methods* (London: Sage, 2001), 111.

talks about. No further questions are to be asked in session 1, but one can use 'facilitative non-directional support' in order to enable the interviewee to tell their story.[29] Wengraff has found that most interviewees will not just go on telling unless encouraged. The interviewer must listen *actively* by giving verbal and non-verbal acknowledgement of receiving what is being told. This involves posture, eye contact, intonation and the use of 'hmms'. One may tentatively offer words to mirror the person's experiencing. 'Such words might fit or they might be useful by provoking the interviewee into getting a better self-expression for themselves.'[30] One must allow silences, so that the interviewee can continue talking about the topic, or introduce a new one. Only after a break, in which one reviews the topic noted down, in session 2, can a semi-structured interview take place. However, this must be performed according to a strict format: one attempts to elicit more narrative material about each topic. The way of doing this is to 'push for PINs'. This means that one must ask specific 'questions pointed at narrative' rather than mere open-ended questions that may 'allow narrative'.[31] For instance, if one of the topics raised in session 1 was 'my mother', then a question that only *allows* narrative would be something like 'can you tell me more about her?' or 'what are your feelings about her?' A PIN, on the other hand, would ask: 'Can you remember any event involving your father.' The way such a PIN is introduced, is by repeating something the person said about that topic in session 1: 'you said […], can you remember/tell me in detail how that happened?'

BNIM specifically aims to *elicit* stories. The aim of PIN-questions is to 'discourage a non-narrative response, such as the production of a theory, an argument, an unhistorical description, a justification, a declaration of values, an expression of felt emotions'.[32] I did not wish to discourage such 'non-narrative response'. In fact, I regard reflection, declaration of values or expressions of emotions as integral parts of narrative. The narrative consists of more than representations of action. I therefore did not strictly adhere to the format. In my view, the principal aim of PINs in BNIM is to move the interviewee from an iterative to a singular mode of narration.[33] Iterative narration tells of something that usually or often happens, whereas the singulative focuses on particular incidents. As such, one could say that Intimate Reading starts at the equivalent of Wengraff's session 2. In responding to the question 'has a book changed your life?' the intimant is already at the beginning going to tell me about a particular incident she has experienced. I accordingly opted for an open-question 'allow narrative' approach rather than an exclusively 'story-pointed' one. A strict adherence to Wengraff's approach would not be possible owing to the decision to include the reading of significant passages into our dialogue. However, the main reason I reject the strict 'story-pointed' procedure is that it is too 'mechanical'; it prevents a more fluid and

---

[29] Ibid., 122.
[30] Ibid., 129.
[31] Ibid., 125–30.
[32] Ibid., 127.
[33] See Gerard Genette, *Narrative Discourse: An Essay in Method*, trans. Jane E. Lewin (Ithaca, NY: Cornell University Press, 1980), 113–60.

spontaneous dialogue in which I attempt to communicate my empathic understanding to the intimant.

Hence, what I take from the method is principally the SQUIN. Therefore, I do not regard my interview method as 'semi-structured'. Conventionally, qualitative interviews are differentiated along one dimension only, ranging from *structured* to *unstructured* – based upon the number of questions prepared beforehand. In my view, this continuum must be supplemented by another: that of *form*. An unstructured interview need not be formless (which would be tantamount to a normal conversation). Instead, it may have a definite, although intangible, form. The structure I attempted to create in my interviews was one of *concentration*: a mutual focus upon a literary text. The form I attempted to create was one of *deepening*: facilitating a gradual move from talking *about* the experience, to talking *from* and *within* the experience. This 'forming' involves a gradual usage of softer voice tone, slower pacing and silences to facilitate emotional deepening 'because an ordinary voice implicitly signals that the speaker is not attuning sensitively to the delicacy of the listener's experience'.[34] These elements are not explicitly apparent in the transcript, nor the textual narratives.

Shared Reading of Significant Passages

The challenge for me was to develop an interview form in which I could invite the intimant to tell me about their reading experience in the context of their life-situation, and at the same time invite a dialogue around the literary work that they had cited as life-changing. *How does one bring the book into the interview?* The sociologist Dempsey discusses the use of stimulated recall in interviews as a technique to bring informants 'a step closer to the moments in which they actually produce action', or experience something, by 'jogging memories'.[35] This is done by playing back to the participants a recording of themselves engaging in interactions. My approach can of course not involve such stimulated *recall*. Instead, by inviting the intimant to read out loud passages that she deemed significant in her reading experience, I intended to facilitate 'stimulated remembrance': the affective memory of the experience would be revitalised, so that they could speak *from* and *within* the experience. In practical terms, this was similar to certain elements from a shared reading session: invite the participant to read out loud and to relate the work to her own personal experience. I would gently respond with my own comments to their responses or alternatively point to other aspects of the passage read. If the intimant did not explicitly comment upon the passage read, but merely communicated deictically by pointing to the passage as important, I would interpret that passage as saying something about the person's experience.

---

[34] Bruce Ecker, Robin Ticic and Laurel Hulley, *Unlocking the Emotional Brain: Eliminating Symptoms at Their Roots Using Memory Reconsolidation* (New York: Routledge, 2012), 51.
[35] Nicholas P. Dempsey, 'Stimulated Recall Interviews in Ethnography', *Qualitative Sociology* 33 (2010): 349–50.

Presentation of Narratives

In going from transcript to text, another narrative layer was added. Instead of presenting the narrative as a dialogue in which the intimant is the narrator and I am the narratee, I have added a narrative frame. This frame consists of an *intro* and an *outro*, plus section headlines. Technically speaking, such a frame is an extradiegetic level of the narrative; it is outside of the level of dialogic exchange (the intradiegetic level[36]) in which the intimant is an autodiegetic narrator and I am the narratee. Why have I chosen to include the extradiegetic element? It was done in an attempt to reflect the fact that I made pre- and post-interview memos in which I noted my principal expectations and impressions. By including the extradiegesis, where I am a homodiegetic narrator, I wish to represent that I have prepared for the meeting and that it continues to 'live' after we have said goodbye. It is a way of showing that I am not a 'neutral observer', without exaggerating the importance of my presence. I am not sure that this was the right decision. I could have simply excluded this extradiegetic dimension and provided the same information in my interpretation of the narrative. In these extradiegetic introductions I attempt to synthesise the information I possessed prior to the interview, as well as my response to the work in question, and the location and time/atmosphere of our meeting. In the codas I attempt to convey the immediate impression and concerns I had following the interview.

According to Polkinghorne, there are two ways of using narrative data and including them in the research report. Either one uses 'paradigmatic' analytic procedures to produce categories out of the common elements (coding-based approaches), or the researcher produces a narrative, as in a case-study report.[37] I find this dichotomy far too coarse. What both these approaches have in common is that *excerpts* or *segments* of a participant's story is included in the researcher's discourse – either to exemplify a category or as direct quotes in the reporter's scientific report. My approach belongs to neither of these types. I present the *entire* dialogue as a narrative, and subsequently interpret this as a whole text. I find it to be a general problem in qualitative studies that the reader is presented with quotes from participants, as if they could unproblematically be taken out of context. Moreover, such quotes are used to *illustrate* a point and are presented as if the utterance was transparent and not in need of interpretation. Thus presenting the intimant's whole narrative is an integral part of subsversation.

Philology and the Manuscript Matrix

'Edited texts', argues Stephen Nichols, are 'rational products of philological endeavour'.[38] He advocates a 'new philology' that returns to the medieval origins of philology in a

---

[36] See Gerard Genette, *Narrative Discourse: An Essay in Method*, trans. Jane E. Lewin (New York: Cornell University Press, 1980), 227–34.

[37] Polkinghorne, 'Narrative Configuration in Qualitative Analysis', *Qualitative Studies in Education* 8, no. (1995): 5–23.

[38] Stephen G. Nichols, 'Introduction: Philology in a Manuscript Culture', *Speculum* 65, no. 1 (1990): 2.

manuscript culture. In the 'old' view of philology, represented for instance by Auerbach, philology was seen as a Renaissance enterprise to collect and edit manuscripts of the ancient world. Philology represented a technological scholarship made possible by print culture, aiming to move away from the multiplicity and variance of a manuscript culture in order to achieve exactitude based on a fixed and transparent text. In the manuscript culture, according to Nichols, adaptation or *translatio* was central: 'the continual rewriting of past works in a variety of versions, a practice which made even the copying of medieval works an adventure in supplementation rather than faithful imitation'.[39] Integral parts of medieval text production were images and annotations of various forms, 'rubrics, captions, glosses, and interpolations'.[40] What Nichols terms the manuscript matrix contained different systems of representation, such as commentaries in the margins. The scribe 'improved' upon the original manuscript rather than engaging in a 'straightforward act of copying'; thus the scribe 'supplants the original poet, often changing words or narrative order, suppressing or shortening some sections, while interpolating new materials in others'.[41] I believe that the transformation of the interview into a textual narrative is an example of such a 'new philology'. The transcript along with the recording and memos constitute the manuscript matrix to be interpreted, and from which the edited text is created. The text supplants the transcript, the recording and my memos to produce a narrative. Several different texts could be created from this matrix, just as a variety of different transcripts can be created from the same recording. What is important is not arriving at the single correct and transparent text, but arriving at *one* justified version, which I authorise through explicating my decisions. This version then becomes the authoritative text to which any interpretation must refer. Regarding the choices involved in turning the raw transcript into text, the main concern was *ethical*: maintaining the integrity of the intimant's voice.[42]

Critical Selection of Narratives for Interpretation

The source of homogeneity in my study is of course the past life experience the participants must have in common: that of a life-changing experience of reading fiction. The inclusion criteria are thus only two: that the person be of adult age and that she or he has read a work of imaginative literature (poetry, novel, novella, short story, drama or what may be loosely called fiction). All 16 transcriptions satisfy those criteria. These are all narratives of life-changing reading experiences of imaginative literature. However, for both practical and theoretical reasons, there must be a process of critical selection of narratives. Firstly, it is impossible within the scope of this study to perform an in-depth idiographic interpretation of 16 different narratives. Secondly, the construct of LCFRE

---

[39] Ibid., 3.
[40] Ibid., 7.
[41] Ibid., 8.
[42] Because I discuss this issue in-depth elsewhere, I have decided not to elaborate on these choices here. Instead, I refer the reader to my article 'Intimate Reading' in Josie Billington (ed.), *Reading and Health* (London: Palgrave Macmillan, 2019).

must be defined precisely, and the data qualified. This does *not* imply that some of these experiences are 'better' or 'more authentic' than others. It simply means I must ensure that narratives selected be narratives of the same thing.

It is not the responsibility of the interviewee to satisfy the construct criteria of the researcher. This is an analytic process to be undertaken a posteriori. This problem has not been discussed in qualitative research literature. It is naively assumed that interviewees speak about the same phenomenon. Although one has a homogeneous life-history sample, this is no guarantee that persons will describe the same phenomenon. One must therefore find a way of ensuring *construct validity*.

Psychologists Angus and Greenberg define autobiographical reasoning as a narrative structure or schema that organises 'the ever-unfolding cacophony of lived experience into bounded episodes that by definition have a beginning, middle and end, and enable perspective taking and reflection'.[43] They regard the self as being continuously constructed in a self-organising process and emerging from more basic elements:

> Embodied emotional experiencing and narrative organisational processes are both fundamental components of a higher order synthesis that ultimately determines who we create ourselves to be. Constructing a sense of self involves an ongoing process both of identifying with and symbolising emotions and actions as one's own and constructing an embodied narrative that offers temporal stability and coherence.[44]

Angus and Greenberg have developed a taxonomy of different kinds of stories that, although it refers to a therapeutic context, I find useful for a preliminary analysis of the 16 narratives. All of the 16 stories of the intimants belong to the category of 'self-identity change story': a positive transformation in overall narrative plotline of their life story and view of self. As such they are all stories of life-changing reading experience. However, Angus and Greenberg find that some stories are 'empty stories': they are not told from a place of feeling. Moreover, some stories are 'broken': there are conflicting plot lines. The person may tell a story of positive change, yet at the same time there is another plot line pointing to standstill or negative change. Also, not all stories have 'unique outcome': it can be difficult to ascertain what the actual consequence of the experience was. An 'untold story' is one that has not yet been told. There is also a category of 'unfinished story', which still has not arrived at resolution. Finally, there are incoherent stories, which the reader struggle to make sense of the internal subjective experiences in relation to events.[45] I used this taxonomy as a sensitising point of departure when performing a preliminary analysis of the 16 narratives. I would consider an interview as empty if there was not a sufficient 'deepening' of the intimation (see section on interview method). I would consider the story to be broken if I was not sure that the change should only be ascribed to the book. I would consider that the story did not have a unique outcome if

---

[43] Lynne E. Angus and Leslie S. Greenberg, *Working with Narrative in Emotion-Focused Therapy. Changing Stories, Healing Lives* (Washington, DC: American Psychological Association, 2011), 25.

[44] Ibid., 25.

[45] Ibid., 109.

I could not sufficiently comprehend the nature of the change. I would consider the story unfinished if the person was still in crisis or in a process of transformation. I would consider the story to be incoherent if I could not sufficiently fathom the subjective experience of the intimant.

The Construct of Life-changing Fiction Reading Experience

When undertaking a preliminary analysis of the 16 narratives, it became apparent that there was variation with respect to the following eight factors:

Proximity: How close to the work does the dialogue take us? Does the intimant point to specific passages and discuss the work in depth in the interview? Or does the intimant speak of his or her story without much reference to the work? For instance, there are some who do not 'weave' the book into their narrative to any significant degree.

Ascription: When reading the narrative, is it reasonable to attribute the life-change to the reading of the book rather than to contextual factors? Naturally, any life change will objectively be multi-determined. However, if for instance the reader is at the same time in counselling, so that the advice from other sources may be deemed to be of equal significance, then the change may also be ascribed to the counselling context.

Concentration: If the dialogue diverts too much away from the life-changing reading experience, then the narrative is not sufficiently concentrated. For instance, if the intimant talks too much about an exciting future project and very little about the life-changing experience itself, then the interview may be excluded.

Coherence: The narrative must have sufficient coherence. If I during the interview or in reading the transcript afterwards find it difficult to gain a sense of coherence as to what the life-change is all about, or to understand what the person means, the narrative must be excluded.[46]

Integrated memory: The reader must have represented the reading experience as life-changing prior to the interview. For example, one of the intimants reported that it was only upon seeing the question posed by my poster, 'has a book changed your life?', that he began to think of his reading experience as life-changing. The experience of life-change should not be 'co-constructed' in the interview.

Resolution: The reader must be judged to have achieved a stage of resolution of crisis, so that the experience is 'complete'. Thus, if the person says the reading experience helped her through her depression, and yet at the time of the interview she is still receiving psychiatric treatment, then the crisis may not be fully resolved.

---

[46] According to Angus and Greenberg (109) markers of narrative coherence include: a clear sense of the beginning, middle and end of the story; descriptions of the internal subjective experiences; an explicit understanding of causes or factors that contributed to conflicting emotions, actions and intentions of self and others; and, finally, an inner felt sense of resolution.

Love of the book: The reader must still harbour strong positive feelings associated with the book. If the intimant has largely forgotten about the book, merely regarding it as instrumental in bringing about change, then the work itself may not have made a lasting, deep impression. The reader must intimate that she or he has been deeply moved by the book.

Shared reading: I must have read the work in question prior to the interview, in order for me to be able to follow the intimant in her reflections on significant passages.

Based on a consideration of these factors, which of course are not 'hard' criteria, I developed the following construct of an LCFRE narrative:

> A narrative is of an LCFRE if the work of imaginative literature is proximal in the dialogue; the change can unequivocally be ascribed to that work; the dialogue is highly concentrated on the experience; the narrative is coherent and intelligible; the experience was already integrated in memory as life-changing; the crisis has been resolved; there is a lasting love of the book; and the person has shared the affective experience of reading significant passages from the work in our dialogue.

Only six narratives fully met these criteria, and were therefore selected for idiographic interpretation. Because Camilla's experience is a composite one involving two different novels, however, I decided to exclude it here. The narrative of Sue is about a reading experience that happened in a shared reading group. Naturally, the group environment will have impacted on the experience. However, as her story revolves around her meeting with the poem, and not on the discussion with the group, I have treated this narrative as an LCFRE like the others.

I must emphasise that the critical deselection of these 11 narratives by no means implies that these are not stories of profound life-changing reading experiences. The exclusion is not based on the degree of change or quality of engagement with text. Nor does exclusion mean that these interviews are not 'information-rich'. Each of them is fascinating in its own right. What is the case, however, is that the five selected narratives fulfil the entire list of inclusion criteria developed in the preliminary comparative analysis. These data are *qualified*, and are therefore the *best* data for idiographic interpretations and subsequent theory-building. But my understanding of the other 11 narratives of course also inform my 5 interpretations.

Analysis of Narrative Structure

I conceptualise narrative analysis as the first stage of the hermeneutic arc, that of explanation of the internal relations. It is therefore merely preliminary to the idiographic interpretations. As such, I engaged in a critical narrative analysis of the interviews in the process of selecting the five narratives for interpretation, and in editing them for presentation. In comparing the 16 transcripts, one could say that I excluded 11 of them on the basis of a hermeneutics of suspicion. Moreover, I narrativised the edited transcripts by introducing an extradiegetic level. Therefore narrative analysis was part of the data production process. Furthermore, in my approach there is also an explanatory stage of structural analysis prior to the idiographic interpretations. In a comparative analysis of the five narratives, a common structure became apparent: that of *crisis – transaction – resolution*. This structure, based on that identified by Colaizzi, became the orienting principle for my interpretations.

Hence I decided to structure my interpretations accordingly; I divided them into three parts: (1) crisis, (2) transaction with the literary work and (3) resolution. The consequence of this is that in addition to the syntagmatic axis of before – during – after, I could develop a paradigmatic axis in which I related the different crises, transactions and resolutions to each other. In my preliminary analysis I also employed the analytic distinction so central to narratology: the distinction between discourse and story.

Idiographic Interpretations of the Narratives

The terms idiographic and nomothetic were introduced by the philosopher Wilhelm Windelband to differentiate between two scientific approaches. Although they were meant to designate approaches typical for the humanities and natural sciences, respectively, what is important is that whereas the nomothetic aims to derive laws to explain types or categories of objective phenomena, idiographic approaches attempt to understand the meaning of unique and often subjective phenomena.[47] Allport imported the terms into psychology, where the idiographic approach endeavours 'to understand some particular event'.[48] Both approaches are common in the social sciences under a variety of different terms. Riessman operates with the terms *case-centred* versus *category-centred* models of research. Narratively oriented inquiries represent the former, as narrative researchers keep a story 'intact' by theorizing from the case rather than from component themes or categories across cases:

> Narrative study relies on extended accounts that are preserved and treated analytically as units, rather than fragmented into thematic categories as is customary in other forms of qualitative analysis, such as grounded theory. This difference […] is perhaps the most fundamental distinction: in many category-centred methods of analysis, long accounts are distilled into coding units by taking bits and pieces – snippets of an account often edited out of context. While useful for making general statements across many subjects, category-centred approaches eliminate the sequential and structural features that are hallmarks of narrative. Honoring individual agency and intention is difficult when cases are pooled to make general statements.[49]

---

[47] See Hans Thomae, 'The Nomothetic-Idiographic Issue: Some Roots and Recent Trends', *International Journal of Group Tensions* 28, no. 1 (1999): 187–215.
[48] Gordon W. Allport, *Personality: A Psychological Interpretation* (New York: Holt, 1937).
[49] Riessman, *Narrative Methods for the Human Sciences*, 12.

Bryman points to two criticisms of the coding approach to qualitative data analysis: the problem of a fragmentation of data, so that the narrative flow of what people say is lost, and secondly, losing the context of what was said.[50]

Each of the five narratives presented in this book were interpreted based on the narrative analysis of the previous stage of the arc. I sought to preserve the uniqueness and particularity by presenting the whole narratives, so that these may be read separately before one reads my interpretations.

---

[50] Alan Bryman, *Social Research Methods*, 3rd edn (Oxford: Oxford University Press, 2008), 553.

Chapter Three

VERONICA'S BRUISE

Veronica got in touch with me after someone had told her about my project. She said that reading Lady Chatterley's Lover had made her decide to break out of an unhappy relationship. With that information I sat down to read the novel. Imagining what her reading must have been like, while at the same time remembering my own previous reading of the novel, was an immensely rich and moving experience. Our dialogue took place in a quiet and pleasant meeting room in her office building, on a blustery morning in November. My first impression of Veronica was of a warm, outgoing and confident person.

Thor: I appreciate your being willing to share your experience with me.

Veronica: My pleasure. I've been quite excited about it, actually. When I heard about your project, I thought, oh yeah, brilliant. I first read the book a number of years ago and I wish I'd had the readerly understanding that I do now, to be able to process it a bit better. So, yeah, I'm looking forward to it.

Thor: Good! As you know, I want to find out how books can change readers' lives. So therefore, I'd just like to basically hear about your reading experience. It's up to you where you want to start. But one way we could start is, if there's a passage that you remember particularly well, if you could please read that for me.

Veronica: Initially let me just give you a bit of background, then. The reason that *Lady Chatterley's Lover* really resonated with me is that I read it for the first time about maybe nine or ten years' ago, something like that, when I was in my mid-twenties. I was in a long-term relationship in which I felt very trapped and at the same time had resigned myself to the fact that this was just what life was going to be. I was going to end up getting married, and I probably wouldn't be happy forever, but it was just … that was real life, and maybe romance was a bit of a fantasy. You know, this is what reality was going to be.

And then I read this book. I think it followed on from having read *The Unbearable Lightness of Being*, which was another wonderful book for how I could sort of break free. Not necessarily by, you know, having an affair with the gamekeeper, but just wanting to be proactive and actually put myself on a different path. And it massively has. So the relationship broke up many years later, well, about a year after that.

And yeah, I just, I feel really free, now *(smiles)*. And I can imagine that maybe if it wasn't for the book, if I'd continued on that path then I probably would be married now, have some children, just be unhappy and feel trapped, so I really feel quite lucky that this book found its way to me when it did, at the right time.

We each open our copy of the novel, and start looking at significant passages together. Veronica reads a passage out loud, and then reflects on its significance, before moving onto another passage.

'And It Frightened Her'

Clifford looked at Connie, with his pale, slightly prominent blue eyes, in which a certain vagueness was coming. He seemed alert in the foreground, but the background was like the Midlands atmosphere, haze, smoky mist. And the haze seemed to be creeping forward. So when he stared at Connie in his peculiar way, giving her his peculiar, precise information, she felt all the background of his mind filling up with mist, with nothingness. And it frightened her. It made him seem impersonal, almost to idiocy. (p. 52)

The way that she reacts to him, her feeling that she's looking at him like he's an idiot, I remember almost seething, looking at my partner and thinking, Oh my God, he's an idiot. What stupidness am I going to marry? But even then it was 'I'm going to marry.' I couldn't see myself being strong enough to get out of it. I just felt even more trapped, because I could see myself still going ahead with this.

I'd been in this relationship for about three years, and that was my second ever boyfriend. It was the first time that I'd ever really felt that I was in a grown up relationship, you know. I'd had a boyfriend when I was around 18, but that just felt like a bit of a first love and I knew it wasn't ever going to be forever. But this guy I thought was my guy. We'd made plans and there was going to be a family, and things were definitely set. There was a future that I thought was going to happen for me, and was planned out to a certain extent. Initially they were joint plans, very much so. Then I realised that I still wanted those things but not necessarily with him. I definitely wanted a family, I wanted some stability, I wanted to feel settled and content. I think initially I saw him as a vehicle to be able to get those things, and have that with him. And then as things changed between us, I realised that those things I still wanted, but not with him. We went on holiday together for the first time and went to stay with some family of mine in France. For both of them it was their second marriage, and they got married when they were a bit older, and then had children. I remember looking at those two as a couple and thinking, oh that's so wonderful and they've got such a great life. And then I looked at my partner, just realising I'm never going to have that with you, even if I get the house and I have the children and we move abroad. The connection isn't going to be there, and again that's similar to Connie. She has all these things, she's intelligent, she has a good education and she's well raised, she comes from a good background, so she has all the things that you'd think an independent smart-minded woman could ask for. And she marries well, but still, even with all those trappings, it's not there.

'Slowly, Slowly the Wound to the Soul Begins to Make Itself Felt, Like a Bruise'

And dimly she realised one of the great laws of the human soul: that when the emotional soul receives a wounding shock, which does not kill the body, the soul seems to recover as the body recovers. But this is only appearance. It is really only the mechanism of the reassumed habit. Slowly, slowly the wound to the soul begins to make itself felt, like a bruise, which only slowly deepens its terrible ache, till it fills all the psyche. And when we think we have recovered and forgotten, it is then that the terrible after-effects have to be encountered at their worst. So it was with Clifford. Once he was 'well', once he was back at Wragby, and writing his stories, and feeling sure of life, in spite of all, he seemed to forget, and to have recovered all his equanimity. But now, as the years went by, slowly, slowly, Connie felt the bruise of fear and horror coming up and spreading in him. For a time it had been so deep as to be numb, as it were non-existent. Now slowly it began to assert itself in a spread of fear, almost paralysis. Mentally he still was alert. But the paralysis, the bruise of the too great shock, was gradually spreading in his affective self. And as it spread in him, Connie felt it spread in her. An inward dread, an emptiness, an indifference to everything gradually spread in her soul. (pp. 52–53)

It's about her husband's war experience, which is like a bruise. The bruising and the almost like aftershock coming through, it really stuck with me. It's in a very, very deep place and then, slowly over time, the colours start to show and that's when it really comes out. Initially you're here, letting you get on with things and you're OK, but then the stuff that is deeper, that has gone deeper, takes longer to come out. That I think would describe the trauma afterwards of these bruises coming to the surface. And that was the real pain, that was the real hurt coming to the foreground in my relationship. My mum had died when I was 12, and that happened a long, long time ago, but then in my mid-twenties, my mum's Will stated that that was the time that we had to sell the house, when the youngest had turned 18, and divide up all of the estate. So I was going through all of that, it was incredibly painful. I felt like I was grieving all over again, it was very, very raw, and very upsetting for me. And I didn't feel that my partner supported me enough, or really understood. He wasn't there for me in the way that I would have liked, and that for me was just something that I almost couldn't get past. We couldn't really get through it because it made me think, although this situation isn't going to happen again in our relationship, something similar might. And if this is how we deal with our problems, or you deal with my grief, then this isn't going to work long-term. The grief was the big thing for me and that for me was the connection about the bruise. Although I'd suffered the grief of my mother many, many years beforehand, it was that bruise, it was coming to the surface now. Well, if he couldn't handle that part of me, then we weren't going to make it.

After my mother died, I was raised by her sister, my aunt. She was a maiden aunt, never married, never had any children of her own, didn't do the best job, but you know, did all that she could. She was estranged from my father who lived abroad and was a sea captain. And he would come home and, yeah, be abusive in his own way and then go off. When my mother died we didn't have any grief counselling. It wasn't handled very well I think by the family as a whole. They come from Irish stock and it was just […] you get on with it, you don't discuss it. So it was very much me finding my own way.

So I had a lot of different things going on within my past, and my partner had almost this idyllic home life with one younger brother, a mother and father that were still together and still very happy. His mum was a retired primary school teacher, which is what I was doing at the time, just qualified as a teacher, and his dad was a museum curator and they lived in the Wye Valley and had this beautiful country life and it was just so very different from my own upbringing. I think when he first saw my family, he couldn't understand how we were that way with each other. And rather than maybe either not saying anything, or maybe trying to be diplomatic, he just was very negative and would say negative things about my family or moan to me about them, which I just didn't find helpful.

We had to sell the house at the start of the year, that's when the proceedings begun. It was all done by May. Then we went to stay with his parents for the holidays. His mum told me this story about how she had read *Lady Chatterley's Lover* many years ago. It had fallen out of a bag when she was on the train in London, but because it was such a scandal at the time to read it, she daren't pick it up, and had walked away from it. And I thought that's such a funny story, I'll have to read this book. So that was the reason why I ever first picked it up. I was reading it just to see if it would be quite funny, or how risqué it was going to be. And actually, the sexual parts they're part and parcel in a certain way of the connection between the two, but it wasn't anything that I ever remember about it or take from it, it was just very much her sort of escape and the enlightenment that she gets. I was reading it in Leeds, also on the train quite a lot, as I was travelling back and forth for the weekends. I'd go back to Bristol a lot just to see my family and to see my sisters who were over there, and I guess deal with the aftermath of splitting up the house. So there were lots of pressures and stresses and strains. And as I struggled with my emotions and what was going on, I just felt this gulf grow between us. My partner had come with me for a lot of visits while we were physically emptying out the house and doing all that stuff, but then afterwards he stayed in Leeds and I would be travelling over on my own, and so that's when I would do a lot of my reading, on the train. I find that trains in particular, I can't read on the bus because it makes me nauseous, but trains are just very good thinking spaces for me.

'She Felt She Was Being Crushed to Death'

> Connie really sometimes felt she would die at this time. She felt she was being crushed to death by weird lies, and by the amazing cruelty of idiocy. (p. 120)

In the beginning there's her growing disdain for her partner and her wanting to get away. And, you know, she starts off by having the affair with the guy that comes round at the beginning, I can't remember his name. And she's not particularly emotionally attached, but it's fine and it sort of serves a purpose there. Even then she knows that's maybe not enough, but she starts off by trying to tell herself that'll be enough and if I just do this, then I can still stay with Clifford and it'll be fine. And we don't have to be a partnership, I can just function with him as a pair and then I can tell him when I've met someone else. And I guess for me, you know, I could see that as well, I would think maybe we're not going to be close forever, but he's intelligent and we can have a conversation and whatever. But then even that slipped away from me. So in the book it goes from that being enough, to her then meeting Mellors. And the way that he almost changes something inside her, the way that her feelings then sit. Her emotions sit differently within her stomach and she reacts to things differently. There's a part where she's almost become a bit of a zombie, everyone's quite worried about her and it looks like she's quite ill and her sister comes along to intervene, to take her away. And again, that was something that I could connect with. With all the other emotions that were happening, I fell into a depression, so I had that sort of fuzziness around me where I was just getting through and could do my day-to-day stuff, but just felt quite numb, to the outside world.

My partner knew that I'd had counselling in the past and that I was depressive. But it was not something that he'd ever experienced first-hand, so I think he found it difficult to understand. Once I started to take medication, I think he felt that that would then make it go away and it'd be all right very quickly. Obviously that's not how it works, but once I'd got to the point where I'd tried to talk to him a few times, and we hadn't communicated effectively, for me then I just felt that part shut down. I thought well I'm not going to try anymore, because it's not going to get me anywhere. So again that was another way of distance coming between us.

Connie is thinking that if she has a child, then that will fix things. And there was a point, when we moved house, where I did wonder if that would be an option. Maybe if I just brought a new life into the world it would give me something to love and make things better and bring a positive out of a negative. Connie thinks that that could be an option, but then at the same time she realises that it could be quite a terrifying thing, just to have the child for the sake of a child, and not to have it as something born out of love. She describes it here as feeling like she's being crushed, and I can remember my dark patches, just feeling like a sort of physical weight on me, and feeling that everything that I said was a lie. That I was merely pretending, oh aye, yeah, I'm fine. Wanting to speak to people without being able to express myself fully. It was like a physical *weight*, it was like a *weight* on my chest, just within me, that I was carrying around. Which I guess was sadness, depression and whatever, really feeling like Connie does in this passage.

It does feel a bit idiotic when you're depressed, or there's a sadness that you know that you should logically be able to reason yourself out of, but you can't help the way that you feel. And if you're depressed or if you're in your dark place, you know when you think: if I just tell myself enough times that I'm OK with things, then I'll be happy.

Thor: So if you can understand why you're unhappy then logically you should no longer be so?
Veronica: Yeah.
Thor: But that doesn't work?

Veronica: No, no. And then it's getting to the root of the bruising, as it were, and really, just thinking deeper, and digging deeper. I think the tablets that I was on and the lifestyle that I was living served the purpose of just numbing those outward feelings, but never really addressing what the root of it was. And therefore the cycle continued, and then I felt more stupid and more of an idiot for not being able to get myself out of this rut that I was in.

Thor: So you were hammering yourself over the head with a …

Veronica: Yeah, really punishing myself. Not forgiving myself for feeling that way, and not being able to forgive other people for not understanding, or not wanting to be with me, or not wanting to help me get out of it.

Thor: It's a very dark place to be?

Veronica: Yes, it was a very dark place. I think I've had numerous bouts of depression throughout my life, and I'd say that was …

Thor: Since your mother died?

Veronica: Since my mother died, yeah, and I'd say that's one of the darkest. Because at that age, it was probably the first time that I really had an understanding of what depression was and how it made me feel. Looking back I think I'd probably suffered depression through my teens as well, after her death, but hadn't understood it. I thought it was just hormones, it was anger or it was just rage at whoever was bringing me up. The understanding wasn't there then, but at this point in my mid-twenties, I could understand what it was. And I was able to read around the subject and do research and find all these things out. None of which were actually effective in changing the way that I felt, however. I could see that a big part of the trapped feeling that I had, came from this relationship that I was in and feeling that I was almost on a set path of unhappiness, and wasn't able to come away from it. Hmm, ooh, I feel tingly now.

Thor: What happened there? Did the tingling come as you were talking about this now?

Veronica: Yeah, I could feel a nervous energy, like a flutter in my stomach. Just like a remembered feeling, of what that was like. I know I don't feel like that now, I can still remember the pain, I remember the kind of physical sensations of it, mmm, yeah.

'Weird and Gruesome'

Connie always felt there was no next. She wanted to hide her head in the sand – or, at least, in the bosom of a living man.

The world was so complicated and weird and gruesome! The common people were so many, and really so terrible. So she thought as she was going home, and saw the colliers trailing from the pits, grey-black, distorted, one shoulder higher than the other, slurring their heavy ironshod boots. Underground grey faces, whites of eyes rolling, necks cringing from the pit roof, shoulders out of shape. Men! Men! Alas, in some ways patient and good men. In other ways, non-existent. Something that men should have was bred and killed out of them. Yet they were men. They begot children. One might bear a child to them. Terrible, terrible thought! They were good and kindly. But they were only half, only the grey half of a human being. As yet, they were 'good'. (172–73)

Veronica: In this part they talk about one England blotting out another, a part of the industrial age changing, and the new England's taking over, and that changing aspect of the land and the feeling of the people. Here it compares this to, or I compared this to, Connie.

That part for me was like there just being no next. When I was on my path, then I thought that I couldn't get off it. Just not being able to see more than a couple of years' ahead. Almost not wanting to have the foresight because it wasn't something that I wanted to really think about, or connect myself to. And being unhappy in my relationship, being unhappy because of my depression, it was very much just like your world closes in. So your concept of friendships, and other interactions around you, become numb. The physical feeling was numbed. And seeing men as being an answer potentially to happiness and to finding a way out, but also being a way to make you feel more trapped and crush you, and not that you'd be who you'd need to be, that was weird and gruesome.

Thor: Weird and gruesome.

Veronica: Yeah, I guess anything, if you think about it in so much detail, can become that. On my first reading it I found it quite a romantic book, just because Connie and Mellors are so absorbed in one another and they have this little hideaway. It is just those two against the world and nothing can really get them. That seemed quite a nice idea, haha, to be able to just hide away. Maybe if you did have a grand estate with acres and acres and acres, you could just have your little life and not let the world affect you, but that's not real, is it? It's not real life, even in this with Connie having to go into the real world, going to the pits, going to the village and interact with different people. You can't, you can't escape. Now that I'm reading it again, I notice more Mellors, and his awareness of the outside world. He knows that it may not end well and that there's going to be problems. And that regardless of how much they care about each other, he's always going to be a gamekeeper and there's this class divide between them. I think I'd maybe glossed over that a little bit more in my first reading because I was so, just thinking about myself as Connie and feeling trapped and wanting to escape. But, I guess, I didn't want to think about the reality of the world outside, hmmm.

'But with a Hopeful Heart'

Well, so many words, because I can't touch you. If I could sleep with my arms round you, the ink could stay in the bottle. We could be chaste together just as we can fuck together. But we have to be separate for a while, and I suppose it is really the wiser way. If only one were sure.

Never mind, never mind, we won't get worked up. We really trust in the little flame, and in the unnamed god that shields it from being blown out. There's so much of you here with me, really, that it's a pity you aren't all here. Never mind about Sir Clifford. If you don't hear anything from him, never mind. He can't really do anything to you. Wait, he will want to get rid of you at last, to cast you out. And if he doesn't, we'll manage to keep clear of him. But he will. In the end he will want to spew you out as the abominable thing.

Now I can't even leave off writing to you. But a great deal of us is together, and we can but abide by it, and steer our courses to meet soon. John Thomas says goodnight to Lady Jane, a little droopingly, but with a hopeful heart. (pp. 335–36)

Veronica: At the end of the book, you know, you're hopeful of them two going off and having a child together and doing their own thing, but you're aware that it probably isn't going to be an easy ride.

Thor: It's quite an open ending isn't it?

Veronica: It's hopeful. Certainly this third version anyway is hopeful. And that was another thing, you know, realising that, OK, it was going to be tough for me to break away and forge a new path, and it would be painful, and that would be the reality, but, that that wouldn't be forever. And it would be better to have a few years of pain with the happier future, the longer term, than to just carry on being unhappy for a longer period. I remember thinking gosh if I come out of this relationship, then I'm going to be probably late twenties, maybe early thirties before I find a new partner and is that going to be too late if I want to have a family, do I need to just do it now, while I'm the right age? And I thought, no, it's better to be single when I'm 30 as opposed to divorced when I'm 35, and then start all over again. And that was a real active choice for me to make: Potentially cause pain now, but pain for the right reason and with a good ending forever down the line. I think that's what Connie's aware of, or maybe not aware of, I think maybe Mellors is more than she is. He's proud of her, at the end, and wants people to know about her, and not just being this kind of secret that's kept in the little hut. That feeling of relief, when you make up your mind about something, once you've made a decision, even if it's not actually happened yet, just the choice has been made.

Thor: Can you remember when that relief came, when you had that particular feeling?

Veronica: I think it was when I finished the book, and was just digesting it. And then the feeling arose: OK, I know what I need to do now. This is something different, I feel differently now. And I can remember putting it down and, the way I do with a book, I tend to just, I guess I cradle it and hold it a bit, haha, especially if it's been a good one, it's just that kind of instinctive, you want to bring it up to your chest.

Thor: It's … a physical thing, isn't it, reading?

Veronica: Yes. And if there's a particularly good passage I'll almost like stroke the page, haha, and obviously connect with it. When I went travelling, I was away for a month and I put a few books on an iPad, thinking oh that'll be easier, and then just didn't read them because I just want the book. It's not the same, doesn't smell the same, doesn't feel the same, you get the same information, but the feeling's different. When you think, what it physically does to you … I'm trying to think. It's like when I meditate. When I'm going to meditate, you get in a certain place, and you get in a certain position and there are certain kinds of physical things about yourself and your environment that are created, for that space to happen at its best. And for me when I'm reading, just the act of, I guess, sitting a certain way, or physically picking it up, the way that I physically hold myself, the physical process of turning the pages, makes me physically feel that I'm in it. The way that I can touch the page if something good happens, the way that I can sort of close it and turn it away from me. If it's electronic, or if it's something that I'm just looking at, it just feels more 2D, I can't get my hands into it, and maybe that's something kinaesthetic, I don't know. Books are just made to be held, aren't they? Holding a book, that just feels good, doesn't it?

So, yeah, afterwards, when I was digesting it, the days after I'd finished it, and just feeling, feeling a noticeable difference within me, from how I had been at the beginning of the book, to coming to the end. And that does happen with other stories that I've read since, and then I guess it sort of fades off, it peters out, but that's almost the thrill I think of it as well, when you finish it, and a sadness, when I'm reading a book that I love. And with this book, I sometimes plough through certain passages, because I'm really keen to know what's happening and I'm absorbed and I want to find out what's coming next. However, when you get to the final few chapters, I find that my pace really actively slows down, because then I don't want it to end yet, I'm not quite ready for the story to finish. And much as I wanted to find out what would happen with Connie and Mellors, I didn't want them to not be in my head anymore, so I wanted to slow it down and go back and read certain bits again.

Thor: You said at the start that the first time you read it, you were so caught up with Connie, or concerned for her, and then you realised that, hey, I should feel the same way about myself, is that right?

Veronica: Yeah, absolutely. I can remember almost wanting to shake the book, come on Connie, you can do it, sister, gearing her on to just get away, just get out!

Thor: So it was a physical response where you …

Veronica: yeah, just like, argh come on woman, what are you doing? And I guess that was just my own frustrations being projected. I remember there being a real kind of crystallising moment for me, thinking if I can want this for a fictional character, then surely I can want it for myself. And that it shouldn't just be, pardon me, a fantasy or like a 'maybe one day', or 'I'll get there in the end'. I realised that if I was going to make any changes, then it would have to be by my own hands, by my own doing. There wasn't going to be a wonderful man to whisk me off and make me feel differently about myself, it had to come from me and from within. And it helped me find that, I'm not saying straightaway, but it certainly gave me the spark to make me to want to go and find it for myself and see what that would look like.

It wasn't for a few months afterwards that I decided to terminate the relationship, but the decision for me internally had been made, that this wasn't good enough and that I had to do something. I wasn't sure exactly what it was at that point, but my willingness to tolerate the status quo sort of evaporated, and something solidified in me about wanting to make a change. It manifested itself I guess initially in me just being a little bit more distant, a bit grumpier, not as willing to just let things wash over me, or let things go. I became more assertive, certainly, and making my position felt, expressing things that I was unhappy about. Which came as a bit of a shock to my partner, because I think I'd been quite submissive up until that point and maybe just whimpered a little, but never really vocalised what I was thinking. When I did, initially it had the desired reaction, and I felt that we kind of connected a bit better, because we were more honest. I subsequently realised that that really wasn't enough, however. Just talking about it wasn't going to change the things that were fundamentally wrong between us, and that I still needed to go.

We broke up about six months after I'd read the book, and then ended up getting back together, about two months after that, and then split up for good. So the first time we broke up it was quite amiable, and it was kind of agreed that it wasn't quite right. I think he thought that I was just having a funny half hour, and that I would then change my mind. And then when we broke up for the second time, it was very – what's the word? – unfriendly. So we haven't spoken since.

Thor: After the intermittent period when you tried to get back to the relationship finally ended, where you frightened then, or did you feel lonely?

Veronica: All of the above I think. Yeah, it was very scary, it was very lonely. When we broke up it was very difficult, there was a complete shutdown. Obviously we'd been together for about three and a half years by that point so, it was quite a big divide. We still lived very near to each other, and still had lots of shared friendship groups that then had to see us separately, so it was very, very painful. I'd say probably for about ooh, like a good year, it was very difficult. I was very sad, I found work very hard. I'd just qualified as a teacher, so I just threw myself into my work and buried myself a little bit, but still held on to the idea that this was just a rough patch, and it was all going to be worth it because I'd be able to come through it, later down the line, and be better for it. And even though it was incredibly painful, and because I tortured myself for a bit when we kind of ended as well, because I'd been the one to call it. I am a hundred per cent certain that I'm better off now than I would have been. I do think back sometimes, gosh, if we had stayed together, where would I have been? I know we'd be married and really unhappy, I'd still be a teacher probably, a head somewhere really stressed and having a horrible time. Yeah, I'm really thankful that I found that book, or it found me.

'The Book Awoke Me and Enabled Me'

Thor: You said that your partner at the time didn't have empathy with your situation, your feelings, but then you had that empathy with Connie, wishing for her to be happy.

Veronica: Yeah, I was really rooting for her.

Thor: And your empathy for her, you could then transfer to yourself?

Veronica: It helped me see myself, something I may not have before, or not be able to recognise anyway. I certainly felt frustration and unhappiness and I guess anger, at certain points, but I couldn't see past that. That was what my emotion was, but feeling hopeful for Connie, and wanting better for her, that certainly made me want that for myself. It helped me understand it, almost like a mirror, like it reflected back into real life. Yeah, and it almost just seemed like such an obvious thing as well. You know, when you have that realisation, of course, come on, why can I feel it for her and not feel it for me? I think that was part of my depression and not being able to feel good about myself or feel that I was worthy. I felt that Connie deserved happiness, but maybe before reading it I didn't feel that I did. I felt like I just deserved to keep going with what I was doing. Hmm, so Connie's a great girl, haha. For me she is anyway. I remember talking to my sister about *Lady Chatterley's Lover*, and she doesn't like it. I said I think she's really great and there's some great ideas. I was really surprised, impressed, by how much more I took from the book than I thought I would.

Thor: So there's a feeling of gratitude that you found each other. And it certainly sounds as if that book has changed your life.

Veronica: Massively, I do believe so, definitely. I think it's serendipity, I guess, how certain books just come to you at the right time. They find you or you find them. Perhaps if you read the same book a year later, or a year beforehand, it wouldn't have the same impact, but just sometimes that kind of connection happens and it can't be copied, there's nothing else like it. So, yeah, I love this book, I cherish it and I'm really, really happy that I'm enjoying it as much the second time round, even though I'm getting very different things from it.

Thor: When I speak to people about the nature of the change, they use different verbs. Some readers say that the book saved their life, some people say it shaped their life. What about you?

Veronica: I feel like the book … mmm, what's the right word? …. *Awoke* something within me. I'm not going to give it all the responsibility, because I feel that I need to take some of it myself, haha, but it certainly awoke something in me. Is the word 'enlightened'? Perhaps. Would that work without sounding too religious? It enabled me to find something inside that I didn't think I still had or didn't have the ability to find. Yeah, it awoke something within me. That's a few verbs there, sorry. Awoke and enabled, I think, yeah, that's great.

Thor: So if I offered you the verb, saved, then that wouldn't feel right?

Veronica: mmm, no, not saved. It makes me think that if something saved me, then that's the only possibility, that there's nothing else that could have done the job, but I'm not sure if that's the case. In that it enabled and awoke something within me, it certainly helped my life for the better. I'm very grateful to it, and to D. H. Lawrence, God Bless him. I'm not actually religious, but yeah, it's wonderful. And I'd love to know if this book has had a similar impact on anybody else. I wonder, I'm not sure it would have, but again it's such a personal thing, isn't it?

After a lengthy pause Veronica tells me about another profound reading experience that occurred several years later.

'A Winter's Tale'

Veronica: Years later I read *The Winter's Tale*, which I'd never read before. I had glossed over it in school as a text, but never sat down and read it for pleasure. We'd studied Macbeth for GCSE and that just, argh, took all the fun out of anything for me. But I chanced upon it and there's a part at the end where, I can't remember the names now, Hermione comes back to life and it's the first time that she's seen her daughter. And it was around about the time of the anniversary of my mum's death and it had been 21 years this year. As I read it, I just completely lost it, tears just rolling down my cheeks, couldn't hold myself together. I could just completely relate to the mother, to see her daughter for the first time and then imagining myself, what if my mum could come back to life and if I could just see her for one day and just have that in a meeting with her. And whoa, all this emotion just came out. I was crying so much. I've had counselling for a number of years to deal with my grief and my loss and my upbringing, and it's just so rare, even in a counselling session, to have that release and have that connection. To think that an equally strong emotion can come from just reading fiction, without there being a psychotherapist or a psychologist there is such a powerful thing, and I really wish that more people could get to it. To actually experience it, and to feel it within you, is something that I think is quite hard to shake off, and it makes me want to learn more about it, so that I can understand it better, looking into research and dig deeper.

Thor: What would you like to find out then, how you can have such a strong connection with literature?

Veronica: I think the psychological theory behind it, what happens in your brain, what are the kind of electronic impulses that are happening when you're reading that, is it influence making, is it memory, what kind of connection? I would love to understand more about the theory behind it, of reading, and how that works and what it physically is that's going on inside us, but I think that's how my brain works, I just like to know all the facts.

Thor: You said that you can see a psychotherapist or you can read a work of literature, how come reading *The Winter's Tale* can work better?

Veronica: I think when you're in therapy, you're either being asked questions, which you then have to consider and think about and process, and you're maybe trying to juggle, is this the right answer? Is this really what I think? Are they going to judge me, or what? What judgements are they making based on what I'm saying? You are aware, even if they say that you're not, you are aware that you're very vulnerable and kind of giving things up that you're maybe not sure if that's even what you really think. Whereas with reading *The Winter's Tale*, it's almost like the kind of realisations that you make about yourself or your feelings, they rise up unannounced. You're so involved in the story, and being with the characters, and your mind's eye is just picturing a story, it almost gives you that distance to think about yourself, not in the third person but just from a different perspective and slightly further away. But looking at it through the eyes of the characters, and

I think it's often easier, for me anyway, to think about other people than about myself. You're very good at giving advice to other people but then you never take it yourself, do you? People can often come to you for advice and I'm very good at helping people and talking things out, but then doing it for myself is often very different. So just having that other person to channel it through maybe takes away some of the danger, takes away some of the risk. And even if you can't say this is really painful for me, it is possible to say that must be really painful for her, or I can understand how that would feel. Some of the words as well that was in *The Winter's Tale*, there's one line where Hermione comes alive and she doesn't go to her husband that's banished her and thinks she's dead. Straightaway, she goes to the daughter and is like, how can this be? How can you be my daughter? How have I not seen you? It's just, yeah, that would be your first thought. I think it might be just a feeling of agreement, a feeling of shared consciousness, a feeling of recognition. So that as you recognise something that a character or person in the book is feeling, it enables you to register that within yourself that maybe you wouldn't have before. I feel like it's a place to enable your own realisations to come through, almost like a gramophone: something that just amplifies what's inside. Because even when you're trying to be conscious and self-aware and observe, that still takes practice, that's not a natural way of going about things, whereas just reading a story feels natural, because from infancy you're used to stories. We use traditional tales, it's part of language acquisition, it's part and parcel of our life, even if it's stories that you hear about your aunts and uncles and mums and dads, when they were children, stories are just part of humanity.

Rereading Lady Chatterley's Lover

Veronica: Re-reading the book, it brings it back up to the surface. Reading it again, it's perfect, just as if it all fell into place. I didn't think I would read it again, because I was worried about what it would be like.

Thor: To try and protect that experience perhaps?

Veronica: Yeah, absolutely. So that exhalation when you finish a book and that buzz in everything being in your mind, yeah, there's a worry that it won't be the same or it'll be a bit different. There's a, oh what is it? There's a turn of phrase, I think it's something in Italian, and it literally translates as, cold cabbage or something like that. It indicates when you have a relationship with somebody or like an old flame or, and then you try to go back to it and reignite that, and it just doesn't work, it's just never the same, and it's like trying to re-heat cabbage, you can't do it. And I think that's the worry for me, if I go back to a book that I've connected with very strongly, there's the worry that it won't be the same or that it will taint the wonderful memories that I had from it before.

I just had a feeling, however, that it was a good time to read it again, and so I did. I spent my birthday on a beach in Mexico reading it. And just even reading the introduction, just falling in love again with the characters and with the story. And it just felt perfect to come back to it. I was a bit nervous at first, because I knew that

I'd had such a strong reaction to it the first time around. I felt a little bit nervous that perhaps it wouldn't connect with me in the same way, or that I wouldn't enjoy it and then it would sort of taint my memory or my experience. I was worried that if I didn't enjoy it again, then it would just completely take away from the love I'd had for it the first time, so I was really excited and pleased to get those positive feelings again when I read it. And just straightaway, when you're reading, you can feel a smile come across your face, yeah, it's great. Haha. I'd kept reading and then stopping and just exhaling and going, yes this is why, this is why, and for different reasons. I certainly connect with it differently the second time round as well. Initially I was very much connecting with Connie's perspective, and then this time around seeing or understanding a lot more kind of his perspective and his disappointment with the violence and the war and the more kind of political aspect of things. I don't really think that I connected with that as much, I was very much just the emotional female, that part in it was my kind of go to, and now I can see more in all of the characters that come through.

Thor: The second time you read it, do you pay more attention to how it's written, to the style?

Veronica: Hmm, a little bit. I found the introduction to this very interesting because it talked about the three versions, whereas I've only read the one, so I was more aware of that. I am interested in the characterisation a little bit more, and seeing more of the other characters come to life for me. As I said before, I was very much Connie focused. Connie was my protagonist that I was channelling it all through and experiencing it through, whereas now, when I'm reading I can sympathise with the other characters more. I've got more empathy for Clifford, I don't particularly like him, but I can understand why he is the way that he is. And I certainly feel more of a connection with Mellors as well. I see that he's probably got so much more appealing for me now in this second reading than he was in the first time, I can see that they're a good match and that he empowers her. I see the same vulnerabilities about being scared about who they are, and about going forward. The introduction, by Mark Surer, talks about the importance of isolation, which I certainly hadn't picked up on when I was reading it the first time. Being older and having to do a lot of reflection, that's something as well that just seems to make sense now, which I would never have connected with the first time round. I think it's absolutely vital to have this quiet space that you need to reflect and to process feelings and emotions. Just to gain your perspective on the world around you, and certainly Mellors is doing this. He's living on his own in the little hut and it might be deemed initially as him kind of escaping because he doesn't like the society he's had to come back to after the war, but actually, it's him recognising the importance of just having some time to yourself. Maybe not forever, but there will be periods when you just need to have nobody else around you, and I think that's important, in the modern day as well, to have those gaps, to have those quiet points, to go away and just have your own mind for a little while. Which is what I was doing when I was travelling, to get some headspace. D. H. Lawrence I love, and *Lady Chatterley's Lover* was the first book by him that I'd read. And again, being afraid to read the same one, I read others of his since, so I do like his style, I like his prose. But this is the first time I've gone back to the same text, and if I honour that I want to read the other versions, to see. But then there are so many great books out there, there's not enough time in the day, is there?

Thor: Sadly, no. So taking a step back, what's it been like to talk about this here and now?

Veronica: I've really enjoyed it. It's very helpful, it's helped me to gain more of an understanding. It certainly brings the book to life for me, it enthuses me to read more and to just absorb it all. And it just helps me understand. Vocalising something helps you process and helps you think things through, and connect with stuff that you probably wouldn't if you were just thinking about things internally. So I've loved it, yeah, thank you.

After the interview is over, I go for a long walk, mulling over in my mind the immediate impressions Veronica's story has made on me. I am left with many questions, yet I feel certain about one thing: any initial scepticism as to whether the novel had liberated her or just seduced her into seeing herself as trapped, has been dispelled. And I imagine that D. H. Lawrence, had he been able to listen in, would not only have shared my conviction that Veronica was truly empowered by what Lady Chatterley's Lover had awoken in her, but would also have felt understood by her.

Listening to the Heart

Crisis

Admitting That She Is Trapped and Finding the Strength to Leave

Veronica's opening summary of her experience is that she was 'in a long-term relationship in which I felt very trapped'. Before reading the novel she had resigned herself to her fate. The book made her realise how she could 'break free', like Lady Chatterley, by 'wanting to be proactive and actually put myself on a different path'. She decides to terminate her relationship, which turns out to be a good decision. This process of admitting and solving a problem through commitment to action seems to fit nicely into the trans-theoretical model of change elaborated by Prochaska and Di Clemente.[1] Veronica's relation may be understood as the progression from pre-contemplation (not yet having admitted to a problem) to dedication by comparing herself to Connie: from 'growing disdain', to admitting the 'lack of connection', to weighing up the pros and cons of leaving ('it would be better to have a few years of pain with the happier future in the longer term, than to just carry on being unhappy'). This process takes her to the stage of determination ('a real active choice for me to make'). A few months later she takes action ('it wasn't until a few months afterwards that I decided to terminate the relationship, but the decision for me internally had been made'). She must then pass through a difficult maintenance

---

[1] See James O. Prochaska and Carlo Di Clemente, 'Trans-Theoretical Therapy: Toward a More Integrative Model of Change', *Psychotherapy Research & Practice* 19, no. 3 (1982): 276–88.

stage: 'We broke up about six months after I'd read the book, and then ended up getting back together about two months after that.' According to Prochaska and Di Clemente, this kind of relapse is common – most people need to reaffirm their commitment and re-enter upon the course of action before the change is solidified. Thus, when they finally 'split up for good' Veronica goes through a very difficult period 'for about a good year'. The successful outcome of the action-maintenance sequence leading to completion is understood to be predicated upon the person's self-efficacy.[2] Efficacy expectations are internalised cognitive-affective resources that can be used to maintain commitment in the face of obstacles: the more effective the individual sees herself in dealing with difficulties, the more likely she is to resist relapse. Veronica has the internal resources that enable her to stay firm in her decision. 'I just threw myself into my work and buried myself a little bit, but still held on to the idea that this was just a rough patch, and it was all going to be worth it because I'd be able to come through it, later down the line, and be better for it.' However, our understanding of Veronica's inner process of change is restricted by viewing it through this framework. It is not the entrapment in a bad relationship itself that is Veronica's deeper concern. It is through the relationship that Veronica's underlying issue becomes apparent to her: the 'bruise' surfaces to manifest an inner crisis of insecurity. As such, breaking free is a necessary dialectic step in order to face the crisis: the emotional wound, which she has carried since losing her mother, can no longer be 'numbed'. Greenberg and Goleman differentiate between two different core affective schemas, one related to identity and the other to attachment.[3] Daniel Stern also points out that in infants there is a system of self-organisation that differs from the attachment system.[4] A crisis related to attachment does not have to be pathological, but can arise from the early loss of the primary caretaker. According to neuropsychologist Jaak Panksepp, who has researched the fundamental affective systems, the grief system will be activated when the child is separated from its mother, and when this loss is permanent will also activate the fear system.[5] The child will experience great psychic stress related to the loss, but this will be exacerbated by the absence of another caretaker who can regulate the emotional pain related to this loss. The activation of the attachment system is meant to solicit required help in order to regain security and regulate the emotional stress of the loss. When this fails, it can lead to a core emotional schema of fear of being alone. Such attachment insecurity will result not only in fear of being abandoned, but also in other secondary emotions such as rage. Judging by Veronica's account of her childhood after the loss of her mother, it seems there was no one else to give her adequate support in coming to terms with the loss:

---

[2] Albert Bandura, 'Self-Efficacy: Toward a Unifying Theory of Behavioral Change', *Psychological Review* 84, no. 2 (1977): 191–215.
[3] Leslie S. Greenberg and Rhonda N. Goldman, *Emotion-Focused Couples Therapy: The Dynamics of Emotion, Love and Power* (Washington, DC: American Psychological Association, 2008).
[4] Daniel N. Stern, *The Interpersonal World of the Human Infant: A View from Psychoanalysis and Developmental Psychology* (New York: Basic Books, 1985).
[5] Jaak Panksepp and Lucy Biven, *The Archeology of Mind: Neuroevolutionary Origins of Human Emotions* (New York: W.W. Norton, 2012).

> After my mother died, I was raised by her sister, my aunt. She was a maiden aunt, never married, never had any children of her own, didn't do the best job, but you know, did all that she could. She was estranged from my father who lived abroad and was a sea captain. And he would come home and, yeah, be abusive in his own way and then go off. When my mother died we didn't have any grief counselling.

It is therefore understandable that she has a deep insecurity in her relationship: will he be able to support me emotionally?

'Slowly, Slowly, the Wound to the Soul Begins to Make Itself Felt, Like a Bruise'

'I couldn't see myself being strong enough to get out of it,' Veronica says. She does *not* say that she was not strong enough at the time. She knows now, in light of subsequent events and in retrospect, that she did possess the strength and the self-efficacy. What her formulation appears to imply is that she is not in touch with the part of herself that listens to the impulses that come from within. Veronica experienced a conflict of needs: 'I definitely wanted a family […] some stability […] to feel settled […] I saw him as a vehicle to get those things.' She needs the stability that she's never had; given her account of her early loss of her mother, the absent father and the emotionally cold atmosphere at her aunt's, it is a reasonable conjecture that she has not been allowed to develop secure attachment in an empathically attuned relationship to her primary caregivers. Her partner is not seen as an individual in his own right, but as 'a vehicle' to shore up her own insecurity. The other horn of the dilemma is that she has an inner need to break free and become her own person: 'to feel differently about myself'. There are thus two opposing deep needs of her psyche: she must come to terms with the fundamental emotional wound of losing her mother, as well as the insecurity and loneliness stemming from growing up without a family; she must also become her own person, being able to rely on her own feelings so that she can establish true connection with others.

The *bruise* of her mother's death is coming to the foreground for Veronica: 'I felt like I was grieving all over again.' It is the bruise coming to the surface that brings it home to her that there is no real connection with her partner: 'The grief was the big thing for me […] If he couldn't handle that part of me, then we weren't going to make it.' He seems unable to receive and validate her core experience. Like Connie, Veronica subsequently falls into a depression, increasing the distance between them. Her attempts at communication fail, thus, 'for me then I just felt that part shut down. […] I am not going to try anymore.' In the passage quoted from the novel, Connie only dimly realises the psychic law of the bruise. The word 'realised' is ambiguous here: it could mean 'to cause (something) to become real' rather than 'to understand or become aware of'. Her *life* realises it, because all her experiences point to it. It may something she knows without being able to put into words. It is something her body knows. Connie is suffering from the effects of the bruise; they affect her outlook: everywhere she sees the lack of 'a manifestation of energy' (p. 53). It is only later, when she has fallen in love with Mellor, that she can see something different: 'Shall I tell you what you have that other men don't have, and that will make the future? […] It's the courage of your tenderness, that's what it is.' To which

Mellor responds: 'Ay!' he said. 'You're right. It's that really. It's that all the way through.' (p. 307). He feels true compassion from her here; what she says resonates deeply with him, as if she has formulated something that he knew but had yet to verbalise. He is able to recognise this as truth precisely because he has the courage of his feelings, that is, he can listen to what his feelings tell him. And in this, perhaps, lies Connie's enlightenment: instead of lamenting the (lack of) manifestation of spiritedness, she can now recognise and feel that which allows spiritedness to emerge, the very seat of spiritedness. She learns to listen to and trust her heart.

Let us note here that Lawrence was deeply concerned with the sense of touch and interoception – his focus on physical intimacy and sensuality has its roots in a desire to restore an emphasis on the body, and bring it into balance with what he judged to be Western civilization's over-emphasis on the mind through the dehumanising effects of modernity, industrialisation and instrumentalisation. His emphasis on vitality, spontaneity and instinct springs from this concern with emotional health and its dependency on contact with a bodily way of knowing. His treatment of sexuality was thus a part of a larger picture. 'I always labour at the same thing, to make the sex relation valid and precious, instead of shameful,' Lawrence wrote in one of his letters.[6] Sexuality is thus not the main aspect, but a vital part of a full life. This larger picture was connected to his religious experience: '[…] primarily I am a passionately religious man, and my novels must be written from the depth of my religious experience.'[7] He felt that a sense of wonder is our sixth sense, and 'it is the natural religious sense':

> My great religion is a belief in the blood, the flesh, as being wiser than the intellect. We can go wrong in our minds. But what our blood feels and believes and says, is always true. The intellect is only a bit and a bridle. What do I care about knowledge. All I want is to answer to my blood, direct, without fribbling intervention of mind, or moral, or what-not.[8]

When we look at the narrative structure of *Lady Chatterley's Lover*, we see that it most closely corresponds to the ironic type of *mythos* delineated by Northrop Frye. The ironic mythos 'attempts to give form to the shifting ambiguities and complexities of unidealised existence.'[9] Connie must escape from a world in which common sense is lost, dominated by the coarseness, brutality and coldness of rationality brought about by war, modernity and civilisation. The novel is not romantic in that it sets up a better, authentic world in contrast. The woods in which she meets up with Mellor is a transitory realm, a place to which Mellor has retreated in escaping from the lower world of the real. The ironic lies

---

[6] D. H. Lawrence, *The Letters of DH Lawrence*, vol. 6, March 1927–November 1928, ed. James T. Boulton and Margaret Boulton (Cambridge: Cambridge University Press, 1993), 8.
[7] D. H. Lawrence, *The Letters of DH Lawrence*, vol. 2, June 1913–Oct. 1916, ed. George J. Zytaruk and James T. Boulton (Cambridge: Cambridge University Press, 1981), 165.
[8] D. H. Lawrence, *The Selected Letters of DH Lawrence*, ed. James T. Boulton (Cambridge: Cambridge University Press, 1996), 53.
[9] Northrop Frye, *The Anatomy of Criticism: Four Essays* (Princeton and Oxford: Princeton University Press, 2000), 223.

in the distancing from the world of Connie's husband, which represents the social order. The ironic perspective sees this world as 'full of anomalies, injustices, follies and crimes, and yet is permanent and undisplaceable'.[10] This is not a life-sustaining order and she must escape from it. According to Frye, the hero must escape from such a world without being able to transform it. Moreover, the hero can only negate this world, not knowing what the alternative to which she turns will be.

Transaction with the Literary Work

Connection

Veronica regards her situation as 'similar' to Connie's. In the first passage quoted, Clifford seems to Connie 'impersonal, almost to idiocy'. And Veronica remembers looking at her partner, thinking 'he's an idiot'. Furthermore, relating an anecdote to illustrate her realisation that something is wrong in her relationship, she concludes: 'The connection isn't going to be there, and again that is similar to Connie.' She enumerates several other parallels:

> 'Connie is thinking that if she has a child [...] I did wonder if that would be an option';
>
> Reading about Connie's illness: 'again, that was something I could connect with';
>
> Like Connie, she feels 'crushed';
>
> 'I compared this to Connie';
>
> 'thinking about myself as Connie and feeling trapped and wanting to escape.'

Her evaluation of Connie is that she 'is a great girl [...] For me she is anyway.' She indicates several times that she processes the story through Connie's perspective: 'Initially I was very much connecting with Connie's perspective.' Her understanding of this is that 'I was very much Connie-focused. Connie was my protagonist that I was channeling it all through and experiencing it through.'

From these excerpts we see that the main verb she uses for her relation to Connie is 'to connect'. There are enough similarities for the two of them to connect on an emotional level. To connect implies an active process of joining, tying two parts together in order to establish a relation and close interaction. This kind of joining together may be otherwise described in terms of the Ancient Greek verb *symballein*, which means 'to put together'. This term forms the root of 'symbolic', and designates an act of uniting, joining and converging. Thus, the two parts are not identical, but 'fit together' and form a unity. Veronica never uses the verb 'to identify with'. Still, it would seem apposite to understand her connection in terms of Jauss' theory of interaction patterns. Veronica's story may be viewed as an example of a progressive sympathetic identification with the protagonist. Sympathetic interaction is characterised by compassion for an imperfect heroine: 'By sympathetic identification, we refer to the aesthetic effect of projecting oneself into the

---

[10] Ibid., 226.

alien self,' according to Jauss.[11] Furthermore, this process 'can inspire feelings in the reader that will lead him to a solidarization with the suffering hero', and thus the reader 'can recognize the scope of his own possibilities'. The identification is progressive if it evokes moral interest in the form of a readiness to act, through the reader's solidarity with a specific action.[12] If it had been regressive, it would instead have led to a tranquilizing self-confirmation by means of a sentimental engagement only. Veronica takes action to terminate her relationship through an active engagement with Lady Chatterley's project to break free from her entrapment.

However, the term 'identification' remains vague – in Jauss's account as well as in other ones. Jauss's 'pendulum movement' bears a clear resemblance to the dialectic of immersion and reflection described by Christina Vischer Bruns.[13] However, both sides of the pendulum, identification/immersion and reflection/distance, remain rather ambiguous terms that adumbrate a plethora of phenomenological experiences. Identification may entail a feeling of sameness or similarity, and may pertain to situation, predicament, personality, values, worldview or project, as well as to how the narrator relates to the character. It is not just that Connie acts and intends in certain ways, but the narrator is attuned to her experiencing so that one gets the sense that the narrator knows Connie better than she knows herself.

Veronica quotes at length from the passage about the bruise. Who does she identify with here? She does not comment upon the narrative technique used by Lawrence in this passage. But it is perhaps significant that in the second sentence the narrator reverts to the present tense. He appears to slip out of free indirect discourse here, thus reverting to speaking in his own voice. He is the one formulating the psychic law. It is almost as if the narrator himself chances upon the discovery of this law through empathising with Connie. The narrator's statement, 'and when we think we have forgotten' seems to be a statement directed to the implied reader above the head of the character, a universal law that would include every reader. Moreover, does the reflective distance point of the pendulum swing involve reflecting on the discursive and stylistic aspects, or on the nature of the identification itself? I find that the concept of metaphoric self-implication by Kuiken et al. comes closer to Veronica's transaction with the text.

Self-Compassion through Discovery of Compassion for Fictional Character

In the following passage Veronica makes a general reflection about her reading experiences:

---

[11] Hans Robert Jauss, *Aesthetic Experience and Literary Hermeneutics: Theory and History of Literature*, vol. 3 (Minneapolis: University of Minnesota Press, 1982), 172. There is however a problem with this: Jauss understands 'the readiness to act' in terms of taking pro-social action on behalf of others, based on compassion. It is quite clear in Veronica's case, that her process is not one of admiring emulation.

[12] Ibid., 59.

[13] Christina Vischer Bruns, *Why Literature? The Value of Literary Reading and What It Means for Teaching* (London: Continuum, 2011).

You're so involved in the story, and being with the characters, and your mind's eye is just picturing a story, it almost gives you that distance to think about yourself, not in the third person but just from a different perspective and slightly further away. But looking at it through the eyes of the characters, and I think it's often easier, for me anyway, to think about other people than about myself. You're very good at giving advice to other people but then you never take it yourself, do you? People can often come to you for advice and I'm very good at helping people and talking things out, but then doing it for myself is often very different. So just having that other person to channel it through maybe takes away some of the danger, takes away some of the risk. And even if you can't say 'this is really painful for me', it is possible to say 'that must be really painful for her', or 'I can understand how that would feel'.

In a similar vein to how the narrator declares that Connie 'realised one of the great laws of the human soul', Veronica seems to have come upon another such great 'law', akin to the one stated by Diogenes Laertius: 'When Tales was asked what was difficult, he said, "to know one's self". And what was easy, "to advise another".'[14] It is as if she is looking at herself through the eyes of the characters. Self-empathy must be channeled through another person or fictional character: 'even if you can't say this is really painful for me, it is possible to say that must be really painful for her.' This channeling appears to alleviate a risk, a 'danger'. What is this danger? This is something that perhaps I should have probed further into during the interview. Is it the danger involved in acting upon your own advice (making the wrong choice), or that of misunderstanding one's own feelings, an inability to 'know one's self'? Or does it have to do with the very intersubjectivity of the formation of the self, and the psychic danger involved in not experiencing empathic attunement from the environment?

We observe that Veronica describes herself as 'really rooting for' Connie, and she can remember going '"come on Connie, you can do it, sister," gearing her on to just get away, just get out!' Her appraisal of this is couched as follows: 'I guess that was just my own frustrations being projected.' Then, significantly, Veronica experiences a moment of truth: 'I remember there being a real kind of crystallising moment for me, thinking that if I can want this for a fictional character, then surely I can want it for myself. […] I realised that if I was going to make any changes, then it would have to be by my own hands, my own doing.' When I invited her to elaborate on this, she says:

> It helped me see myself, something I may not have before, or not be able to recognise anyway. I certainly felt frustration and unhappiness and I guess anger, at certain points, but I couldn't see past that. That was what my emotion was, but feeling hopeful for Connie, and wanting better for her, that certainly made me want that for myself. It helped me understand it, almost like a mirror, like it reflected back into real life. Yeah, and it almost just seemed like such an obvious thing as well. You know, when you have that realisation, of course, come on, why can I feel it for her and not feel it for me? I think that was part of my depression and not being able to feel good about myself or feel that I was worthy. I felt that Connie deserved happiness,

---

[14] Diogenes Laertius, *The Lives and Opinions of Eminent Philosophers*, vol. 1, books 1–5. Loeb Classical Library No. 184, trans. R. D. Hicks (Cambridge, MA: Harvard University Press, 1925).

but maybe before reading it I didn't feel that I did. I felt like I just deserved to keep going with what I was doing.

She implies that there is no direct identification of a sameness-relation. First she feels hopeful for Connie, she feels compassion for her. Then, remarkably, in an act of meta-cognition, she catches herself in this act of compassion. And she realizes that this way of relating to Connie is something that she is not as yet able to do for herself. This complex operation seems to involve more than just a pendulum between reading about Connie and relating it to herself. Veronica employs the commonplace simile of 'almost like a mirror'. It is as if Veronica's actualisation of Connie creates an inner entity that has reflexive compassion for her, in a double movement. The element of metacognition, of recognising the pendulum movement in full swing, so to speak, is what leads to the discovery of the need for self-compassion. Not a straightforward identification with the character's project, followed by a desire to do the same thing, but recognition of the need to listen to herself, through recognition of empathy with the other. This is not simply a back-and-forth movement between identification and reflection, it is a turning point: Veronica reads her own reading, and then interprets what implications this meta-cognitive act must have for how she relates to herself. (Let us bear in mind, however, that her description of this is also a 'reading': there may well be a gap between experiencing and narrating I). It is as if Veronica's internal *dia-logos* follows this movement:

> *Connie and I are similar: None of us are happy.*
> *I really want her to be happy, she deserves it.*
> *That means I have compassion for her.*
> *If I can have compassion for her, I ought to have compassion for myself.*
> *How would this self-compassion manifest itself? I am making myself unhappy if I stay in this relationship. I owe it to myself to finish it.*

Veronica does take action, and she does say her reading was channeled through the perspective of Connie. However, the decision to leave, and the concomitant action-maintenance sequence it precipitates, may not constitute the essence of the life-change. Ending the relationship may just have been a necessary, but not sufficient, step needed for her to be able to develop an inner security. And perhaps the interaction paradigm leaves vital aspects of Veronica's reading process unaccounted for. Veronica declares that what she took from the reading of *Lady Chatterley's Lover* was 'her sort of escape and the enlightenment she gets'. So far, I have thematised her experience in terms of the process of *escaping* from entrapment by deciding to act. But what kind of *enlightenment* does Connie, and Veronica, get? When Veronica subsequently makes the following appraisal of her experience, 'it awoke something within me,' what is this something?

Veronica's understanding of Connie's encounter with Mellor is that 'he almost changes something inside her, the way that her feelings then sit. Her emotions sit differently within her stomach and she reacts to things differently.' I think this interpretation is crucial for an understanding of Veronica's transformative reading experience. What does she mean by emotions sitting differently in the stomach? Reflecting on her experience of reading *The Winter's Tale*, Veronica evaluates this as 'a feeling of shared consciousness, a feeling of recognition':

> So that as you recognize something that a character or person in the book is feeling, it enables you to register that within yourself that maybe you wouldn't have before. I feel like it's a way to enable your own realisations to come through, almost like a gramophone: something that just amplifies what's inside. Because even when you're trying to be conscious and self-aware, that still takes practice.

This is an interesting formulation: 'to enable your own realisations to come through'. As if they are located/stored elsewhere, but you need something to let them come through to you, to be able to hear the signals; as if the sound of that voice inside you is barely audible, and needs to be amplified. Is this not a different form of knowing than the meta-cognition that enabled her to act self-compassionately, one that is predicated upon having practice in listening to one's own realisations?

The Bodily Aspects of Reading

Upon finishing the book Veronica could feel 'a noticeable difference within me, from how I had been at the beginning of the book, to coming to the end'. As she is digesting the experience, another feeling arises: 'OK, I know what I need to do now. This is something different, I feel differently now.' She now *knows*, on a deep emotional level, what must be done, because she *feels* differently. And this knowing brings another shift with it: 'That feeling of relief' once the choice has been made.

Throughout, Veronica employs a viscerally oriented discourse to describe important aspects of her reading experience. For instance, the physical environment of the reading act is important to her: 'trains are very good thinking spaces'. When I agree that reading is a physical experience, she relates that she will stroke the book if it is good, and that holding a book feels good. She talks about digesting the reading experience, and that her pace slows down towards the end. The engagement with the characters has a visceral manifestation: 'I can remember almost wanting to shake the book.' She confirms that her response was physical through her use of non-verbal utterances: 'argh, come on woman, what are you doing?!' Moreover, she describes the 'exhalation when you finish a book'. About re-reading it, she said she could 'feel a smile come across your face'.

During her depression, she 'felt numb'. When Veronica describes how she experienced her depressive state, she employs a physical metaphor: 'like a weight on my chest'. She uses 'weight' three times, literally putting weight on this word through her emphasis. And, remarkably, as she is telling me about this 'dark place', she can contact a 'remembered feeling' of the physical sensations of what it was like: she catches herself 'feel a nervous energy, like a flutter in my stomach'. She is clearly now in contact with a deeper part of herself, whereas previously there was simply a heavy weight on this chest region. Veronica's interpretation of Mellor's effect on Connie could also hold true for her own process: the reading experience 'almost changes something inside her, the way that her feelings then sit. Her emotions sit differently within her stomach and she reacts to things differently.' Self-compassion manifests itself in this ability to listen to herself differently. What is this ability, and what part of herself does she listen to?

The Felt Sense: On the Edge of Awareness

In an attempt to 'carry forward some of Merleau-Ponty's crucial insights'[15] the American phenomenologist E. T. Gendlin has elaborated a process which he terms 'focusing': how we can learn to contact, at the very edge of our awareness, a special kind of internal bodily awareness. The term he uses for this awareness is 'felt sense'. According to Gendlin, Merleau-Ponty 'greatly enriches and enlarges what can be meant by "perception". He finds the body's interaction and intentionality prior and presupposed in perception.'[16] Thus, Merleau-Ponty's achievement was that he 'rescued the body from being considered merely as a *sensed* thing among other sensed thing (as it still is in physiology). For him the body, sensing from inside, is an internal-external orienting center of perception, not just perceived, but perceiving.'[17] Gendlin aims to build on this theory in order to 'understand how the body can think beyond anything ever formulated before – how it senses on the edge of human thinking'. Steps towards change come when a person focuses on an unclear 'felt sense', one's bodily awareness of the ongoing life experience. A felt sense is the body's sense of a particular problem or situation. According to Gendlin, 'the felt sense comes in the middle of the body: throat, chest, stomach, or abdomen'[18] and for most people can be difficult to contact. It constitutes the centre of personality, residing 'between the usual conscious person and the deep, universal reaches of human nature, where we are no longer ourselves. It is open to what comes from those universals, but it feels like "really me".'[19] The process of focusing on the felt sense may lead to a 'body shift': 'a distinct physical sensation of change, which you recognize once you have experienced it' "[20] Focusing is different from merely getting in touch with one's emotions, as it concerns a different kind of inward attention to what is at first sensed unclearly. The experience of something emerging into awareness from this felt sense is one of 'relief and a coming alive'.[21] Veronica's resolve does not stem from a rational deliberation of alternatives, but from arriving at a deeply felt sense of knowing what to do: as she has finished the book and is "'igesting' it, 'then the feeling arose: OK, I know what I need to do

---

[15] Eugene T. Gendlin, 'The Primacy of the Body, not the Primacy of Perception', *Man and World* 25, no. 3–4 (1992): 341.
[16] Ibid., 342.
[17] Ibid., 349.
[18] Eugene T. Gendlin, 'The Client's Client: The Edge of Awareness', in *Client-Centered Therapy and the Person-Centered Approach: New Directions in Theory, Research and Practice*, ed. R. L. Levan and J. M. Shlien (New York: Praeger, 1984), 79.
[19] Ibid., 82.
[20] Eugene T. Gendlin, *Focusing* (London: Rider, 2003), 7.
[21] Ibid., 8.

now. This is something different, I feel differently now.' She can feel 'a noticeable difference within me, from how I had been at the beginning of the book, to coming to the end'.

At first the felt sense is a wide and vague feeling, before the core of it reaches awareness; concomitant with the awareness is a shift, something is now different inside. A felt sense does not come to one in the form of thoughts or words, but as a single and whole – albeit complex and puzzling – bodily sensation. Therefore, says Gendlin, it is difficult to describe in words: 'It is an unfamiliar, deep-down level of awareness that psychotherapists (along with almost everybody else) have usually not found.'[22]

How does this gradual deepening process, which follows Connie's own, to the point where there is a clear felt sense of what to do, tie in with the movement thematised earlier, of self-compassion through an act of metacognition? There appears to be two different, and somewhat contradictory, processes recounted. The turn of perspective in which Veronica discovers that what she can do for Connie, she also must do for herself, is described as a 'crystallising moment'. The other process is something arrived at after the reading experience has been digested. The time of the 'crystallising moment' is not specified, but it is a fair assumption that it occurred during the act of reading or before the 'digestion' of it. Thus we may assume that they occurred at different points in time. The metacognition was the result of sympathy: of hoping that Connie would escape. The feeling different within is the result of a complex process: of an empathy with Connie's deepening experience: a realisation that once the bruise has been acknowledged, one can start to develop contact with the bodily awareness.

The felt sense that brings Veronica in contact with a deeper part of herself is a meditative mode of engagement with the work that lies beyond the aesthetic pendulum of identification and distance that Jauss identifies as the progressive movement of interaction. A concept which might encapsulate the affective-visceral involvement of one's deeper self-modifying feelings is Susan Stuart's *enkinaesthesia*. Enkinaesthesia emphasises the direct and non-dual/blended experience of the other, as well as the background dimension that makes transaction possible. This dimension is primarily affective and kinaesthetic, since we mutually understand the intentionality of actions through our motor capacity. Stuart's concept encompasses two concomitant processes:

(i) the neuromuscular dynamics of the agent, including the givenness and ownership of its experience, and (ii) the entwined, blended and situated co-affective feeling of the presence of the other(s), agential (for example, human, horse, cat, beetle) and non-agential (for example, cup, bed, apple, paper) and, where appropriate, the anticipated arc of the other's action or movement, including, again where appropriate, the other's intentionality. When the 'other' is also a sensing and experiencing agent it is their – in this case, the pair's – affective intentional reciprocity, their folding, enfolding, and unfolding, which co-constitutes the conscious relation and the experientially recursive temporal dynamics that lead to the formation and maintenance of the deep integral enkinaesthetic structures and melodies which bind us together, even when they pull us apart.

---

[22] Ibid., 33.

Such deeply felt enkinaesthetic melodies emphasize the dialogical nature of the backgrounded feeling of being.[23]

Thus we may say that through a process of enkinaesthetic engagement with the work, which leads to a crystallisation through the experience of felt sense, Camilla achieves an ability to *listen to her heart*.

Resolution

Thumos

In Plato's conception of the tripartite nature of the human soul, *thumos* is the white horse that, along with the black horse of the appetites, must be guided by the charioteer of reason.[24] There seems to be no modern equivalent of the term *thumos*. In *A Study of Thumos in Early Greek Epic*, Caroline P. Caswell shows that it is difficult to 'adequately express what was intended by the Greek. And yet the uses of *thumos* are so varied, covering almost every important aspect of inner human experience.'[25] For Plato, *thumos* was closely associated with the courage to conquer and endure fear and pain of all sorts, and not simply related to anger. However, according to Barbara Koziak, modern interpreters of Plato 'often script *thumos* into a submersed narrative of anger, justice, manliness and the military life', and she criticises interpretations that translate *thumos* as 'spiritedness' expressed in 'anger against violations of one's honour or as a desire for recognition'.[26] Koziak's conjecture is that such a narrow view may be based on a superficial understanding of the *Iliad*, which of course famously opens with the emotion of rage. According to Koziak, Achilles undergoes a transformation: 'where Achilles was liable to the pathologies inherent in the dominating emotion of anger among heroic warriors, in the last book a calm settles [...]. Now a surprisingly empathetic compassion, a sharing of sorrows turns Achilles' *thumos* [.]'[27] Translations of the Iliad reveals how our own psychological vocabularies impact on our understanding of the emotions depicted. This has been demonstrated by Alasdair McIntyre in a review of the famous scene in which Achilles considers whether to draw sword against Agamemnon when the

---

[23] Susan Stuart, 'Enkinaesthesia: The Essential Sensuous Background for Co-Agency', in *Knowing without Thinking: Mind, Action, Cognition and the Phenomenon of the Background*, ed. Zdravko Radman (Basingstoke: Palgrave Macmillan, 2012), 167.

[24] In his dialogues *Phaedrus* and *The Republic* Plato allegorises *thumos* as one of the three constituent parts of the human psyche. In the *Phaedrus*, Plato depicts *logos* as a charioteer driving the two horses *eros* and *thumos*. In the *Republic* (Book IV) the soul is partitioned into *noos* ('intellect'), *thumos* ('passion') and *epithumia* ('appetite'). To its appetitive part are ascribed bodily desires; *thumos* is the emotional element in virtue of which we feel anger, fear, etc.; *noos* is (or should be) the controlling part which subjugates the appetites with the help of *thumos*.

[25] Caroline P. Caswell, *A Study of* Thumos *in Early Greek Epic* (Leiden: E. J. Brill, 1990), 1.

[26] Barbara Koziak, 'Homeric Thumos: The Early History of Gender, Emotion, and Politics', *Journal of Politics* 61, no. 4 (1999): 1069.

[27] Ibid., 1070.

latter threatens to seize Briseis.[28] As Achilles is deliberating, 'he weighed in *phrenes* and *thumos* these two courses' (1.193). George Chapman, in his sixteenth-century translation, represents Achilles's reaction as a conflict between two thoughts in his 'discursive part', whereas Alexander Pope depicts a battle between reason and passion in his eighteenth-century version. In Fitzgerald's modern translation, Achilles is torn between conflicting passions. However, the conception of *thumos* depends on an integration of emotion and reason: it entails a configuration of affect, sensation, feeling and deliberation.

In her study of psychological conceptions in Greek poetry and philosophy, Shirley Sullivan has found that *thumos* is 'the most prominent psychic entity' in the epics of Homer. Sullivan says that *thumos* can be an agent, a location or an instrument within the person. It is a vibrant source of energetic action and a seat of vital energy that can fill a person: *Thumos* is 'placed like other psychic entities in the chest, it is able to inspire, direct and guide the person'[29]; 'very often does it "order", "stir up", "urge on" or "drive" someone'.[30] In the epics of Homer, outside forces and agents can often affect *thumos* 'as it proves open and vulnerable. We see the person very much heeding *thumos*, sometimes needing to control it, and even talking to it directly.' *Thumos* can encompass and contain all the emotions. But it is also related to cognitive activity, as a person can ponder things, make plans and consider choices in his/her *thumos*. Athena says she knew in her *thumos* that Odysseus would return home. According to Sullivan, '*thumos* is the location where possibilities become apparent and it contributes to the decision that is formed',[31] and in a poem of Archilochus 'we see *thumos* connected with knowing or realizing a truth'.[32] Gregory Nagy, in his investigation of key terms in Homer's epics, consistently renders *thumos* as 'heart'.[33] However, *phrenes* normally encloses *thumos* in order that *thumos* act appropriately. Caswell accords with this view, stating that 'when the *thumos* is not contained in the *phrenes*, the intellectual function is impaired and the emotions become uncontrollable. Hence no doubt the later semantic developments of *thumos* which came to be thought of as violent emotion *per se*.'[34]

Such a conception of *thumos* is, in my view, essential for an understanding of Lawrence's novels, and for Connie's experience in particular. Curiously, the modern reduction of 'heart' to 'spirited anger' as analysed by Koziak seems to be paralleled in the narrow view of Lawrence as being primarily concerned with spiritedness, vitality and the appetites. Connie's 'enlightenment' may be said to consist of a realignment with her *thumos* as she learns to listen to and trust her heart. Accordingly, Veronica appears

---

[28] Alasdair MacIntyre, *Whose Justice? Whose Rationality?* (South Bend, IN: University of Notre Dame Press, 1988), 17.
[29] Shirley Darcus Sullivan, *Psychological Activity in Homer: A Study of Phren* (Ottawa: Carleton University Press, 1988), 55.
[30] Ibid., 58.
[31] Ibid., 56.
[32] Ibid., 62.
[33] See Gregory Nagy, *The Ancient Greek Hero in 24 Hours* (Cambridge, MA: Belknap Press of Harvard University Press, 2013).
[34] Caswell, *A Study of Thumos*, 50.

to undergo an analogous deepening process. I believe that what Gendlin describes is a form of awareness closely akin to that described in terms of *thumos*. The felt sense may be another way of formulating the '*phrenes*-encompassed' *thumos*.

In the Fullness of Time

There is an intriguing complexity in ascription of agency and meaning in Veronica's account of the encounter with the book:

> 'And I can imagine that maybe if it wasn't for the book [...] so I really feel quite lucky that this book found its way to me when it did, at the right time.'
> 'Yeah, I am really thankful that I found the book, or it found me.'

The book found its way to her – what does she mean by that? She sought one thing ('I was reading it just to see [...] how risquè it was going to be') and found another. She was motivated by curiosity, but perhaps also had other, unconscious motives. Her mother in-law had started it, but had to 'walk away from it': that story itself fascinated her and pulled her into the book's orbit. The book found her – as if it were an agent. In other words, as if it were the intention that she read that book at that time. Retrospectively, it feels as if she was meant to read it. And it happened 'at the right time': she was ripe to receive this experience, and can now be thankful that it happened. While one may intuitively relate this notion of 'the right time' to the concept of *kairos*, I think it may more precisely be designated as *horatic*. In his philological review of the etymology of the word 'hero' in ancient Greek epics, Gregory Nagy discusses the meaning of the word *hora*, the precise moment when everything comes together for the hero. *Hora* means 'season, seasonality, the right time, the perfect time; beauty'. According to Nagy, *hora* 'stood for natural time in a natural life, in a natural life-cycle. The English word *hour* is derived from ancient Greek *hora*, as in the expression "the hour is near".' Hera, the goddess of *hora*, 'was the goddess of seasons, in charge of making everything happen on time, happen in season, and happen in a timely way'.[35] This seasonality is also the mark of maturity and of ripeness.

The encounter is felt to have come about through a combination of fate, grace and luck. Veronica uses the word *serendipity* to describe this experience:

> I think it's serendipity, I guess, how certain books just come to you at the right time. They find you or you find them. Perhaps if you read the same book a year later, or a year beforehand, it wouldn't have the same impact, but just sometimes that kind of connection happens and it can't be copied, there is nothing else like it. So, yeah, I love this book, I cherish it.

The word serendipity has somehow *found its way to* into the common vocabulary. It was coined by Horace Walpole in 1754, based on his interpretation of a fairytale, *Peregrinnagio*

---

[35] Nagy, *The Ancient Greek Hero*, 32.

de tre giovani figliuli del re di serendippo.³⁶ The *New Oxford Dictionary of English* defines serendipity as 'the occurrence and development of events by chance in a satisfactory or beneficial way, understanding the chance as any event that takes place in the absence of any obvious project (randomly or accidentally), which is not relevant to any present need, or in which the cause is unknown'. According to James L. Schulmann, in his introduction to a major scientific study of serendipity, the concept is difficult to define: 'Serendipity can be about finding something of value while seeking something entirely different or it can be about finding a sought-after object in a place or manner where it was not at all expected. The word is always about what Walpole called "happy accident", but the exact mixture of wisdom and luck [...] varies.'³⁷ It seems to designate a complex phenomenon of fate, luck and sagacity intertwined. It depends on the capacity to creatively connect the finding to other things as much as on luck, and it may feel as if one was fated to discover it, or that grace was operative, thus giving rise to feelings of gratitude. It is important to note that she did not approach the book looking for a solution to her problem. Her motivation was primarily what is loosely termed 'reading for pleasure'. Yet she did happen to read it during a time of crisis: she was travelling back and forth on the train, having to deal with sorting out the property left by her mother. When she was in a state of readiness, the right book came to her. She acknowledges that the reading experience could well have been different had it occurred a year earlier or later. At the same time, she also thinks that she could have had the change experience without this particular book.

The Mother Perspective

On being asked whether the book saved her, she responds: 'no, not saved. It makes me think that if something saved me, then that's the only possibility, that there's nothing else that could have done the job, but I am not sure if that's the case'. The question is a productive one, in that it precipitates an instance of contra-factual thinking. Furthermore, she does not ascribe the facilitation of change to the book alone: 'I'm not going to give it all the responsibility, because I feel I need to take some of it myself, haha.' Thus, it is evident that she acknowledges that a different facilitative agent or crystallising event could have precipitated the change, and that the change must be ascribed both to the unique qualities of that work, and to her sagacious capacity to utilise that reading experience. Robert Merton asserts that 'the word serendipity sums up well that prevalence of unknown causes for unanticipated results'.³⁸ As Veronica emphasises, the results of her reading were highly unanticipated. And the causes of her change cannot be known, all we can do is to interpret her relation of how it happened. Within the narrative configuration

---

³⁶ Walpole describes in a letter to a friend how he found this word when reading a fairytale about three princes. The princes, however, do not make a happy discovery by accident. They happen to be able to solve a problem because they have paid attention to things along the way.

³⁷ James L. Schulman, 'Introduction', in *The Travels and Adventures of Serendipity: A Study in Sociological Semantics and the Sociology of Science*, ed. Robert K. Merton and Elinor Barber (Princeton, NJ: Princeton University Press, 2004), xiv.

³⁸ Ibid., 238.

created in Veronica's story, we see that her decision to break out of her relationship is a resolution of the crisis. At the same time, it enables her to face a deeper crisis. The resolution of the crisis of the wound left by the loss of her mother occurs only much later, in the form of her story about *The Winter's Tale*. This story was told by Veronica unbidden, and for her was closely linked to the bruise in *Lady Chatterley's Lover*. In the account she gives of this reading experience, there appears to be a homologous movement to the one described as 'the crystallising moment'. Here, Veronica seems to experience love for herself through imagining not what it was like for the daughter to see her mother again, but, in a turn of perspective, for the mother to finally see her lost child again. Let us look at what she says: 'I could just completely relate to the mother, to see her daughter for the first time, and then imagining myself, what if my mum could come back to life and if I could just see her for one day and just have that in a meeting with her.' What does she mean by 'have that'? What she is expressing here is not so much a desire to have her mother back and to tell her something; rather, she is relating to Hermione's perspective: what it is like for the mother, sprung back to life, to see her daughter. She is experiencing the encounter from the vantage point of the mother: imaginatively entering into, and tuning into, what it must be like for her to see her own daughter. 'How can you be my own daughter? How have I not seen you'? Then she can transfer this experience to her own life: what would it be like for her own mother to see Veronica again? For Veronica now to empathically imagining her mother missing her as well, releases something in her. The sorrow is released through imagining the mother's, rather than her own, grief. This is not simply a case of thinking about an imaginary scenario, this is living through the experience, an expressive enactment of a sharing of love that has evident healing effects. This is a resourceful, creative act: by relating the play to her own inner experience, she manages to address her own need by imagining her mother's love for her. My interpretation of her encounter with *The Winter's Tale* is that it allowed her to finally heal the bruise of the loss of her mother. Thus, this experience brings to completion the change initiated by reading *Lady Chatterley's Lover*. Without the prior act of self-compassion, she might never have had this healing encounter. And without the healing encounter, she would not have been able to construct a coherent narrative of positive life-change. The healing of the bruise through reading *The Winter's Tale* was made possible by the acknowledgement of the emotional pain underlying her relationship insecurity, discovered in reading Lawrence. It was by turning back to her old wound that she could free herself from what trapped her. As such, her story has the shape of an *anamorphosis*, a turning back to bring up what was hidden. Anamorphosis implies a perspective requiring the viewer to use special devices or occupy a specific vantage point (or both) to reconstitute the image. The word 'anamorphosis' is derived from the Greek prefix *ana-*, meaning 'back' or 'again', and the word *morphe*, meaning 'shape' or 'form'.

Her change story was not simply about ending an unsatisfactory relationship, but about beginning the process of restoration of *thumos*. An essential part of the integration of the experience into her life-story was the actual re-reading of the book. This was something she was wary of, feeling the need to protect the experience as if it may be 'tainted' or ruined by going back. What she discovered, however, was not only an enriched understanding of the book, but the resolution of her own story.

Chapter Four
NINA'S LIFE-LONG FRIEND FLICKA

An acquaintance put me in contact with Nina. My Friend Flicka had meant so much to her, and she was willing to meet me and tell me about it. I had never heard of the book beforehand, and was surprised I enjoyed it so much. I imagined that she must have read it as a young girl, and that the memory had stayed with her ever since. Our meeting took place in my office one afternoon in February. I made us tea, and we sat down in comfy chairs. We talked for a long time.

Thor: Could you please tell me all about your relationship with *My Friend Flicka*.
Nina: It's a bit difficult. I don't quite know how old I was when I first read it, but I was a young child. Let me have a look at the book – it says it was printed in 1973. It may be that one of my brothers had it first. So I don't know when it came into my hands, but it's like it's always been there. My mother loved reading out loud, she had taken lessons, but I preferred reading on my own. I am born in 1967, so I must have been seven or eight. Perhaps my mother read it to me the first time. But I clearly remember reading it when I was nine, ten, eleven, twelve. I can't recall what it was like arriving at a particular chapter, for instance – the feeling of 'oh, what's going to happen now?' I have a general memory of the world of the book, a world of horses, which was my dreamworld. Where I grew up, only the rich people had horses, so that was beyond even thinking about as something that would come true. My cousin and I would play at having a ranch full of horses. It's not that I really wanted to live on a ranch in Wyoming, it was just a different world to dream about. But now that I live in the countryside, I can remember all the little descriptions of scenery and animals which at the time would merely serve to colour my reading experience; they now happen before me all the time, making me think sometimes that 'Oh, I live in Flickaland.'

But to get to the essence of what this is about, I would say it's a classic coming-of-age story, about arriving at something, about overcoming something, on both the inner and outer level. And I think it was that process, and the fact that for Ken the inner world was so important, he was a dreamer. In spite of this, he managed to achieve something that I didn't: He fought for his dreams on the outer level. He could sit at the breakfast table and say out loud to his father: 'I want that horse.' He had the courage to express his deepest wish. Even though sometimes he dared not to look his father in the eye, and they would fall out. As if it was a continuous falling in and out of grace, so to speak. For me it was the greatest heroic tale I could possibly read. Not that I was fully conscious of this at the time. I wouldn't have told myself this at the age of 11. But it was the combination of admiring him for the richness of his inner life which was entirely his own, and that, incredibly for me, he could share it with his mother. He'd tell her about his feelings. His mother understands him very well, almost guessing his thoughts, and at the same time she pulls him towards reality, represented by his father. He gets so happy when he can fulfil some of his father's expectations. It's not looked upon as a fault that he is a dreamer, because that is who he is at the deepest level. At the same time, he manages to lift himself up into the reality of the outer world. That double movement, for me, was essential. And I think that on a general level that is what literature can do, it brings out what we carry on the inside, the stuff we think we are all alone with. The realisation that 'ah, this exists out there for someone else, too: Someone has written it down'. And at the same time it is just fiction.

The Great Struggle

There's much more to it than that, of course. That's why I have returned to it over and over again, I reckon. Because I have carried this inner struggle. I have always had a rich inner life, but I have believed that I had to shut it off from the world. That it would be lost to me if I tried to reveal it to someone. When I face the world I have to put all that to the side and be someone else. This has been a crucial life-issue for me during the last 10 or 15 years. I have based myself on the premise that in order to be in the world I must play according to the rules. Which means that all the things you dream about, all the things you can imagine, they are not valid. So the book gave me immense support for the way I saw the world. That it was a valid way of being. And at the same time it made me realise that it is possible to come out with the things one has inside. It's not as if Ken climbs up on a rock and declares to all the world the contents of his inner images, but he does stand up for himself and his true wants. After his pneumonia, which almost becomes a kind of purification, he manages to bridge the gap to reality. Let's see what it says on page 230 – it's strange isn't it, because I still return to this book – where it says about his illness. He's been out watching the stag – you probably won't remember all these details – but he's been out looking for a stag. That is when he decides to […] to come back to the world:

But sometimes, kneeling beside the child's bed, the sight of him made hot tears sting her eyes. It was not only the sickness of his face, the fever, the difficult breathing and dry, bluish lips, it was the utter weariness of him. It had been too much for him, this summer, this desperate striving to alter the pattern of thought upon which his life formed itself.

What a great struggle that is! And it makes me think, 'yes, he … yes, he.' I read myself into it, you know (*in tears*). How he has all the time been thinking that – or I don't know, because he also has fought his corner – at least *I* have been thinking that my inner life is something I must keep to myself. I cannot come out with it and just be myself. It's good that it says this specifically. It is such a massive struggle to change the patterns of thought that your life has followed. But this is something that I noticed only recently. It didn't register in the same way when I was twelve, I don't think. It's a new discovery.

Thor: So that is something you discovered recently?

Nina: Yes, I see that now. It's something about the whole stance, the attitude that pervades the book. That understanding of life. The enormous process of turning things around. This awareness has been there the whole time, regardless of whether I have formulated it in words. It is what made me seek that book. Let me take a breather … (*Pause*). Did you like the book?

Thor: Yes, much more than I had thought. I really loved it.

Sacrificing One's Self

Nina: This is a special book for me. I may as well tell you the history of the book itself. It's a bit touchy, this, but it's ok. When I was 16, I joined a group of Christians. They were a bit too Christian. Something about this youth milieu attracted me, there was a togetherness that appealed to me – difficult to find elsewhere. But it just got more and more confined and strict. It started off as a nice youth club, and we lived in a commune. But gradually it evolved, to the point where one was not allowed to have anything but God. You were to smash up your rock'n'roll records. These boys who were 20, they told me how this music corrupted me. We were not to trust our own will, and the life of the body was sinful. You didn't have to burn your books, because books were not as bad as music; music was of the devil. 'There is no end to all the books being written,' it says in The Ecclesiast. I had been dreaming about writing books ever since childhood. And I love music. So it meant I had to do rather severe things against myself. In fact, I burnt this book in the stove in my own house when I was 18 (*in tears*). I sat down and pondered: What is my dearest treasure? Because we were to sacrifice our most valuable possession. In the Old Testament it says 'Go sacrifice the best, and the next best of your livestock.' This conscience, which took possession of me, also conquered my home turf. Until then I had been good at leading a double life where I would be able to feel free in my own home, at least. But now even that was taken over. No one witnessed me do it, although I felt sure that somehow someone would see it. It was my own choice. But it must have been done in an attempt to become good enough. Because I went to this book to draw strength, rather than go to the Bible, I simply had to burn it. So I threw it onto the fire, hoping this would make me a better person. It didn't work, needless to say. So this copy I've got here – it's the same edition – was given to me by my cousin many years later. Prior to that I did procure another copy, but of a different edition. She has written this greeting on the title page: 'Of love and theft' (She's a Dylan fan): 'Dear Nina. I stole this book from my sister many years ago. It has endured a lengthy existence in a cellar, and survived a flooding. I have dusted down every page and tried to piece it together as best I could. It now deserves a better destiny, and I want nobody but you to have it. Happy Birthday.' What a wonderful gift that was (*in tears*). Her gesture of generosity and empathy was important. She knew my story. A different edition is not the same thing at all, it *had* to be this particular one.

Thor: So it matches the original edition you had as a child?

Nina: Yes, the same as the one I burnt. So it has become almost a symbol. That I was willing to sacrifice the most precious part of me. And that I have been able, bit by bit, to reclaim it, to piece things together. That was the gift I received. It's quite a profound experience.

Thor: To regain your book?

Nina: Yes. It is a long process to take back ownership of oneself.

Thor: So you went from sacrificing the most precious to reclaiming yourself.

Nina: I loved music, listening to it and playing music with my brother. My home was full of books and music. But I destroyed my records. So when I moved out, I didn't bring any books or records. The very things that meant the most to me. That really *were* me. They were my wells, my sources. It was explicitly said that we should cut ourselves off from our sources. I don't think I understood how much comfort I derived from those sources, how it had kept me alive in a way. Being a creative soul, they were my conversation partners, and of immense importance. That is also why it is fantastic to speak about this here today, because I have missed it. I mean, I have had plenty of books and music since, but to be inside that sphere. When that is cut off, then all that remains is the interpersonal game-playing, which depletes me. In the Old Testament it says: 'If your brother, or your friend, or your wife say that we shall worship other gods, then do not spare him but smite him down.' I underlined that with an orange marker. If my brother invited me to a concert, it created an enormous inner dilemma for me. 'If I do that, then I am worshipping false idols.' It must have created a lot of damage. I wanted to play in a band, like my brothers did. I read about double tracking on the Beatles for Sale album, and I was fascinated. I wanted to learn about these things.

When my brother turned 50 I went up on stage and performed 'This is my life' to great applause. And after that I had the feeling of 'Yes! Now it is mine.' It's all been like a long-distance love affair with my own life, almost. The theme of my life. So I think this book has been quite like a bridge. The fantastic thing about the book is that regardless of anyone else acknowledging its significance, it is out there. Someone has given a voice to this. Someone writes about it, so it is not just me. That is wonderful. Instead of just being locked inside one's own private dilemma, it can be shared. I have in some ways been struggling with my own place in the world all the time while reading it, and simultaneously finding it delightful to read it. The voice who relates the sorrow, whether it's in music or literature, it becomes both sadness and solace simultaneously. The language is the solace. There doesn't have to be a happy ending to the book, because it's the language, the telling, which gives consolation. There are other, more recent, books I could have chosen, but I reckon my relationship with books was born with this one. *(Pause)*. Please feel free to ask me questions, I like that. I will go down my paths anyway.

Thor: Yes, I will. I want to give you the room to both talk and reflect. My understanding of what you have said is that Ken represents what you felt was your situation, and he points to a way forward, he represents the courage you need.

Nina: Actually, yes. I didn't articulate that, because I wouldn't have dared to, but yes. He is a real hero, that such a sensitive person can also be an active agent in the world. Literature is more than just fiction, it is something very intimate. The book made me respond: 'Is that really possible?' Can one really lift up something so … all that you think you're alone with? And the wonderful thing about literature and music and art is that it creates such a delight as well. It is not like reading a self-help book. You become someone else, somehow. It is like dancing, in a way, a particular way of moving. You are permitted to draw threads to yourself, but at the same time you are allowed to let yourself go, to dissolve into it, to dance with what comes. You don't think throughout that 'Oh, that is just like me.' You actually get away from that, but those threads just *are* there. You simply know that. There is a great freedom in it, I find. You receive recognition of yourself. All my life I have been after a sort of 'It is ok that you exist. That you are you. It is ok that you draw from the wellsprings you do.' If only one could realise that once and for all. Then one would have been much more serene. But it is so good to experience it. To go into the library, find a book and open it, and just go: 'everything's just fine'. A strong experience.

Ken's Transformation

Thor: Surely we can say that Ken goes through a transformational process. How does he manage this, after being very ill?

Nina: Yes, it's a transformation. I haven't thought so much about his period of illness. It's not really then that it happens, although it forms a backdrop. So many things have happened to him this summer, and he can't just jump from one thing to the next. He has to let all this sink in. It is too much for him, and it also involves him thinking that his foal will die. And his father is God, the ruler of his universe. There is nothing to be done about that. One can dream, but if the father decides that the horse must die, then die it must. This is of course also in relation to myself, but I think that when so much have happened to him, it also demands a lot from him, to be able to change with it. It's some struggle. So that when he, of course he gets very ill from being submerged in the water, but also … The closest he can get is to sneak out the night before to the horse. He cannot say 'No, dad. Please let's not shoot the horse.' That is not a possibility, but what he can say is: 'Can we wait until tomorrow?' Yes, ok. He does have the freedom to do that. Because he has more influence over Gus than over his dad. And then he goes to bed, only to sneak out later. This is the limited room to act that he has got. And as fate wills it, it so happens that not only does he sit with her, but he actually saves her life. The dramaturgy here is excellent. He has shown great courage, in relation to his perception of his role in life. He has dared a lot when he managed to postpone the shooting and also sneak out at night when the others are sleeping. He cannot do more than that. And when he has done what he may, Fortune lends him a helping hand. The enormous strain on him – having lost her and got her back, over and over again. The father opposing it. They take her in, but she turns ill. A classic plot, in a way. And when that man comes to buy those prairie horses, he says: 'I can fit another horse onto the car.' And then his father asks him: 'Do you want me to sell Flicka too?' Then Ken says: 'No, I want to keep her.' Then his father responds: 'If you say you really want to keep her, we will do.' He is fair like that. Which is a good thing. Because it's so hard for Ken to look his father in the eye and declare his wishes. A big achievement for him. So I reckon that with all that has passed, and everything he's been through, he must, if he is to move on, he has to have a period of inward turning. The illness actually helps him in this respect. He was supposed to have gone back to school in three days, which would have been absolutely impossible. Then he would have just collapsed and broken down. He would have failed, he would just have sat there in his dreamworld, and been all confused. The illness is a real help. And it also does something to his parents, to his father. So I think the transformation happens before that, but it takes root during the period of illness. It makes him able to carry his new identity. That's what it does. He is able to hold and encompass that courage. It is magnificent when his dad takes him outside and … I mean, I have had three years where I was incapacitated, just lying on the floor, barely venturing outside. And suffered from terrible anxiety every time someone tried to contact me. So I know something of what it is like. How he is unable to take the world in. The world is too much with him, it's overwhelming. I can recognize that. He has protected himself from the hardness of the world outside, and against his father. He has used his dreams to protect himself against reality. Those inner images can be a fantastic resource when they get channelled, for instance into art. But they can also be an escape. A fantastic way of dealing with the world. Ken has managed to negotiate reality by just staying there in his dreams. In a way, he has also been courageous before, even though it may not have been a conscious decision. Early on in the story he is just stood watching the foals run away. And then his dad reproaches him: 'Why didn't you turn them?' He didn't because he was lost in dreams. He is not so terrified of his father as to be totally submissive, he allows himself the liberty of being distracted. He has the strength not to do what he is told. There is a power in that to, albeit negative. Because it was the only way of escape from the strict regime, the constricted world. He didn't plan to do it, it just happened, but he let it happen. I think his daydreams are also a form of creative activity. Imagining things is a form of recognition of your own creativity. By entering those dreams he is opposing his father's wishes. He knows that. It's not as if he is thinking: 'I am strong because I have my dreams and I don't do what dad wants me to.' But still there is a will there. The will not to be formed by others. I can recognise some of myself in that. It is a potentiality, because it is not given any kind of form. What he gains by dreaming is lost in his father's estimation of him. But it is from this part of himself that he finally takes the courage to stand up to his father and say: 'Yes, dad. I want her.' He must have had another room inside than the one that has been socialised into the family. And

I think that is where the transformation is. The teacher says something about the daydreaming, let me find it. On page 231 there is a dialogue between Rob and Nell about what Mr Gibson had said about Ken having a brilliant mind.

'Did you know it, Nell – that Ken is brilliant?'

'I suspected it.'

'What on earth made you think that? He has always failed at everything – till this summer.'

'Well –' Nell spoke slowly, thoughtfully, 'a dreamer – you know – it's a mind that looks over the edge of things – the way Ken can do what he calls "getting into other worlds"; gets into a picture; gets into a drop of water; gets into a star – anything .'

Rob sat looking out of the window.

He doesn't have any response to that. But it is marvellous that she has seen it.

Thor: What enables her to do that?

Nina: I reckon it's because she's a bit like that herself.

Thor: Yes, the book relates how she can be lost in looking at things, but she has the ability to gather herself when needed.

Nina: That is right. She has the healthy balance. She is such a fantastic character, you know. Yes. And he has told her much more about these things than he has to his father. Nell's been important to me, really. She has a great role, because to a large extent she acknowledges Ken's perception of reality. At the same time, and this is crucial too, she *lets* him be, she leaves him in peace. She has tremendous respect for him. She's not always hot on his heels to check on him, in that 'How are you now?' or 'Are you lost in that picture now' kind of interfering way. So I think she has a very fine way of involving herself in his life, recognizing his individuality. And she is not, she has her own issues: in the following books she becomes more fragile: It's quite strange in a way, there are marital problems and she develops a form of anxiety. Interesting that that is part of it too. That was not what I was most concerned with then. But it does make me think about who this author is, and what her life is like. So Nell develops. No, I think she is very good to and for him, because she lets him be a dreamer. And I think he knows that she knows.

Thor: So he can trust her with his secrets?

Nina: Yes, and sometimes she just asks him. There is a passage somewhere, where he is not even surprised to learn that she knows. She's always guessed his thoughts. But she never invades him, thankfully.

Thor: An interpretation on my part: The way she relates to him, is that the way the book relates to the reader?

Nina: Yes, it's … That is a good question. Yes I think it is. I think you are right. Because the thing is that the holding places we find in literature and music, it is up to us to regulate the distance. We can come and go, and that's vital. It is not the case that if all people were good to each other we would not need these books. We need the human aspect in them, but also that they are not people. There is a freedom in that.

Thor: So reading is not a substitute for interpersonal relationships?

Nina: Sometimes perhaps it can be. But it has its own unique value. If I only had people to relate to, I would end up very confused and depleted, and if I only had books I would of course get lonely. But you put it well. Nell is in that way. Obviously she has a closeness that a book cannot have, but still. You are allowed to grow into it, she doesn't try and keep him overly attached to her, holding him back, and neither does she try to tear him out of his dreamworld, the way his father does. The father wants to force him to grow up. She is there for him. And if she had been too tied to him, she may have become scared to see him change.

Thor: Early on in the book it says that both boys are astonished that Nell can tell their father what she wants. Even though he gets angry, she does not give in. Do you think Ken draws courage from that?

Nina: Hmm, I do reckon it becomes a kind of a bridge for him. Mother can speak to dad. And mother speaks to me, ergo … A little bridge over to the father. Especially when Ken says he wants that horse. Rob just says: 'I hoped you would make a sensible choice.' Whereas Nell just pretends not to know that horse, treating it like any other choice of horse. That is a beautiful moment. A conscious counterweight to Rob.

Thor: What do you think about the portrayal of the father?

Nina: One understands very well why Rob has this power. He is impressive in a way, with a magnificent personality. And he is described respectfully too, I think. In a way which gives us an insight into the society in which they live. He has been to West Point, so they must address him as 'sir'. Actually, I believe in him as a character. Nell is fantastic, almost better than any mother can be, but Rob needs her. I think one needs both parents. I think you need one parent who fully validates you, and one you must stretch towards. He knows in many ways that he has his mother's recognition, but there is also a lot of anxiety in wanting to be good enough for dad. But if father is a just man, and his actions make sense, then it is a real test of manhood, or test of personhood, to stand upright in front of dad. Because when you go out into this world, you don't meet mothers everywhere, only fathers. It is great if someone does understand you, but it may well be that no one does. There will be people who don't see your soul and understand you, who will demand something from you. I do not perceive Rob to be inhuman or unfair. He is not unrealistic in the demands he places on his son.

Thor: And he is not implacable, either?

Nina: No. He also undergoes a certain development, in that he does not go out and shoot the horse when he realizes that Gus has failed to do so. I would say that his parental project, so to speak, does make sense. The importance of being brave, and I think Rob must be very proud of his son, when he makes a choice. 'You know what I think about selling her, but what do you think?' And then Ken says: 'I want her.' It's not the choice he would have made, but he has let Ken make that choice. He is proud of his son for showing courage, I think. If you have a mother like Nell, then perhaps you can handle having a father like Rob. She becomes a sort of interpreter between the two, she says: 'But you must realise that Ken will thrive on the responsibility.' She understands these relationships much better, and she can conceive solutions that please both father and son. She's not asking Rob to simply give in to Ken's whims. She is asking him to meet Ken's real developmental needs. Ken needs something to really care for. Not just to be commandeered around the farm, and to be punished for not managing things right. He is a dreamer and will never be as good as his brother when it comes to dealing with affairs and practicalities. But if you give him that chance to grow, and this is something that I am thinking here and now as we speak, it is a fabulous message she gives her husband when speaking on Ken's behalf, it is not just a way of protecting Ken's fragility but of enabling him to grow into a human being. That he has the opportunity to use his dreams, to actualise some of them, that he has to find a way to dream realistically. In dreams everything is perfect. The dream is pure. But you dream about a reality. You must struggle to tolerate the real. All the good things in life demand struggle. It's a transformation. You must be able to tolerate that reality is imperfect.

Thor: So it is not about renouncing the dream, but of finding a way to bring it into the world by acknowledging that you must let go of perfection?

Nina: Yes. My dream has been to be on stage, as a musician. And that is great, I love being on stage. But it is the whole process of getting there. There are loads of people you have to deal with. Phone calls and practicalities. All this took me a long time to overcome. There is something anaesthetic about dreaming, or it is a privileged situation. There are so many things you don't have to deal with then. Then you create the whole story yourself. Nell has a wonderful attitude, whether it is by instinct or deliberation. She does not bow to Rob's demands. She wants Ken to become responsible, but she also wants him to be happy. Rob seems to think that happiness comes as a result of mastery. He is a bit more instrumental in outlook. That's what I reckon, and I haven't really articulated that before. That is the great thing about this conversation. I think he needs at least one period of illness to manage this transformation. At first he was just dreaming about having the horse and stroking it. But when he gets full responsibility for her, and she turns ill because of what's happened, then that's a different kettle of fish. The first thing he says to her is: "We didn't mean to kill you." He is looking after her, that's why he is not moving. And it is the boy who draws the conclusion, not the father. The boy says that he is responsible for her. He's been allowed to articulate that himself. Ken wakes up, and then I think he realises. His dad has talked to him about strength of spirit and acting like a man, trying to communicate this in a good way. So then I reckon Ken realizes that that is what it means to own something. Acknowledging the sense of responsibility. He doesn't exactly think that, but probably experiences it nevertheless. In his new life, so to speak, having chosen the object for which he is responsible, rather than just having responsibility thrust upon him, he is in an entirely new position. Rob takes many things for granted, he doesn't realise how privileged his background is. Nell has something to teach everyone in the helping professions. If you are allowed to use your own inner motivation, then you can achieve so much more.

Thor: Another thing is that Nell sees that Ken also is similar to Rob.

Nina: Yes, he is just as stubborn and unruly. The way it comes out is different. Nell almost sees too many things. She is such a special person. And perhaps that is the very strength of the book: When you come back to read bits of it, over and over, this universe is always there, even if your own family and all else is far away and all your points of contact dissolve. Ken and Rob and Nell are always sitting there at the kitchen table, and the horses are grassing till all eternity. In all turbulent periods for me this has been like a place to come home to when I have been run down. 'Ah, yes, here I am.' Can you imagine? I know what they are going to say, still it is delicious to read it again.

Thor: So you don't have to reread the whole book?

Nina: I have read it all several times. So I can just open it at random.

Where Does the Need to Hide Come From?

Thor: I don't know if you'll be able to answer this question. I understand that you have felt a need to protect and hide your inner world, whereas Ken can share it and reveal his deepest wishes. Where do you think this need to protect yourself comes from?

Nina: Oh, that is a huge question. I think it has something to do with what Hanne Ørstavik says: 'There must be someone there who can mirror the child's perspective.' It's to do with the way I grew up. Because when I joined the group of Christians, it was not the first time I experienced something like that. Not everyone would have joined this group. I entered a place where people said: 'This is the way things must be here.' It never occurred to me to express my own views of God. I thought, if I am to belong here, then I must be like them and believe what they believe. Whereas Ken manages to preserve himself, saying to himself that 'this is what dad wants, but I must also be myself'. I haven't been able to do that. It was ill fortune that I joined that group, but it was also ill fortune that I grew up to believe I must be like that. My dad was very much a realist, earthy and sensible. He was not an authoritarian. My maternal granddad was very authoritarian. Good job my mum married someone who never was angry and aggressive. Quite the opposite, if there was something he couldn't deal with, he would just go quiet. He just would not respond, assuming that to be a neutral position to take. It was mum I trusted to when it came to personal things, although she had her problems. And I could trust my dad when it came to all material things. If he said he would be home at 4:30, then he would be. Everything was in order and very reliable. Later on I understood that not everyone's home was like that. He was a university professor, worked in the Museum of History. He recognized me for my cleverness. I used to do a lot of work for him. I couldn't talk to him about feelings. I would talk to mum about literature. But he had a better grasp of reality. So he sort of demanded that I had that too. I got the impression that I must always be ready to deliver. And if there is something he doesn't like, then I must sense that and not speak about that. That is how I experienced him, I cannot say that that is what he was really like. So what I said about Rob was quite empathic of me, because I found it really hard to accept that in my own dad. My mum could get quite hysterical and had a lot of anxiety, which freaked my dad out. If she began to cry, my dad wouldn't ask her how she was, it was more like 'it's not that bad, get over it'. I never saw him console her. So I think I must have realised that my mum was frail, and decided not to upset him. I loved my mum, but I saw that it was difficult, that he was uncomfortable, so my job was not to make him uncomfortable. Then he could be a better dad for me. That was heavy work, I tell you. So I must have been very glad that Ken in a way surpassed that. Although my dad was not very similar to Rob. When they shouted for Ken to come downstairs, he would be lost on the landing, looking at that picture. Even if he got told off for it, that was a real reaction. Whereas with me, if they called out 'dinnertime!' I would immediately get up. Even though I might be reading this book. But we always had a very friendly and inviting dinner table, especially when my brothers were home. My parents were not strict. But when something happened to them, then I had to accommodate that. Not the other way round. Of course if I had really cried out for help, they would have come. They were not negligent. But emotionally they did not really see me. I must have made a rule for myself: 'If you release what is inside you, then the world will collapse!' I think I must have felt too strong, too much for them.

My dad strongly wanted me to become a correspondent travelling the world. But I couldn't. I dared not tell the stories from my own standpoint and perspective. I had been to Bosnia, experienced a terrible amount of things. My mum said I ought to publish articles about it. But I was not capable of doing that. I could not write for the public – imagine if anyone thought it was erroneous? It just made me so frustrated and furious. I had all these experiences, yet dared not tell them to the world. It has been a massive struggle. My parents thought it was terrible that I joined that group. I was baptized as a 16-year-old, but did not tell my parents as they would have disapproved. I prayed to God: 'Dear God, don't let me will what I will.' We were not meant to go to university, that was not God's will. So I found a job as an au pair, the only way to fulfil my dream of moving out and have my own home. When I eventually did start studying at university, it was after one of the others paved the way. He said: 'Well, we can sit here and wait for God, but in the meantime I think I'll go and get a degree.' Half a year later I did too. I went on to study Spanish at Uni. And then I wanted to travel and do social work in Spain. I chose to work at a Christian orphanage. My group actually collected money on my behalf. I stayed for a year. Then started to study Russian after I came back. The group began to dissolve as central members left. Gradually I began to realise that I was free to decide for myself what to do. It was terribly frightening. Apropos Ken's incubatory period, it was no easy matter saying, 'Now I can do what I want.' I had some incredibly rootless years. I bought a small apartment. How do you go about living your own life? I didn't know. And I still lived this double life. If I brought someone home, then the minute they left the door I no longer knew them. I didn't share anything of myself. Then at 32 I enrolled in a one-year creative writing course in a different town, a great experience. I loved talking about literature and texts. But it was only towards the very end of the year that I was able to write anything. It was a boarding school, though, which was very problematic for me. I couldn't keep on living in parallel worlds. I got a boyfriend there, but in the dining hall I would pretend not to know him. Through this course I was confronted with myself, and met things in myself that I had not touched before. Quite a journey. So when I got back after that year, I entered a real crisis. I could barely move for three years. It was only at the age of 38 that I discovered I was a musician. Which is a fair while ago now, almost ten years. I started playing music. Before that I was almost immobilized, spending my time on a carpet on the floor. If I attempted to get up, all the thoughts would flood over me. As long as I remained lying there, I had mercy. If I stood up, the relentless churning started. The thoughts were so painful.

Thor: It felt painful.

Nina: Yes, very painful. Because everything else would well up. I had to stay down to just keep myself together. But then I somehow found a way. I asked myself: 'What *is* all this stuff inside me? If I have kept so much stuff pent up, what is it made of?' What then transpired were complaints and grief. And on the other side of that, creativity. After a lengthy period of recreation, walks in the woods, looking out onto the sea, talking to the flowers, I started making music. Initially, I couldn't talk to anybody about this. For fear of destroying it if I shared this with anyone. Imagine that. My inner life became much more real to me. Before I joined the Christian collective, my inner life was a natural part of me. But then this conscience burrowed its way into my innermost privacy, to the extent where it controlled even what I dared to articulate to myself, inside my head. That's why I burned the book, and smashed up my records. Do you understand?

Thor: Yes, I do …

Nina: It's one thing when an authority says you're not allowed to listen to music, and you then do it surreptitiously. It's another when you yourself is the one instigating the ban. My inner life was bombarded by the Christian collective. Sometimes they would say wonderful things, other times horrible stuff, and I got all confused. However, what happened when I took ill, and hit the ground, was that I reconquered that inner space. This was crucial to me. I carried on these conversations with myself to sort my thoughts out. So if the phone rang I would suffer acute headaches, because it made me think I had to let go of the interior processing. And I refused to do that. So after a while people would stop contacting me. And even now I will sometimes be startled when the phone rings. Anyway, I managed to conquer an inner space for myself. It was fragile at first. And then I registered my account on MySpace, where I could use a pseudonym. I didn't want to use my own name, because I associated it so strongly with the girl who had helped her dad with his manuscripts. On MySpace I could just be myself, be a musician. It was fantastic. It was a community of musicians at that time. I would wake up one morning, log on and be greeted with a message like: 'Your stuff is fabulous! Your song really inspired me! Greetings from Australia!' Wow. My music had meant something to a Latin-American living in Australia. That was huge. Gradually I gained the courage to share this with other people. I was *terrified* that this would be crushed, when I came forward with it.

Thor: It just struck me now: MySpace truly meant 'my space' to you …

Nina: That's right. (*Pause*). I seldom read on trains, for instance, or in public places. It is too existential a thing for that, because something happens when I read. It's a way of working through my own inner stuff. I want to be by myself. I need to be able to let myself go, to weep or whatever. I'll read for a while, and then something will happen inside me. And if I am surrounded by people, then that movement will not have enough space. So I have a very intimate relationship to books. Sometimes I wish I could just read and let it just pass. Just to pass time and relax, not think so much. But I seek out those books that give that kind of existential experience.

The Innermost Question

I think I did happen to read this book a bit too much, at times. It gave me solace, but then I would cling onto it rather than summon the courage to act. I would stop myself from taking action almost before I knew what my intention was. I would just hold tight. But then I had an inner voice that told me: 'Now you are stopping up on purpose.' It's about knowing the dividing line between needing to recuperate and just wanting to escape. I wouldn't be happy if the only thing I'd done all these years was read this book. However, it is a valuable thing to have something to hold onto. 'At least I've got you.' Then the act of reading is just about wanting to stay where you are. Other times I discover new things in it. For instance, when I needed to cry I would turn to page 144.

Thor: When you needed to cry you opened the book?

Nina: On page 144. It's a bit of a strange story. I still cry a lot, but I think there is something about me that gives me a physiological need to shed tears. I need it to reduce tension. Crying is very restorative. I suppose that my whole life I have been interpreting things psychologically, looking for psychological causes for my feeling states. But I have found out that I have a skeletal problem which means it is difficult for me to stand straight, giving me physical difficulties when it comes to breathing. Maybe this made me feel insecure and unsafe. I still need to cry, even when I don't feel sad or there is a reason to be sorrowful. As a child there were many things I felt sad about without knowing it. I didn't know the reason why, just that I wanted solace and release, so I turned to page 144. Should I read it to you?

Thor: Yes please, that would be lovely.

Nina: Let's see. We'd best start on page 143, then. She is baking, and Ken enters the kitchen. At the bottom of the page, where it says: 'If Flicka's really loco' – can you find it?

(*Reads*).

His appearance shocked Nell. The look in his eyes was direct, almost staring – nothing like Ken. He was looking at her now to drag facts from her.

That's it! I hadn't thought about that before, but *there* is that firmness. Now he is really intent on finding out.

Thor: You discovered this just now?
Nina: I discovered it now.
Thor: 'The look in his eyes was direct …'
Nina: 'Almost staring – nothing like Ken.'
Thor: 'Nothing like Ken.' So here we see things from Nell's perspective? She's thinking that …
Nina: Yes. He *wants* to know. It is incredible. 'He was looking at her now to drag facts from her.' There you are.
(*Proceeds to read on from there.*)

'Well, Kennie?'

'If she's loco?'

'It's a bad lookout for her, then, isn't it?'

There was a long silence. He struggled. 'If she *really* is, Mother –'

'If she really is, Ken, then not all the king's horses and all the king's men –.' Nell didn't finish, but flung the dough out on the table, floured the rolling pin and began to roll it out.

Ken watched her, hooked on that terrible IF.

'Mother, is there anything you want – *terribly*?'

Nell paused, looking out of the window, then began rolling the pin lightly over the dough again.

'Kennie, there's something I've wanted – *terribly* – for a long time.'

'How long?'

'Since a few years after you were born.'

'But Mother! I didn't know you *wanted* anything!'

'Most everyone wants something, dear –'

'But not you, Mother. You're grown up, and married and you've got Dad and us – why, you're finished –'

Nell laughed. 'And I shouldn't be wanting still then, if I'm finished, should I? But people do, Kennie.'

'Everyone? Always, Mother? Don't you ever get really finished?'

Nell again put down the rolling pin, and stood with a far-away look in her blue eyes. 'I wonder. Sometimes for a minute or two.'

That brief experience of peace and fulfillment that came, she thought, now and then unexpectedly and unaccountably. Why should one, at a certain moment, be held in the stress and ceaseless striving and wanting? And the next be almost swooning in desireless bliss – open, drinking, basking –

'Mother –'

'Well?'

'*Do* you? *Will* I?'

'Will you what?'

'Get through wanting?'

'What do you want now, Kennie?'

There was a feeling in his chest that his breath was too much for it and crowded it.

'Mother, I do so *want* Flicka to be all right and not loco.'

Nell looked at him, rolling the dough thinner and thinner.

In his eyes she saw a question. He was asking if it wouldn't come true, if he wanted it hard enough; and his face was strained in anguish.

Right now, she thought, narrowing her eyes against the tears that came so quickly, stinging them, *right now* – to let him know, once for all, that wanting and wishing can't buck a fact.

'Perhaps she isn't loco dear, we don't know yet for sure. But if she is, Ken', her words came slowly, '*wanting* won't change it.'

Ken turned away and walked out of the kitchen with his chin tucked down into his neck.

'Come back when the cookies are baked, dear,' she called after him. 'There'll be some hot, crisp, brown, crumbly ones –'

She went on rolling out the dough, cutting the cookies, putting them on tin sheets in the hot oven. But she had really gone away with Ken, up the Hill, into the woods, face down on the pine needles, hands clawing at the ground, salt tears burning –

'No, Kennie – not all your love and longing – not all the wishing and wanting –'

But she didn't know that Ken was seeing the deep hollow shaft of the mine on the hillside, with a horse going down into it – not Rocket.

He couldn't stand it. There must be a way out … there always had been …

Ken turned over on his back and looked up at the sky. It was close, it was a deep blue, but not opaque; it looked as if you could go into it, farther and farther… Thinking this way, just drifting, he began to feel better. There were well-trodden paths in his mind that led out and away from the real, and on and into limitless worlds of fancy. He stopped thinking about Flicka. Stopped thinking about anything real. In that other world of fancy, there were colts and fillies too. He wanted the make believe colt that couldn't hurt itself, that could fly over six-foot fences, that needn't be broken and trained, *that couldn't be loco*, that would carry him on its back as easily as a bird carries one of its own feathers … He began to feel comfortable and free … this was the way … this was the way…

> It is fantastic. It is wonderful to read it aloud. What really moved me when I read this – it is a sad subject, of course, but what I think was my dream in all this, was that one could talk like that with a parent (*in tears*). That there would be someone who would come – that one could really ask about it. Because I didn't know what my questions were, so it was like a secret dream for me. I was of course immersed in the story itself. But in addition there was a secret dream: Imagine if one could formulate one's innermost, deepest question, and then be met with a response like that. Also, I was allowed a glimpse inside Nell. I think that is a vote of trust in young readers, that we are permitted access to her perspective. Another thing that strikes me about it – lest I kill it with talking too much – there are so

many significances to this scene – I thought that 'a situation is not so difficult if one can share with someone that it is difficult' (*in tears*). 'If you can tell somebody that things are difficult, then they are no longer so threatening.' When you have spent so much time dreaming, there is much you have not lived, in a sense. I believe that … there is an incredible happiness in that meeting, between the two. It is lovely to witness that she accompanies him in her thoughts: 'But she had really gone away with Ken, up the Hill, into the woods.' That's where he's gone. 'But she didn't know that Ken was seeing the deep' – I mean, it's just what I said earlier. She accompanies him, in her thoughts, as far as is possible - but not all the way. Because you can't do that with another person. And then he switches on his world of fancy, it's fantastic how he does that. And then, 'the lines of strain on his face relaxed'. That is in fact what I experience. I have so much tension pent up in my body. Always have had. And when I open a book, when I need to read, that is what I experience: the release of tension. I am tempted to call it the Nell-gaze, the look of acknowledgment, that the *great* reality inside me that I love, it does exist. It is great. So I have been given this. It is weird to have something like this.

Thor: Thank you for reading it to me.

Nina: I thought it was important to include this bit, but I didn't want to do it straight off. It was good to read it towards the end of the interview.

Has the Book Saved Your Life?

Thor: Would you go so far as to say that this book has saved your life?

Nina: Hmm. That has to be a hypothetical question. At least I can say that, during these last few years and when I was younger, it has made unbearable times bearable. I can go at least that far, to say that it made things bearable. I think I am too much of a coward ever to have taken my own life. I have dreamed of dying, but never been tempted to go beyond the brink. But it has carried me through unbearable times as an adult. As a child, it was something to hold on to. It has been someone to turn to in all kinds of situations. Or, in those situations when I needed someone. I do believe that a life-giving message can save you. I have a rough draft of a novel I wrote many years ago. It's about a girl who loves music, but is utterly confused. She's around 17–18, on her way to a religious service. There is a verse in a Psalm which goes: 'When the disquiet thoughts in my heart grow many, your solace brings comfort to my soul.' Fantastic, I think. In her congregation there is a pair of twins, of whom only one is a Christian. She visits the other one in his home, and he plays Janis Joplin's *Little Girl Blue* to her. When she listens to this song, tears well up in her eyes, and her hand reaches out to him. She can't say anything, she just sits there. But she receives such great solace from the song, as they listen to it together. And yet she cannot recognise it as solace, because it does not come from God.

Thor: So she cannot receive the consolation?

Nina: Well yes, she can. But she cannot admit that she does. She cannot say thank you to him. Afterwards she is going to the service, and they'll tell her to search for the source of purity, and free herself from the impure ones. But it is precisely in these impure sources that she has found consolation. Now I have reclaimed the right to find my sources where I need them. A massive difference. In the Gospel of Thomas, it says that 'If you bring forth what is within you, what you bring forth will save you. If you do not bring forth what is within you, what you do not bring forth will destroy you.' Whereas in our group, you had to remove what was inside you, and replace it with their version of God.

As a musician it is of course nice when someone says that I play the piano well. But one time this person came up to me and said: 'When you played that I could experience the world, and that is a rare thing for me.' That makes me happy, because I know how much music and literature has given me. A meeting where presence can be felt, where all the noise and distraction and misunderstandings and intentions clear away. I think art can save lives. The mirroring experience of art is absolutely vital, I think. To save a life – it is not just on a physical level. A friend of mine told me his mother had wanted to top herself, but a man had intervened and talked her out of it. In my experience, I too killed myself when I was 17, although not literally. I killed my soul, and installed a being-good-mask instead. And since then I have been working to restore, to reinstall, those original parts. So being dead can have different meanings. And it's just not for my own sake that it is a shame that I haven't had the courage to live. But for the people around me as well. If you don't reveal yourself, you also make it harder for others to do so. I don't think I would be dead now if it weren't for this book. But I would have been even more lonely as a child. And with all that that does to you over time. I would have been less able to listen to myself, to have self-belief, and to have hope that I could find myself at last. I wouldn't have harboured the hope that there is a way for me, without this book. So it has supported me and changed me.

Thor: I must say that this is a remarkable story. That you destroyed the book that meant the most to you, only to regain a copy many years later. Thank you for generously sharing this with me.

Nina: Yes, it is a strange story. It is good to talk about it. When you ask me about it, it is as if the canvas expands. A good question can somehow extend the frame. I feel strong for having done this, and am grateful for the opportunity.

Afterwards I am amazed: this book has accompanied her all her life – loved, burned, regained. And yet she still discovers new things in it. I cannot help but think about the biblical associations. About Abraham's reprieve from sacrificing the most precious. And about some words from Matthew 16:25. Whoever loses her life, shall regain it.

The Nostos of MySpace

Crisis

The Great Struggle: 'This Desperate Striving to Alter the Pattern of Thought upon Which His Life Formed Itself'

I have carried this inner struggle. I have always had a rich inner life, but I have believed that I had to shut it off from the world. That it would be lost to me if I tried to reveal it to someone. When I face the world I have to put all that to the side and be someone else. This has been a crucial life-issue for me during the last 10 to 15 years.

Nina expresses fear that the most precious part of her would become lost if it were brought into the world. She experiences the need to keep this part of her intact. Nina knows that in order to 'build a bridge' from the continent of Dream over to the land of Reality, the inner life must be shared with somebody, it must be both validated and subject to revision in dialogue. But if she does this, it may be put to death or destroyed; this risk is too great to take, as reality is ruthless. We note in this passage that Nina says she *has* had this inner struggle: subsequently she changes to the present tense: 'when I face the world'. Is this because she still carries this belief, or is this a case of using dramatic present tense? I judge it to be the latter, as she again reverts back to the past tense: it *has* been a crucial life-issue. It is only now that this has been resolved: This use of dramatic present tense reveals that it is only in the last 10–15 years that she has become aware of this inner splitting, and started the arduous search for a way to reveal her true self to the world. And yet, a deeper part of her has known this all along: 'This awareness has been there the whole time, regardless of whether I have formulated it in words. It is what made me seek that book.' Retrospectively she can see that 'all my life I have been after a sort of [...] recognition' that has not been forthcoming. Tragically, there can be no such recognition unless she reveals herself. Instead, she adopts a false self: 'In order to be in the world I must play according to the rules,' concluding that her dreams and imaginations 'are not valid'. It is only now, through 'a new discovery', that she can see that her journey has been about 'the enormous process of turning things around'. I understand her great struggle to be one of identity crisis. She must find a way to overcome her split between the false self and the inner dreamer, in order to arrive at identity achievement.

Erikson's model of psychosocial development, an epigenetic model in which each stage occurs only when the previous one is completed, was the first theory to recognise the criticality of identity development. According to Erikson, 'there is no feeling of being alive without a sense of identity'.[1] This fifth stage of his model, if negotiated successfully, should lead to identity consolidation, a person's self-definition consisting of the goals, values and beliefs to which she is committed. Failure to complete this stage results in role confusion, an inability to settle on an identity; this is characterized by vague commitments and a feeling of being disconnected from one's inner self, as well as low self-esteem. As Nina says of her former self: 'When I face the world I have to put all of that [rich inner world] to the side and be someone else.' Samuel and Akhtar have developed an assessment inventory of identity consolidation. They argue that identity consolidation, by which term they probably intend the identity status of achievement, depend upon sufficient 'psychic structuration having taken place in an individual'.[2] They delineate the following significant features of structuration: subjective self-sameness; consistent attitudes and behaviour; stable body image; authenticity; and temporal continuity. Identity diffusion will thus show up as low scores on these dimensions. Of particular

---

[1] Erik H. Erikson, *Identity: Youth and Crisis* (New York: Norton, 1968).
[2] Steven Samuel and Salman Akhtar, 'The Identity Consolidation Inventory (ICI): Development and Application of a Questionnaire for Assessing the Structuralization of Individual Identity', *American Journal of Psychoanalysis* 69, no. 1 (2009): 53.

relevance in relation to Nina's self-description are the features of subjective self-sameness and authenticity. An unstable self-image is revealed in affirming such statements as 'I feel like I can't put the different parts of my personality together', and lack of authenticity in statements such as 'I feel like I am living someone else's life rather than my own'; 'I imitate others rather than act like myself.'

Later researchers on identity developments have extended and expanded on Erikson's theory to elucidate both process and content variables.[3] Marcia, in a seminal study of the process of identity formation, conceptualised and operationalised Erikson's theory as a dialectic between exploration and commitment that could produce four different *identity statuses*: foreclosure, diffusion, moratorium and achievement.[4] Achievement is the result of going through a period of exploration that leads to firm commitments. In diffusion there is no focused exploration and there is lack of commitment. Individuals in identity diffusion are described as less autonomous and more sensitive to external pressure compared with persons in the other statuses. According to Waterman, such diffusion may be accompanied by negative emotional states such as pessimism, apathy, boredom, unfocused anger, alienation, anxiety, confusion and hopelessness.[5] Moratorium, while also low on commitment, is an active search for alternatives that may lead to commitment choices. Foreclosure is commitment without preceding exploration. Exploration is the process of finding relevant information about oneself and the environment so that one can make a decision about an important life-choice. In the views of Marcia and Waterman, foreclosed individuals tend to adopt others' goals and beliefs, and may fear to question these. Commitment is the degree of personal investment in a given choice.

In a meta-analysis of developmental patterns of identity status change, Kroger et al. found that although most studies point to progressive forms of change in identity status over time, which tend towards achievement, there also occur anomalous patterns of regression and stasis. Moreover, it is not the case that identity crisis is resolved by the time of young adulthood: 'Assessments of identity status change showed that relatively large mean proportions of individuals had not attained identity achievement by young adulthood.'[6] Kroger et al. distinguish between three types of regressive development: disequilibrium (from achievement to moratorium); rigidification (from exploration to rigid closure); disorganisation (from any status to diffusion). There are several factors that may impinge upon these movements. The conditions that may facilitate or impede progressive development, suggest Kroger et al., are a combination of one's specific life experiences with 'individual personality factors, such as one's degree of identification with a parent or significant others, openness to new experiences, one's level of resilience, general level

---

[3] See Seth J. Schwartz, 'The Evolution of Eriksonian and Neo-Eriksonian Identity Theory and Research: A Review and Integration', *Identity* 1, no. 1 (2009): 7–58.

[4] James E. Marcia, 'Development and Validation of Ego Identity Status', *Journal of Personality and Social Psychology* 3, no. 5 (1996): 551–58.

[5] Alan S. Waterman, 'Identity Development from Adolescence to Adulthood: An Extension of Theory and a Review of Research', *Developmental Psychology* 18, no. 3 (1982): 341–58.

[6] Jane Kroger, Monica Martinussen and James E. Marcia, 'Identity Status Change during Adolescence and Young Adulthood: A Meta-Analysis', *Journal of Adolescence* 33, no. 5 (2010): 694.

of ego strength and other such factors'.[7] There are individual differences in how this diffusion is experienced.

There is disagreement and variance in how overall identity is constituted. Based on Schwartz's integrative review of neo-Eriksonian identity theories, one may say that identity comprises at least seven domains: occupational, intimate relationships, lifestyle, political, religious, gender and ethnic.[8] An important distinction is made by Waterman between instrumental/pragmatic choices and personally expressive ones. Waterman holds that personal expressiveness be considered as a third dimension of identity development alongside exploration and commitment.[9] I think this is an important adjunct vis-à-vis Nina's sacrifice. The demand for personal expressiveness, that one's commitments be an ideal reflection of one's true self, may paradoxically cause rumination and hinder commitment. Perhaps the personal expressiveness-demand may lead one to focus everything within one domain, or trying to develop in too many domains simultaneously. Alternatively, the emphasis may be on commitment within domains that are estimated negatively within a given cultural context.

Initially, we may adopt this framework of identity statuses as representing four stages of Nina's struggle towards identity achievement. Her conversion and sacrifice of her own will may be understood as a foreclosure of identity exploration. Although it may have been an attempt at moratorium, in effect it turned out to be a foreclosure. Her subsequent apostasy, a gradual defection as the group dissolved, may be understood as a diffusion experience causing great distress. Her moratorium was instigated by being 'confronted with myself' in the creative writing course, instigating a three-year period of 'real crisis' during which she could 'barely move for three years'. Her identity achievement then happened at the age of 38, when she 'discovered that I was a musician'. Berman et al. have studied a condition they label 'identity distress': those instances in which identity development is highly problematic, 'a tumultuous time of existential anxiety and depression, fraught with fears and uncertainty'. They label this a crisis. They have found that identity distress is highest during moratorium, in the active phase of exploration. Commitment was found to be negatively correlated with identity distress.[10] However, although there clearly is distress during moratorium, there can also be great distress due to the inability to enter moratorium, as evidenced by Nina's 'terribly frightening rootless years'.

Carlsson et al. refer to the anomalous, regressive movement patterns as 'the dark side of identity development'. In their study they explored qualitatively what long-term identity diffusion means to people. Among their findings was that 'individuals who stay in long-term identity diffusion […] may be described as their lives are on hold, as if

---

[7] Ibid., 696.
[8] Seth J. Schwartz, 'The Evolution of Eriksonian and Neo-Eriksonian Identity Theory and Research: A Review and Integration', *Identity* 1, no. 1 (2009): 7–58.
[9] Alan S. Waterman, 'Personal Expressiveness: Philosophical and Psychological Foundations', *Journal of Mind and Behavior* 11, no. 1 (1990): 47–74.
[10] Steven L. Berman and Marilyn J. Montgomery, 'Problematic Identity Processes: The Role of Identity Distress', *Identity. An International Journey of Theory and Research* 14, no. 4 (2014): 241.

their unwillingness or inability to form and maintain a sense of identity prevents them from wholeheartedly investing themselves in anything that move them forward in life.'[11] They also indicate that these individuals experience little increase in meaning-making and therefore 'engage in very little identity work'.[12] However, is it not possible that people stay in diffusion and experience great distress in spite of engaging in soul-searching and constant identity work? Several studies differentiate between those who are troubled and those who are not. According to Luyckx et al. troubled individuals show ruminative tendencies and psychological distress. It is the striving for identity itself, and the concomitant rumination, that causes distress, rather than the diffusion itself.[13] Beyers and Luyckx found that ruminative exploration is a major risk factor for maladjustment: 'Adolescents high on ruminative exploration experience difficulties with active and purposeful exploration of alternatives. When confronted with identity questions, they brood and worry constantly without being able to close down this exploration process and make strong commitments.'[14] They also identify a second risk factor: reconsideration of commitment, in which unsatisfactory commitments are compared with possible alternatives. They conclude that 'a clear differentiation needs to be made between adaptive forms of exploration and maladaptive forms'.[15] In my view, both these maladaptive forms, one relating to exploration and the other to commitment, are connected to rumination. Rumination results in ineffective exploration and in commitments that are not allowed to take root and grow. In my understanding, the concept of rumination is essential in understanding Nina's lengthy diffusion phase after the apostasy. Let us look at Nina's account of her conversion experience and how it affected her. Whereas a successful conversion experience may be regarded as achievement of identity, Nina' story of 'de-programming' indicates that in her journey it only resulted in a foreclosure of exploration.

Conversion and Apostasy: A Failed Foreclosure Leading to Diffusion

Nina's account of her conversion emphasises that she gradually became the victim of psychological coercion. Yet her initial motivation was social: 'Something about this youth milieu attracted me, there was a togetherness that appealed to me, difficult to find elsewhere.' At the same time, 'my parents thought it was terrible that I joined that group.' There is a clear act of rebellion involved. She makes an active choice. It appears that there was no form of coercion in her upbringing, neither mother nor father were authoritarian.

---

[11] Johanna Carlsson, Maria Wängquist and Ann Frisén, 'Life on Hold: Staying in Identity Diffusion in the Late Twenties', *Journal of Adolescence* 47 (2016): 227.

[12] Ibid.

[13] Koen Luyckx, Seth J. Schwartz, Michael D. Berzonsky, Bart Soenens, Maarten Vansteenkiste, Ilse Smits and Luc Goossens, 'Capturing Ruminative Exploration: Extending the Four-Dimensional Model of Identity Formation in Late Adolescence', *Journal of Research in Personality* 42, no. 1. (2008): 58–82.

[14] Wim Beyers and Koen Luyckx, 'Ruminative Exploration and Reconsideration of Commitment as Risk Factors for Suboptimal Identity Development in Adolescence and Emerging Adulthood', *Journal of Adolescence* 47 (2016): 170.

[15] Ibid., 176.

Nina says that for a while she was 'good at leading a double life'. I take this to mean that she initially obtained something valuable; she had a sense of belonging to the community, without having to fully commit to the beliefs and values of the group leaders. 'But it just got more and more confined and strict […] one was not allowed to have anything but God'; 'This conscience, which took possession of me, also conquered my home turf.' She succumbed to psychological coercion and internalised the beliefs of the group. It is noteworthy that Nina uses the passive form in elucidating these commands: 'It was explicitly said that we should cut ourselves off from our sources', and 'we were to sacrifice our most valuable possession'. She portrays her subsequent journey as one of de-programming this coercion: 'I too killed myself when I was 17, although not literally. I killed my soul, and installed a being-good-mask instead. And since I have been working to restore, to reinstall those original parts.' She needed to belong, but did not think it was possible to have both togetherness *and* her own personal will and beliefs.

According to Long and Hadden, there are two general models that attempt to account for why people join unconventional religious groups. In sociological research, the social drift model, which emphasises wilful deviance on the part of the novice, takes precedence; whereas in psychology there has been more reliance on the 'brainwashing' model, which looks at the coercive means and deprivations employed to exercise mind control over new converts. Long and Hadden argue that both models carry partial truths. The coercion model studies how members are stripped of their identities, their willpower is corroded, they become dependent on group and they are programmed with beliefs: 'Converts are thought to be so radically and permanently transformed that only "deprogramming" will sever their allegiance to the cult.'[16] According to Snow and Machalek, there are several shortcomings in the coercive persuasion account: 'It is inconsistent with the finding that most conversions are voluntary and occur in the absence of confinement' and there is a high incidence of defection. Moreover, this model is primarily based on information from ex-converts who have been de-programmed. 'Accounts of apostasy are no less retrospective or transformative than accounts of conversion, and they are therefore no more reliable as sources of data.'[17] The social drift model, on the other hand, holds that people convert 'gradually, even inadvertently, through the influence of social relationships, especially during times of personal strain. Conversion is viewed as precarious and open to change in response to shifting patterns of association.'[18] Implied in the social drift model is the view of conversion as a compensatory move: 'an attempt by the individual to solve serious personal problems or to deal with disintegrating intrapsychic conflicts'.[19] Nina's identity diffusion after leaving the group may therefore be due to two

---

[16] Theodore E. Long and Jeffrey K. Hadden, 'Religious Conversion and the Concept of Socialization: Integrating the Brainwashing and Drift Models', *Journal for the Scientific Study of Religion* 22, no. 1 (1983): 1.

[17] David A. Snow and Richard Machalek, 'The Sociology of Conversion', *Annual Review of Sociology* 10 (1984): 179.

[18] Long and Hadden, 'Religious Conversion and the Concept of Socialization', 1.

[19] Brock Kilbourne and James T. Richardson, 'Paradigm Conflict, Types of Conversion, and Conversion Theories', *Sociological Analysis* 50, no. 1 (1989): 5.

different factors: withdrawal from the emotional investment, and suffering from having internalised 'their God', both factors leading to rumination. Why may Nina's reference to the 'conscience which took possession of me' be equated with rumination? In his theory of meta-cognitive therapy, Adrian Wells refers to a maladaptive cognitive attention style the central aspect of which is rumination, characterised by automaticity of negative thoughts and beliefs, 'difficult-to-control repetitive negative thinking' that is 'marked by engaging in excessive amounts of sustained verbal thinking and dwelling in the form of worry and rumination'.[20] Such rumination, locking attention on to warding off negative thoughts, clearly go at the expense of exploration.

Sacrificing the Source of Strength: Burning the Book

> Before I joined the Christian collective, my inner life was a natural part of me. But then this conscience burrowed its way into my innermost privacy, to the extent where it controlled even what I dared to articulate to myself, inside my head. That's why I burned the book [...] Do you understand?

On telling me why she ended up burning the book, Nina imploringly asks me: 'Do you understand?' I answered affirmatively. And yet, did I really understand? My 'yes' was probably first and foremost an acknowledgement of the severity of her crisis. Also I felt I could understand that only by an injunction from an outside force would she sacrifice her most precious possession. Still, the reasons for burning the book are complex. On the one hand, her understanding points to a process of psychological coercion. On the other, she describes it as her own choice. One may argue that it is only when the person comes to feel that it is her own choice that the internalisation process is complete, and that therefore it is mere compliance with a group norm. Is it possible, however, that Nina was hoping to be truly converted by going through this ritual?

Nina says it was 'because I went to this book to draw strength, rather than go to the Bible, I simply had to burn it'. Does she burn it to penalise herself for having worldly pleasures – or does she burn it in the vain hope that the Bible subsequently will take on the role of source of strength? She has already smashed up her records and thus fulfilled the obligation to get rid of sinful things. Hence it is reasonable to conjecture that she performs the sacrifice in the hope of receiving a greater reward, of being 'purified': 'So it has become almost a symbol. That I was willing to sacrifice the most precious part of me. And that I have been able, bit by bit, to reclaim it, to piece things together.' Nina makes the sacrifice in the hope of 'becoming a better person', not in order to live up to the demands of a punitive Superego. It is done in order to overcome an inner divide, by sacrificing one pole of the self. Nina 'wanted to play in a band', but this was impossible as it would amount to 'worshipping false idols'. Why did she find herself in this impossible dilemma? She is afraid to express her own views, both in the group and later when being unable to publish anything: 'imagine if anyone thought it was erroneous?'

---

[20] Adrian Wells, *Metacognitive Therapy for Anxiety and Depression* (New York: Guilford Press, 2009).

Nina relates this coercive belonging to a personal vulnerability: 'not everyone would have done this'. Is her conversion an 'escape from freedom' or is it an attempt at repairing a felt deficit, an 'active pursuit of a self-transformation'? By finding togetherness and relinquishing personal responsibility, one manages to defend against the disintegrating tendency. Both models account for parts of Nina's experience. However, they seem to miss an important aspect. Nina may precisely have been hoping to be changed through joining this group. A number of social scientists have posited a 'seekership' orientation that predisposes certain people to conversion. These seekers 'are more likely to undergo conversion precisely because they are in active pursuit of just such a self-transformation'.[21] As such it is not merely a defensive coping strategy meant to solve a tension-inducing life-problem, but rather a quest for development and meaning. The group gives her a sense of belonging and togetherness. But many affiliations can fulfil this function – why did she choose to convert? She must have been seeking more than belonging. One may conjecture that this 'more' is a purpose in life, a direction. According to Paloutzian et al., 'the weight of the evidence from a number of studies is that many if not most converts to one of the new religions do so for serious reasons that correspond to the personality issues of self-identity and improvement'.[22] Thus there arises the possibility that Nina was not only seeking togetherness and willing to adopt 'their God' in order to obtain it. She was actively exploring a way to overcome the painful condition of her inner divide.

My question 'where do you think this need to protect yourself comes from?' may not be a particularly good question, as it seems to invite speculation. She cannot be fully aware of the roots of her needs. Still, the question acknowledges that after an experience of apostasy and sacrificial burning, *she* will have expended a great deal of psychic energy and thought on asking *herself* that question – why she 'grew up to believe I must be like that'. Predictably, she relates it to her parents' interactional styles. She says she had to accommodate the feelings of her parents, 'not the other way round': 'emotionally they did not really see me.' And so she must always 'be ready to deliver'. Her account is centred around a deficit: a lack of self-esteem and clear values and purpose. She is afraid of expressing herself, lest she be criticised: 'imagine if anyone thought it was erroneous? It made me so frustrated and furious. I had all these experiences, yet dared not tell them to the world.' When we put together her account of her childhood and her subsequent conversion, we have a picture of a fragile self-structure.

In my interpretation, Nina's conversion was an attempt to shore up the fragile self-structure by a compensatory strategy. She attempted to merge with the group and its unrealistic demands for perfection, thus giving in to archaic idealisation needs. At the same time she felt the need to deny her ambitious needs for making music, due to her low self-esteem. Her decision to join the group and try to merge with their beliefs and standards, at the same time denying her own ambitions and creative needs, may be understood as a lack of self-cohesion. It is a compensatory strategy, in which her need to merge is so strong

---

[21] Snow and Machalek, 'The Sociology of Conversion', 180.
[22] Raymond F. Paloutzian, James T. Richardson and Lewis R. Rambo, 'Religious Conversion and Personality Change', *Journal of Personality* 67, no. 6 (1999): 1062.

that she refrains from any expression of dissent. Moreover, it is an attempt to avoid her own needs for creativity. Kohut's theory of the self as a mental-affective system or process that organises a person's subjective experience in relation to a set of developmental needs, emphasises that self-cohesion is dependent upon certain self-object needs being met. Consolidation of cohesiveness provides a sense of identity and permanence, and it enables self-regulation. The process towards cohesion takes place along three axes: the mirroring axis, the idealisation axis and the alter ego-connectedness axis. Adequate mirroring allows for a stable sense of self-esteem, ambition and creativity. The idealisation process leads to a system of values and ideals. The connectedness axis refers to the ability to form authentic relationships and become part of larger groups.[23] These three configurations serve to maintain a healthy self and are mobilised in service of restoring cohesion when the self is depleted. If these self-object needs are insufficiently met, the self-structure will be fragile. As a result, the ability to express one's true feelings, formulate realistic goals and to develop a sense of connectedness will be underdeveloped. In experiential terms, such fragility means that the person will 'become focused on their deficiencies, extremely vulnerable to criticism and failure, and overwhelmed by negative emotions, pessimistic thoughts, and feelings of alienation and loneliness'.[24] When parents fail to satisfy these needs well enough, powerful archaic needs will remain. 'The psyche continues to cling to a vaguely delimited image of absolute perfection.'[25] This means that these needs must either be expressed in an unmodified form or be denied. For instance, the person may have a strong need to 'identify with a powerful other' rather than 'develop her own system of ideals and goals and maintain a sense of direction in life'.[26] In an empirical study designed to measure insufficient structure along the dimensions of grandiosity and idealisation, Robbins and Patten found that not being able to value one's own importance and lacking goal directedness was significantly associated with low self-esteem and problems in identity formation.[27]

Transaction with the Literary Work

Moratorium

Nina says of *My Friend Flicka* that 'it's a classic coming-of-age-story, about arriving at something, about overcoming something, on both the inner and the outer level [...]

---

[23] Heinz Kohut, *Self Psychology and the Humanities: Reflections on a New Psychoanalytic Approach* (New York: W.W. Norton, 1985).
[24] Erez Banai, Mario Mikulincer and Phillip R. Shaver, '"Selfobject" Needs in Kohut's Self Psychology. Links with Attachment, Self-Cohesion, Affect Regulation, and Adjustment', *Psychoanalytic Psychology* 22, no. 2 (2005): 224–60. In this study, the authors found empirical evidence for Kohut's tripolar conception of self, although the study was based on subjects' self-reports.
[25] Ibid., 228.
[26] Ibid., 227.
[27] Steven B. Robbins and Michael J. Patton, 'Self-Psychology and Career Development: Construction of the Superiority and Goal Instability Scales', *Journal of Counseling Psychology* 32, no. 2 (1985): 221–31.

And I think it was that process that was so important to me.' Together Nina and I look at Ken's transformation process, and by doing so implicitly also discuss hers: 'This is of course also in relation to myself.' One must arrive safely at one's destination, and in order to do so one must overcome many perils and suffer much pain. It takes her many years and many returns to the universe of the book to accomplish that process of finding the courage to undertake such a journey for herself. 'It was the greatest heroic tale that I could possibly read.' In Ken's story she finds her own challenge plotted, in terms of Ken's starting point and his arrival. Nina identifies with his personality: 'For Ken the inner world was so important, he was a dreamer.' In this they are similar. But the difference is that he has the means to overcome the challenge of healing the split between dreamer and responsible agent: 'He managed to achieve something that I didn't: he fought for his dreams on the outer level [...] he had the courage to express his deepest wish.' Thus, initially, she can identify with his way of being in the world, and she can daydream about having his courage. This is her go-to source of strength, prior to sacrificing the book. 'Is that really possible?' is an expression of admiration and wonder, but first and foremost of Hope. Without hope, nothing is possible. Nina has hope, this book is her book of hope, her Bible, so to speak. Ken is like her, she is not alone. And he has found a way, therefore there is hope! The book validates her sense of self: 'You receive recognition of yourself'; 'so the book gave me immense support for the way I saw the world. That it was a valid way of being.' The dreamer is who she is, not the false self that she has tried to be. 'And also it made me realise that it is possible to come out with the things one has inside.' The book shows her that she does not need to give up on her inner self, nor that she must give up on forming an identity, but that she can arrive at a point where she can be herself. My understanding is that these two different gifts occur at very different stages on her journey. The book all along has been a support-system, but it is only with the advent of her crisis of 'lying on the floor' that she realizes the possibility of coming out with who she is inside. Upon regaining the book, her reading of it evolves and deepens, as she comes to understand where Ken gets the courage from, and what it takes for him to transform himself. Nina's view of his courage shifts from being something he has and she doesn't, to being something that he *gains*, and by imaginatively empathising with that process, she can gain it too, and 'find myself at last'. For there is another aspect of Ken's situation which she finds to be crucial: in addition to 'admiring him for the richness of his inner life', there is the fact that 'incredibly for me, he could share it with his mother'. Nina emphasises that Ken really needs a period of withdrawal, 'to let it all sink in'. 'I think the transformation happens before that, but it takes root during the period of illness.' This is necessary after 'the enormous strain' of his 'great courage' in coming out with what he wants. Ken's withdrawal is in fact a moratorium. I think Nina sees her own period of 'lying on the floor' as a similar 'letting it all sink in'.

The protagonist's descent to the underworld to confront forces of death or to gain knowledge is one of the richest motifs of classical literature, being at the core of the epic tradition from *Gilgamesh*, *The Odyssey* and *The Aeneid* to the *Divine Comedy*. The catabasis is related to both initiatory themes and the theme of quest. Raymond J. Clark divides catabasis narratives into two traditions: The 'fertility tradition', which concerns the descent to bring back a lost divinity of vegetative life, and the 'wisdom tradition', which concerns the descent to acquire knowledge about the ways of the dead. The hero contemplates the fates of those whose lives are ended, and consults them on matters pertaining to his own future.[28] Nina's (and Ken's) moratorium may be said to constitute a catabasis. She is 'on the floor' for three years, disconnecting from the outer ('upper') world of day. She has to contact a part of her that has gone underground, that is hidden from her normal self. This catabasis has a twofold function: to bring back a lost part of her, her 'inner life that was a natural part of her', and also to learn about her destiny, how to journey forward towards identity achievement. I think it is instructive in this regard to consider the *Nekyia* episode in the *Odyssey*. Odysseus receives different kinds of knowledge about his home from meeting different visages: Circe, Anticleia and Teiresias. It is a gradual piecing together, 'bit by bit', of the resources he needs in order to manage his return. According to Clark, 'in heroic mythology a catabasis may happen once in a lifetime at most'.[29] According to Judith Fletcher, who argues that catabasis is a powerful metaphor of maturation, the renewal or achievement of identity is 'a recurring feature of catabatic narratives and one that has obvious parallels with coming-of-age stories'.[30] Rachel Falconer argues that the catabatic imagination is central in the Western tradition; it constitutes a 'worldview which conceives of selfhood as the narrative construct of an infernal journey and return'.[31] Falconer maintains that in classical catabasis 'the descent to Dis or Hades is about coming to know the self, regaining something or someone lost, or acquiring superhuman powers or knowledge'. This descent culminates in 'the collapse or dissolution of the hero's sense of selfhood'.[32]

What is the transformation that ensues? 'It makes him able to carry his new identity.' Ken manages to *bridge* two needs: he is able to assume responsibility and prove himself to his Dad, while at the same time realising his dream of having his own horse. Previously, however, he had 'used his dreams to protect himself against reality'. This was a regressive, compensatory strategy: 'It was the only way of escape from the strict regime.' Now, Nina has all along been able to recognise this strategy in herself. The essential difference lies in 'the Nell gaze'. Nina says that 'what made me seek the book' was the related to its 'understanding of life' and 'the enormous process of turning things around'. In the passage on page 230 that she quotes, it is Nell who acknowledges Ken's 'desperate striving to alter the pattern of thought'. Nell deeply understands Ken's inner world, and 'incredibly for me, he could share it' with her. At the same time she 'pulls him towards reality, represented by his father'. It is this double role, dream sharer and reality-softening negotiator, that allows her to *bridge* the two poles of Ken's self so that he may both 'arrive

---

[28] Raymond T. Clark, *Catabasis: Vergil and the Wisdom Tradition* (Amsterdam: Grüner, 1981). These traditions are not exclusive, however. There are myths that combine them, such as the Hymn to Demeter.
[29] Ibid., 77.
[30] Judith Fletcher, 'The Catabasis of Mattie Ross in the Coen's True Grit', *Classical World* 107, no. 2 (2014): 244.
[31] Rachel Falconer, *Hell in Contemporary Literature: Western Descent Narratives since 1945* (Edinburgh: Edinburgh University Press, 2005), 2.
[32] Ibid., 3.

at something' and 'overcome something'. The book shows her two vital things: that she has given up on her most precious self, the dreamer, in a desperate attempt to fit in. And that there is hope, she can regain that part and be herself; the book has been 'like a bridge'. The metaphor of the bridge is repeated twice: Nell 'becomes a kind of bridge for him […] There forms a little bridge over to the father.'

There is a divide between two worlds: Ken's dreamworld and the reality of the father. Ken is, initially, subject to the sirens' song of his inner world, and to the fear of his father's harsh demands and expectations. He learns to take responsibility for the horse, earning the respect of his father and at the same time harnessing his dreams of freedom. Rob learns, reluctantly, to see that Ken 'is brilliant'. Nell is 'the bridge' between these two worlds. 'She becomes a sort of interpreter between the two.' There are two immense psychic dangers: first, of adapting to this reality by giving up and renouncing the world of dreams. Second, of refusing the world of reality by staying within the dreamworld. These dangers are the Scylla and Charybdis of ego development. The first leads to an over-adapted false self cut off from the source of inner vitality and meaning, the second to a pathological condition of maladaptation based on maturity fears, where adulthood signifies losing the most precious part of oneself. A bridge over troubled water is needed. A bridge has two ends: at the one end of the bridge there is the sharing of one's nascent dreams and ideals so that they can be moulded and given shape and concretised. At the other end, the demand must also be softened: you need not be perfect. Thus both worlds must be modified and transmuted. Over time, Nina's view of Ken and of Rob is modified. She becomes more empathic and understanding of Rob, and she comes to see that Ken needs to transform his relationship to the world of dreams. Symbolically, with time Nina comes to embody Nell's perspective on both Ken and Rob, rather than Ken's perspective on the world. It is this passage that reflects Nina's coming-of-age. We could say that she goes from loving Nell in the naïve way that Ken does, to loving Ken in the empathic-compassionate way that Nell does – a Kopernican turning.

Transmuting Internalisation

In Kohut's theory of transformation, the archaic self-object needs are modified through a transference, in which they undergo what Kohut terms 'transmuting internalisation'. This is a taming process whereby the needs gradually lose their raw intensity and find symbolic outlet. And so the individual slowly becomes able to internalise and perform vital functions of self-regulation. This is a two-stage process: first there must be a strong relationship so that the transference can unfold. Next, through manageable and minor failures of the object to conform to the expectations, a process of 'optimal frustration' ensues.[33] I think it is fruitful to employ the concept of transmuting internalisation to account for what happens to Ken through his moratorium. He comes to realise that his mother too has her own dreams, different from his. And he comes to see his father

---

[33] Heinz Kohut, *The Restoration of the Self* (Madison, CT: International Universities Press, 1977).

as someone amenable to softening. And by going over this ground over and over again, Nina can both revisit a permanent ideal universe and discover new bits that she then internalises. Even while we read it together in the interview, the book is 'the living word' as she makes fresh discoveries. In her catabasis the book is something to hold onto, a safe haven to return to; and importantly, by seeing new things in it she also receives confirmation that she is making progress. She needs to internalise 'the Nell gaze' in relation to her own life. She must see both the 'Ken pole' of herself, the pole of ambition, and the 'Rob pole' of ideals, in a new light. In literature on perfectionism it is common to distinguish between a normal and adaptive kind, 'defined as a striving for reasonable and realistic standards that leads to a sense of self-satisfaction and enhanced self-esteem' on the one hand; and a neurotic or maladaptive perfectionism on the other, 'a tendency to strive for excessively high standards and is motivated by fears of failure and concern about disappointing others'.[34] We may say that the maladaptive one is like Rob one cannot negotiate with, the adaptive kind is like Rob after he realises that Ken is both brilliant and responsible. As Ken changes, 'getting into other worlds' goes from being a defensive manoeuvre to being a source of creativity. Nina admits that it has taken time for her to be able to see Rob empathically, as well as to fathom the importance of the 'Nell gaze'. But the fact that she is able to do that is testament to the transmuting internalisation she has undergone. This has been a great struggle: to free herself from the internalisation of 'their God' and to grasp the full extent of the source of strength inherent in *My Friend Flicka*.

In a fascinating passage, Nina says:

> Nell almost sees too many things. She is such a special person. And perhaps that is the very strength of the book: When you come back to read bits of it, over and over, this universe is always there, even if your own family and all else is far away and all your points of contact dissolve [...] In all turbulent periods for me this has been like a place to come home to when I have been run down.

What I find peculiar here is the word 'and', ostensibly there to logically connect two thoughts, and yet the associative jump is apparent; it switches from talking about her affection for Nell, to musing on the self-sustaining importance of this fictional universe. Is this merely a flight of thought? What does the 'and' mean here? That she is such a special person, and that the book becomes special in a like manner? My understanding is that Nina, through a deepened appreciation of Nell, becomes aware of the extent of the Nell gaze and how vital it is. And although she always has come home to this book, now she has also come home to herself, able to be her own Nell. To conceptualise this process of a deepening engagement with the work through repeated re-readings, by which a transmuting internalisation takes place, I propose the term *palilexia*. One of the rhetorical figures of repetition is *palilogia*, which signifies a figural repetition in order to increase general

---

[34] Gordon L. Flett and Paul L. Hewitt, *Perfectionism: Theory, Research and Treatment* (Washington, DC: American Psychological Association, 2002), 11.

fullness or to communicate passion.³⁵ And in one of Heraclit's fragments, we come across the word 'palintropos': 'They do not understand how, though at variance with itself, it agrees with itself. It is a *backward-turning [i.e., palintropos]* attunement like that of the bow and lyre.' This palintropic attunement is how I understand Nina's mode of engagement with the work. So *palilexia* means a repeated reading of deepening attunement.

My initial understanding of the above passage, in which she says that 'this universe is always there, even if your own family is far away' and 'a place to come home to when I have been run down', is that this is an expression of *nostalgia*. As she says elsewhere, 'as a child, it was something to hold on to. It has been something to turn to in all kinds of situations. Or, in those situations when I needed someone.' Is it nostalgia?

Resolution

Nostos *and* Algos

In a psychoanalytic context, nostalgia was viewed as a maladaptive, regressive condition conceptualised as an acute yearning for the pre-Oedipal mother, or as an incomplete form of mourning for a lost object. In recent years, the beneficent aspects of nostalgia have come to the fore in psychology. Theorists have increasingly begun to view nostalgia 'as an adaptive response to stress or change'.³⁶ Cavanaugh considered nostalgia to represent 'a cognitive attempt to recapture a time when life was good, safe, secure, and contented', and 'one of the ways that one develops and maintains identity'.³⁷ Hepper et al., using a prototype approach, examined the lay conception of nostalgia. They found that 'lay people view nostalgia as a self-relevant and social blended emotional and cognitive state, featuring a mixture of happiness and loss'.³⁸ That nostalgia is self-relevant indicates that it may serve several adaptive functions. Two main empirical approaches to studying its adaptive functions have emerged: those who focus on its *security-providing function* – nostalgia's potential to act as a psychological protection from threatening self-relevant cognitions; and those who explore the *growth-providing function*. Sedikides et al. have undertaken several studies to find out whether nostalgia can counteract loneliness. They found that nostalgia had a restorative function. Although individuals may find it difficult to cope with loneliness directly through strengthening social support, nostalgia may work as an alternative coping strategy. They conclude that nostalgia 'restores social connectedness by increasing subjective perceptions of social support'.³⁹ This was particularly

---

[35] See Brigham Young University's rhetorical lexicon: http://rhetoric.byu.edu/Figures/Groupings/of%20Repetition.htm.
[36] Krystine Batcho, 'Nostalgia: The Bittersweet History of a Psychological Concept', *History of Psychology* 16, no. 3 (2013): 6.
[37] Cited in Batcho, 'Nostalgia: The Bittersweet History of a Psychological Concept', 6.
[38] Erika G. Hepper, Timothy D. Ritchie, Constantine Sedikides and Tim Wildschut, 'Odyssey's End: Lay Conceptions of Nostalgia Reflect Its Original Homeric Meaning', *Emotion* 12 (2012): 102–19.
[39] Xinyue Zhou, Constantine Sedikides, Tim Wildschut and Ding-Guo Gao, 'Counteracting Loneliness: On the Restorative Function of Nostalgia', *Psychological Science* 19, no. 10 (2008): 1028.

so for resilient individuals. In another study they found that nostalgia provides security through four key aspects: 'It generates positive affect, elevates self-esteem, fosters social connectedness, and alleviates existential threat.'[40] Baldwin and Landau have investigated the possibility that nostalgia may promote psychological growth understood as cultivation of potentialities, seeking out optimal challenges and integrating new experiences into the self-concept. They tested the effects of 'experimentally induced nostalgia' on growth-oriented self-perceptions and behavioural intentions. They found that nostalgia indirectly increased growth by increasing positive emotion through drawing on positive self-regard.[41] What is not discussed in this research, however, is what happens when one lacks this positive self-regard and the resilience that allows one to contact the resource bank of positive memories. Nostalgia is viewed exclusively as looking back on one's own past. Might a fictional universe assume this role by proxy? Svetlana Boym defines nostalgia as 'a longing for a home that no longer exists or has never existed. Nostalgia is a sentiment of loss and displacement, but it is also a romance with one's own fantasy.'[42] If it is a longing for something that never existed, may one then create it? Moreover, this research neglects a feature of nostalgia that has been prominent throughout the history of the concept: that it may sometimes serve a regressive function. Nina says that

> I think I did happen to read it a bit too much, at times. It gave me solace, but then I would cling onto it rather than summon the courage to act. I would stop myself from taking action almost before I knew what my intention was. But then I had an inner voice that told me: 'Now you are stopping up on purpose.' It's about knowing the dividing line between needing to recuperate and just wanting to escape [...] Then the act of reading is just about wanting to stay where you are. Other times I discover new things in it.

We see here that this universe to which she can always return sometimes has a regressive function, at other times a progressive function. With time she has learned to listen to the inner voice that wants her not to move forward in life. Can these two tendencies really be subsumed under the same concept? The concept of nostalgia has journeyed from designating a painful pathological condition to indicating the inner resources one draws upon in order to sustain the psychological distress involved in psychological growth processes.

Krystine Batcho has traced the historical trajectory of the concept of nostalgia from its origins as a medical disease to a psychological concept, and from a malevolent, regressive experience to a benevolent emotion that can strengthen the self. From its origins derived from the *Odyssey*, the concept has itself undergone an odyssey without yet finding a secure home. She shows the changes from viewing homesickness as a normal and admirable feeling to inscribing it in medical pathology for ideological reasons. When subsequently this disease is subsumed under a larger category the term

---

[40] Constantine Sedikides, Tim Wildschut, Jamie Arndt and Clay Routledge 'Nostalgia: Past, Present and Future', *Current Directions in Psychological Science* 17, no. 5 (2008): 307.
[41] Matthew Baldwin and Mark J. Landau. 'Exploring Nostalgia's Influence on Psychological Growth', *Self and Identity* 13, no. 2 (2014): 162–77.
[42] Svetlana Boym, *The Future of Nostalgia* (New York: Basic Books, 2001), xiii.

is freed up for reconceptualisation within the field of psychology. It is still a disease, but no longer related to yearning for home. Instead it comes to mark a pathological regressive state. However, another reversal takes place. The term now goes from signifying an abnormal condition to becoming normalised, coming to mark a sentimental longing for an irretrievable past. The concept undergoes yet a further transformation: as its valence changes from bitter, via bittersweet, towards sweet, it changes its meaning from a malevolent or neutral state to a benevolent process serving adaptive means.[43] Batcho emphasises that 'confusion of different constructs designated by the same term has continued to obstruct progress in empirical research on nostalgia'.[44] She therefore proposes that '*homesickness* and *longing for one's past* represent different, albeit related, constructs'.[45] This confusion was inherent from its conception, however, as *nostalgia* collapses two different states into one: the safe return and the pain of being in exile. Theories of nostalgia always point us back to the concept's origin in the *Odyssey*. *Algos* denotes a painful condition (the Algea were the personifications of pain, sorrow and grief). In the beginning of Book V of the *Odyssey*, the long-suffering Odysseus is said to suffer this pain. He is a prisoner in the house of Calypso, without 'the power to regain the land of his fathers'. He is in exile, cut off from his homeland, without the means of returning home. He is unable to achieve *nostos*. The *algos* is due to the very impossibility of *nostos*. Only when he receives help does he have a choice: whether to stay on Ogygia and have immortality, or return home. Anna Bonifazi has inquired into the double meaning of *nostos*: it signifies both the safe return after a dangerous journey, and the telling of the tale about it. It is a poetic genre, of which Bonifazi lists the following motifs as central: the sailors initially plan to reach a particular place; the journey is diverted by a storm; there is a shipwreck and many of the crew perish; the survivor arrives in an unknown land and collects certain goods there; he stays in this place for some time; he receives help in reaching home. She argues that *nostos* is a foundational concept in the *Odyssey*. Bonifazi, summarising the various meanings and associations of the term *nostos* – safe journey, coming back (home), saving oneself – says that 'return' is common to these meanings. But what she identifies as the core meaning of *nostos* is 'surviving lethal dangers'.[46] Therefore, she argues, *nostos* is connected to the idea of salvation. She maintains that 'translating *nostos* and its cognates as "return home" is not sufficient, and in several instances it does not even make sense'; it is 'because of the frequent Homeric associations with a backward movement and with the idea of home' that it has come to mean 'homecoming'.[47] *Nostos* is the quest to reach one's destination after a perilous journey in which one suffers many *algea* in one's heart. I suggest that we therefore derive the following terms to differentiate states and conditions.

---

[43] Batcho, Nostalgia: The Bittersweet History of a Psychological Concept', 1–12.
[44] Ibid., 7.
[45] Ibid., 9.
[46] Anna Bonifazi, 'Inquiring into Nostos and Its Cognates', *American Journal of Philology* 130, no. 4 (2009): 492.
[47] Ibid., 497.

The pain of being in exile and the accompanying homesickness may more accurately be termed *oikalgia*[48]. The yearning to return home may be termed *hiemenos*. The refusal to head this call, opting instead for 'immortalisation' by hiding to oneself one's true self, is *kalypsis*. And the arrival at one's destination, by having helpful resources, to tell the tale, is *nostos*. These four terms respectively sum up the four concepts historically embedded within nostalgia. Also, they sum up the various stages on Nina's quest for identity. Foreclosure is at the bottom a *kalyptic* state; diffusion is *metoikalgic;* moratorium is *oikad hiemenos;* and achievement is *nostos*, arriving at one's destination after suffering many perils. In my interpretation, the resolution of Nina's crisis is a *nostos*.

MySpace: Homecoming

Her homecoming is metaphorically symbolized by her account on MySpace:

> I managed to conquer an inner space for myself. It was fragile at first. And then I registered my account on MySpace, where I could use a pseudonym. I didn't want to use my own name, because I associated it strongly with the girl who had helped her dad with his manuscripts. On MySpace I could just be myself, be a musician. It was fantastic. […] My music had meant something to a Latin-American living in Australia. That was huge. Gradually I gained the courage to share this with other people. I was terrified that this would be crushed, when I came forward with it.

In this passage she formulates the true nature of courage: to come forward *despite* the terror of being crushed. This is what it takes to achieve identity and to find one's way home from inner exile.

Nina is reluctant to say that the book has saved her life, because 'I am too much of a coward ever to have taken my life'. She thus understands 'saved' to mean 'resqued from death'. Still, the book has 'made unbearable times bearable'. In my view that is a form of salvation – of reaching nostos, arriving safely after experiencing many perils and algea. And in fact Nina proceeds to acknowledge that 'to save a life – it is not just on the physical level'. She says that since she killed her soul, she has 'been working to restore, to reinstall those original parts'. Her 'great struggle' was that 'I haven't had the courage to live'. She couldn't dare to reveal herself. Without the book she would have been 'more lonely as a child', 'less able to listen to myself, to have self-belief, and to have hope that I could find myself at last'. Thus, we may conclude that the book has changed her – she has found self-belief and the hope that she could achieve her quest for *nostos*. Her challenge was twofold: first, to 'reconquer that inner space', and then to reveal to others what was in there: creating a 'My Space' and come forward, courageously. Nina's narrative may thus be said to be an *Odyssey*. The plot has a circular shape; it is structured according to three stages: having the book, sacrificing it, and regaining it.

---

[48] From Μετοικεσία: a removal from one abode to another, especially a forced removal. *Hiemenos*: the word used in the *Odyssey* for Odysseus' yearning to return home.

Chapter Five

ESTHER'S EPISODE

I happened to read an essay Esther wrote for a Norwegian magazine about youth, identity issues and relationship problems. I was struck by her mentioning how important poetry in general, and Episode *in particular, had been to her own development. So I contacted her and told her about my project and asked whether she felt the poem had changed her life. She confirmed this and consented to an interview. I had read some of Hagerup's poetry before, but enjoyed the opportunity to read up on it. I found* Episode *very moving in its simplicity and truthfulness. I drove out to her home on the outskirts of a large town in the eastern part of Norway. She greeted me warmly. The interview took place in her study, surrounded by all her books.*

Thor: I've brought the poem. Would you like to read it for me?
Esther: Fantastic! Yes, I would. Should I perhaps find the book in which I first encountered the poem, though?
Thor: Yes please, that would be great.
Esther: Right. This book of poetry is the one we used in school. This must have been in 1967. We had to read Wergeland and Welhaven and all that. Which was nice. Look, the book opens almost of its own accord onto that particular page! I'm not sure how old I was then, I must have been 16 or 17, when I was in the gymnasium. One is quite green at that age, haha. The poem made a really deep impression at that time. Should I say something about why it did?
Thor: Please do.

Kitchen Sink Drama

Esther: I grew up in the 50s. I was born in 1951, into what was then a typical family, where mum was a housewife and dad went to work. And he came and went, as men did in those days. She was, I would say, placed by the kitchen sink by coercion. Because she did not really want to stay at home. She had an education and wished to work, but that was entirely out of the question. She had studied at a college of commerce, which was regarded as a good qualification then. And she had several years of experience from the accountancy department in the little town where she lived. So when she met my dad she had in fact more intellectual capital than he did. She was also an avid reader. However, when people got married then, and they got married in 1947, it was very common in the post-war years for the female to become a housewife. And she had to move in not just with him, but his mother, too. This was forced upon her. Which was terrible for her, I think. As I was born, they finally moved into their own home. I think they were quite happy those first few years in their new home, before the great disappointment happened. It registered quite profoundly in her life, being a person who was meant to just stay in the house and clean and cook and tidy up. An awful life, really, for a lively soul such as her. Awful. So she would read a lot, but she was terribly angry and resentful for much of the time. *Frightfully* angry, and sad, I think. But the two of them had the kind of marriage that is very difficult to grow up with as a child, because they communicated so poorly with each other. They would scream at one another, or they would stay silent for weeks on end. And that was *very* frightening, I must say. I remember my sister and I, we would talk about it a lot: 'What's the point of such a miserable relationship, why are they together?' and stuff like that. In between, there'd be bright moments, when my dad played the guitar and they sang. Then we were happy, because it felt like a clearing in the woods and we could just *be* – things were all right then. But then another thundercloud would form. And he always went fishing. Every weekend during the summer, on those long summer evenings, he would be off on a fishing trip. Leaving her there, on her own. So that was a massive let-down and caused much bitterness in her life. Also, and how can I put it, they were brought up in emotional ignorance, like so many others of that generation. They did not understand their own emotions at all. They could not understand themselves, and they could not understand each other. They were concerned with not standing out. A real peasant mentality. When you grow up in a home environment like that, then as a child you learn nothing about what you feel. They wouldn't know anything about that, and besides there was a culture of obedience in those days. They would go: 'Shhh!, be quiet!', 'Far from it', 'That's rubbish', dismissing our feelings and perspectives. If we as children had beliefs or opinions that did not accord with theirs, that is the reaction we were met with. They were scared of everything that was strange or different. And as we moved into the 1960s, for them the changes were scary. The advent of rock and the hippie movement in the States, and the Beatles – all this was terrible. Horrid music and unacceptable hairstyles. There must have been a lot of anxiety in the parental generation. So there was no help to be had when it came to working out one's feelings; What's going on inside me, am I angry or sad or scared?" No help at all.

Thor: So they could not acknowledge or validate your emotions?

Esther: No. And just imagine how important that is for children and their development. But when you think about the generation before them again, they *really* received no help from their own parents. My mother grew up in an orphanage. I don't think she had much emotional comfort there. My dad had a mother who would just sew all the time and a dad who drank, so there was not much guidance to be had from them. So to all intents and purposes they were still children themselves, who no one had looked after properly. When they had children of their own they didn't know how to do it.

Led into the World of Books

So, what can you do, when you're lucky enough to be born after the war and education is available to all? You can read books.

Thor: When did you start to do that?

Esther: As soon as I had learnt to read. I could sing all the lyrics in the songbook when I was three, but I didn't know how to read. They would point to the picture, and then I would sing the song. I remember I was longing to be able to read it myself. The first book I took out from the library was when I was five. It was called *The Golden Book*, about a family of mushrooms in the woods. I've never forgotten that, getting a library card and opening that book. That was big for me. I grew up in a small town in the Eastern part of Norway, where I spent the first 11 years of my life. So I was five when my reading life began. And my mum would read to me, aloud. She sang and recited nursery rhymes and read aloud. She was very good at that. I haven't given that much thought, actually, but that's something that she did very well. She led me into the world of books. That was brilliant.

Thor: She made it come alive for you?

Esther: Yes. And she was an avid reader herself as well. I noticed a book just here on this shelf now, this is the sort of stuff she would read: Susan Lennox. Books about women who suffered, you know. And David Graham Phillips, these were on our bookshelf when I was a kid. This one's from 1950.

Thor: Opening it at random now, it says here: 'Are you going to go on with this life? She asked'. So this must have resonated with her?

Esther: Oh, yes. Reading about a woman who is unfairly treated, and placed in a difficult situation. There were many books like that on her shelf, which I went on to read as soon as I was able to. Clearly, this was *her* life. She found solace there, I think, in literature. Because she was so stuck in a rut. Because she could not go on to receive further education or continue to work, it was brought to a halt. It simply stopped. At a fairly young age I must have thought: 'I am not going to end up like that.'

I was five when my sister was born. I don't know whether all the shouting and screaming had started at that stage or whether they were still all right. However, I read a book called *Bobby Bear Runs Away*. It's about a bear who feels that he is treated unfairly. He then runs away from his nan and Lotte. The dog runs away with him, because he has been locked up in the cellar for being naughty. I remember thinking that is a *very* good idea. I remember thinking: "No one else has parents as stupid as mine.' I packed a knapsack, and proceeded to walk out of the town, all the way to the hospital. I regretted not having brought a lunch bag. But then I walked into the woods and found something to eat. Kids in my day knew what we could eat in nature, so I found fresh green spruce shots and green leaves. But then I heard the screeching of car brakes, and before long my dad had found me. He was not angry, though, just silent. When we got home I was treated to cakes and cocoa. So it paid off, haha. I was only five then. They probably didn't handle it too well having another child to look after, so I think it was just too much for them, for my mother.

Thor: Which meant the older child was neglected a bit?

Esther: Yes, then she was invisible, and must have felt she didn't belong. So she ran away. After that things were much better for a while, haha. I think they realised that they had not handled things very well. They were much kinder afterwards. Like Bobby Bear, I was comforted when I came home. So that book inspired me at the time. It didn't save my life, of course, but it inspired me to protest. That's the first time a book made a deep impression on me. Other books would follow.

Thor: Before you started in the gymnasium, what did you read?

Esther: Comics and books for boys, Tarzan, Davy Crocket. There wasn't much for girls then. Until Nancy Drew came along, finally. Later on, Norwegian authors came into my life. First Johan Borgen and then, regrettably, Jens Bjørneboe. One should not offer Bjørneboe to vulnerable young people. That's not good. After I started the gymnasium I read all of Bjørneboe, *History of Bestiality* and *Jonas* and all that. Which was not good for me. This was not literature that saves, rather it served as confirmation that the grown-ups were bad and the world was terrible.

Thor: Because you had no resistance against it?

Esther: None at all. It confirmed a negative worldview, a negative self-esteem. All the negative things were just absorbed. I had a feeling that everything was hopeless. Bjørneboe was a very depressive writer. And young people would take all of it to heart, we believed him.

I took much solace from Hans Børlie. I have always loved the woods, having grown up next door to it. Børli really saved me, actually. Because his writings were warm. His poetry was full of warmth, in contrast to Bjørneboe with all his hopelessness. There was a sense of hope in everything Børli wrote. I read to bits the little collection of poems I got when I joined the Monthly Book Club when I started the gymnasium. I've still got it here, his *Selected Poems*. Let me see, what year's this from? It must have been in the late 60s that I got this. At that time it probably wasn't the forest poems that interested me most. And some of them I found too difficult. Like the one called *Words and Life*, which I have appreciated more as I got older and understood what he meant. But one that I particularly loved then was the poem *Distance*. I've bookmarked it: 'I watch the sky on a spring night, the flight of snipes. What wonder. The greatest star is just a tiny thing, a birch leaf can cover it. Distance – distance is what makes the eternal bearable. How good that such a wide shade is cast by that which is small and near.' I felt that was lovely. I thought about it a great deal. If one were to think about all the terrible stuff all the time, one wouldn't be able to go on living. I found that he described those feelings so well. And *On a Night in June*, too – with them two sitting on the stairs, saying they have to hurry up and be together, because life for us humans is so short. Things like that I just loved. His universe was a human one. And he … connected the human and nature. Bjørneboe didn't do that. He just entered the emotionally black, whilst

Børli managed to place the human within nature in a way that really appealed to me. And whenever I am stressed or exhausted, I go out wandering in meadowland or woodland. Picking mushrooms in the woods is what I love best. What Børli tried to communicate really resonated with me. So there I found a poet who could help me.

Thor: In Børli's poems, two of your loves – the woods and words – met?

Esther: Yes, precisely. Just so. And – how can I put it – that was much *healthier* than the depressive style of Bjørneboe. Apart from them, I would read a lot of female authors. Once a week I went to my local library and took out all books by an author – Remarque, say. 'So that's where you're at just now, then?' the librarian would say.

Episode

Esther: There was also a lot of misery connected to Inger Hagerup, actually. She wrote this poem, *Episode*, while she and her husband were struggling severely, I learnt later on. It just seems so, so autobiographical. It simply can't be something that she just invented. This is not about the couple next door, that's for sure. It's about *her*, just cut straight out of her own life. But reading it, it was not dangerous in the same way as Bjørneboe, because it gave me such a profound insight. It made me able to understand the complexity and contraries of my parents' terrible marriage.

Thor: Had you read anything else by Inger Hagerup before you found 'Episode'?

Esther: Yes. All her children's stuff and her nursery rhymes. Then all of a sudden I discovered that she was about more than that: In fact she wrote marvellous poems for adults! That's when she opened another door for me. I remember seeing her in a new light, thinking why hasn't she been more highly regarded? But that's how it was: she was female, and she wrote in rhymes. And she probably drank too much wine as well […] So it was something people looked down their noses on a bit. What she wrote was pure genius, however. Afterwards I read all of her work. *Episode*, though, that was – how can I find the right word – that was *enlightening*. It really was. It enlightened me about those two poor souls at home. My parents.

Thor: Did you have that feeling immediately?

Esther: Yes, I think so. I learnt it by heart, it meant so much to me. Quite simply. I had an instant illumination: 'Yes, this is them! Two forsaken people.' 'Oh, my God!, is that how it is?' And I also thought: 'So *I am not the only one* to have experienced something like this. It can't be just them two who are like that. It must be universal.' Yes, I realised that this experience must be common to all people. All of a sudden I could see them as they were, as human beings. As two vulnerable people. That there was a reason why they were like that. And that there was a depth there; something went on beneath the surface behaviour. I could see this, because the poem describes precisely how they would act.

106   LITERATURE AND TRANSFORMATION

Esther reads the poem out loud:

> EPISODE
>
> Theirs was not a quarrel, not in the slightest.
> Of course not, he said. – Thank you for the meal.
> And though their polite words were uttered lightly
> They gleamed with old hate under icy seal.
>
> You are welcome, was all that she replied.
> She pushed the chair up to the table, intending
> With narrow mouth and lips so firmly tied
> To build a fence behind her words, unbending.
>
> They stood silent for a moment, on guard,
> Both searching for new weapons, the most searing
> phrase conceivable, to be thrust so hard,
> A poisoned dagger-blade through love's woof tearing.
>
> She felt venomous words well up inside.
> A yellow delight at the thought of harming
> Him rose up in her so ruthless and snide.
> Then fingers fumbled through his hair, disarming
>
> Her – and now, suddenly, her eyes were filling
> In a powerless, inexplicable pain.
> She sensed deep beneath all the hate so chilling
> The tensed cord from his heart to hers again.[1]

As she finishes, she has tears in her eyes. It is a highly charged moment, and we sit in silence for a good while.

Esther: It is fantastic, you know, to be able to write this. It is absolutely moving. It moves me. I guess I must have felt so sorry for them. A realization went through me: 'poor mum and dad. They must be suffering so.' The poem helped me over – into that experience. The weird thing is, and you'd best not write this – well actually you may, no harm in it – when I was 17, just after I had read the poem, I still didn't know that my mum had grown up in an orphanage, because she'd never told me. I had no idea at all why she did not have any family relations. The shame was too great, you know. Every single Christmas a lady came round with a large

---

[1] My translation from the Norwegian original, in: Inger Hagerup, *Samlede Dikt* (Oslo, Aschehoug, 2007). I have endeavoured to keep the original's pattern of alternating masculine and feminine rhymes, since it bears on the thematic concerns of the poem.

bouquet of flowers. And every year I'd ask her: 'Who are the flowers from?' Oh, just somebody she knew. In actual fact it was from her half-sister. She had always felt so guilty, since their mother had kept her, and put mum away in a home – because she could not keep them both. So my mum always felt rejected and cast aside. Chosen away. She had always felt inferior and full of shame because of it. She couldn't find the courage to […] My dad knew about it, but neither my sister nor I knew. We knew nothing. Everything to do with her family and upbringing was shrouded in utter secrecy. Not a word was spoken of it.

Thor: A secret life?

Esther: A secret life! And she didn't know who her father was. That was a secret that was never disclosed. Not even on her deathbed did her mother divulge who the father was. So my mum did not know who she was. Literally speaking, you know. Imagine, it would make anyone weird, that. But then, one day, when I was 17, just after I got home from school, she broke down in the kitchen. She told me the story, because she had decided to tell me before I turned 18. I remember that I had read about children who are cast aside, and children who are abused, and children who suffer and orphans and everything. So I just said: 'But why didn't you tell me? Did you think we would renounce you because of it? It wasn't *your* fault!' She thought of course that there was something wrong with her, that that's why they'd put her there. So then she broke down when she realised that it wasn't to do with her, that we didn't love her any less because of it, but that's what she had thought the whole time. In all the years since she had us, she believed she must keep it a secret. That if we found out about it, we would reject her. And this was at her core, she had a massive issue to do with rejection. And, you know, when you are not told anything about your parents' backgrounds, and you do not understand, then obviously they become alien to you. So because of that incident and the poem, I gained a much better insight into who she was as a human being. And that made it much easier for me to deal with the anxious-laden bitterness of this chain-smoking, furious mum. Whom I had previously judged, thinking, 'What the hell is up with you?' So then everything fell into place and connected, with help from Inger Hagerup and with my mum's subsequent confession. Which must have happened just after I read the poem, when I think about it. Things clicked. And that was quite life-saving for an adolescent who can't work herself or her parents out at all.

Thor: You had a feeling that everything made sense, knowing what was under it all.

Esther: Yes, indeed. This was a very, very helpless mother. Who didn't understand herself, who didn't know why she was placed where she was. And who almost never had had any contact with her own mother. And this was to be kept secret. No one must know, it was too shameful. Shame, shame, shame. It also made me understand more of that fear of being different, the fear of being wrong, and the extreme conformism. She did all she could not to stand out, by being always dignified, always neatly dressed, always speaking proper. She had to be immaculate. Lest anyone 'arrest' her. All this I began to understand then, although that would take many years and I had to move out and start my own life. Which I did as soon as I could. Because it was still a burden to live in the conflict zone between my parents. Her silence and anger, and having to listen to all her moaning and complaining about how awful he was. He was almost frightened of his wife, he was. And she would scream at him what a coward he was. We had to cover our ears on occasions, to protect ourselves.

Thor: In your essay you describe literature as a form of theory of passion. I find that interesting with regards to Hagerup. The word 'heart' seems to be found in nearly all her poems. The language of the heart, is that what it is?

Esther: Yeah, wow. Now researchers have found out that heartbreak causes actual damage to the heart. If you suffer from lovesickness or you've been betrayed and you feel that your heart is about to break, it's almost as if it literally does. It does make you ill.

Thor: In the poem it says 'and suddenly …"' It's the language of the body. He is despairing.

Esther: When he, he puts his hand to his head, yes, and strokes his fingers through his hair. Then suddenly she becomes aware that he is not out to hurt her. He doesn't understand much either, and really he feels quite helpless, doesn't he. And so she no longer feels the urge to say the poisonous things she had intended to. I saw very little of that with my parents. Not much reconciliation. There were these intermittent flashes where dad brought his guitar out and they sang some old jazz tune, which they were both very fond of. But there were long, protracted periods of silence and bitterness that exhausted my sister and me. The silences and the smoke-filled bitterness and the stinging remarks wore us down. So they were moments of happiness and relief when suddenly there was a form of reconciliation. A physical relief: 'Ah!' As if the stress and tension would leave our bodies too. Because we had been walking on eggshells. Tip-toeing around the home, in an atmosphere of impatient rustling of newspapers and sighing and moaning. It's very stressful for a child or an adolescent. It makes you tied up in knots. And so it's a wonderful relief on those rare occasions of release. And that's what happens in the poem. In the last stanza.

Thor: What about that tensed cord? It can only be pulled so far?

Esther: Yes, but that's when they feel – and this is something that I only thought much later, not when I first read it – what she feels then is the emotional tie between the two, which is a tie that holds them, it has not been torn asunder despite all the pain they have undergone. And *that* is what I realised was the case with my parents too. My sister and I, we discovered that if we said something to attack their relationship that could be a very smart strategy. If we said: 'Goodness me, you are always bickering and arguing. We have never heard anyone else as bad as you.' Then they'd go, 'What, I've never! What impertinence.' And she would say to him: 'Have you ever heard such nonsense?' and he'd agree with her and all of a sudden they would be a united front. United against an external attack. Then we would chuckle and be pleased and go to our rooms. We did that almost on purpose just to get some peace. When we criticised them they would respond with: 'You have no idea how lucky you are to live in a house where one is able to let off steam and express things!' As if they were able to do that, but they must have thought so. 'You have no idea how good it is to have parents who can argue and make up.'

Thor: Because they saw this in relation to their own upbringing?

Esther: Yes, they compared it to their own past experiences, when the culture of obedience was more extreme. In that respect they had a fair point, of course.

Thor: I find it fascinating how she has this sudden insight in the poem, and you have a sudden insight about your parents when reading this.

Esther: They were in need of compassion. That's what I suddenly understood. They weren't to blame for it! There *was* love there. And this love was very hard to understand for a young person. Is this love, all the shouting and the silences and the black, black moods? Can there really be something warm, true goodness, underneath it all? Yes, there was. And that's when I realised: 'There is a good reason why they are together.' It has helped me ever since. When I have been working with couples who apparently hate each other's guts, when one of them screams: 'I hate you!' – I never believe that to be the case. That affect is a form of camouflage emotion. 'Deep below hatred and cold' there is that emotional chord that binds them. But what surfaces there is their primary emotions. The enormous sorrow and grief over all the time they have spent being nasty to each other. It falls away, all her […] Because the secondary emotion, that is the anger and contempt. The urge to say something cruel to him, you know. That is a result of all the sorrow and disappointment that's been built up, perhaps because the love has never been met. Naturally, in this poem she is unable to say: 'I love you, and it's a terrible shame that we are acting like this. It's just that I get so upset and disappointed and hurt, you see. And then I react with anger and bitterness and enmity.' She cannot say that.

Thor: No, the poem does not have a sixth stanza.

Esther: She just cannot say it.

Thor: You don't imagine that she will afterwards?

Esther: No, she won't. And neither could my parents. They did not have that emotional awareness. They didn't know how they felt. Thus they assumed that all the secondary emotions, what is visible – anger, irritation, boredom, exasperation – that that was what it was about. But it wasn't so. My dad was terribly frightened of an angry woman, what with his own mother having been such a monster. Not a monster, of course, but very domineering. He was a very obedient, subservient boy.

Thor: So they mutually reinforced each other's weaknesses?

Esther: Terribly so. So when his wife turned out to be verbally combative as well, he'd leave the house. If she batted an eyelid he'd be off like a shot, to go fishing. And as soon has he retreated, that activated her feelings of contempt. That he was a coward who couldn't face things, and who had never stood up to his own mother. Who had let his wife live with her mother-in-law for so many years, trapped, inactive. She felt he'd trapped her. Every time he withdrew, it activated her 'coward!'-response. All this was revealed to me when I read the poem. 'Oh, my God, this is what's going on!'

Thor: So then you could see the perspectives of both of them?

Esther: Yes, that he was avoidant. How could he not be, always having been told what to do. And mum could be very venomous, which had to do with the contempt she felt regarding the perceived cowardice. Whereas he didn't know what else to do.

Thor: When this realization came to you, do you think it gave you the room to explore who you were and your own feelings aside from those connected to your parents?

Esther: Yes, it did. And I remember no longer having to be so angry with them. The anger would return, of course. I was angry with them hundreds of times after that, but each time I could acknowledge that they were two poor souls tied to each other, without sufficient emotional awareness. When my mum died, in 2000, there was of course no bitterness or anger left in me. She complained throughout her life, but she was very ill. And she suffered from a lack of self-understanding and self-compassion, which pained us to witness. My dad's avoidance strategy was so fundamental that when he passed away at the age of 94, he didn't have a care in the world. Nothing ever got through to him. What saved his life was that river he'd retreat to every summer and every Sunday. The flyfishing really was a therapy for him. While she was sat at the kitchen table, smoking filterless South State, fuming. That was not therapeutic. She did not have a release valve. Although she did lots of charity work, for the housewives' association, raising money, that kind of thing. And she was well respected. She was a tough woman. She'd help people in need and she'd defend people. She was brave. I can remember on the bus if old ladies or pregnant women didn't get a seat, she would make sure they did by telling everybody off. She was tall and imposing.

The Language of the Heart: Psychology versus Literature

I was lucky, being an avid reader, because of that poem and many of the things I read later on. I went on to study psychology, because I thought: 'I have to find out why people act the way they do. What on earth is driving them? What is going on with human beings?'

Thor: So you had a real existential need to understand the driving forces in people?

Esther: Yes, to understand the psyche. However, that psychology degree was not very good at throwing light on this. It was a massive disappointment in that respect, to be honest. It was mostly about behaviourism and cognitive psychology. There was hardly anything about feelings, about emotions. Rats, and Skinner, and things like that. And of course there was all that Freudian claptrap, which did not appeal to me. That tiny children should have these terrific sexual fantasies – I thought: 'that just cannot be the case. What a load of nonsense.' It just made me angry, so I rejected it. Consequently I missed out on some of the clinical training, since I did the social clinical programme on language and communication and systemic theory. I did not learn about emotions there either. So then what do you do? Yes, you read. I kept reading literature until my eyes were sore, running down the library. There was no other way.

Thor: So that's where you found the language of the heart, in fiction?

Esther: Yes, it was there I found it, the language of emotions. The word 'love' was not a part of psychology. I find that a lot of poets and novelists have more wisdom when it comes to these matters. I would go so far as to say that I learnt hardly anything that's of use to me as a psychologist, in the department of psychology. I learnt far more from literature and from conversation with friends. Long and deep conversations, hundreds of conversations with friends.

Thor: Does that mean that the encounter with poetry, with fiction, is a form of dialogue?

Esther: It absolutely is. It really is a form of dialogue, where you taste it, chew on it, digest it. And you talk with it. You don't talk with the author, because when you are young you're not concerned about the person who wrote it. You are just reading the work, and it is the person in the book that is alive to you. That there is a person named Steinbeck, you do not care about that. I wasn't bothered about finding out about his life. Who was he? Didn't interest me, but what he wrote in *Of Mice and Men*, and the *Grapes of Wrath*, that was of intense concern. So I think it's the persons, the characters, that you're concerned with when you're young, not the authorship. That's only as you get older, at least that's how it is for me. You have a dialogue with the characters in the books, an exchange. As you read you shout out inside yourself: 'No, no, no!'; 'Stop being so bloody self-destructive!'; 'Don't be such a coward, come on!'; 'You have to break free, be courageous!'; 'You mustn't put up with this'; 'You can be free!' There's a lot of that. You care about the characters, and you address them and talk to them. Yes, that's what it's like.

Thor: As if it were a real person?

Esther: As if it were a real person, yes. Without your being psychotic and not being able to distinguish. The wrath and anger at the world and its injustice, I remember how furious reading Uncle Tom's Cabin made me as a child. We were so angry with those people who hurt Tom, and with the white people. It made us very aware of racial discrimination, which was politically very important then. Later on women's literature would become very important for me, as well. But my degree in psychology, it didn't give me that much. It could explain group dynamics and cognitive processes, attribution and things like that. Which of course is crucial for understanding the mind. But it didn't help me understand relationships, and love. There was also little developmental psychology. Our hero John Bowlby, we learnt very little about his work. I loved reading about his research on attachment, and Mary Ainsworth's studies of children, but there was not enough emphasis placed on this. It wasn't until way into the 1970s that one stopped hospitalizing children without their parents. But this research had been done in 1951. So to graduate and go out there and practice as a psychologist with so few tools was no easy task. I had to find my own way. I had a lot of knowledge, admittedly, but I knew so little about my own feelings, and how I reacted when in a situation with people in great distress. How to deal with that?

Emotion-Focused Therapy: The Subtext of 'Episode'

Thor: The poem represented a life-saving moment for you in your adolescence. But also, when considering your vocation as a couples' therapist, it has followed you throughout your adult life. Has the poem accompanied you into the therapy room?

Esther: Yes, all the way, you know. It's exactly what I work with. It informs my work. I have developed, in collaboration with others, a course for new parents, where the poem is used. A lot of nurses around this country read this poem in their work with young couples, young parents who are angry and exhausted and can't get through to each other. I don't read the poem out loud to people, but I have used it when training therapists. Inviting them to look at the ending of the poem.

Thor: I wonder what the next stanza would be like, maybe it would be a good exercise to have them write that.

Esther: That's a good idea, because that is how I work. I work according to Emotion-Focused Couples Therapy. There I encourage each partner to articulate these feelings. Then we record them, and they have to watch it afterwards. For instance, I will get her to say: 'When I withdraw, it's because I get frightened.' And then I get him to say: 'When I get angry, it's because you pull back from me. I think you don't love me anymore.' So we work a lot with that. And I also work with what I call subtext. What is underneath the surface expressions. The primary emotions are the subtext. So instead of saying that 'this is the primary emotion,' I will say that 'this is the subtext. If you regard what we see, the anger or the irritation or the defense, as the headline, then what we cannot see, the sadness, sorrow, shame, feeling abandoned, lonely, invisible, is the subtext.' That's a concept I use. So in this case the subtext is her sorrow and his helplessness. When she sees his helplessness, her aggressiveness dissipates, as well as her desire to be contemptuous. That's what's referred to as 'softening moments'. In therapy we create and bring about softening moments.

Thor: And they enable people to find other ways to interact?

Esther: We call that 'corrective emotional experience'. Quite simply. Where you suddenly realise that the other person is not indifferent. In the poem she may consider him ungrateful and indifferent. He eats his food and then leaves the table. When she realizes that his withdrawal is due to helplessness rather than apathy, immediately her need to wound him goes away. Then she is able to feel: 'I do love you. What I am afraid of is your retreat. I take that as a sign of your not caring about me.' That is a softening moment, when she suddenly sees his underlying feelings. And the unmet attachment needs beneath that again. We conceptualise this using the metaphor of a loop. The notion of a vicious circle is insufficient to explain why people act like that. It is like a loop. If he is avoidant, and she is pushy and contemptuous, then his manifest behaviour elicits her underlying feeling of loneliness, the primary emotion, but it will come out as contempt and anger. And when he sees her contempt and anger, it elicits fear and shame in him, which makes him withdraw even further. He will then think: 'she doesn't care about me anymore, and no matter what I say or do it will be wrong, so I may as well just retreat.' When he does so, that again will elicit feelings of desperation and separation anxiety in her, which come out as shouting and complaining. And so on it goes, like the infinity sign. So we work to uncover what is beneath this. At the very bottom lie the unmet attachment needs and identity confirmation needs. It produces great anxiety when the person we are attached to does not acknowledge our identity. It is as if we disappear. We are evicted into darkness. That is a great psychic danger.

Thor: In your essay you talked about armoured hearts. Do the softening moments melt away the armouring?

Esther: Hmm. Yes. It takes nothing for the armour to melt. We naturally assume that it is very hard to penetrate an armour. But it is not difficult at all. It is just a protective shell, and the very moment you realise that you don't need the protection, when your brain realises that you are not in danger, then it just falls away. As if it evaporates. So the notion that you have to break through the armour by force is erroneous. The more you beat the armour the harder it gets. If the other recognises that you wish them well, then the armour glides off. It may of course return, because this is not a permanent state. But the person has had a corrective emotional experience. I had an experience like that with my husband yesterday. We had a conflict, but managed to repair it after a couple of minutes and we could both laugh. It only took us minutes, whereas it would have taken my parents weeks.

Literature as Corrective Emotional Experience

Thor: So the poem does the same thing as the therapy, it provides a corrective emotional experience? So the poem becomes an objective correlate: 'Oh yes, there is someone else who feels as I do'?

Esther: Yes, that's right. I think that is very important. It was crucial for me when I was young and reading, that I was not the only person in the world to have strange feelings. I was not alone in being anxious, angry, confused, feeling abandoned etc. So in families where you don't get adequate help to understand your feelings, and there are a lot of families like that even in today's society, then reading is a way of gaining greater affective awareness. It was for me at any rate. Both affective awareness and solace and recognition, and maybe also courage to act differently. I think when you understand more about yourself, you also become a better person. You become kinder to your husband, warmer in relation to the people you work with, kinder to your kids. So by understanding more, you becomes more caring, more empathic. As a young reader, it's mostly about consolation, recognition, identification - and then as you get older it's about corrective experiences, and learning, and expanding the empathic space. At least that's how I think it's been for me. And another important thing: self-compassion. To be able to feel: 'Poor me, who was in that state.' To be able to forgive one's own follies. For instance, I thought that I was very tough when I was young, but later I realised that really I was quite frightened. It was just a secondary emotion: 'I don't mind, it doesn't affect me at all.' But reading has broadened my horizon. I think I have become a better partner and a better human being by reading literature. I understand myself better.

Thor: If I understand you correctly, you're saying that first you experience empathy from the book, and then that makes you more empathic towards others? That sounds like a loop, too?

Esther: Hmm. Yes. Empathy with oneself and with other. Yes, like a good loop. Much more positive than the one I described, which is very bad.

Thor: To sum up, then, literature has saved your life?

Esther: Yes, it has, in a way. I would say so. In a way. Because I think that if I hadn't read so much, my foundation would have been smaller and less solid. I would have had a poorer understanding of life. I am forever in debt to libraries, for giving me access to all these books. And this poem, *Episode*, helped me to understand my parents and myself, and the complexities of love.

In the car on the way back, I reflect on Esther's story. My first impulse is to try to evaluate the interview: Did I listen carefully enough? Did we get close enough to the poem? But soon my worries give in to my fascination with the actual story. To think that she read Episode *nearly fifty years ago – and she has carried it in her heart ever since! She said she 'learned it by heart'; I find that such a telling expression. What at first was a personal truth that helped her understand her own parents and get to grips with her own identity, has accompanied her into the therapy room, where she is trying to help people read its 'subtext', to sense the tensed cord and to move and be moved from discord to concord.*

From Discord to Concord

Crisis

Bjørneboe versus Børlie

Esther immediately accepts the invitation to read the poem aloud. She does, however, offer to 'say something about why' the poem 'made a very deep impression at that time'. This offer could partly be made in an attempt to compose herself and defer the emotionally charged moment of reading, but more likely she feels the need to provide background information so that the recipient may understand what was at stake for her, and thus be enabled to empathise with the depth and ramifications of her realisation. As such, it has the function of an orientation sequence about 'that time'. The implicit assumption is that before we can understand the reading experience itself, we must know what situation she was in when she encountered the poem. What, then, does Esther deem relevant to provide sufficient orientation? There are two main aspects: firstly, her parents' marital discord and its effects on her; secondly, her reading history as a series of significant experiences. These two strands seem to be intertwined: not only is there conflict between her parents, but she also experiences a conflict between two poets and their opposed worldviews.

The parents' conflict is narrated from the perspective of the mother, who is portrayed as 'terribly angry and resentful'. It must have been very difficult not to takes sides in the parents' conflict, and her mother is to a certain extent presented as the protagonist of the story. This mirrors the narrative structure in the poem, where *She* is the focaliser in the last two stanzas. Her mother's story is contextualized in terms of gender issues, and we are told her 'secret story'. Esther points to two important consequences of growing up in this 'conflict zone': it was 'very frightening' and she could not understand 'the point of such a miserable relationship'. Moreover, she repeatedly emphasises that the feelings this frightening atmosphere instilled in her is – 'anxious, angry, confused, feeling abandoned' – were ones she could not process: 'when you grow up in a home environment like that, then as a child you learn nothing about what you feel'. Thus, she thought she was 'the only person in the world to have strange feelings'. Esther cannot recall the onset of the intensification of the conflict, but it appears that in the course of her first few years she internalised a relatively secure attachment pattern. She relates a significant childhood memory: her elopement. 'The first time a book made a deep impression' was when Bobby Bear 'inspired her to protest'. She could not have run away from home without having faith that she would be alright, and clearly she evidences strong coping resources. Interestingly, she seeks shelter in the woods.

An internal conflict between two worldviews is configured in the form of an opposition between two poets of great importance to her: Bjørneboe and Børlie. Bjørneboe gave her 'a feeling that everything was hopeless', although he did not so much instill this feeling as 'confirm a negative worldview' that was forming in her at the time.[2] Børlie on the other hand, gave her hope. His distance from human affairs through communion with nature offered a respite: 'If one was to think about all the terrible stuff all the time, one wouldn't be able to go on living.' Børlie 'managed to place the human within nature' for her. There are at least two ways in which this worldview conflict can be connected to the parental conflict. When she escaped from the place of hopelessness and conflict, she went into the woods, where the complications of human relationships recede into the background – precisely the experience Børlie confirmed in his poems. Alternatively, it is almost as if Bjørneboe and Børlie come to represent one parent each: the fatalism and depressiveness of her mother is reflected in Bjørneboe, while the retreat into the vast stillness of the outdoors, her father's strategy, is represented by Børlie.

---

[2] Jens Bjørneboe also had a life-changing reading experience, albeit not of the redemptive kind. In his autobiographical novel *The Silence*, he writes: 'Then there's something else, which keeps popping up. It happened thirty-eight years ago, and changed my whole life. I was fifteen years old at the time, and it was all because of a book. I read it through in one day; it wasn't that long. It was a thin book with contents of a descriptive sort; and even though I had been quite depressed in the previous fourteen years as well, still I can say that since reading this book I've never been happy again, or only for brief moments […] It may be the most important book I've ever read, and it put an end to my childhood.' Jens Bjørneboe, *The Silence*, trans. Esther Greenleaf Mürer (Chester Springs, PA: Dufour Editions, 2000), 164. The book in question was Wolfgang Langhof's account from the German concentration camp Sachsenhausen, *The Peat Bog Soldiers*. The impact of the war on many Norwegian writers of that generation was major.

Deleterious Consequences of Inter-Parental Conflict

Naturally, we have no means of establishing the objective level of the frequency and intensity of marital conflict in Esther's home. However, given Esther's account of her upbringing, both in terms of the emphasis placed on the parents' relationship and her descriptions of how it affected her, it is entirely reasonable to conjecture that the subjective impact was highly significant. Interparental aggression and conflict is common and has deleterious consequences not just for the marital dyad, but for the entire family.[3] Children who are exposed to such conflict have been shown to have a higher incidence of emotional and behavioural problems.[4] Children's coping responses to such stressful events as marital discord are linked to the level of their psychological adjustment, having a severe negative impact on self-worth and leading to externalizing behaviour and proneness to depression. Bishop and Ingersoll found that this link is a stronger predictor of adjustment than for instance non-traditional family structures.[5] Rogers and Holmbeck investigated the moderating effects of children's cognitive appraisals and coping strategies on their adjustment to interparental aggression. They found that problematic beliefs about interparental conflict (such as blaming one parent, fear of divorce and abandonment, feeling of personal responsibility) and ineffective coping strategies were related to greater maladjustment, particularly resulting in negative self-worth and depression. They 'expected that children who lived in highly conflictual homes but who had adaptive appraisals and coping strategies would have relatively better emotional and behavioural functioning than their counterparts who had problematic beliefs and ineffective coping strategies.'[6] Their hypothesis that perceived peer availability and the use of social supports could buffer the negative effects of the parents' conflict received tentative support. The study does not define what is included under the term social support, but it is unlikely that reading fiction and poetry is one of them. However, Esther's reading experience may well be counted as a coping strategy and adaptive appraisal. It is quite clear from Esther's account that she did harbor 'problematic beliefs' such as fear, guilt and despair – to an extent where we are justified in describing her situation at the time as a crisis. The parental conflict holds her back, where all the energy needed to focus on the challenges of the psychosocial stage of development is not available to her. Emotions of fear, guilt and confusion are likely to result from being reactively embroiled in the conflict. However, alongside these problematic beliefs she also had bountiful coping resources in the form of reading and seeking the comforts of nature.

---

[3] E. Mark Cummings and Patrick T. Davies, *Children and Marital Conflict* (New York: Guilford Press, 1994).

[4] John H. Grych and Frank D. Fincham, 'Marital Conflict and Children's Adjustment: A Cognitive-Contextual Framework', *Psychological Bulletin* 108, no. 2 (1990): 267–90.

[5] Sue M. Bishop and Gary M. Ingersoll, 'Effects of Marital Conflict and Family Structure on the Self-Concepts of Pre- and Early Adolescents', *Journal of Youth and Adolescence* 18, no. 1 (1989): 25–38.

[6] Mary Jo Rogers and Grayson N. Holmbeck, 'Effects of Interparental Aggression on Children's Adjustment: The Moderating Role of Cognitive Appraisal and Coping', *Journal of Family Psychology* 11, no. 1 (1997): 125–30.

Thus her crisis can metaphorically be represented as *Bjørneboe versus Børlie*: an internal struggle between despair (negative self-worth and lack of belief in self-efficacy) and inner security.[7] She cannot protect herself from 'the negative worldview' as long as she views the most important relationship in her world as 'terrible', and she has to suffer the 'burden' of living 'in the conflict zone'. How did the destructive parental relationship of 'shouting and screaming' play out? Her dad, having grown up an obedient and subservient boy under a domineering mother, was frightened of his angry wife. The wife was tough, brave and imposing. Her strategy of being 'verbally combative' would make him hide in silence or go off to 'that river he'd retreat to every summer and every Sunday'. This in turn would activate her feelings of contempt and make her more confrontative, 'fuming' and 'venomous'. According to John Gottman's research on predictors of negative future trajectories of marital relationships, facial expressions of negative emotion, particularly one of fear on the husband's face and one of contempt on the wife's, is a primary indicator of divorce. Habitual negative ways of expressing one's emotions lead to stable destructive patterns in interactions. Critical angry blaming on the part of one spouse will be followed by an avoidance of emotional expression and withdrawal by the other (what Esther later on refers to as the negative 'loop').[8] Susan Johnson has found that whereas in secure relationships 'protest at perceived inaccessibility is recognized and accepted', insecure attachment responses are organized along two dimensions: anxiety and avoidance.[9] Based on Esther's portrayal of her parents, it is reasonable to conjecture that these two responses correspond to that of her mother and her father, respectively. Of the first strategy, Johnson says:

> When the connection with an irreplaceable other is threatened, attachment emotions, particularly anxiety, can become hyperactivated. Attachment behaviours become heightened and intense; anxious clinging, pursuit, and even aggressive attempts to obtain a response from the loved one escalate. Even when the loved one responds, the response may not be completely trusted, and a heightened emotional sensitivity to relationship cues may remain. This response can be momentary or it can become chronic and develop into a habitual way of dealing with emotions and engaging the partner.

The second strategy for dealing with the lack of safe emotional engagement, especially when hope for responsiveness has been lost, is

---

[7] It is important to note here that her evaluation of Bjørneboe is not shared by everyone. There are bound to be many Norwegians of that generation for whom Bjørneboe was felt as a real help in coming to terms with problems relating to identity, depression or conflict.

[8] John Gottman, 'An Agenda for Marital Therapy', in *The Heart of the Matter: Perspectives on Emotion in Marital Therapy*, ed. Susan M. Johnson and Leslie S. Greenberg (New York: Brunner/Mazel, 1994), 259–96.

[9] Susan Johnson, 'Extravagant Emotion. Understanding and Transforming Love Relationships in Emotionally Focused Therapy', in *The Healing Power of Emotion. Affective Neuroscience, Development and Clinical Practice*, ed. Diana Fosha, Daniel J. Siegel and Marion F. Solomon (New York: W.W. Norton, 2009), 264.

to try to deactivate the attachment system and suppress attachment emotions and needs, focusing on external tasks and avoiding attempts at emotional engagement. [...] If this affect regulation style becomes generalized, it effectively cuts off the person from an awareness of his or her emotional responses and needs and shuts out the partner.[10]

Johnson notes that these two basic affect regulation strategies – the anxious heightening of emotion eliciting hypervigilant behaviours, and the detached avoidance – tend to pull for confirming responses from a partner. Thus, these are the experiences Esther brings to the reading of the poem.

It is reasonable to suppose that underneath her despair, accentuated by her reading of Bjørneboe, there was self-confidence and assertiveness that could not be accessed. My understanding of her crisis is thus that the despair is a secondary emotion produced by the fright and loneliness stemming from the fighting atmosphere, and masks the primary emotional adaptability needed to answer the demands of identity development. Underneath the reaction of hopelessness, there seems to be secure attachment. Shaver and Mikulincer note that people who are securely attached can 'reappraise situations, construe events in relatively benign terms, symbolically transform threats into challenges, hold onto an optimistic sense of self-efficacy and attribute undesirable events to controllable, temporary or context dependent causes'.[11] After her reading experience, Esther evidently was enabled to do just that.

Transaction with the Literary Work

Metamorphosis

Esther's reading experience took place in a classroom. One may imagine a panoply of different responses made by the students to the reading of *Episode*. Perhaps one student will have related the poem to the poet's own life and marriage, another will have accurately placed it in terms of era and genre. A third may have analysed its stylistic features, perhaps even relating the form to the content: how the alternating feminine and masculine rhymes appear to mirror the subject matter. Perhaps also the students were well-versed enough in modernist aesthetics to appreciate the openness of the poem's ending. Perhaps they saw the poem as a springboard for discussion of gender issues and the sociopolitical context of the poem. All this without the poem necessarily having left a *deep impression* upon them. Nor could the teacher know that among the schoolchildren there was one girl who was forever changed by the experience. How did the reading of the poem make her 'able to understand the complexity and contraries of my parent's terrible marriage'? What is the content of her revelatory realisation?

When reading the poem, the experiencing I's initial impression is: 'Yes, this is them! Two forsaken people.' The interaction described in the poem mirrors that of her parents

---

[10] Ibid., 264.
[11] Philip R. Shaver and Mario Mikulincer, 'Adult Attachment Strategies and the Regulation of Emotion', in *Handbook of Emotion Regulation*, ed. J. J. Gross (New York: Guilford, 2007), 450.

closely. We cannot know at which point during the reading process this moment of recognition took place. But we can imagine that this occurred before the last stanza. Her appraisal of the couples' – and by extension her parents' – situation is that they are 'forsaken people'. What is meant by 'forsaken'? They have not abandoned each other; they are not so much forsaken by the other as they are together in their forsakenness: they are left to their own devices, without anyone to help them. As Esther remarks of her parents, 'They did not understand their own emotions at all. They could not understand themselves, and they could not understand each other.' She describes the next moment in her realisation thus: 'Oh, my God! Is that how it is?' Through experiencing the poem, she has gained an inside perspective. Whereas before she was 'very angry' with them, and did not understand 'the point of such a miserable relationship', she can now feel how it must be like for them to be in this marriage. 'All of a sudden I could see them as they were, as human beings. As two vulnerable people.' This change of perspective may be called a metamorphosis: the parents' appearance has changed for her.

In her article 'Emotion in Romantic Partners: Intimacy Found, Intimacy Lost, Intimacy Reclaimed', Marion Solomon describes transference by recourse to the metaphor of 'putting old faces on new people'.[12] It is as if each partner puts a mask on the face of the other, distorting their true identity by changing them into a character in an inner drama stemming from the past. Thus, their interaction pattern, consisting of his withdrawal and her angry pursuit, bears a resemblance to certain transformations famously depicted in Ovid's *Metamorphoses*. When Apollo acts condescendingly towards Cupid, he retaliates by shooting two arrows 'of contrary purpose: one is for rousing passion, the other is meant to repel it'. The first 'smote to the core of Apollo's being' and caused him to fall in love, the second was 'implanted in Daphne's bosom', and made her flee 'from the very thoughts of a lover'.[13]

Apollo pursues her, but Daphne rejects him. When Apollo persistently pleads, Daphne cries out to her father, the river, for help, and he responds by transforming her into a laurel tree. Only thus can she survive. In the story of Io, the young nymph tries to flee from Jupiter, but he rapes her. To evade the suspicious Juno, he turns Io into a 'snow-white heifer'.[14] Juno then demands Io as a present, and appoints Argus to keep watch over her. Upset by Io's suffering, Jupiter sends Mercury to kill Argus. Is it too fanciful to suggest that it is as if Esther's father withdraws from his wife by appealing to the river, whereas she becomes like Juno, angry that he prefers the company of the nymphs and dryads of nature to hers, castigating and trying to change him?

In Ovid, these myths contain a second transformation. Eventually, Io is transformed back into a nymph. And Apollo, realizing that he cannot have Daphne, transforms his disappointment by turning the laurel into a symbol. *Episode* may be interpreted as such

---

[12] Marion F. Solomon, 'Emotions in Romantic Partners', in *The Healing Power of Emotion: Affective Neuroscience, Development and Clinical Practice*, ed. Diana Fosha, Daniel J. Siegel and Marion F. Solomon (New York: W.W. Norton, 2009), 250.

[13] Ovid, *Metamorphoses*, trans. David Raeburn (London: Penguin, 2004), 29.

[14] Ibid., 36.

a relation of a double metamorphosis of the two characters. One can imagine the first metamorphosis having taken place prior to the narrated scene, where they go from showing open love for each other to retreating into fixed roles of defensiveness. Then, suddenly, a world opens up behind this pattern. Esther's transport is analogous to the movement within the poem: She goes from only seeing a persona with a cold and stiff mask, a solid armour, to seeing the human being behind the mask, as it suddenly melts away and leaves exposed the vulnerable person underneath. Instead of two opponents who seem less than fully human, the objects of fear, anger, scorn and contempt, her parents are transformed into two rounded characters in their separate identities, worthy of compassion, understanding and love. Her parents' manifest behaviour is now understood as just the surface level of their relationship, hiding a great depth: 'That there was a reason for why they were like that. And that there was a depth there, that something went on under the surface behaviour.' The realisation that 'went through' her presumably tied her perceptions of their interaction to a meaning she had felt but had not connected to previously: 'Poor mum and dad. They must be suffering so.' The softening moment that Esther the therapist sees between partners is also what takes place in Esther as she is reading, with regard to how she related to her own parents. The anger makes way for compassion, and therefore opens up for forgiveness: 'They were in need of compassion. That's what I suddenly understood. They weren't to blame for it!' She no longer blames them, because they are forsaken: The discord is not their fault. They cannot truly see each other, but only the projection of a mask created by their own past experiences.

Revelation: Anagnorisis

Esther describes the effect of her reading experience as 'absolutely *moving*'; giving her 'a *profound insight*'; '*an instant illumination*'; it 'was *enlightening*'. 'A *realisation* went through me.' 'All this was *revealed* to me when I read the poem.' (My emphasis). There are several knowledge-words here related to inner vision: insight, illumination, enlightenment. What was shrouded in darkness is suddenly brought to light. But this is not merely a cognitive realisation. It is also an *affective* experience, as she employs metaphors of depth and movement: she was deeply moved, and the realisation 'went through' her. 'To realise' means to become fully aware of, to bring into concrete existence and to make the potential actual. When we become fully aware of something, we take a potential truth and turn it into concrete actuality, and we take a general truth and make it personal.

Intuitively, it would seem apposite to call Esther's 'instant revelation' an 'epiphany', in accordance with McDonald's findings from his study of 'epiphanic experiences'.[15] The antecedent state he describes as marked by 'periods of anxiety, depression and inner turmoil' ties in with Esther's experience. And her reading experience did lead to 'an acute awareness of something new, something that the individual had previously been blind

---

[15] Matthew G. McDonald, 'The Nature of Epiphanic Experience', *Journal of Humanistic Psychology* 48, no. 1 (January 2008): 89–115.

to'. And it was a momentary experience which resulted in 'an experience of profound change and transformation' for Esther, 'made significant and enduring by the ascription of personal meaning'.[16] The precondition for her epiphanic leap is the depth of the emotional significance for her of her parents' interaction. 'Emotional predisposition is required if the reader is to make the epiphanic leap,'[17] Longbaum declares. It is unclear what he means by 'emotional predisposition' – whether this is an innate trait or an antecedent emotional state. However, it is reasonable to assume the latter. Longbaum argues that epiphany is an 'inevitable concomitant' of realistic fiction and poetry, since 'the reader must be relied on to transform the details into visionary significance [...]. When the transformation does not come off, it is because the author has not supplied the necessary structure for transformation.'[18] Esther does seem to imply such a leap: 'The poem helped me over – into that experience.' Clearly, there are strong resemblances between the descriptions of epiphany and Esther's experience. Furthermore, Irene Hendry remarked that with regard to epiphanies in modern narratives, the most common technique is a sudden revelation of character 'through an apparently trivial incident, action or single detail',[19] which is precisely the device employed by Hagerup in *Episode*. However, in these descriptions of epiphany there is little emphasis placed on the affective-bodily component so marked in Esther's account. Therefore, I think it better simply to designate Esther's transformative experience as a *revelation:* It is a sudden, unexpected appearance that carries strong affective components.

Esther says later on in her narrative, that in the rare moments of happiness in the home, the children experienced 'a physical relief. "Ah!"'. As if the stress and tension would leave our bodies too. Because we had been walking on eggshells.' And this kind of 'release' is 'what happens in the poem. In the last stanza.' Implicitly, a part of the affective experience of reading was a physical release of tension. 'There can be no knowledge without emotion. We may be aware of a truth, yet until we have felt its force, it is not ours. To the cognition of the brain must be added the experience of the soul,' wrote Arnold Bennett in his journal in 1897. We may know something to be true, but we have to feel its force – before that it is not *our* truth. Although elicited by a trivial incident, the sensuous experience of the fingers stroking through the hair, it enacts a metamorphosis. Metamorphosis is inevitably an affective-bodily experience. The poem says: 'then his fingers stroked through his hair', not that *he* stroked his fingers. As if the fingers acted without his conscious knowledge or consent – seemingly appearing out of nowhere.

What is 'the necessary structure for transformation' that the author has supplied Esther with? She says that 'the poem describes precisely how they would act.' The poem's title, *Episode*, may carry two different meanings. The etymology of the word is given as

---

[16] Ibid.
[17] Robert Langbaum, 'The Epiphanic Moment in Wordsworth and Modern Literature', in *Moments of Moment: Aspects of the Literary Experience*, ed. Wim Tigges (Atalanta, GA: Rodopi BV, 1999), 44.
[18] Ibid., 40.
[19] Irene Hendry, 'Joyce's Epiphanies', *Sewanee Review*, 54 (1946): 461.

directly from Greek *epeisodion* 'an episode', literally 'an addition', noun use of neuter of *epeisodios* 'coming in besides', from *epi* 'in addition' (see *epi-*) + *eisodos* 'a coming in, entrance' (from *eis* 'into' + *hodos* 'way'). Transferred sense of 'outstanding incident, experience' first recorded in English 1773.

From this 'addition', we can see how it has come to connote a passing incident of no great consequence in a person's life. Its actual denotation, on the other hand, is of a narrative unit within a larger dramatic work – the material contained between two choric odes in the Greek drama. It is precisely these two meanings that are played upon, and played out, in the poem.

The poem's opening line is an ironic statement, denying that it is in fact a quarrel: 'It was by no means a quarrel.' Who makes this statement? This is an instant of free indirect discourse. The words seem to be the narrator's, but whose perception is it? It could be focalised through the *He* person, and thus directly continued in the next line, in which the denial is clearly coming from him: 'Absolutely not, he said.' However, it may also be her judgement, which he then responds to. If the focalisation in the opening line is attributed to her, then they both agree that it is not a quarrel. Then, ironically, the poem starts with pseudo-agreement. Thus, we have an *in medias res* opening: an open conflict must have preceded this scene, and now the two revert to familiar reactive patterns in the wake of the argument. The polite words mask feelings of animosity. He retreats into silence, cutting off communication by denying that there is a conflict. For an instant, it seems that they will leave it off there, as her mouth is 'compressed'. However, that is merely an interlude while they are both 'searching for new weapons'. She is preparing an attack, looking for ammunition in the shape of venomous words, when she has her metamorphic revelation. (This moment perhaps makes us having to read the third stanza again: it was focalised through her, and thus it was her assumption that he was also preparing an attack. However, we do not know what goes on inside him at this point. He may no longer be looking for 'a cutting phrase'.) Why the *in medias res* opening? It means that there is an untold scene preceding the narrated one, something that occurs prior to the poem and which the reader must surmise, and by implication it therefore hints that there may be a succeeding scene, also to be completed by the reader's imagination – in other words, the poem is an episode within a larger, untold drama.

The fingers stroking the hair could have been merely a 'coming in besides', and simply have been a passing incident that confirms the habitual aspects of their cohabitation – there will be many more episodes like it. However, it is transformed into a moment of utmost significance through her revelation. Because 'there is no sixth stanza', the poem does not explicitly tell us the outcome of her revelation. Will she be able to communicate it to him, and how will he respond to this? Whether her internal change will precipitate a lasting change in their marriage can only be determined by the reader. The revelation as such only marks the potential for reconciliation. If they miss the opportunity opened up, then the revelation is reduced to a mere 'episode'; if they grasp the opportunity to turn the tide, then *Episode* becomes an *episode,* the turning point in a dramatic structure. In Aristotelian terms, there is *anagnorisis*: she recognises his true identity – he is still the person who loves her. A famous example of such an anagnorisis of the loved one occurs in the *Odyssey*, as the identity of the hero is recognized despite his disguise, through a small detail.

Whether there be *peripeteia*, a reversal of their fortunes, from being caught in a 'vicious loop' to entering a virtuous cycle of increased intimacy and (relative) harmony, the poem thus seemingly leaves undecided. If the poem is read as a lyric, it is concerned with the moment of revelation. However, if the text is understood as a narrative unit within a larger drama, it may be interpreted as a turning point in their relation – in which case this episode will be followed by another 'ode', where love replaces strife. Seen in this light, the poem is made into an episode in a comedy. Given the title and the narrative structure, the second reading is perhaps more likely. In this case, the *peripeteia* is a natural consequence of the *anagnorisis*: It has made such a deep impression upon her that she will have to act upon it and communicate it to her husband. However, Esther is adamant that this will not happen: 'in this poem she is unable to say: "I love you, and it's a terrible shame that we are acting like this. It's just that I get so upset and disappointed and hurt, you see. And then I react with anger and bitterness." She cannot say that.' When I asked whether she will be able to do so *after* her sudden realisation, Esther rejects this possibility: 'No, she won't. And neither could my parents.' It is important to note here that Esther also perceives a difference between her parents and the couple in the poem. Commenting on the turning point in the poem, she says:

> Then suddenly she becomes aware that he is not out to hurt her. He doesn't understand much either, and really he feels quite helpless, doesn't he. And she no longer feels the urge to say the poisonous things she had intended to. I saw very little of that with my parents. Not much reconciliation.

The statement is equivocal. Here she indicates that the poem ends with reconciliation. She seems to say that there was no evidence of anagnorisis manifest in the parents' relationship, because the poisonous things continued to be said – therefore reconciliation could not take place. On the other hand, the lack of reconciliation does not exclude the possibility of anagnoristic knowledge of the 'tensed cord' of love, only that they were unable to act upon it. Esther says that the emotional tie that binds them "has not been torn asunder despite all the pain they have undergone. And that is what I realised was the case with my parents too.' It is unclear here what is immediately realised and what she 'only thought much later'. What is evident is that the experiencing I realises three things through her revelatory moment:

> 'I realised that this experience must be common to all people [...] I am not the only one to have experienced something like this.'
> 'I could see them as they were, as two vulnerable human beings.'
> 'There was a reason for why they were like that.'

Thus, the realisation that the elements of forsakenness and vulnerability, and latent feelings under the surface behaviour, are *normal*, changes her. When asked if this change gave her 'the room to explore who you were, and your own feelings aside from those connected to your parents', she confirms this. Anger gives way to compassion; problematic beliefs regarding her own isolation are replaced by feeling connected to the common lot. Thus, the secondary feelings of despair and confusion dissipate, leaving her no longer adumbrated by the shadow of her parents' relationship, but free to venture forth in search of her own separate identity. My interpretation of Esther's reading is thus that although she explicitly denies reconciliation and a leap out of the 'loop', this is based on her real-world knowledge of typical interactions. The *effect* the reading experience has on her is an affective realisation of the comic pattern: the move from confusion and discord to union.

Comic Katharsis

The form of comedy has two different tendencies, according to Northrop Frye: on the one hand towards irony and satire, on the other towards romantic comedy. In the former, the emphasis is on the blocking characters, in the latter it is on the scenes of discovery and reconciliation.[20] We may say that Old Comedy represents the former, whereas the latter is represented in the comic tradition established through Menander's New Comedy. In Menander, the transport from confusion, contempt and despair to joyful reconciliation is the primary plot structure. In this genre, the central characters are ordinary people with their follies and problems in marriage and relationships. Identity confusion over what is a mask and what is the true self is resolved – or dissolves – to be replaced by clarity and union in love. Of the characters in comedy, Frye remarks: 'it is more frequently a lack of self-knowledge than simple hypocrisy that characterizes them.'[21] The fundamental movement of comedy is from illusion to reality, hence the importance of creating and dispelling illusion. The comic ending, according to Frye, is generally manipulated by a twist in the plot, and will often 'involve metamorphosis of character'. Psychologically, says Frye, the ending of comedy 'is like the removal of a neurosis or blocking point and the restoration of an unbroken current of energy and memory'.[22]

It is my argument that it is precisely through this comic form that we may understand not simply the poem's dramatic structure, but also the 'necessary structure for transformation' that brings about Esther's anagnorisis. The dialectic of emotional development in romantic partners described by Solomon, 'intimacy found, intimacy lost, intimacy reclaimed', is the dramatic structure of *Episode*. This reflects the tripartite structure that, according to Cristopher Booker, characterises the comic form. At first the characters live under the shadow of confusion and despair because they are shut up from one another. Gradually, there is a tightening of the knot: the discord deteriorates until the pressure of darkness is at its most acute and everyone is in a nightmarish tangle. Suddenly the resolution happens: with the coming to light of things not previously recognised, perceptions are radically altered. Shadows are

---

[20] Northrop Frye, *The Anatomy of Criticism: Four Essays* (Princeton, NJ: Princeton University Press, 2000), 166.
[21] Ibid., 172.
[22] Ibid., 171.

dispelled, the situation is transformed and the characters are brought together in a state of joyful union.[23] This structure is clearly borne out for instance in Shakespeare's *A Midsummer Night's Dream*, a play that takes much inspiration from Ovid. Hermia and Lysander initially love each other, but under the shadow, in the enchanted forest, confusion is created and nobody can see each other clearly. In the resolution, confusion dissolves and there is a return to love. William Carroll, in his study of Shakespeare's comedies, argues that 'although metamorphosis is not exclusively a comic theme, [...] few critics have considered metamorphosis as central to a definition of comedy'.[24] According to Carroll, metamorphosis is different from mutability and maturation. It requires that somebody recognisably changes their nature. The explicit change may be man turning into animal, but it may also be the assumption of a mask of disguise, or a psychological shift. 'Above all, metamorphosis prompts questions of identity. The boundaries transgressed, the shapes dissolved, may be physical and external – man to wolf, woman to water – but the equally frequent inner transformations may be more significant than the outward ones.'[25] Carroll says that masking and disguise dramatises how identities can shift, collapse and reform, and that 'disguise always constitutes an encounter with the metamorphic'; therefore it 'does not merely represent metamorphosis: it *is* metamorphosis'.[26]

Although there is 'not much reconciliation' between her parents, the poem allows her to experience the transport from confusion to clarity: the veil of illusion is lifted, and the lost intimacy can be reclaimed. She can imagine a different outcome to the 'realistic' one she has witnessed in her family home. The revelation leads to a comic anagnorisis. It is brought about by (re-)metamorphosis; suddenly and abruptly, a twist in the plot occurs that leads to a special form of insight: one can see the face through the mask. The revelation of the true identity is 'deeply sensed'. The hardening mask of coldness, bitterness and hatred that had previously transformed the lovers into personae less than fully human, melts away to reveal the underlying emotion of love and restore the vulnerability and openness of the characters. This recognition may be understood to affect a katharsis in Esther. 'Sympathy and ridicule' is purged, leading to a purification of the underlying feeling of tenderness. By 'ridicule' we must here understand the way Esther saw her parents: as caricatures, living in a pointless marriage, the subjects of blame. By 'sympathy' we must here understand the resulting secondary emotion of despair: growing up in this atmosphere of hostility, it is hard for her to differentiate her feelings about self and world from those about her parents. According to Susan Johnson, one of the originators of emotion-focused therapy (EFT) for couples, an attachment theory perspective is adopted vis-à-vis partners in conflict:

---

[23] Christopher Booker, *The Seven Basic Plots: Why We Tell Stories* (London: Bloomsbury, 2004), 107–52.
[24] William C. Carroll, *The Metamorphoses of Shakespearean Comedy* (Princeton, NJ: Princeton University Press, 1985), 37.
[25] Ibid., 25.
[26] Ibid., 26.

many extreme emotional responses in distressed couples are seen as primal panic or secondary reactive emotions to this panic. This approach differs from other perspectives, wherein these responses might be seen as signs of immaturity, a lack of communication skill, a personality flaw, or a sign of 'enmeshment' in the couple's relationship.[27]

Thus, rather than judging the response, one meets it with empathy. When judged, these responses may be met with contempt, and seen as ridiculous – or with fear, and seen as threatening. In both cases there is confusion. The difference in the two attitudes of empathy and judgement may be said to correspond to the difference in perspectives before and after Esther's katharsis, in as much as the latter is evidence of implicit 'ridicule' – the persons are judged as base and inferior.

Through the metamorphosis, these feelings are revealed to be only secondary, as no longer belonging to her, and can be cast out. The 'joyful' feeling is one of being freed up to find one's role in society. Moreover, Esther manages to mobilise her creative resources. This crisis is now turned into a quest to 'understand the psyche': 'I have to find out why people act the way they do. What on earth is driving them? What is going on with human beings?' It is as if Esther has to go in pursuit of 'the sixth stanza' or write the subtext to the poem.

'Readerese'

Gradually she realises that 'the language of emotions' can only be learnt through dialogue: through conversations and reading literature. Her twofold description of her way of reading literature is interesting in its complexity. On the one hand, she relates it as a dialogue with the characters in the book: 'You address them and you talk to them.' Esther states that for her, 'reading is a way of gaining greater affective awareness.' And the talking she engages in with characters is highly affective: an inner shouting of support, admonition, encouragement: ' "Stop being so bloody self-destructive!", "You mustn't put up with this!" ' As if they can hear her, and respond to her, 'as if it were a real person'. This is how 'care about the characters' shows itself, in active intersubjective engagement. It is reminiscent of 'motherese', the manner in which mothers talk to their babies in communication of affect.[28] They wholeheartedly engage in dialogue, attributing mental states and feelings to the baby, long before the baby has acquired language, as if the baby understood every word and in fact responded in kind. This is what the developmental

---

[27] Johnson, 'Extravagant Emotion', 264.
[28] 'Motherese' is a term that 'has historically referred to the prosodic exaggerations that are typically found in mothers' speech to their infants and young children', according to Robin P. Cooper, Jane Abraham, Sheryl Berman and Margareta Staska, 'The Development of Infant's Preference for Motherese', *Infant Behavior and Development* 20, no. 4 (1997): 477. Mothers use rising pitch contours to engage the alert infant in interaction, and falling pitch contours to soothe a distressed infant. The primary functions may thus 'be the elicitation and maintenance of the infant's attention and the communication of affect', argues Anne Fernald. See Anne Fernald, 'Four-Month-Old Infants Prefer to Listen to Motherese', *Infant Behavior and Development* 8, no. 2 (1985): 181–95. However, motherese can be said to include more than prosody.

psychologist Daniel Stern refers to as 'infant-elicited social behaviour'.[29] What mothers have always known, that the baby is born with awareness specifically receptive to subjective states in another person, was put forward as the theory of innate intersubjectivity when researchers found that mother and infant, as early as two months, 'while they were looking at and listening to each other, were mutually regulating one another's interests and feelings in intricate, rhythmic patterns, exchanging multimodal signals and imitations of vocal, facial and gestural expression'.[30] Furthermore, the regulation of this primary human communication, argues Trevarthen and Aitken, 'depends on an innate 'virtual other' process in the infant's mind'.[31] This virtual other in the mind finds its correlate in the mirror neurons of the brain. Gallese et al. argue that present evidence of mirroring neural systems for 'reading' another's intentions, linguistic expressions, emotions and somatic sensations points to 'neuronal mechanisms whereby the observation of another triggers an automatic and unconscious 'embodied simulation' of that other'.[32] From this we can conjecture that Esther experiences an embodied simulation of these characters by engaging in an affectively tuned 'virtual other' process that may be termed readerese. Not only is the *readerese* experience of dialogue marked by a bodily affective attunement, it is also figured metaphorically in terms of the body as a process of eating: 'You taste it, chew on it, and digest it.' We are reminded here of how she described the manner in which the revelation occurred to her: it 'went through her'. Although there is sudden illumination, it must also pass through the whole system and be digested. Perhaps we can therefore say that her journey after she leaves her home is one of digesting the entire reading experience.

Ascription of Meaning to the Reading Experience

An important element of Esther's narrative is her mother's secret story. Her mother's disclosure closely coincides in time with the reading experience: 'which must have happened just after I read the poem, when I think about it'. That 'things clicked' in a way that 'was quite life-saving for an adolescent' is attributed to both factors: 'So then everything fell into place and connected, with the help from Inger Hagerup and with my mum's subsequent confession.' Thus, when asked whether literature has saved her life, she replies: 'Yes, it has, in a way. I would say so.' How are we to interpret the qualification or reservation implied by 'in a way'? I think this must be read in the light of her opening move, when she says she will 'say something about why' the book created a deep impression. She uses the word 'why', but does not proceed to explain why – she tells the story

---

[29] Daniel N. Stern, *The First Relationship: Infant and Mother* (Cambridge, MA: Harvard University Press, 2002), 24.
[30] Colwyn Trevarthen and Kenneth J. Aitken, 'Infant Intersubjectivity: Research, Theory, and Clinical Applications', *Journal of Child Psychology and Psychiatry* 42, no. 1 (2001): 5.
[31] Ibid.
[32] Vittorio Gallese, Morris N. Eagle and Paolo Migone, 'Intentional Attunement: Mirror Neurons and the Neural Underpinnings of Interpersonal Relations', *Journal of the American Psychoanalytic Association* 55, no. 1 (2007): 131–76.

of her upbringing. It is not presented in causal terms. The background is presented as an antecedent state. And the mother's secret story is presented as a concomitant factor of great importance. My interpretation is that she must reserve herself against a causal relationship: Her upbringing was not the cause of the reading experience, and the reading was not the cause of her being saved. The logic of narrative is a different one, the transformational sequence is catalytic rather than causal. When she relates the enlightenment the poem gave her, Esther says: 'I could see this, because the poem describes precisely how they would act.' She switches from the past tense to the present, probably without being aware of it. This slide, however, I find deeply significant: the poem not only spoke the truth about the experience *then*, all those years so long ago, but still does, *here, now*. It is where the experiencing and narrating I meet in union. Not only is the plot of her life story circular – she leaves the interparental conflict of the home to become a couples' therapist, and finds a therapeutic language informed by *Episode* – but also the telling of it. When Esther the narrator relates her previous experiences, they are inevitably coloured by her looking at them through the theoretical lenses of EFT. Her reading experience, her narrative and her therapeutic practice are all embedded within the same figurative matrix.

I note her formulation when remarking on the difference between reading Bjørneboe and Hagerup's poem: 'It was not dangerous in the same way as Bjørneboe, because it gave me such a profound insight. It made me able to understand the complexity and contraries of my parents' terrible marriage.' Interpreting this passage is problematic; her judgement of Bjørneboe conveys that she sees the danger as residing *in* the poem, it's an objective aspect of his work, whereas with *Episode*, Esther clearly portrays her own active contribution in creating meaning. Does she mean that poetry, when it gives the reader a profound insight, cannot be dangerous? Or perhaps she means that Bjørneboe only touched the surface of things, her 'problematic beliefs', and not her heart. Therefore, reading Bjørneboe only reinforced her previous understanding, whereas Hagerup revealed the subtext. When asked whether the profound illumination happened immediately, Esther replies: 'Yes, I think so. Because I learnt it by heart, it meant so much to me.' From her words it seems as if she says that the illumination happened because it was something she learned by heart – that she read it with her heart. What she probably means, however, is that because the poem was so important to her, she decided to memorise it. Still, even though it meant so much, it does not naturally follow that one wants to commit it to memory, as she has kept that volume of poems after all. Sadly, the meaning of the expression has changed in the course of history. Today it carries the meaning of rote learning, of mindless repetition until something finally sticks to the wall of memory. *To learn by heart* was used by Chaucer in *Troilus and Criseyde* (1374), and must have been proverbial long before that. For the ancient Greeks believed that knowledge resided in the heart; the heart was the seat of memory and intelligence. 'To record' etymologically has the same meaning: to engrave upon the heart. She needs to interiorise it, to keep it in her heart. She also described the realisation as 'going through her'. Normally one would say that it touched the heart, as if the heart was on the receiving end. But here the heart has been active, she has placed all of herself into the poem. She learnt it by heart because she had read it with her heart and from the heart. Over and beyond her appraisal of the reading experience as 'profound', her life bears witness to the truth that this poem has been learnt by heart.

Resolution

The Quest for 'the Language of Emotions'

The plot of Esther's story of what happens after the transformative reading experience assumes the shape of a quest. She ventures forth in search of the key to understanding the psyche, to learn the language of the heart. At first there is great disappointment: she does not find it where she expected, in the psychology graduate programme. 'I did not learn about emotions there either.' When Esther finally discovers the 'language of emotions', Emotionally focused therapy for couples (EFTC), this turns out to be a kind of 'subtext' to 'Episode'. It now transpires that the poem 'is exactly what I work with. It informs my work.' Thus, she went on a quest and eventually discovered that she was already in possession of the treasure. The focus of the therapeutic process is to effectuate 'softening moments' – the metamorphosis of the armour, the mask, into open and vulnerable persons in dialogue. The EFTC-theory envisages the relationship as consisting of two layers: a surface one of secondary emotions, and a latent one of primary emotions. Esther has translated the psychological concept into a literary one of 'subtext', what is 'underneath the surface expressions'. She goes on to articulate one of the main theoretical underpinnings of EFT: 'At the very bottom lie the unmet attachment needs and identity confirmation needs.' She encourages each partner ('for instance, I will get her to say: "When I withdraw, it's because I get frightened." And then I get him to say: "When I get angry, it's because you pull back from me. I think you do not love me anymore."') to experience what the *she* person in the poem does: that behind the overt behaviour there is a 'tensed cord'. A central procedural premise is one analogous to Aesop's fable of the Sun and the Wind.[33] 'The more you beat the armour the harder it gets. If the other recognizes that you wish them well, the armour glides off.' The armour is a 'protective shell' that will 'just fall away as if it evaporates' when softening moments are created. Esther talks of the negative loop, where the armoured partners will react to one another in an Ovidian game of pursuit and withdrawal and countermoves. The metaphors of armoury, shells, gliding off and evaporating are all visceral. The softening moment is a revelation brought about by metamorphosis. Two armoured warriors dissolve into two naked lovers, disarmed by the recognition of each other's vulnerability. It is important to note here that 'softening' is a visceral term, a bodily felt term, not a visual one. A metamorphosis is a change of bodily aspect, and it registers affectively, in and through the body.

The originator of EFTC, Leslie S. Greenberg, writes that 'expression of underlying vulnerable emotions was seen as central in changing interaction and in re-establishing the couple's emotional bond.[34] It is quite remarkable how closely connected the theory

---

[33] Cf. Aesop's Fables, Harvard Classics (1909–14).
[34] Leslie S. Greenberg, *Emotion-Focused Therapy*, Theories of Psychotherapy Series (Washington, DC: American Psychological Association, 2011), 7.

of hardening and softening, of evaporation of illusion and the removal of secondary emotion to reveal primary emotions, correspond to the comic plot. The role of the therapist is cast as one of precipitating softening moments and of guiding the couple to a *peripeteia*: a reversal where they get out of the negative 'loop' and into a virtuous cycle of open communication. According to Frye, a comedy often

> begins with some absurd, cruel or irrational law [...] which the action of comedy then evades or breaks. Compacts are as a rule the conspiracies formed by the hero's society; witnesses, such as overhearers of conversations or people with special knowledge [...] are the commonest devices for bringing about the comic discovery.[35]

It is indeed absurd, cruel and irrational, the almost lawful repetition of the negative loop of marital conflict. People with special knowledge, the therapist, is here the device that brings about comic discovery, the revelation of the softening moment that leads to the anagnorisis of the other's true identity.

Episode gives shape to Esther's life. It was a transformative reading experience when she first read it, but we may also say that her adult life has been about translating the affective patterns embedded in the poem, and helping other people to discern these patterns at work in their relationships. I referred to the anagnorisis of the loved one's true identity as a kind of metamorphosis. What kind of shape unfolds in Esther's story, how may we conceptualise its plot? In order to see the true image of the other, one must come to occupy a different vantage point. And Esther, through EFT, came to find a particular vantage point from which to regard emotional interaction. Through her work she helps couples see the underlying patterns of their interaction, thereby recreating the experience of metamorphosis she experienced. I therefore suggest that the master trope that organises the emplotment of her story is *metamorphosis*. Throughout her life, she has come back to the experience of *Episode,* and helped other people realise the perspective inherent in its dramatic structure.

---

[35] Frye, *The Anatomy of Criticism,* 166.

Chapter Six
JANE'S VISIONARY READING

While doing voluntary work for the Reader Organisation, I met Jane, the director and founder of the Shared Reading model. She told me that literature had transformed her life. She immediately accepted my invitation to participate in the project, and also offered to help me find other people to interview. She said that reading Shikasta, *by Doris Lessing, had been an awakening, and that it had changed her whole world-view, literally overnight. When I read the novel, I found it difficult to get into at first. As it were, I found it rewarding once I had worked my way into it. I was familiar with the aspects of Jane's story, having read an article about her prior to our meeting. The interview took place in a room in the attic of the Georgian mansion that is the home of the Reader.*

In Medias Res: *The Encounter with the Book*

Thor: I am very happy that you are willing to take part, and also very excited to meet you. I always read in advance the book the person has stated was important for them. So I brought this along. (*I produce my copy of Shikasta*). What I want is for you tell me all about your experience. Also, if there is a passage that you remember, that stands out, would you like to read it for me, please?

Jane: Yes. There are quite a lot of passages. The first bit is in Doris Lessing's introduction, which is called *Some Remarks*, at the very beginning, and when I read this for the first time I was absolutely … an atheist. I don't think I would even describe myself as an agnostic, I just think I didn't like the idea of religions or God. I loved Doris Lessing and had been reading her novels for many years, so when I came across this paragraph, I was really shocked by it, and also deeply affected:

> *Shikasta* has as its starting point, like many others of the genre ['that's Sci-fi'], the Old Testament, it is our habit to dismiss the Old Testament altogether, because Jehovah, or Jahve, does not think or behave like a social worker. H. G. Wells said that when man cries out his little 'gimme, gimme me, gimme' to God, it is as if a leveret were to snuggle up to a lion on a dark night. Or something to that effect.
>
> The sacred literatures of, of all races and nations have many things in common. ['And then it goes on:'] Almost as if they can be regarded as the products of a single mind, it is possible we make a mistake when we dismiss them as quaint fossils from a dead past.

So when I read that, I felt as if I was being asked to consider, at the deepest of levels, the very basis of everything I thought I was. And at the same time, while that was quite frightening, I also absolutely recognised something in it as true. Because I didn't … believe in God or have any of the apparatus that religious people must have, mental apparatus I mean, I couldn't really think about it, I just *felt* it. So I didn't have the equipment to think the thoughts, it was beyond my ken, but the sense that 'as if a leveret were to snuggle up to a lion on a dark night', I just thought: 'Hmmm, that's true.' If I and all humans are that leveret, the little soft creature, there is a lion (*laughs*). And I'm afraid of that. And I felt: 'Wow, this is making me think something I've never thought before.' So even that was a massive change. And I think reading it took place on a bus, between getting on the bus in the city centre, by the Philharmonic Hall, and getting off at Princes Road. So in that short distance … (*laughs*). I started reading, and then I came to this bit, and these are also just so, so real. The other thing is, there's a dedication in this at the very beginning, and this was the first bit of it I read, which I also thought, wow, mmm, this is true:

For my father, who used to sit, hour after hour, night after night, outside our house in Africa, watching the stars. 'Well,' he would say, 'if we blow ourselves up, there's plenty more where we came from!'

And I love that because I've always been interested in space, and I do believe that there is life in other parts of the universe, or I … no, I don't even know if I believe it, but I think it must be, because it's so vast. So I just like that and I like the sense that we're not the only chance, though it may be better for us if we thought we were. Then, going to the novel itself – I am still on the bus – I probably read about down to the bottom of the first page maybe. And at this part, the other bit I would have as a significant passage – there are millions of things in here that I sort of have in my memory – but this one, Johor is talking about the colonies:

I have been sent on errands to our Colonies on many planets. Crises of all kinds are familiar to me. I have been involved in emergencies that threaten species, or carefully planned local programmes. I have known more than once what it is to accept the failure, final and irreversible, of an effort or experiment to do with creatures who have within themselves the potential of development dreamed of, planned for […] and then – Finis! The end! The drum pattering out into silence.

And I don't think I knew it at the time, but I think I've worked it out since then … I was reading this as I was in the first year of University, I think, but it might have been the year before, when I was just thinking about going, and I'd be about 23 or 24. By the time I was 27 my mother had died of alcoholism, she was 51 when she died.

A Very Hungry Person

Jane: My mother was the daughter of a docker. She went to public school after she got a scholarship. She loved reading, trashy novels as well as classics. During my childhood, before things became too bad, she read to me. One of my most vivid memories is of her pulling her hair down over her face and then recited the witches from Macbeth: 'Where the place? / Upon the heath / There to meet with Macbeth.' We would all scream and hide behind the couch. I was the oldest of four children. My parents divorced when I was ten. So I grew up in a poor and quite chaotic single-parent family. My local library in Toxteth became a refuge. When I was 12 they let me take out adult books. I remember really getting into Beckett. I loved *Happy Days*. I think I knew that somehow I was in that story. I recognised it. So from way back my reading has been about making sense, although I didn't realise it at the time.

So she was in the high throes of the end of her life by the time I read this. She lived next door but one to me and I had a lot to do with her. I'd recently had a conversation with her about her dying. Basically, I thought she'd been drinking so heavily for 15 years it was like a form of suicide, it was like 'I'm going to drink myself to death.' Though she spoke about it more in terms of pleasure and a lifestyle choice, but really, it was suicide. So I was very conscious that that was happening, and my three younger siblings were still teenagers, and conscious that their lives were all turning into lives that were connected more to smoking dope and drinking than to going to school. And so when I read that, I was very, very moved by it. I suppose I was imagining as part of the story, I was thinking about galaxies and alien life forms and so on, but at the deepest level, I was thinking: 'Hmm, yes, this happens. Life, some lives fail, and they fail to achieve their potential.' And that certainly is the case of my mother, and it was, I think, also the case of my siblings.

Thor: You were fearing that they would go down the same road.

Jane: Yeah, and even for me, you know, would my life also do that. I don't think I had any of that in proper consciousness, but I do now think I knew it. So it didn't feel like a pleasure to read it, well it did in a way, but it was more like a very *hungry* person, finding something they really needed to eat.

Thor: Like you just *had* to read?

Jane: Yeah, and further down, where is it … Yeah, this bit:

This is a catastrophic universe, always, and subject to sudden reversals, upheavals, changes, cataclysms, with joy, never anything but the song of substance under pressure, forced into new forms and shapes.

So that sentence, again I felt I, wow, I recognised it was just true: It is catastrophical, or it was to me then at that age, that my life had been full of sudden reversals, upheavals, changes, cataclysms. I wasn't aware of joy being … 'the song of substance under pressure', but when I read it I thought: 'Yes, when things are under pressure, they *are* forced into new shapes.' I don't know, weirdly it both allowed the terror of some of my experiences of life, and the possibility: Here I was, about to start at University and what became a complete change of life. So the book and where I was in my life came together at exactly the right sort of point to interact with each other and make a major change.

Thor: You said you'd already read books by Lessing, and you loved those. So you had a sense of …

Jane: I *trusted* her.

Thor: You *trusted* her. So does that mean that even though you found that kind of uncomfortable to read …

Jane: It was more like going, *huh!!!* (*Laughs*). It was like a shocked recognition.

Thor: Let's say that you'd picked that book up and it was not by Doris Lessing, but some geezer you hadn't heard of, do you think it would have felt like that?

Jane: Yeah, it might have, because if it was exactly written like this, I think some of those sentences would still have got me. And I think it may have been that in a sense my life was at a point of change anyway. I'd been living in a feminist commune, and I'd been ordering my life through the ideas of feminism and to a certain extent things to do with Marxism and socialism or anarchism. Though nobody who was part of that world would ever have thought of me as a real member of it, because I was too disaffected and anarchistic (*laughs*), and naughty, but that was the framework I inhabited. Before that I'd had the framework of my family which was about … (*exhales*). Enjoy yourself, drink, eat, be merry, for tomorrow we die. That was the philosophy in our house. And so those political frameworks I inhabited from about the age of 18 onwards, gave a different kind of structure and meaning, but I didn't *really* believe in them. I believed in some things about feminism, but I certainly didn't believe in some of the Marxist stuff. And anyway, the commune had come to an end, and I suppose that left me in a strange place where I knew I wasn't going to go back into 'eat and drink because tomorrow we die'. I had a child. I knew I'd done well in one of my 'A' levels, I had been to college, had a teacher who'd said to me, 'hey you're clever,' so something was going to change. And maybe I was just ripe to … maybe if I'd met an evangelical Christian preacher, I might have gone for them, who knows. I don't know. But luckily, I got this.

Thor: So this was then like a third kind of worldview, after 'eat, drink, be merry' and feminism.

Jane: Hmmm, yeah. And Doris had been in the feminist, Marxist world, obviously with the *Golden Notebook*. But she'd also had all those sort of weird, slightly mystical, slightly sci-fi books like *Briefing for a Descent into Hell*, which is about, really, the truths that come through nervous breakdown. Which I'd absolutely also just thought: 'Wow, all this is *true!*' So there were things about understanding what a life might be, that were already happening, that were changing anyway. I already liked sci-fi, so it was easy for me to read it, and I was so excited by it.

The Big Dream: Everything Matters

And then I got home, and I can't remember what time of day it was, but anyway, after my daughter had gone to bed and it was evening, I just sat and read the whole book, haha, from cover to cover. And it was, you know, 3 o'clock in the morning or something by the time I'd finished.

Thor: You were completely immersed in it?

Jane: Yeah. And then I had this very, very weird dream. I just stayed up all night to finish it, and then went to sleep. And I had this dream that I was looking down on my daughter's school playground, but from quite close to it, so maybe 20 feet up in the air onto it, and so I could see all the children, maybe speeded up, moving about, and then I just went higher up, and then I could see the cars in the streets round it, and then higher than that, and then I could see the whole city, and then, haha, I could see the *whole* world, and, and then the whole *universe*, haha. And it was really exhilarating and terrifying. I don't remember what else happened. It has just made me think now, I wonder if I wrote it down. I might have done at the time, I might have it in a journal somewhere, what the rest of the dream was. But that's all I can remember, that sense of going up and up and up, and it getting bigger and bigger and bigger and being able to see all, still see all the parts of it.

Thor: And you can remember feeling in the dream both exhilaration and fright as well?

Jane: Yes! So when I woke up in the morning, I was, partly through the reading and partly through the dream, my mind had *shifted*. And then I was really *scared*.

Thor: That's the kind of dream you only have a couple of times in a life, isn't it? So you were scared of it all?

Jane: Yeah, and I was scared because if the book is true, if it *matters* what each individual *does* in their life, which is really the premise, *then what would I do*? So, I was scared that I didn't know how to even interact with people anymore, that if everything mattered, if I'd gone from a state of either nothing mattered, so enjoy yourself, or political determinism to now *my* individual acts all mattered, every single one of them, I was really scared to even go to the shop to buy bread. Because I was thinking: 'I can't go out, to the shop or anything, because I don't know how to behave in this new universe, I don't know how to.' That's why I say it was a bit like a religious conversion, because it was, it did feel vulnerable. And when they say in religious settings, 'born again', and things like that, the main feeling I remember of that is of immense vulnerability. Of being like somebody with very soft skin, or no … And as if I would have to learn how to *be* … I don't think I went out, I don't know. I don't know how my daughter got to school, I can't remember. I'm going to go and look at my old diaries, because I may have written all that down, but it's interesting that I can't remember.

Thor: Yeah, you had that feeling of soft skin, like everything is open and …

Jane: And as if it might hurt me or I might hurt it. It was as if a great deal of, I suppose, moral thinking would have to come about or even moral *practice* maybe. That literally I'd have to learn how to do it, if everything mattered, and if how I conducted myself mattered. It's like starting again, and everything you did you'd have to think, have I done that right? Was that right? Normally of course, one has a kind of continuation through life and people teach you what is right, and you act, but this is like having to start again as an adult. I would just have to find out what the rules were. So it was very frightening, and I just thought, well, the only thing I can do is, I'll write to Doris Lessing and just say 'hey, can you help me, please?'

Thor: So that is what you did?

Jane: I did. I wrote her a letter. You know, she was a Sufi, that was her religious practice, and I wrote to her and said: 'I know you're a Sufi […].' I can't remember what was in my letter, but it was, you have a teacher, are you my teacher? Is this what I have to learn? Can you help me? What shall I do? And so she wrote back, after a few days, I think within the same week. I don't know, but I feel as if I was still indoors all that time, that may not be true, that may be a strange memory. And she said: 'No, I'm not your teacher, I'm just a student and not a very good one. I'm a writer, for God's sake, pull yourself together. Grow up. You remind me of myself when I was young, very hysterical.' It was quite a sort of cold water…

Thor: Not what you expected?

Jane: I didn't know what to expect. I really didn't know, I don't know what I wanted. I wanted her to take notice of me, that this thing had happened to me. Which she did, though it was a strict response. And later I got to know her, and that was a big part of her character, haha. She said: 'I'm a student of Idries Shah, you should read his books, I'll send you some money for them, if you can't afford them. Just concentrate and get serious and get on with it', that was basically the gist of the letter. I hadn't read any books by Idries Shah, and I was very attracted to the idea of Doris Lessing sending me money, I thought that would be a nice relationship, haha. But I also thought, that's not a good start to my new life, is it? So I'll go down the library and see if there's any books in there, which of course there were. And I got them all out and read them all and just thought no, this isn't it, this is not for me. It might work for her, but it doesn't answer what I want and need. So then I just got on with reading, and reading other things. I was at University and I began – without at first realising it, but gradually with more consciousness – looking for other things that connected to the things I'd learnt in this book. And so for example when I got onto reading George Eliot, it was clear to me that there was a relation between the two things. In *Middlemarch*, it's all about *vocation*, about finding what you are meant to do, and Dorothea even says to Will about her religious ideas, 'Oh I don't want to tell you about it, you'll say they're Persian,' or something. And I remember thinking, 'oh that's like her with her Sufism,' and me sort of thinking, no I don't want to *solidify* it in any way. I really identified with Dorothea as somebody who had to find a way of *being*, but I also identified with people in the book like Fred Vincy, who's just, you know, morally dubious and weak. So this book, *Shikasta*, gave me a kind of prism to read a lot of other things and eventually that became my PhD. So in a way I wrote about what, for me, leads up to *Shikasta*, which I didn't know when I read *Shikasta*. Because I did it the other way round, I read this, and *then* I read English Literature. But actually, you can see that something like this starts way back and it starts as she says really with the Old Testament, and it's in everything, but I didn't know that, then. (*smiles*)

Necessity: Integration of the Vision

Thor: Just to clarify one point, you said that everything matters, that means that it must matter to someone, or some being.

Jane: Good point, mmm.

Thor: And then you mentioned George Eliot.

Jane: I really waiver between whether I believe in God or don't believe in God. So when you, as soon as you say Someone, I just think, I don't believe in that, I don't believe in *Someone* … If it was more like a kind of pattern, or … principle or direction of energy, or underlying template, or structure, maybe I find that easier than something personal. I have wished I could become a Christian, but I can't, something in me gets just like a horse, just won't jump. But I … when I look at earth, I think there are underlying patterns of goodness and wholeness, and connectivity and things like that. And I know that includes dying and rats eating ladybirds and things that you'd think are bad, but I don't know whether they are … I think the experience of beauty must somehow be connected to human beings and what we can *do* with ourselves. So usually now, when people would – if anybody would – ask me, do you believe in God, I usually say yes, just because I definitely believe something, I just don't know what it is. I think it's better to believe than not to believe – well, it is for me at any rate – and that's partly to do with behaviour. Also the thing I would like about being a Christian is that it'd be quite good for me to be someone who was committed to living by some rules, I'm not very good at that by myself. One of the rules that's in *Shikasta* is the rule she calls the need, the Necessity.

> What the Natives were being taught was the science of maintaining contact at all times with Canopus; of keeping contact with their Mother, their Maintainer, their Friend, and what they called God, the Divine. If they kept the stones aligned and moving as the forces moved and waxed and waned, and if the cities were kept up according to the laws of the Necessity, then they might expect – these little inhabitants of Rohanda who had been no more than scurrying monkeys half in and half out of the trees, animals with little in them of the Canopean nature – these animals could expect to become men, would take charge of themselves and their world when the Giants left them, the work of the symbiosis complete. (40)

I think that was one of the things I recognised in the book, each according to the need or you do it according to the Necessity. And still, 30 years on or more, I think that's true.

(*Long pause*).

Thor: You said this book gave you like a prism, and your searching and reading afterwards have been a matter of …

Jane: Collecting more stuff into that container, yeah. In a way one of the best things about that have been religious poetry, which before this I couldn't read. I would just think, 'oh, not relevant to me, don't want to be doing that.' But since maybe about five years after this, I've been reading George Herbert, Milton, Dante and they are, in many ways, bigger than this and *better*. So yeah, I love it, and I wouldn't like to say it wasn't the best, because it was my *darling*, but the *Divine Comedy's* the same story, in a different way. So I feel as if what the book did for me was open an area of life and thinking of human experience that was closed, and then I went in and found it was full of this amazing stuff in there. And reading George Herbert for many, many years has probably done more than anything to make me understand what God might mean to people who believe in God, and when I'm reading

George Herbert, that's the closest I get to being ... I don't think it's still a Christian, it's a *believer*.

Thor: Is there a particular poem by Herbert?

Jane: Yes, there's *The Flower*: 'And now in age I bud again, / After so many deaths I live and write; / I once more smell the dew and rain, / And relish versing: O my only light, / It cannot be / That *I* am *he* / On whom thy tempests fell all night.' That feeling, that you've been through hell, and in time it was only a few hours, but it was forever, wasn't it? That's a real human experience, and I love the way that the poem *suffers* the experience and imagines a pattern that makes sense of it. That imagination of the pattern is a wonderful thing. And I also like the *Temper*, where he goes from a kind of resolution at the end of *Temper I*, to suddenly begin *Temper II* with something like, 'it cannot be!' And I'm thinking: 'oh you've just solved it in the first one,' haha, and then immediately can't, it's gone broken again. That's fantastic, the relation between those two. I like the Affliction poems, 'broken in pieces, all asunder, Lord hunt me not'. And sometimes when I'm teaching that I'll think about trying to take people to understand what *Lord* means in that poem, if you don't believe in God; well, it means *necessity* or the *truth* or *reality*. They're fantastic.

Thor: With this book in hand, so to speak, you come into literary studies, and there's already a book that's blown you open and in a sense given you a key to all kinds of literature. How was that experience, then, where things were formalised?

Jane: The first two years at University were very difficult for me, because much of the study was sort of unreal. And I kept thinking, oh I don't like this, I think I'll leave, and then being afraid to leave. I didn't want to be someone who just always started things and didn't finish them, which is what I'm like, and it then was very much what I was like. And then, in the third year, Brian Nellist became my teacher. His whole life has been made by books. I don't know whether he'd say he was *changed*, every book probably changes him. But he's a great person. I suddenly realised: I'm going to learn something here, and then suddenly I really wanted to do it. I worked my socks off in the third year; I'd found a way to do the thing I was interested in, through his inspired teaching. He always just gives you the opportunity to see if there's anything for you. He presents everything as if he *loves* them, everything. Later I found out there were some other things he'd taught me that he didn't love, and I was really shocked. And he said: 'But I have to do that, so that you can if you want to, because if I told you that I don't think much of this, what would happen? You would immediately not read it.' I thought, hmmm, that's a good way, *love things*! And while he's doing it, he does love them, he looks through everything that's *good* about it and gives it to you. So that was a great experience and it taught me also how to be a good teacher, I think, how to be a good reader: Try and find things you *love*. I brought this book, *Shikasta*, to Brian at that point, during the third year of University, and got him interested in it.

Thor: Because you were talking passionately about it?

Jane: Yeah, and saying: 'This is *Shikasta, Shikasta!*' And then, I don't know, it just became obvious that I would probably do a PhD. I was in an amazingly lucky, unusual position, I think, which was that I had a *real* problem that I wanted to work on. It was not theoretical, it was not academic, it was *my* genuine line of thing I needed to find out about, and so the PhD was very, very *real* to me: what *do* I think about this? It was a real experiment for me of where, whatever this is, *where* is it? And where can I see it elsewhere? And how do you get there? And why is *Middlemarch* connected to it? It was three years of really being able to stay in one place and think through all the thoughts that had arisen that night when I had the terrible dream. The PhD, 'Visionary Realism: From George Eliot to Doris Lessing', became the combing out of lots of strands of it into, I suppose, an order or a *framework* by which I could *be*. And it was immensely useful and you know, even now, I'm still proceeding on the basis of what I did in that PhD. What a *lucky* girl! To have that chance.

Thor: It's as if this is sort of a kernel or bundle of energy, and you spent a lot of time just unpacking it.

Jane: Yes, so, yes, almost like *what is religious experience*? The PhD is essentially what happens to God if humans don't believe in God? What happens to religious experience if culturally you don't believe in God. Surely the religious experiences of everybody are the same wherever we come from, or whatever our cultural background. Is there an underlying reality? You know, I wrote about, for example, in *Middlemarch*, the conversion experience where Dorothea tries to, and does in fact momentarily, convert Rosamond to being good. It just doesn't last, it can't last. If that whole experience had been conceived within a religious framework, somebody could have made that same experience into an evangelical understanding of life, couldn't they? However, George Elliot is trying to think without God. I was interested in, does religious experience go away if we don't believe in it, or is it still there? I suppose I didn't make it explicit in the PhD, but as we speak now I suddenly think: 'Well of course I was writing about my own experience, really.' Was it a religious experience? I think anybody would say it was, though if you don't *believe* in religion, oh God, it's a hard thing to understand.

Thor: I suppose you could always redefine it as a spiritual experience. But then you're still faced with the same problem. I suppose this is what William James is trying to work out as well.

Jane: Yeah. (*pause*). Hmm.

Thor: So if you were to find the right verb for describing what your reading experience has meant to you, would you say it has changed your life, or saved your life, or something else?

Jane: (*Pause*). It was part of a saving, but there's probably more than a 50/50 chance that I would have saved it anyway, somehow. I think I was on the route to saving my life, the book certainly became a big element of that, but I think it seems better to say something like it's *made* or *shaped* my life. In that I think I would have still had my life, and I think I would have … done something with it. But it wouldn't have been what I *have* done. The book made me realise that there is a spiritual dimension to life, and it made me see that you have life for a purpose, and you've got to find out what that purpose is, and then you've got to *do* it. So I think it's given me a very, very strong sense of purpose, and that purpose has *made* my life. Not just with the Reader Organisation, although the Reader's a massive expression of that now. But before I started the Reader, I just had a private life as a part-time teacher and a reader and writer.

(*Pause*) One of the other things I really remember loving in the book is the festival of the child, do you remember that part?

Finding the Purpose: Shared Reading

(She reads excerpt from 'ILLUSTRATIONS: The Shikastan Situation [This Report by Johor seems to us a useful addition to the Illustration]. Archivists.')

While even a few years ago this festival was entirely for the children, the economic pressure of the tourists has operated so that there are entertainments and food and drink for the adults as well. This year, for the first time, there were television cameras, and because of this, everything was more elaborate than usual. When the statue had been taken in and put away into its cupboard, dancing begins again, and continues until midnight.

This is a pleasant enough festival, and offers much needed relief to people whose lives are hard indeed. It has not become much more elaborate since the report of Emissary 76, four hundred years ago. But we must expect that while tourism lasts, every year will show new feats of imagination.

There is no use left in this festival from our point of view. I could not prevent myself wondering as I observed these scenes, what would happen if I were able to stand forward and relate the real origins of the festival. (208–209)

Jane: It starts with the Canopean saying each child has a lot of potential, this child can become anything, but it ends up as a sort of strange European Christian thing where they parade round with a child on a pedestal. I love that sense that way back, there was a real piece of information in it, and now we just have these vestiges of ceremony, or, I love that child potential thing.

There was a moment in the summer school, the first time we did the summer school here two years ago, where one of the little boys who's aged twelve had to be given Ritalin every day. And it was my job to do that. In the morning the social worker gave me a packet of pills, and said you must give it him at 12 o'clock. And then I had to do that. (*pause*) (*tears*). That's made me feel sad. That seemed like a moment from a book like this, where it's small, it's not going to change the world in any way. It was good for him to come to the summer school, if we didn't give him the Ritalin he wouldn't be able to come, nor we to have coped with him. But, it was *wrong*. It was wrong in the larger sense that that child needs something else, something that I and his social workers and everybody can't give him. Anyway, that boy is one of the children who is now getting one-to-one reading through the Off the Page project with volunteers. And the lady who's reading with him really likes him. I got a message two weeks ago, saying – he can't read or anything – we've been reading the Witches from Macbeth this week, and he really loved it. And I can remember trying to even make him look at a picture book, during that beginning, two years ago. So that feels like *something*.

I started the Reader in 1997 with the *Reader Magazine*, and that was really an expression of something that was happening in teaching at the University. I don't think we've got the first edition here because it's very rare now. No, it was a little sort of homemade looking thing. We were teaching in this particular way, the way that has partly come out of this book, reading as a way to understand yourself and your life, or everything – personal reading. Behind our idea of teaching was always the question: Can it help? We'd been doing that for, I don't know how long, and I kept thinking we're doing something really *good* here, people should know about it. At the same time literary theory in the main part of the School of English was the big thing, with people all going round strapped up in this apparatus of theory, and we were just sort of weird ladies on the sidelines. So the idea was to start the Reader to try to get what was in the classes out more visible. During that period of life, from when I got married in the early 80s and I had done my PhD, I was just reading and teaching and writing. Teaching twice a week, not being a member of the department, I never went to a staff meeting, I never had any formal connection with anything at all. I was like a hermit, really. I had my children and my husband, didn't really have any social life, didn't want any. I just wanted to read and write. During that period, from 1983 to 1997, I was writing novels. I wrote five novels over a 15-year period, and that was my main activity. When I realised I'd never get of any of these novels published, I thought I'll just stop writing them. And then I just found I couldn't stop writing. I started writing poetry. What I now think is that that whole period, that 15- to 17-year period, was assimilating … the Big Bang. And that was something to do with, I don't know what, whether that's … Well anyway, it's your *inner* self, that's what was being made in that time. It's almost as if there's a whole massive thing, and then there was this long period of building up energy or …. yeah, let's call it energy – and then eventually starting up the Reader. When I thought: 'I'm not going to be a writer, just stop doing this,' that energy and the backlog of energy, the full battery if you like, fully charged now, just immediately began to come into this. And I think this is a much better expression of passing on the Big Bang, the energy of the Big Bang. Though in many ways – until we had this conversation – I've done it without realising the connection of it and without making a lot of that very explicit. (*Pause*). I don't know if it's just myself, but I'm really interested in that story and I would like to *write* it one day. It's an interesting story, I think.

Thor: Yes it is, it is a very interesting story.
Jane: I'll write it when I retire, haha. When I did well in my Degree and I was top of my year, it's the first time I was ever very successful at anything I'd ever done. At school I was nothing, and I hardly had any qualifications when I went to University. It was the absolute bare minimum to get in. So realising that I could be very good at something was an amazing and immensely encouraging thing. Finishing the PhD, which I did in three years flat, I finished the PhD at the end of August, had my son on the 16th of September, and I'd been thinking all the time that if I don't finish this before I have that baby, I'll never finish it, I must finish it. So that was a wonderful practical piece of discipline. That was the first major piece of writing

I had ever finished and I'd been writing since the age of ten, always starting stories, and novels and so on, and never, never finishing them. I guess that must have been a sore point in me, though I didn't really know it was. But I knew when I finished the PhD, wow, this means something, now I could finish a book, couldn't I? So then I started writing the first novel almost straightaway. It was an achievement to me to write those five books, and to finish them, every single one of them is finished.

Thor: Have you had any of them published?

Jane: No. I tried to get all of them published, but they're probably not very good, and they were definitely not very marketable. I'm sure there are worse books that are published, but those worse books are sellable, haha. Whereas mine were probably poor attempts to be George Elliot, in my own time. Not fashionable, nobody wants to read it, plus whatever was their own deficiencies. But I wanted to write them, and in fact probably needed to, and they also were a part of the response to this. Almost as if what the books became were a series of human situations, where moral problems were what I needed to work out: If this, then what? If you don't wash the dishes, then what? Even at that silly level, then what? So, it was good for me to do all that working out, and it helped me realise I was somebody who could finish things, even though it didn't become a life as a writer. When I started The Reader Organisation properly, I mean the actual work of the organisation, I think that 15-year apprenticeship as writing those novels, and working out those problems, has really helped me with this. I was learning to believe in, and to build, structures. To think, you can take an idea and make it into a thing; you, Jane, you can do that. And now it's almost as if in some way the moral problems are the real people that I'm working with. Where you think, oh what am I going to do about the fact that X is always late for work, yet when they get here they're good? That's one of them, isn't it? So it's still part of the *Shikast*a story. So I suppose the reverberations then, of the book having *made* or *shaped* my life, those reverberations are interestingly now all in this organisation in lots of ways. So that's a powerful thing, isn't it? (*Pause.*)

Recognising the Signature

The best thing in it, from my point of view, is the *Signature*. They are given the Signature and it can flash, and as soon as you show it, people recognise it:

And I gave her the Signature, saying they must regard this as more important than – but what? Life? They did not have that conception: the thought of death as an ever-present threat was not in them. This came from Canopus, I said. It was the very substance and being of Canopus and must be guarded at all times, even if they were to lose their lives doing it. Thus I held Death before them, using it to create in these creatures a sorrow and a vigilance where there had been none. Sais put the Signature reverently into her belt and kept her hand there on it, as she stood in front of me, her eyes on my face, listening. When they reached a settlement, I said, she must first of all speak of Canopus, and if the word was enough to revive old memories and associations, and if her hearers could listen because of that word alone, then she could give her message and go. Only if she could get no one to listen, or if it seemed that she and her father might be harmed, then she might show the Signature. And when they had been everywhere, and spoken with everyone even hunting bands they met, or solitary farmers or fishermen in the forests or by the rivers, then they must bring the Signature back to me.

And then I spoke to her carefully and slowly about the concept of a task, something which had to be done – for I was afraid that this might have lapsed from her mind altogether. This journey of hers, I said, the act of making it, and carrying the Signature and guarding it, would develop her, would bring out in her something that was buried and clouded over. (85)

> I believe there is a sort of signature, though it's sadly not a physical object, but people do recognise it, when you show it to them, haha. I think that we are here *to know*. I don't mean intellectually, a lot of our knowing is in our gut, in our heart. You've already got your feelings, sometimes you just haven't got any language for them. Something happens to you in Shared Reading, a sudden moment – a feeling of recognition, of seeing written down something you had as nameless (and therefore in a sense unknown), taking some form in the visible world, so you can begin to know it. And there is something so important about that – it's a form of consciousness. There is a big thing to be done intellectually for humans – which I think George Eliot's already done, but no one has noticed – which is to make sure that we understand that *feeling* is the deepest form of knowing. That's what literature does for us. It makes us feel, so we can know. I think one of the beautiful things about shared reading is that it has a bit of signature in it. I was in Amsterdam at a conference a few days ago talking about it, and you can see as you begin to tell people about it, some people really recognise something, it's like something they already know and then you tell them.

Thor: So The Reader has grown from the start from one group in a Library, then spread across Merseyside, across this country and then into Europe, how does that feel?

Jane: It's amazing. It has grown out of and from the wonderful compost of sadnesses, breakages, losses and terrors of my own real life and the lives of others I have known. I was in Belgium earlier in the year, I went over because they had organised a get together and training weekend for their volunteers. I think there were about 30 of them at a residential place in the country. I read in a group with some people there, and just listening to each person saying, oh, I'm a school teacher and I do this on Saturday mornings, in a poor district of my town, I work in prisons and I do this as part of my job, I'm a psychiatrist, and I use it with my patients, and so on, I was just thinking, Christ, these people are all *really* doing it! It was a powerful, moving feeling of just thinking, whoa! It doesn't feel particularly connected to me, it feels more like people *recognise* the *thing*, and that's a lovely feeling. It's like having unearthed a little bit of reality that, I think, we'd just forgotten about. I think humans did already know it, because I think that's what for many hundreds of years the Bible was, people *shared* it, and other sacred text books, but I mean because we're Europeans let's say the Bible. It was read aloud, people all knew the same stories, people all knew Daniel in the lion's den, people all knew Ruth, and it's a terrible loss, a loss of the cohesiveness, not having a body of shared stories.

And I think it's almost as if we've just *stumbled* into a way of having that, so it feels great, haha, it feels really good.

Thor: So do you think, then, that what they recognise, is the signature of literature?

Jane: Yes, how well you've put it. (*Pause*). I suppose, it's a funny thing because I remember once I'd gone to lobby at one of the political conferences, and somebody I was speaking to said to me: 'I hate the idea of sharing reading, reading's private.' And I bet a lot of people who are keen readers probably feel that, and I know in groups people who are very good readers already find it quite difficult to get into the same gear as everybody else. Sometimes you can see people really struggling with that, and I wonder about that, about the sort of individuality of reading as it has largely been for most people, and the strangeness of making it a social activity. I think we haven't been very good at making more of that somehow, and it's a very different experience. (*pause*) Lots of readers are solitary, and maybe people who are struggling with social connections go into books, don't they? Well, I know I did.

Thor: Maybe it's more to do with protecting something because you fear that some people want to step on it or misunderstand or whatever.

Jane: Yeah, and also the actual experience is an individual experience, so it happens to you, even in the group. And when you're a private reader, or a private religious person, I would imagine, when I'm reading George Herbert by myself, the experiences of one soul or mind with the other thing. What's amazing sometimes in shared reading is that you witness that extremely *intimate* experience. (*Pause*). And actually some of my best reading experiences now come in groups, rather than by myself, because I think I'm more able to concentrate in the group. I'm just thinking about last week when I was reading some George Herbert with some colleagues, that the responsibility and desire to make the good thing happen, which if it was just me by myself at home might happen, but I don't think I would concentrate as hard, because I have to make it happen for all these people. Is that like being a musician or something? If you're a performer, a Yo-Yo Ma, you would have to practice at home all the time by yourself before you gave it to everybody, wouldn't you? And yet the giving, the doing it … I don't know, that's interesting.

Thor: Your life-changing reading experience has led to so many other people's lives being touched by literature. That is very inspirational. Thank you so much for sharing.

Jane: That's great, I've really enjoyed talking with you. And thanks for the opportunity to think it through. Definitely over Christmas I'm going to look up those old diaries, and just see if I was writing all the time at that point. I'd be amazed if I haven't written something about it. Won't it be weird if it's different than I remember? That sometimes happens.

As I walk out of Calderstones Park, I turn back and look at the stately Georgian mansion. It seems to me that the entire place, housing a large organisation of people dedicated to sharing literature, is connected to a Substance of We Feeling. I feel uplifted, not only because I have listened to Jane's story but also because I have witnessed the materialisation of her vision. And, thinking of all that she has told me – the childhood memory of the mother reading aloud to her children against the backdrop of hardship, trouble and neglect; the readiness for change described as a hunger for truth and meaning; the propitious encounter with Shikasta *on the bus and the ensuing dream that left her vulnerable; the shocked recognition of a world-shattering ineffable truth; the undergraduate professing the wonders of* Shikasta *to her professors and going on to achieve a PhD on her own terms; writing five novels in order to work out a personal solution to life's exigencies; ultimately finding her life's purpose after she put the pen down, spreading shared reading and the love of literature across Merseyside and far beyond – I say to myself: yes, this is an interesting story.*

The Big Bang and the View from Above

Crisis

Kairos *and* Metanoia

Jane, at the time of encountering *Shikasta*, did not consciously experience herself as being in crisis. It is only afterwards that she is enabled to see that she was *hungry* for change. The summary of her background is preceded by a reflexive differentiation between the experiencing I and the narrating I: 'And I don't think I knew it at the time, but I think I worked it out since then.' It is a careful consideration of what she was able to know then and what she knows now: 'I think' acknowledges the fact that she cannot now remember the past as it actually was then. Yet, further on she nuances this by saying: 'I don't think I had any of that in proper consciousness, but I do now think I knew it.' She here appears to distinguish between two levels of knowing: conscious knowledge and tacit knowing. So there is both a horizontal gap, between then and now, and a vertical division between levels of knowing/awareness. What did she unknowingly know? That some lives tragically fail, 'they fail to achieve their potential'. She seems to imply that she possessed a negative form of knowledge: she knew the 'frameworks' that would lead to failure. And she was now 'hungry' to find a way to achieve the potential she must have suspected was there. Her mother had been awarded a scholarship, yet had chosen the road to suicide. The second framework she had entertained, the Marxist-feminist one, she 'didn't really believe in'. She reaches the conclusion that 'the book and where I was in my life came together at exactly the right sort of point'. This notion of the propitious moment, *kairos*, is an assertion that she shares with many of the other intimants. The ground had been prepared, partly by previous books by Lessing: 'There were things about understanding what a life might be, that were already happening, that were changing anyway.' She had followed Lessing up to this point, sharing her framework and her discovery of the possibilities of sci-fi. Jane was a declared atheist, however. Retrospectively, she can identify this as a kairotic moment. Her life was at a critical point. She also indicates an element of fortune, implying gratitude: 'Luckily, I got this.' In looking back on her experience, Jane can now see that the encounter happened at the right time, in a propitious moment: 'So the book and where I was in my life came together at exactly the right sort of point to interact with each other and make a major change.'

In the fourth book of the *Laws* (709b ff.), in his discussion of the factors that govern human life, Plato declares: 'Chance [*Tyche*] and Occasion [*Kairos*] cooperate with God in the control of human affairs.' Whereas chance has to do with luck and a coming together of events that could have happened at any time, *kairos* points to a particularly propitious moment. Together, they form an ontological element where the moment, although not of human devising, calls for human response. John E. Smith notes three distinct but related aspects of Kairos:

> First, the idea of 'the right time' […]. Second, Kairos means a time of tension and conflict, a time of crisis implying that the course of events poses a problem that calls for a decision at that time, which is to say that no generalized solution or response […] will suffice. Third, Kairos means that the problem or crisis has brought with it a time of opportunity for accomplishing some purpose which could not be carried out at some other time.[1]

According to Philip Sipiora, kairos first appeared in the *Iliad*, where it is connected to vulnerability; 'it denotes a *vital* or *lethal* place in the body, one that is particularly susceptible to injury and therefore necessitates special protection.'[2] Sipiora refers to Doro Levi's study of the etymology of the word, who in his 1923 treatment of kairos in classical literature, traces the etymology of the word to 'death', 'ruin', 'breast', 'the seat of spiritual life', 'to care for', 'to destroy'. Passages from Euripides reveal the transition in meaning from the Homeric vulnerability to 'opportunity' and 'the right time'. There are, relates Sipiora, two different sources for the word: In archery, it refers to an opening, a tunnel-like aperture through which the arrow must pass; in the art of weaving, it is the 'critical time' when the weaver must draw the yarn through a gap that momentarily opens up in the cloth being woven. Thus it is at the same time a momentary opening, creating an opportunity for the weaver or the archer, and a vulnerable spot that needs to be protected; in both instances a sensitivity to the aperture is required for an apt response. It marks a particular moment in time where several conditions become confluent, and whether it presents an opportunity or a special vulnerability, it is vital that one does not fail to respond.

According to Carolyn R. Miller, there are two different conceptions of Kairos within rhetoric. 'In one view […] it becomes a principle of adaptation and accommodation to convention, expectation, predictability. […] In the other view, *Kairos* is understood to represent not the expected but the opposite: the uniquely timely, the spontaneous, the radically particular. […] The timely action will be understood as adaptive, as appropriate, *only in retrospect*.'[3] It is this latter view that is apposite in relation to Jane's situation: the determination of the moment as propitious can only be understood in retrospect. Jane and the book came together at the right moment: the *kairos* of this was beyond the awareness of the experiencing I, just as the crisis of meaning was. Kelly R. Myers

---

[1] John E. Smith, 'Time and Qualitative Time', In *Rhetoric and Kairos: Essays in History, Theory and Praxis*, ed. Philip Sipiora and James S. Baumlin (Albany: State University of New York Press, 2002), 52. Crisis and Kairos are here related, although they are not derived from the same verb. Krinô means to 'separate', whereas keirô, the verb leading to Kairos, means to 'cut', 'cleave' or 'part'.

[2] Philip Sipiora, 'Introduction: The Ancient Concept of Kairos', in *Rhetoric and Kairos: Essays in History, Theory and Praxis*, 2.

[3] C. L. Miller, 'Foreword', in *Rhetoric and Kairos*, xii–xiii.

discusses the close partnership of *Kairos* and *Metanoia* as essential in 'understanding the affective and transformative dimension of *Kairos*'.[4] She argues that it is often neglected that 'the god of opportunity does not work alone. [...] *Metanoia* resides in the wake of Opportunity, sowing regret and inspiring repentance in the missed moment.'[5]

One meaning of *metanoia* is 'afterthought' (from meta, 'after' or 'beyond, and nous, 'mind'). The afterthought 'brings new knowledge and therefore creates a 'change of mind' that can affect the feelings, will, or thought. Thus *metanoia* implies a reflective act in which a person returns to a past event in order to see it anew.'[6] Such a retroactive meaning-making, where an event only gains meaning in light of a later occurrence, seems to have a certain resemblance to an experience recounted by Wordsworth in the Prelude:

> While on I walked, a comfort seemed to touch
> A heart that had not been disconsolate:
> Strength came where weakness was not known to be,
> At least not felt.

In a perspicacious commentary on these lines, Philip Davis remarks: 'The heart had *not* been disconsolate: it is not simply a problem followed by a solution. Deeper and more gently, it is a subtly double experience: he did not know he previously lacked what now he was glad to be given.'[7] Jane, through a *metanoia*, realises both that she was in a crisis, needing spiritual nourishment, and that encountering *Shikasta* was a *kairos*. I will argue that this *kairos-metanoia* complementarity is reflected in Jane's use of the two metaphors of 'framework' and 'hunger'.

Framework

I interpreted Jane's encounter with *Shikasta* as 'a third kind of worldview', which she accepts after a brief moment of mulling it over. This more Kantian term is not the one she used, however. She referred several times to 'framework', apparently implying an entire life-philosophy with an outlook, a set of values and moral implications – something that she 'ordered my life through'. Later on, in recounting the process of working on the PhD, she says it 'became the combing out of lots of strands of it into, I suppose, an order or a *framework* by which I could *be*'. All in all, she leaves behind two different frameworks before finally working out one that allows her to *be*.

The mother, although talented and with a love of reading, had chosen a flawed framework. She passed on the love of reading, however. And now Jane had outlived the two frameworks that the culture around her espoused, leaving her 'a very hungry

---

[4] Kelly A. Myers, '*Metanoia* and the Transformation of Opportunity', *Rhetoric Society Quarterly* 41, no. 1 (2011): 1.
[5] Ibid., 2.
[6] Ibid., 3.
[7] Philip Davis, *Reading and the Reader* (Oxford: Oxford University Press, 2013), 75.

person'. This is the essence of her crisis, which may therefore be called a spiritual crisis. We note that her state or condition at the time is described both in cognitive and bodily/instinctual terms, as she employs the metaphors of 'framework', a mental order(-ing) and 'hunger'.

She appears to equate framework with a way of being and relating to the world, and that there is progression through stages, as if one passes from one framework to the next by climbing up a step on a ladder, each step affording a momentary resting place and an increasingly larger vision and outlook. Within psychology several such theories of frameworks and stages have been propounded, all of them building on the work of Piaget, offering dynamic models of levels of growth where cognitive/moral/psychosocial development progresses through an invariant sequence of qualitatively distinct, hierarchically arranged stages.[8] James W. Fowler has developed a dynamic model of seven distinct stages of faith, attempting to 'clarify the dynamics of faith as the ways we go about making and maintaining meaning in life'.[9] He sees faith as transgressing the boundaries of religion and belief, as a deeper and more personal way of responding to transcendent value. 'Faith is not always religious in its content or context. Faith is a person's way of seeing him – or herself in relation to others against a background of shared meaning and purpose.'[10] Growth and development in faith, adds Fowler, 'also result from life crises, challenges and the kind of disruptions that theologians call revelation'.[11]

Like Piaget's cognitive model and Kohlberg's moral model, it seeks to describe changes in human thought and adaptation in general and formal ways, but attempts to incorporate the structuring of *affective and imaginative modes of knowing* left out of their accounts. Furthermore, it discusses the dialectic between structure and content in development from one stage to another. Fowler argues for faith as a form of imagination:

> Faith is our way of discerning and committing ourselves to centers of value and power that exert ordering force in our lives. Faith, as imagination, grasps the ultimate conditions of our existence [...]. Faith, then, is an active mode of knowing, of composing a felt sense or image of the condition of our lives taken as a whole. It unifies our lives' force fields.[12]

I find it reasonable to compare Jane's notion of framework to Fowler's concept of faith stage. The framework of 'enjoy yourself while you can' is – not so much on account of its content, but because it is the prevailing sociocultural and parental norm with which

---

[8] See for instance Jane E. Loevinger, *Ego development: Conceptions and theories* (San Francisco: Jossey-Bass, 1976).

[9] James W. Fowler, *Stages of Faith: The Psychology of Human Development and the Quest for Meaning* (San Francisco, CA: Harper & Row, 1981), xii. Fowler is inspired by Tillich and Niebuhr.

[10] Ibid., 4. Fowler maintains that 'If faith is reduced to belief in creedal statements and doctrinal formulations, then sensitive and responsible persons are likely to judge that they must live "without faith". But if faith is understood as trust in another and as loyalty to a transcendent center of value and power, then the issue of faith – and the possibility of religious faith – becomes lively and open again' (14).

[11] Ibid., 100.

[12] Ibid., 25.

she grows up – analogous to Fowler's Synthetic-Conventional Faith, where one's identity is a reflection of the group and family norms, and tacitly held. The 'feminist framework' is, moreover, comparable to the next stage, Individuative-Reflective Faith. 'Self (identity) and outlook (world view) are differentiated from those of others and become acknowledged factors in the reactions, interpretations and judgments one makes on the actions of the self and others.'[13] This stage is marked by a capacity for critical reflection on identity and is based on a logic of clear distinctions and abstract concepts, translating symbols into conceptual meanings. The next stage in the model, Conjunctive Faith, is according to Fowler quite rare and unusual before mid-life.

> Alive to paradox and the truth in apparent contradictions, this stage strives to unify opposites in mind and experience. It generates and maintains vulnerability to the strange truths of those who are other. Ready for closeness to that which is different and threatening to self and outlook (including new depths of experience in spirituality and religious revelation), this stage's commitment to justice is freed from the confines of tribe, class, religious community or nation [...] The new strength of this stage comes in the rise of the ironic imagination – a capacity to see and be in one's most powerful meanings, while simultaneously recognizing that they are relative, partial and inevitably distorting apprehensions of transcendent reality.[14]

This stage accepts that truth is multidimensional and organically interdependent, and cannot be encompassed in any abstract theory. It does not take the form of propositions or a set of beliefs, but will often take paradoxical forms of expression and may be akin to a Keatsian negative capability, or the attitude Gordon Allport referred to as 'wholehearted but half-sure'. The term 'conjunctive faith' also has hermeneutical ramifications. Fowler indicates that the conjunctive faith stage has its own way of relating to text and scripture: without giving up or negating one's critical thinking skills, one learns 'to relinquish initiative to the text'.[15] Instead of analysing and extracting meaning, one lets oneself be read by the text. Without attributing any objective status to these stages, one may regard them as a useful way of illustrating the felt development and progress Jane had been through as a qualitative leap in framework. We may say that Jane's crisis consisted of being in transition between the framework of Individuative-Reflective Faith and Conjunctive Faith. She moves to a higher stage, but takes many years to integrate this experience. Her spiritual crisis of transition is experienced as a hunger for meaning.

Transaction with the Literary Work

The Hunger for Reading

Jane is seeking something; it is an instinctual seeking, to fulfil a deep need rather than a passing whim. The nourishment she hungered for, are we justified in calling it 'spiritual', in the same way that Tolstoy defines true art as spiritual nourishment? To eat does not

---

[13] Ibid., 182.
[14] Ibid., 198.
[15] Ibid., 186.

mean to 'swallow whole': it involves a process of preparation, taking a mouthful, masticating, tasting, savouring and digesting before the body can make use of the food as energy. The use of this metaphor to describe the need for reading finds its counterpart in the medieval reading practice of *Lectio Divina*, a personal mode of engagement with scripture, which was revived by Thomas Keating within the tradition of Contemplative Christianity. Gervase Holdaway explicitly links *Lectio Divina* to spiritual hunger and eating food, likening it to 'feasting on the Word': first, the taking of a bite (*lectio*); then chewing on it (*meditatio*); savoring its essence (*oratio*) and, finally, digesting it and making it a part of the body (*contemplatio*).[16] The four stages of the divine reading are thus described metaphorically in terms of the process of eating. I will now look at how Jane relates the way she read *Shikasta*.

Feeling as the Deepest Form of Knowing: Mmm, Wow, Huh!

We have of course no transparent access to what Jane was experiencing as she read *Shikasta*. We must rely on the words and expressions chosen by the narrating I as indicators of important qualities of her reading process. In my view, onomatopoetical expressions such as 'Mmm, that's true'; 'Wow, this is making me think something I've never thought before'; 'Wow, mmm, this is true'; 'wow, I recognised it was just true'; 'It was more like going: huh!' must be interpreted as tokens of a bodily-affective form of responding to the work.

The recurring juxtaposition of *wows*, *huhs* and *mmms* is interesting: A preverbal, guttural expression of visceral reactions and of excited discovery on the one hand; on the other hand are the *mmms* – expressions of contemplation, of mulling it over, tasting, and holding it up for comparison with previous experiences. The 'mmm' has both a pensive and a savoury quality, and as such mirrors the two metaphors of mental framework and eating. It signifies an emotional truth, a recognition of something that rings true, rather than a deliberative being convinced of propositional truths. Although she is sitting in the bus while reading these first few pages, she is not reading hurriedly. She stops to consider the truth-value of each segment that she bites off and chews. *Mmmm* is a signifier of slow reading, of reflection, of a back-and-forth between text and lived experience. It is a form of expressive enactment. And the *wow*, coupled with the *huh*, mark an immediacy of felt reaction. So the *mmm*, with its ' […] ' and the *wow/huh* with its '!', are both components of, and precursors of, perceived truth. She takes a bite, then chews on it (*wow!*), savouring its essence (*mmm*), but then spends ever so long digesting the nature and implications of this truth for her life.

Together, the reflective *mmm* and the immediate reflex of *wow-huh* make up the phenomenology of the deep impression the words are making; a doubleness of immersed reflexivity that bears witness to a great receptivity to the text. So much has happened by the time she steps off the bus, by the time she has even read the first page of the story itself, having barely begun to digest the prefatory remarks. Later on in the narrative, she

---

[16] Gervase Holdaway, *The Oblate Life* (Norwich: Canterbury, 2008), 109.

refers to George Eliot's aim of making us 'understand that feeling is the deepest form of knowing. That's what literature does for us. It makes us feel, so we can know.' How can this deep impression of immersed reflexivity become a knowing, and what would be the linguistic markers of such a knowing? I believe this is connected to her repeated use of 'as if' to describe what it did to her.

The Great 'As if' and Metaphorical Thinking

Jane's first major evaluation of the experience was this: 'I felt as if I was being asked to consider, at the deepest of levels, the very basis of everything I thought I was.' This means that a great demand is placed upon her; she must start again: 'It was as if a great deal of, I suppose, moral thinking would have to come about, or even moral *practice* maybe. That literally I'd have to learn how to do it, if everything mattered, and if how I conducted myself mattered. It's like starting again, and everything you did you'd have to think, have I done it right?' In addition to the 'as if', this evaluation makes use of simile: 'it's like starting again.'

The reading experience not only precipitates this great moral demand, it also gives her something: 'So this book, *Shikasta*, gave me a kind of prism to read a lot of other things and eventually that became my Ph.D.' Furthermore, she says: 'So I feel as if what the book did for me was open an area of life and thinking of human experience that was closed, and then I went in and found it was full of this amazing stuff in there.' The book gave her a prism, and it opened up an area of life, like a key to a hidden room. Thus it is both something to view other things through, and an area to be explored. It colours her perception of the world, but also opens up and expands that world, and it shapes her life.

These, the *starting again*, the *opening up* and the *prism*, are the three central metaphors she uses. These metaphors are themselves embedded in figural thought structures of 'as if' and 'like'. The poet John Ashbery in some of his poems speaks of the 'great as though' and the 'great as if' – as if it is a spacious territory allowing thinking, or is itself a big thought operation. This adverbial subordinating conjunction pertaining to manner recurs on seven occasions in the course of this narrative:

> 'I felt as if I was being asked.'
> 'And as if I would have to learn how to *be* […]'
> 'And as if it might hurt me or I might hurt it.'
> 'It was as if a great deal of, I suppose, moral thinking would have to come about or even moral *practice* maybe.'
> 'I don't know, but I feel as if I was still indoors all that time, that may not be true.'
> 'So I feel as if what the book did for me was open an area of life and thinking of human experience that was closed.'
> 'And I think it is almost as if we've just stumbled into a way of having that.'

Interestingly, the first use of 'as if' comes directly after she has read out the passage where Lessing uses this expression. And Jane repeats this very line, saying she recognised it as 'true', implying that it is the form of thinking, as well as the content, that she recognises. The *as if* signifies a movement of the narrating I into empathising with the experiencing I, feeling her way into her former self. Unlike the word 'seemed' it does not signify that something was illusory or premature and a position which the narrating I has left behind. It is not an automatic, clichéd conjunction that follows upon it. Rather, it has a double perspective, opening up a space, a form of and for exploration of felt sense. It involves both disjunctive reasoning and imaginative bridging. The person must listen to herself first, look for the right expression and weigh it against others. The implication of *as if* is that there could be other possible ways to represent it, but this one *feels* right. It is tentative and explorative, yet very visceral – an embodied, emotional form of thinking.

In his *Philosophy of As If* Vaihinger argued that we cannot find out whether religious or metaphysical doctrines are true in an objective sense; instead one ought to ask whether it is useful to act 'as if' they were true. His fictionalism, although it bears a certain surface resemblance to William James's argument in *Will to Believe*, is however more like a form of 'if-then' thinking, turning 'as if' into a figure of speech. What is more relevant in this context is to establish how *as if* operates as an opener onto a field of explorative thinking and feeling. The *as if* may be understood on two levels. It signals the opening of a process of thinking, where the subject attempts to articulate preverbal feelings and sensations, searching for the right expression. On another level, it has its own feeling. With James we may say that we must inquire into the 'feeling of as if'. In *Practical Criticism* I. A. Richards maintains that the distinction between Intellectual and Emotional Belief is essential: 'As the scientific view of the world develops, we shall probably be forced into making a division between fact and fiction that, unless we can meet it with a twofold theory of belief [...], would be fatal not only to poetry but to all our finer, more spiritual responses.'[17] He proceeds to argue that 'the desirability or undesirability of an emotional belief has nothing to do with its intellectual status, provided it is kept from interfering with the intellectual system. And poetry is an extraordinarily successful device for preventing these interferences from arising.'[18] If we take poetry here to mean imaginative literature in general, we may say that *as if* is the kind of thinking literature makes use of to create the feeling way of knowing that Jane finds in George Eliot. The *as if* is at one and the same time the interference prevention and the opening up of the imaginative-emotive space – the door to a 'visionary realism', perhaps.

To sum up, the narrating I is making use of *onomatopoetica* and subordinating conjunctions of manner to convey aspects of the reading process of the experiencing I. Whereas the onomatopoetica function to take us immediately into this experience, the 'as if' has a double status of highlighting the distance of experiencing and narrating I. Both figurations are expressions of a feeling way of knowing. The 'framework' that she arrives at cannot be determined in terms of a propositional content or a creed. Perhaps it can only be pointed to, and revealed in the use of 'as if'. The 'hunger' that finds spiritual

---

[17] I. A. Richards, *Practical Criticism: A Study of Literary Judgment* (London: Routledge & Kegan Paul, 1954), 279.
[18] Ibid., 277.

nourishment does so through a double temporality of an immediate *wow-huh!* and a slow process of *mmm*-digestion. Not only does the book give her a new way of looking (the prism) and a bigger world to look at, but her evaluations do themselves rely on a metaphorical way of thinking.

The Shocking Recognition of Frightening Truth

We are given a rudimentary account of what her situation was before starting to read the book, consisting of two pieces of information: She describes herself as 'absolutely [...] an atheist', and someone who 'loved' Lessing's work. And she gives us two adjectives to describe her reaction: 'I was really shocked by it, and also deeply affected.' I take this expression not as a use of *hendyadis* for emphasis, but as a case of subordination. She seems neither to have expected the contents and tone of the passage, nor how it would affect her. By saying 'shocked ... and affected' the implication is that there would be two responses to the shock: recoil and turn away from it to protect herself, or to take it on board and let it affect her. Jane chose the latter, allowing herself to be deeply moved by the experience. We note a parallelism between this description, which came prior to reciting the passage, and the one that follows afterwards: 'And at the same time, while that was quite frightening, I also absolutely recognised something in it as true.' She was both shocked *and* affected, it was 'frightening' *and* 'true'. It is not simply a shock of mild surprise, and this is not simply a cognitive truth where a proposition is accepted as corresponding to facts. It is worth pointing out that the part that must have preceded the reading of this passage, the dedication, is only narrated subsequently. Here she indicates that she seemed prepared for receiving it: 'I've always been interested in space.' The contents of this first paragraph would thus probably have come across as more familiar, and more readily enjoyable and unproblematic to process. It is striking that all this has taken place before she has even started on the main body of the text.

Her initial reaction must have been one of surprise: her atheist stance, and her conception of Lessing was challenged. The work places an unexpected demand upon her: it is *as if* the work insists that she must reconsider her life and her sense of self. In the same way she conjoins shocked and affected, she now pairs fright and recognition of truth. In other words, it is an experience that implicates her on both a cognitive and an affective level. 'I couldn't really think about it, I just *felt* it'; 'I was very, very moved by it.' To be moved means then not just simply to have an emotional reaction, as in laughing or crying or being angry or surprised. There is also a shock, the recognition registers deeply in the body/psyche. The position is shifted. And then, in recounting the event of the dream (referred to alternately as 'the weird dream', 'the terrible dream'), she evaluates it as 'exhilarating and terrifying'. We have shock, fright, terror paired with affected, recognition of truth, exhilaration. A polarity of repulsion and attraction, a double movement. 'My mind had shifted, and then I was really *scared*.' Doubtlessly, the dream is inextricably tied to the affective experience. Because the effect seems to be sudden, shocking, frightening and also exhilarating, it seems obvious to describe this as an example of a sublime experience.

Jane's dream bears remarkable similarities to the Stoic exercise Pierre Hadot named 'The view from above'. The Stoics employed a number of perspective-shifting exercises in a philosophical contemplation of the bigger picture. According to Hadot, contemplating *phusis* in order to expand consciousness and achieve greatness of soul, *megalopsychia*, was 'the very essence of philosophy'.[19] The view from above involves picturing life on earth as if seen from high overhead. In a surviving fragment of Cicero's *De Republica* is related the dream of Scipio Aemilianus (185–129 BC), a cultured Roman and a Stoic. During the third Punic War he experiences a strange and mystical dream:

> He ascends to meet Africanus the Elder in the outer heavens and together they look down upon the whole cosmos. Aemilianus exclaims that Earth seems tiny, adding 'I began to think less of this empire of ours, which only amounts to a pinpoint on its surface.' Yet he is filled with awe at the overwhelming beauty and harmony of the universe. Africanus the Elder shows him that the Earth and mortal life are miniscule parts of the whole cosmos and that 'the lips of mankind can grant you no fame or glory worth seeking'.[20]

Jane's dream gives her such a view from above; that which was big becomes small, and that which was not prominent now stands out. Her dream is both frightening and exhilarating. Although she does not use that word, it seems to fill her with awe.

What seems central to Jane's story is that the reading experience itself, and the ensuing dream, together precipitate a 'Big Bang'. This is a metaphor she uses several times. Curiously, given the fact that Lessing places the book within an Old Testament tradition, the central metaphor for the sudden rupture that gradually formed itself into an order, is taken from the scientific theory that shattered the religious cosmogony. The explosion marks an abrupt, unexpected event, a *metaballein*: there was nothing that lead up to it, and everything changed in its wake. Yet, after the Big Bang, an order was created. The order in Jane's life is not that of a religion: an ordered set of beliefs. Her life seems to be ordered around working out the existential implications of the realization that everything, every choice, matters. She says 'that 15–17 year period was assimilating […] the Big Bang'. Considering that Jane's mode of engagement is marked both by a shocked recognition and a gradual digestion of its truth, I propose that we may employ the term *metabolic* to account for it. It encompasses both the *metabolism* of digesting the experience and the *metaballein* of sudden change.

Ekpleksis and Awe

According to Keltner and Haidt there has been very little scientific research on the positive feeling of awe. In their review of what philosophers, sociologists and theologians

---

[19] Hadot discusses the spiritual exercise of the View from Above in: Pierre Hadot, *What Is Ancient Philosophy?*, trans. Michael Chase (Cambridge, MA: Harvard University Press, 2002). See also: Pierre Hadot, *Philosophy as a Way of Life: Spiritual Exercises from Socrates to Foucault*, trans. Michael Chase (Oxford: Blackwell, 1995).

[20] Cited in Donald Robertson, *Stoicism and the Art of Happiness* (London: Hodder & Stoughton, 2013), 216.

have written on the subject, they found that awe nearly always was related to fear and submission in an encounter with something that is larger than the self. Keltner and Haidt therefore concludes that the emotion of awe has two major appraisals; it occurs as the result of these two conditions: *vastness* and *accommodation*. The person will perceive something that is 'vast', that is, either big or powerful; and the vast cannot be assimilated into the existing mental framework, but must be accommodated. In contrast to cognitive processes of assimilation, where new experiences are incorporated into already established mental structures, accommodation is characterised by a need to expand awareness by forming new mental schemas.

> Something enormous can't be processed, and when people are stumped, stopped in their cognitive tracks while in the presence of something vast, they feel small, powerless, passive and receptive. They often (but not always) feel fear, admiration, elevation or a sense of beauty as well. By stopping people and making them receptive, awe creates an opening for change, and this is why awe plays a role in most stories of religious conversion.[21]

Awe makes us open to change. Keltner and Haidt distinguish between the emotions of admiration and elevation on the one hand, and awe on the other. This is because the experience of the former only necessitates accommodation. In the case of admiration and elevation there is no vast entity or force, but rather great skill or moral greatness. Elevation depends on a successful accommodation. Shiota, Keltner and Mossman have found empirical support for this theory. They discovered that awe leads to 'a sense of smallness of the self and the presence of something greater than the self [...] increasing one's sense of self as part of a greater whole – a self-concept that de-emphasises the individual self'.[22] It is quite clear that Jane's experience invokes a need for accommodation. Her metaphor of the 'Big Bang' seems to illustrate both vastness and accommodation. She takes a number of years to integrate the event into her life story. Keltner and Haidt's theory of vastness is very similar to Kant's emphasis on the mathematical and dynamical sublime. However, it is fully possible to experience awe in an encounter with nature, and still assimilate it to an already existing framework such as a religious one; the wonders of nature becoming confirmation of God's existence. I contend that it is not just vastness that characterises Jane's experience. It is the kinetic experience of turning, *metaballein*, from one perspective to a greater one, where the small becomes great and the big pales into insignificance. Moreover, it is the shock, as Jane had not expected such a perspectival turn in her encounter with *Shikasta*. Jane says that she had developed a relationship of *trust* in Lessing and her books, and that she loved her. Jane would have expected to encounter, in taking up *Shikasta*, something that fitted in with her current 'framework'. However, this expectation is not fulfilled, as *Shikasta* brings in a religious vision. This

---

[21] Jonathan Haidt, *The Happiness Hypothesis: Finding Modern Truth in Ancient Wisdom* (New York: Basic Books, 2006), 203. The distinction between assimilation and accommodation is derived from Piaget.
[22] Michelle N. Shiota, Dacher Keltner and Amanda Mossman, 'The Nature of Awe: Elicitors, Appraisals, and Effects on Self-Concept', *Cognition and Emotion* 21, no. 5 (2007): 960.

disruption of her expectation and the ensuing *metaballein* is an *ecstatic* experience, in the Longinian sense, akin to what Kuiken et al. term 'sublime disquietude'. Her experience is 'sublime' – or to be more precise: *ekplektic*. In his philosophy of the *affects*, Spinoza says that wonder 'aroused by an object we fear' is 'called consternation'.[23] According to Spinoza this consternation happens because wonder at something that does not give us pleasure or conforms to our expectations keeps a person 'so suspended in considering it that he cannot think of other things by which he could avoid this evil'. This consternation is contrasted with veneration and devotion. Says Spinoza: 'love joined to wonder, or veneration, we call devotion'. Now, this *metaballein* from devotion to consternation is precisely what I understand Longinus to mean by his term *ekpleksis*. If we take *plexis* to mean mental schema (cf. the terms 'com-plex' and 'per-plex'), then *ek-pleksis* means the frightening disruption of one mental framework or schema and the ensuing felt need for accommodation. In order to experience wonder, Jane must accept the *ekplektic* shock. Because of Jane's veneration for Lessing, she was prepared to follow her into the Universe of *Shikasta*, even though it challenged her entire framework, and demanded that she leave it behind. Thus the awe-experience, the deeply affective recognition of the truth of the vast vision, is predicated upon a prior *ekpleksis*.

Resolution

Spiritual Transformation

Jane has to ask herself the big and complex question: 'Was it a religious experience? I think anybody would say it was, though if you don't *believe* in religion, oh God, it's a hard thing to understand.' Let's look at some of the other comments she makes in discussing the religiousness of the experience. On being scared because suddenly everything mattered, she says: 'That's why I say it was a bit like a religious conversion, because it was, it did feel vulnerable. And when they say in religious settings, 'born again' and things like that, the main feeling I remember of that is of immense vulnerability. Of being someone with very soft skin, or no [...] And as if I would have to learn how to *be*.' Whether the experience is to be appraised as religious remains an open question. She cannot think of a better word to describe the experience, yet she will not accept any belief structure. 'I really waiver between whether I believe in God or don't believe in God [...]. I don't believe in Someone [...] I think there are underlying patterns of goodness and wholeness, and connectivity.' The next comment may be taken as support for Fowler's distinction between faith and belief: 'I definitely believe something, I just don't know what it is'; 'I don't think it's still a Christian, it's a believer.' This leads her to formulate the following question, 'What happens to religious experience if culturally you don't believe in God?' Jane specifically says that she thinks a central aspect of George Eliot's project was to work out the implications of this problem. This paradoxical notion of 'to believe' as an intransitive verb, is in my view an expression of Fowler's Conjunctive Faith.

---

[23] Benedict de Spinoza, 'Of the Origin and Nature of the Affects', in *Ethics*, trans. Edwin Curley (London: Penguin, 1996), 97.

Jane then goes on to read about the Rule of Necessity, of the need to bow to a larger Will. There is a connection here to what she says about teaching Herbert: 'Trying to take people to understand what *Lord* means in that poem, if you don't believe in God; well, it means *necessity* or the *truth* or *reality*.' God is equated with the supreme value. Is this a non-religious conversion or a non-conversional religious experience? According to A. D. Nock's classic study of conversion, religious conversions bring about 'a reorientation of the soul of an individual, his deliberate turning from indifference or from an earlier form of piety, a turning which implies a consciousness that a great change is involved, that the old was wrong and the new is right'.[24] It is true to say that Jane relates a reorientation of the soul and a deliberate turning from the initial framework of indifference and the second framework of atheism. However, there is no condemning of her previous life and no conviction that she has any right beliefs. In his study of narratives of conversion, Gerald Peters finds that the notion of the reorientation of the soul 'comes directly from the Greek *epistrophê*, the word coined by Plato as the goal of a philosophical education and the term adopted by early Christians for conversion'.[25] Perhaps we could use the term *epistrophe* to designate this conversion into a non-believing reorientation to truth. I think it is fair to say that she experiences the event as a form of spiritual transformation – 'the book made me realise that there is a spiritual dimension to life' – from being an atheist to a non-Christian believer. It is a position that is difficult to articulate, possibly because it is no position. It is 'as if' it was a religious conversion: She can enter into that way of thinking, explore it and compare it. It is as if it is the container without the content of a religious experience. Jane's experience of a self-surrender to the Rule of Necessity, without knowing what this is or what it leads to, comes close to what William James saw as the essence of the religious experience: surrender to something greater than oneself, despite the fear of not knowing what this is or what it will entail. Elsewhere James states that 'however particular questions connected with our individual destinies may be answered, it is only by acknowledging them as genuine questions, *and living in the sphere of thought which they open up*, that we become profound. But to live thus is to be religious'.[26] There are questions which we must not answer, but rather live in the sphere they open up. We live in the light cast by the questions. So here the religious is different from a professed faith-content of a conversion. We remain in the open, in a kind of negative capability. If we then understand her non-religious conversion as a spiritual transformation through metanoia, I think that we must include the discovery of Purpose in that process of metanoia.

The Shape of a Life: Purpose

The religious man has an aim. Only activity with a purpose, which is the union of theoretic and practical activity, gives man a moral basis and support, i.e. character. Every man,

---

[24] A. D. Nock, *Conversion: The Old and the New in Religion from Alexander the Great to Augustine of Hippo* (Baltimore, MD: Johns Hopkins University Press, 1998), 7.
[25] Gerald Peters, *The Mutilating God: Authorship and Authority in the Narrative of Conversion* (Amherst: University of Massachusetts Press, 1993).
[26] James, *Varieties of Religious Experience*, 379.

> therefore, must place before himself a God, i.e. an aim, a purpose. He who has an aim has a law over him; he does not merely guide himself; he is guided. He who has no aim, has no home, no sanctuary; aimlessness is the greatest unhappiness. An aim sets limits; but limits are the mentors of virtue. He who has an aim has a religion.

Thus says Feuerbach, in George Eliot's translation. The essence of religion is not a belief system, but the manifestation of a Purpose. Before we discuss the meaning of the Purpose, let us look at how it forms part of the shape of her story. Perhaps the most important and central evaluation Jane makes of her reading experience is the following:

> The book [...] *made* or *shaped* my life [...] The book made me realise that there is a spiritual dimension to life, and it made me see that you have life for a *purpose*, and you've got to find out what that purpose is, and then you've got to *do* it. So I think it has given me a very, very strong sense of purpose, and that purpose has *made* my life.

She says that it has been a transformation: from atheism into realising that there is a spiritual dimension to life, and that this spirituality takes the form of a purpose. I find the idea that life has a shape very interesting. What is the shape of Jane's life, as told in her story? Her narrative of life after *Shikasta* can be read as constituting two stories: the 17 years of assimilating the Big Bang; and 'passing on the Big Bang' in the discovery of her purpose, Shared Reading. We could extend the cosmic metaphor in terms of the imagery of darkness and light, sleeping and waking: at first there is living in darkness, then the Big Bang happens: an explosion of light and energy that it takes a patient and faithful effort to integrate into an order (*religio*), then working to manifest the vision. Thus the shape is of a double journey, a double movement of *katabasis* and *anabasis*. The first movement is an inward turning in order to accommodate the revealed truth, marking a progressive going into the depths of her experience: 'What I now think is that that whole period, that 15- to 17-year period, was assimilating [...] the Big Bang. And that was something to do with, I don't know what, whether that's [...] Well, anyway, it's your *inner* self, that's what was being made in that time.' It is quite clear that Piaget's cognitive concept of accommodation can only partly account for this process. The inner self was being made. There is a turning inward, by means of the 'prism' given to her by *Shikasta*, where both the PhD and the writing of the novels form part of a laborious search for an essence, an answer to the implicit question of what does it imply that everything matters? The answer comes in the shape of the gradual unfolding of the Purpose, the Shared Reading, which points back to *Shikasta* as well as to her significant childhood memory. Thus, Shared Reading can be understood on two levels: Jane shares her reading experience by creating Shared Reading. The way for her to share with us what she experienced in reading, is not to write about it, but to create the conditions for others to have a similar encounter. Is Shared Reading, then, not itself a form of 'visionary realism': The social realism of countering lack of access to cultural heritage, the low levels of literacy, the receding importance of the classics, and the need to provide low-cost mental health interventions?

Against the conventional view of *metanoia* as the lament for a missed opportunity, Myers recasts 'metanoia as an active emotional state [...] the affective dimension of *Kairos*. [...] The experience of *metanoia* involves a transformation that can range from a minor change to a dramatic spiritual conversion.'[27] Thus, *metanoia* may be more accurately translated as 'change of heart' than 'change of mind'. The New Testament *metanoia* calls for a (re-)turning of the soul to God. The meaning of an act of repentance that leads to spiritual conversion, so central to the concept in New Testament translation, may thus be said to be an afterthought to this afterthought: 'Such reflection often brings an emotional response, such as the regret of a failed attempt or the guilt associated with a poor decision, but regret and guilt are only part of the overall experience of *metanoia*.'[28] Alan J. Torrance, drawing on Kierkegaard, differentiates *metanoia* from *anamnesis*: 'Whereas anamnesis denotes the confirmation and ratification of the epistemic criteria immanently within us, metanoia denotes, by contrast, a profound transformation of the epistemic orientation of the whole person.'[29] Edward J. Finlay uses the term metanoia to describe the '"turn" toward understanding characteristic of Plato's liberated cave dweller'.[30] In this he accords with Pierre Hadot, who sees this turning of the whole body or soul as a reference to *metanoia*.

Myers argues that 'metanoia requires that a person look back on past decisions in order to move in a new direction'.[31] Thus, just as *Kairos* has the three aspects of propitious moment, crisis and opportunity for change, so *Metanoia* has the three aspects of retroactive meaning-making, a change of heart, and moving in a new direction to realise one's purpose. In light of this, the anabasis of the story of Shared Reading forms an integral part of the narrative of her reading experience. In the quote above about how her life has been shaped, she makes recourse to the word 'purpose' four times:

> And it made me see that you have life for a *purpose*, and you've got to find out what that purpose is, and then you've got to *do* it. So I think it has given me a very, very strong sense of purpose, and that purpose has *made* my life.

There is a progression involved: first discovering the idea of purpose, then finding out what it is, then carrying it out. Doing so will make your life. For a deeper understanding of what this notion of purpose may mean, it may be useful to turn to Gabriel Marcel's philosophy of Vocation. In his rejection of all forms of –isms, Marcel endeavoured to understand what a person is meant to do with her life, which led him to explore the concept of vocation.[32] For Marcel, says Terence Sweeney, 'vocation opens us up to the reality that the human person is *homo viator*, a pilgrim and wayfarer'.[33] To be such a *homo viator*

---

[27] Myers, *Metanoia*, 2.
[28] Ibid., 8.
[29] Alan J. Torrance, 'Auditus Fidei: Where and How Does God Speak? Faith, Reason and the Question of Criteria', in *Reason and the Reasons of Faith*, ed. Paul J. Griffiths and Reinhard Hütter (New York: T &T Clark, 2005), 38.
[30] Edward F. Findlay, *Caring for the Soul in the Postmodern Age: Politics and Phenomenology in the Thought of Jan Patocka* (Albany: State University of New York Press, 2002), 146.
[31] Ibid., 11.
[32] Gabriel Marcel, *Creative Fidelity*, trans. Robert Rosthal (New York: Fordham University Press, 2002).
[33] Terence Sweeney, 'Against Ideology: Gabriel Marcel's Philosophy of Vocation', *Logos: A Journal of Catholic Thought and Culture* 16, no. 4 (2013): 179.

'is to be in relation to the transcendent while living in the immanent world, a stance that emerges from a sense of having been called'.[34] Each use of 'purpose' in Jane's quoted words marks a different part of this journey.

Marcel opens his *Homo Viator* by stating that a person must be 'acutely conscious that his condition is that of a traveler'.[35] The initial step on the journey is one of 'not-at-homeness'. This is a state of captivity where one is restrained from 'rising to a certain fullness of life'.[36] This state is marked by an ontological exigency: the beginning of openness to the other and to vocation. In discovering that the self is restrained, one becomes able to respond to the call for fullness. This call may be ignored or misinterpreted (leading to a fall into ideology), or the self may open itself up to its vocation. For Marcel, vocation is more than and other than its common usages of religion or career. It has three interrelated aspects: the interior call, the callings of others and the summons of the transcendent. It forms the centre of personhood and is unique to the individual. Yet it is intersubjective: it is a response to something that comes to us from outside and from above. Vocation 'comes both from me and what comes from outside, a connection which is nourishing or constructive and cannot be relinquished'.[37] It means to make oneself available to the other. Vocation is intersubjective: if it is reduced to an inner call, the self cannot reach fulfilment; it also involves a relationship with the transcendent. I think this sense of vocation touches on vital aspects of Jane's 'strong sense of purpose'. It is a call from within and from without: her childhood and her reading of *Shikasta* meets her deep wish that the underprivileged have access to the best that literature can offer, and it requires a deep faith to stake so much on such an enterprise. The double movement of the story, the *metanoia* of accommodating and integrating the Big Bang, and the discovery and manifestation of Purpose, both *turn upon* the experience of reading *Shikasta*. I therefore understand the term *epistrophe* to encompass both the non-religious conversion and the shape of the plot of Jane's life-narrative.

---

[34] Ibid., 179.
[35] Gabriel Marcel, *Homo Viator: An Introduction to a Metaphysics of Hope* (South Bend, IN: St Augustine, 2010), 1.
[36] Ibid., 24.
[37] Ibid., 17.

Chapter Seven

SUE'S BURIED LIFE

I met Sue through the Reader Organisation, where she works as project manager and facilitator of shared reading groups. In a course for volunteers on how to lead reading groups, she related to us her decisive encounter with a poem by Matthew Arnold, The Buried Life. *As she read parts of it out loud, it was evident that her memories of the reading experience were still salient, bringing tears to her eyes. I felt really moved by the poem and the concerns it raises. Afterwards I told her about my project, and asked her whether she be willing to take part. The interview took place in Sue's home. She made us cups of tea and we sat down in her lounge to talk.*

Sue: I was thinking that in a way – because this started from when you were on the Read to Lead course, when we read an extract of it, from 'but often in the din of strife' – that that was kind of the story, you know, so it's a shame that the tape wasn't on then, really. I felt full of feeling at that time. Because we were talking about this issue of breakthroughs, and I still felt strongly about it; it had such an impact on me. I can't remember what I said.

Thor: But the feeling was very present then.

Sue: Yes. This poem, I first heard it on my Read to Lead course which was in January 2009. The group facilitator read it out loud to the group. I can't remember how many of us there were, there might have been sixteen of us or something like that. It took place in a beautiful manor. It was just a lovely place to stay, it was a five-day residential course, so we were there for five days together. I don't know what day this happened, it wasn't early on actually, it was quite a bit late through the course. And I just really, from the moment she started reading, that very first sort of section, I had a strong, strong feeling for it. And I think partly that was because it just felt so current, even though I know he was writing in eighteen hundred something. I don't know when he was writing, but it's quite a long time ago. Still, that first bit, it just somehow really resonated with me, about this idea of two people just struggling, you know, in this relationship. And so already I was kind of captivated.

Thor: Right from the start.

Sue: Yeah, right from the start. Partly because of what the subject matter was, you know that very first bit where he's talking about this mocking war, war of mocking words, and he's, you know, he's crying, he's got tears in his eyes: 'Behold, with tears mine eyes are wet! I feel a nameless sadness o'er me roll.' So that, just the fact of that, but there was something about the fact that he was feeling this two hundred years ago, or whenever it was, that had a big, big impact on me as well.

The Possibility of What Poetry Might Do

Thor: There were two feelings at the same time? That it was like he was speaking to you now?

Sue: Well, yes, like it … it felt very, very current, you know. I felt I completely understood this experience that he was writing of, the experience of struggling to communicate with someone you love, that actually you're in this sort of passionate, this important relationship, but for whatever reason you can't make it work, in terms of your communication. So that really struck a chord with me. But then also the fact that it was happening, well, two hundred years ago or something, that seemed really important as well. And I think for me that was important because I hadn't been someone who read poetry. It was really my first real contact with poetry. I mean, when I first found myself being in a situation where I actually had to pay attention to it. I have a group of very close friends, in some ways I am closer to them than to my own family. That's the most home I ever feel, when I am with these women. They are really into poetry and when we go away at the weekends, we go as a group of sort of seven or eight people, they're all reading it, and I'm ignoring it, because it's never resonated or had any meaning for me. They'd bring along their latest poetry find, and I would wish we could do something else altogether. Poetry just felt like a waste of time to me. But if my friends valued something, then that would make me curious, because then I would think it must have some value. I just couldn't overcome the hurdle. I had never given it a chance, but something about just that very first bit of this poem, it felt like it changed everything really.

Thor: It changed everything?

Sue: Well, it felt like it just changed everything, that suddenly I was awake to this possibility of what poetry might do. I mean it did feel that big actually, yeah. (*Pause*). Obviously I've been reading poetry now for seven years, you know, and a lot of poetry. I read a lot of poetry because I've been reading poetry with people in groups. And initially when I started I knew almost nothing about how to do it, I didn't even know how to read around the punctuation or the comma. Honestly, I knew nothing, but as I've kind of gone through it, I've got more and more tuned into it and I can probably read it fairly well, and I can even understand some stuff that I would never have been able to understand in my way of looking at it. I've grown tremendously, and I can't imagine my life without poetry now, you know. I don't even want to think about my life without poetry now. So yeah, I just think it was the most magical, amazing stuff. Although I do find it difficult to read, you have to really work at it, and I find it much easier to read in a group, and to have that kind of group experience of it.

Thor: Relating to it together?

Sue: Yeah, yeah, and other people struggling with it and working it out, I love that process. Hmmm, so that first little bit of it really was powerful, and then it just carried on really.

Thor: Would you like to read the poem for me now?

Sue: OK, I'll read the second part of it.

She proceeds to read the poem, slowly, meditatively, with restraint, trusting the words to carry the emotion.
From the *Buried Life*, by Matthew Arnold:

> But often, in the world's most crowded streets,
> But often, in the din of strife,
> There rises an unspeakable desire
> After the knowledge of our buried life;
> A thirst to spend our fire and restless force
> In tracking out our true, original course;
> A longing to inquire
> Into the mystery of this heart which beats
> So wild, so deep in us—to know
> Whence our lives come and where they go.
> And many a man in his own breast then delves,
> But deep enough, alas! none ever mines.
> And we have been on many thousand lines,
> And we have shown, on each, spirit and power;
> But hardly have we, for one little hour,
> Been on our own line, have we been ourselves—
> Hardly had skill to utter one of all
> The nameless feelings that course through our breast,
> But they course on for ever unexpress'd.
> And long we try in vain to speak and act
> Our hidden self, and what we say and do
> Is eloquent, is well—but 't is not true!
> And then we will no more be rack'd
> With inward striving, and demand
> Of all the thousand nothings of the hour
> Their stupefying power;
> Ah yes, and they benumb us at our call!
> Yet still, from time to time, vague and forlorn,
> From the soul's subterranean depth upborne
> As from an infinitely distant land,
> Come airs, and floating echoes, and convey
> A melancholy into all our day.
> Only—but this is rare—
> When a belovèd hand is laid in ours,
> When, jaded with the rush and glare
> Of the interminable hours,
> Our eyes can in another's eyes read clear,
> When our world-deafen'd ear
> Is by the tones of a loved voice caress'd—
> A bolt is shot back somewhere in our breast,
> And a lost pulse of feeling stirs again.

> The eye sinks inward, and the heart lies plain,
> And what we mean, we say, and what we would, we know.
> A man becomes aware of his life's flow,
> And hears its winding murmur; and he sees
> The meadows where it glides, the sun, the breeze.
>
> And there arrives a lull in the hot race
> Wherein he doth for ever chase
> That flying and elusive shadow, rest.
> An air of coolness plays upon his face,
> And an unwonted calm pervades his breast.
> And then he thinks he knows
> The hills where his life rose,
> And the sea where it goes.

Thor: Thank you. What was it like to read it here and now?

Sue: It's quite a long time since I've read it in its entirety, actually. Hmmm, I mean, there's lots more in it really, bits that I didn't remember. But it still, it still has the same kind of power for me, you know? (*Tears in her eyes. She pauses*)

The Woman in Prison

Sue: I've come to this feeling that, the sense that ... Because I've had the experience of reading with lots of people now, and I've had the experience of witnessing people have, I suppose, a similar response to a piece of writing ... I wrote an article about an experience a woman in prison had with the poem Bluebird by Bukowski.[1] Where she had a profound experience with the poem. So I've come to feel that there is something for everyone, or maybe there's more than one thing, I'm sure there is. There are bits of writing that have this sort of power to resonate, to move you. They're kind of tuned in, they're the right tune for you and then, when you get one of those, it's like, I don't know, everything sort of *fits*. And then you can't hold yourself back. Like the woman in the prison for instance, she had no interest in joining with me or being with me, she was resisting every step of the way, until that poem was brought out, and she just couldn't help herself, you know. So when I was running groups all the time, that's what I'd be thinking, what does this person need? What does this person need? What can I bring that's going to get past the [...] what's going to be 'the bolt shot back'?

Thor: Do you think you sense what that happens?

---

[1] In this poem, the speaker says: 'There's a bluebird in my heart that/wants to get out/but I'm too tough for him.' See Charles Bukowski, 'Bluebird', in *The Last Night of the Earth Poems* (New York: Ecco, 1992).

Sue: I don't know, I'm not sure if you can predict it, but you can sometimes feel it, or get a sense of it. I think sometimes you can. I know the feeling when you get it right, so I know what that feels like, and often I feel that you can tune in, and get a sense of what people need. I don't always know the right piece of writing, but sometimes I do, or sometimes I hazard a guess. And I take it along and try it, to see what happens.

Thor: So you think it's the right poem for the right person at the right time?

Sue: Yeah, kind of. Hmmm, I do feel like that can happen. That if you knew enough poetry you could. For me it doesn't feel like an intellectual kind of process so much as a sort of feeling, an intuiting process of coming to understand something about that person and then tuning into them. Perhaps knowing a little bit of their story in some way, that might of course be essential. I didn't know that that poem would do that for her, but I did know that the things I had been taking weren't working, and I did know I had to completely change tack, which is what I did that week, and it worked really beautifully, so…

Your Whole Body Is Going to Sing with It

Thor: Would you say that your experience with this poem is important to you in recognising those break-through moments?

Sue: I think so, yeah, because if you've had that experience of being moved by something then I suppose you, well *I*, would like other people to have that experience, for sure. And I think it is a deep thing. I was going to say it does change you, in some way, in a good way. And what I mean by change is, it does make you a different person, it helps you access some part of yourself that you … that has been a bit buried.

Thor: A buried part.

Sue: You know, a bit that's unknown, or kind of … *un-resonated*. That hasn't been … the strings haven't been played, or something – like an instrument that's not been used fully, so … Well, I don't know if that's the right metaphor, I'm struggling to find the right kind of metaphor, really.

Thor: You said un-resonated?

Sue: Hmm, some sort of deep – or because what it feels like is that, when that happens, you – even if you don't tell anyone else, it's like you can't *not* experience it if you get a piece of writing that does that to you. You're just going to, your whole being is going to, *sing* with it.

Thor: Sing with it, yeah.

Sue: Well, it's enlivening, isn't it, it's life-enhancing, you know. I mean you can try and block that, you can try and avoid it or block it, to not have it, but actually that takes quite a lot of energy. So you could just accept it, haha.

Thor: And you felt very able to accept it, then, when it happened?

Sue: Yeah, yeah. I didn't feel any inclination to block it. But I'm thinking of the woman in the prison for instance, who had been very blocking for weeks and weeks, you know, and then this bit of writing comes along, and she just couldn't stop herself, because it just resonated so deeply, and it was so profoundly moving for her. So even though up until then, every time I'd meet her, everything had been rubbish or been boring or crap … I guess what I'm trying to say is that she could have resisted that, but it was so powerful, she couldn't, haha. Does that make sense?

Thor: Yeah, that's an interesting formulation, because she's blocking, she's got a resistance, and then suddenly something …

Sue: So powerful and so resonant, so in tune with what it was that she's in need of. All of her defenses are just gone, you know, and it's quite interesting, because – I'm obviously not in that prison anymore, but one of our colleagues is, and this woman ended up back in prison for a variety of reasons. She'd left when I was there, and then she came back, and so now she's back in the group again. And she was the same sort of sour-faced, resistant person. She'd had a really, really difficult life, this woman, I mean a horrendous kind of life story. And then, apparently, she said to the facilitator, Jo, there's only one poem I like, and Jo, who knew about the Bluebird thing, said, oh, what's that then? I've got it in my room, she said, so Jo said why don't you go and get it, and we'll have a look at it. So she went to her room, and she had a copy of it. I'd actually laminated her a copy of it, as a little bookmark. So she had that, and she brought it back, and read it out in the group. And then again, from then on, she was right there, in the group, able to be. So, yeah, I think it's just incredibly powerful.

Thor: Interesting, because you said 'able to be', so that poem enabled her to be?

Sue: Yeah, absolutely. It enabled her to be in that group in a positive way, in a way that was an act of … she became an act of presence rather than a sort of blocking presence, you know.

Thor: You said you were struggling to find the right words to describe it, and you said that it resonates with, and enhances, your life. Does the *Buried Life* brings you in touch with a depth inside yourself?

Sue: Well, I think there are things in here that have been concerns of mine for most of my life, really. So there are things in this poem that are things that have interested me or, you know, worried me, or have been problems for me. So when I read, when I heard this, and it was read out, for the first time ever, I thought … The idea that someone could be writing about something that was of such concern to me, it's kind of …. well it was mind blowing, really. I suppose because I hadn't read much poetry, and I'd never read anything that kind of personal.

Thor: So you had no expectations that this would do anything for you, but you were open and willing, so to speak?

Sue: No expectations at all. I was there, I went on this course and evidently it was going to be part of my work, even though I hadn't understood that before I went on this course. So I was put on this course basically because of the role I was in. I had never participated in shared reading before. I was living in London at the time. I was completely ignorant, you know.

Thor: How did you come to be on the course?

Sue: Because I got this job, within the library service, to set up these groups. The library service had decided that they were going to have this, what they called Bibliotherapy service, and they'd chosen this model, and then I'd applied for the job, and just happened to be in the right place at the right time. All really, really fortunate, when I look back on it now. I just think, you know, there is a God, haha.

Thor: So that's how you best can express it, there is a meaning, a God, someone led you here?

Sue: Yeah, absolutely.

Thor: Did that feeling arise in you, or grow in you, before you read the poem?

Sue: No. Well in a way. I mean, when I got the job, I was just hugely relieved because I was very new in the UK, I'd only been here a few months, having moved from Australia, and I was struggling to work out how I was going to be here. I didn't even really know that I wanted to be here, I was just here, for a variety of reasons. And then I got this job and I remember, when I got the job, my sister was in hospital, she'd had a very serious accident and she'd been flown to the UK. I was in the hospital with her, and I received the call that I'd got the job, and I actually just burst into tears because I was so relieved, and delighted. And then, within five or six weeks after I got the position, I was on this course. I was relieved to have the job and I wanted the job, although I didn't really entirely know what it was. I was very keen to do it, and I thought I could probably do a reasonable job at that. It was like the job was made for me, even though I didn't really understand what it was about, if that makes sense. And yeah, six weeks later I was on the course, so it's more looking back and at the time I wouldn't have said there is a God. Looking back I think how incredibly fortunate I've been to be able to this, you know, it just doesn't get much better really, does it? In a way it feels like a whole lot of things were leading to this, a combination of things in my life made it all make a lot of sense.

Thor: Maybe it's a leading question, but I just get a feeling that the whole ground had been prepared for this meeting between you and Matthew Arnold?

Sue: Yeah, well, in a way. I suppose it's a meeting of me and shared reading and Matthew Arnold. It was a particular moment and that experience of reading this, of realising that there really was stuff in here. This idea of reading, that the important things in life are in this, are in here – that there's power in it. If I hadn't had the experience with the *Buried Life* on that course, I'm not sure if I would have really entirely got what this was about, what this whole shared reading thing was about. So it concretised it for me, I was made aware of the potency of it, the power of it. I remember after I'd read it, I emailed it to a very close friend of mine, and another thing I did was, I started to think about people who were 'on their own line'. Because I felt like I had this need to identify people who had managed to do it, because you know, some people do manage to do it. You know, to be themselves – being on your own line, this idea of being your truer self, expressing who you are in the world rather than just being some kind of carbon copy of yourself. So I went through this little phase of trying to identify people who had managed to do that.

A Bolt Is Shot Back Somewhere in Your Breast

Thor: He says towards the end, 'A man becomes aware of his life's flow' …

Sue: 'A man becomes aware of his life's flow', oh yeah, of his life's flow, yeah. There's quite a lot of sadness in here as well. This stuff about can I not even sort of have …. 'But we, my love! – doth a life, doth a like spell benumb Our hearts, our voices? – must we too be dumb?' It's like he's almost … I mean, can we not even, if we love each other enough, can we not break through this, whatever this thing is that wouldn't let us communicate with each other.

Thor: Because he says as well that 'Alas! Is even love too weak to unlock the heart, and let it speak?' and there seems to be so much despair in that.

Sue: Yeah, even though you love this person, deeply love them, you know, you still can't … Just – separateness is still, always there. Hmmm, 'And many a man in his own breast then delves, But deep enough, alas! none ever mines. And we have been on many thousand lines, And we have shown, on each, spirit and power; But hardly have we, for one little hour, Been on our own line, have, have we been ourselves –' I mean he's quite hard on; I'm not entirely sure that's true for me, but there's something about the being authentic, you know, being who you really are. And I think that has been a big thing for me in my life, trying to not being some kind of … cipher, or copy, trying to sort of work out what's important for me, what I really think.

Thor: So there's a struggle to find out who you are, and how to be that, in your world?

Sue: Yeah, not just to do what everyone does, but to actually work out what is important for me and, if I was to do anything, what would it be? Rather than just go along. And I've always been a bit like that, I've never really followed the crowd. 'But hardly have we, for one little hour, Been on our own line, have we been ourselves –' … I don't know, I'd like to think I have been myself. Unless I'm not understanding what he's meaning entirely, it's not like I entirely agree with it, but I think there are people who just do what's expected of them. But I don't feel like I've been one of those people, or, I have been at times in my life, probably lots of times, but I've also been someone who's gone against the grain a lot. And I tend to admire people who do their own thing.

Thor: Yeah. And he does find, although he says it's rare, that 'Our eyes can in another's eyes read clear'

Sue: Hmmm, yeah …

Thor: 'And what we mean, we say, and what we would, we know.' So that line there is to me what the authentic self would be, wouldn't it?

Sue: Yes. 'A bolt is shot back somewhere in our breast.' *Bolt. Shot. Back.* - I've never really understood what a bolt shot back means, but it sounds so … *right*. I think it's like, I imagine it to be a shock, a shocking awakening. Like a sort of an aha-moment, a sitting up moment. Or a … it was like a bolt was shot back somewhere in *my* breast,

Thor: It seems you have a clear felt sense of what that means.

Sue: Yeah, I think I've got a felt sense of it, but I would find it a bit hard to describe as well. 'And a lost pulse of feeling stirs again', that's that awakening of the deepest part of yourself, the bit of you that just … if things aren't used, or noticed, they can just sort of fade away, can't they? So a lost pulse is like something that's there, but it's getting weaker and weaker because it's not ever attended to. Hmmm, so it's not putting something new into him, it's not putting within, he's reawakening something that is there already, it's always there.

Thor: So you recognise something rather than find something new?

Sue: Yeah, hmmm. I think that's definitely what this is about, it's not about putting something new in and it's all there, but it's just about whether you are using it or paying attention to it, or, or whether it's kind of fading away. And then there is this bit: 'But often, in the world's, yeah, most crowded streets, But often, in the din of strife, There rises an unspeakable desire after the knowledge of our buried life; A thirst to spend our fire and restless force In tracking out our true, original course'; – So it's like something that's in us, that's always been in us, that's just buried, the buried life, hmm.

Thor: He says that there is a true original course, it's just a matter of tracking it, of finding it – would you concord with that?

Sue: Yeah, yeah. I would, because if I think about people who … When a baby's born, it's like this incredible kind of creative force, and I mean some of them are going to end up in prison, but it's not because there's something in them that's wrong, actually they could just as much end up being, I don't know, some kind of genius. So I think it's in there, but things happen to all of us or, you know, life's hard, isn't it? And that stuff gets laid over, and buried deep often. And the woman in the prison, I reckon it's buried really deep. She had her experiences in her young life, she was only about twenty-four, I think. From what I can gather, what I was told, her mother basically pimped her out, at about eight, and at twelve her mum gave her heroin. So it's just really, really laid over, but even then, even with that, those kind of experiences she's had in her life, still, this bit of poetry, it touches something absolutely essential in her.

Thor: Would you say that, before you encountered this poem, you felt 'an unspeakable desire after the knowledge of your buried life'? Or was it after you read the poem you realised that?

Sue: I think I probably always had that. But that's why it's so powerful, because it's not that I got that from here, it's powerful because someone was speaking about this thing that I always felt. I mean, if I hadn't felt that, and I was reading about it, I'd find that probably interesting and maybe exciting and everything, but it wouldn't feel like it does feel for me, because it's someone speaking about something, writing about something, that's strongly felt. So it's as if it was more powerful because it's something I'm already being aware of. When I read a poem or something where I'm learning or finding something new, something I hadn't known before, or a different kind of experience to what I had in my own life, that's great and really interesting, but it doesn't have the kind of resonance that something like this has.

Thor: When you read this, 'a bolt is shot back somewhere in your breast', is that how it felt?

Sue: Yeah, it was, really. But, I mean, when I remember, I remember first reading it and I think I probably cried, I would have been not particularly wanting people to see that, because it was quite a big room, and there was probably 20-plus people sitting there, it was quite a large group, because there were staff as well. Most of us had been there a few days together, but I didn't feel particularly close to anyone. Yeah, I think I probably did have a weep actually.

Thor: Did anyone pick up on that, or ask you how you felt?

Sue: No, well, it just felt so personal, I actually didn't want anyone to see or notice. I did feel a bit shocked, and I think I didn't really want to talk about it, because there was nobody there that I knew very well. It just felt very, I felt like it was, oh, that it was touching a really tender place. It felt precious. I felt quite protective with myself at the time. When we read it in the group, we didn't spend as much time on the poem as I would have liked. I would have been happy to have a lot more time on it, yeah, but I also would have quite liked not to have anything else be read for a while, so that nothing else took up space in my head, I just wanted this to be there.

Thor: So that feeling of shock, because it was unexpected, that this poem brought …

Sue: I don't think I'd ever had that experience from reading anything before, even novels and stuff which I'd obviously enjoyed. I liked reading but I'd never had that kind of reaction.

Thor: So after this slight shock, were you frightened of the strength of your response?

Sue: No, no, not at all. No, it was like a … it was more like a relief. You know, like I felt a bit less mad, haha. I felt a bit more normal. (*Pause.*) When I'm thinking back to that time, it's almost seven years ago now, and I had only been in the UK for about three or four months at that point, I'd come here because I'd gotten into quite a severe depression. I almost needed to shock myself out of it, so I gave up my job and just, you know, came over. I didn't really know what I was doing, but I was following some kind of deep thread of knowing. It absolutely felt like the right thing to do, I knew it was the right thing to do, but I had no idea what I would do when I got here, I just knew that I was coming, I had a one-way ticket, a tiny amount of money. And so I arrived, and I got a bit of work care giving. But I just couldn't do it, you know, I just had to stop doing that as quickly as possible. And this job came up with the library service. I've never worked in a library, it wasn't like I was a librarian or anything, but just a combination of things meant that I ended up getting it. And that was partly why the emotion when I got the job was so strong. I just burst into tears because it was so overwhelming to have this job; it meant I wasn't going to be doing this care giving anymore, it was quite well paid, and I was going to be doing this amazing thing that I didn't really know what it was, but I knew that I had what it would take to do it. I had this feeling because I knew it involved running groups, and I'd done about 10 years of psychodrama training, so I had a lot of experience of running groups. I just had this sense that I'd be good at that. I was still really in this depression, actually, and it took probably about a year of being here before it really lifted properly. I don't know, something about this poem connected in with that in some way. I'm not quite sure how, but it just felt so enlivening. I mean, with a depression it's like everything is dampened, and there is this weight on you, and it is hard to have anything that really excites you, so I felt this excited me. It was like this broke through all of that.

Thor: So it was a breakthrough that helped to lift you out of that?

Sue: Yeah, I think so. It was enlivening and energising, you know. Anything that did that was a crucial thing, because a lot of the time I did feel like I was wading through treacle, it was so hard to have forward motion.

Thor: When you told me that, I got goosebumps from thinking about the courage to pack in your job and to just travel to the other side of the world, not knowing what …

Sue: Well, it was that or kill myself.

Thor: That's how it felt?

Sue: That's how it felt, it really felt like that. I'll either finish my life now, or I will give this a go, and if that doesn't work, well then I can still kill myself. I mean, I'm joking about it now, but I was in a very difficult place, and so I just decided I'll give this a go, because nothing can be worse than what it is right now. Nothing can be worse, and it might even be better. So it was kind of brave, but in a way it didn't feel brave at the time. Because when things get really, really tough, it's almost like all you can do is just live minute by minute, and just make decisions minute by minute. And I only made the decision to leave eight to ten weeks before I came, so it wasn't like I'd planned it for a year or anything. I just had the thought, oh I could do that, it came to me one day, and then I just started getting ready to go. I had to pack up my house and rent it out, and make sure I had enough money, buy a ticket, you know, just do that kind of stuff. And then I came, and I mean it wasn't easy. That first year was really quite tough, being here away from everybody, obviously I knew nobody, I've got no family here or anything like that. But actually, the amount of energy it takes and effort it takes to create a life, it was like the shock I needed. It was a very helpful thing, to have to struggle so hard in a strange place, to struggle with making money and finding a place to live. I would have sunk otherwise, if I didn't do it. And I didn't really want to sink, I guess I didn't want to, so having to deal with the day-to-day living of my new life – because before I didn't really have to think about it, I had my life, had my work – it was a really, really good thing to do.

Thor: I can imagine the relief then to have that phone call.

Sue: For the job, yeah. I feel like I've always been really, really lucky. I don't know if everybody has this, but I suspect not, in fact I'm pretty sure not, but I've always known, like when I make a good decision I know, or when something's right, I know it.

Thor: So that knowing must come from the very depth of you, yeah?

Sue: Yeah, I think so. I've tuned into that as I've gotten older, but even when I was quite young, I've had this ability to know what's good for me and what's not so good for me, and to make decisions. Well, I haven't always made great decisions but even when I've been making bad decisions, I've known somewhere inside myself that that it's not a good decision, you know, does that make sense?

Thor: I think it does. So when you read the poem, did that strengthen that feeling?

Sue: Yeah. You know, the thing about being on your own line, that was probably the main line for me. The beginning bit was really important, the very beginning of the poem when he's talking about that relationship, that really got me and caught me and got me in, but actually, the line that really had the most impact for me was the one about being on your own line. 'But hardly have we, for one little hour, been on our own line, have we been ourselves' – those two lines really were the lines that stuck out the most to me, even more than the bolt shot back. Because, I don't know, something about that just felt really important, just knowing what your line was, and actually being on it, rather than going along someone else's line, or falling off your own, or not even realising that you're not on it, you know. And it was different in that being on our own line, that was the bit that really stuck out to me, hmm.

Something That I Will Always Carry with Me

Thor: Maybe I'm over-interpreting, but it's almost like this poem describes your journey from being on the other side of the world to engaging in shared reading.

Sue: Yeah, perhaps. I'm not sure if I'm …

Thor: In the sense that it seems to go from a deep despair to …

Sue: Hmmm … Yeah.

Thor: And it ends with …

Sue: It ends quite hopefully, doesn't it? I mean, he does come back into some happy place.

Thor: I like that line where he sees 'the meadows where it glides, the sun, the breeze'. A very visceral feeling of light and air and being out in the open again.

Sue: Yes – 'A man becomes aware of his life's flow, And hears its winding murmur': It's like he's connected into something greater, like he's part of what … like his life flow is part of the life flow of nature, hmmm. Wonderful, I love it. The fact that the poem has travelled such a great distance in time, adds to its power. It makes it timeless, you know, these ideas are timeless, they're about being human rather than being a twenty-first-century person, and that just feels important really, I don't quite know why. I feel like I know this guy, that's the feeling. I actually haven't really read many of his other poems, which is a bit foolish you know, but it'd be quite good to read a lot more of his stuff. I feel like I would, if I met him, I'd really like him. I don't know if I would, but there's something in this poem that communicates his innermost being. I don't think you can write a poem like this otherwise. It feels like it must really come from someone's real heart, the innermost place of a person. I mean, people can create art and still not be people that you might want to have at your dinner table, but something about this feels different, because this feels so true and authentic to me. I don't know, I could be very wrong. I can't see how someone can write this stuff and not really, really embody it as well. He says, 'And long, long we try in vain to speak and act Our hidden self, and what we say and do Is eloquent, is well – but 't is not true!' You can be eloquent but still full of bullshit. I get a feeling with this poem that it is eloquent in its way and it's a beautiful poem, but still it just seems, given the time, very close to how you would actually speak, you know. It's all just pouring out of him really.

Thor: Yeah, pouring out is a good word, because he's talking about that stream and the river and the flow and sort of subterrain. How did it feel when you took this experience with you into the next poem you read?

Sue: Well, I started to look out for things that would have a similar impact. But I don't think I've had that kind of experience again. I mean there are lots of poems that I really, really like now, and there's some poems that I really love, but I'd struggle to name another one to match that. I don't have a technical background, I'm such a feeling person, I don't really go on the intellect of the how the poem's constructed or put together or what's a good poem or what's a bad poem, for me it's just really about feeling.

Thor: What I gather from what you've said, is that this poem has changed your life.

Sue: Yeah, it sounds a bit twee, maybe, but it has.

Thor: Other people have told me the book saved their life. Would you say so too?

Sue: Hmm, I wouldn't say it's saved my life, no. Because ... I wouldn't say it's saved my life, I keep on using the work impact, it's had a really significant impact, definitely. Has it changed my life? It has really, because it's opened me up to the power of the written word, so in that respect it has really. I don't know if it's saved my life, I wouldn't go so far as to say that, I mean, I think my life was already on a sort of upward trajectory by the time I read it. A number of things had happened, even just getting on the plane and coming here, you know. That was like a saving in a way. It's a whole combination of things that have been really helpful. But the poem has really helped me. I love it, because – I mean I love it for itself and I think it's a great poem – but it also has a special resonance for me in that it opened something up in me. Something that I will always carry with me. So I don't think of it so much as saving my life, I think of it more as, I don't know, *reminding* me of something important, getting back to sort of excavating something 'from the soul's subterranean depth'.

Afterwards, as I step out into the din of the street, there are two voices inside my head: one of worry, one of wonder. I question myself: did we manage to recreate that 'fullness of feeling', our original shared moment, in the interview? And even if we did, was it too messy, too scattered? But foremost in my mind is the thought of Sue following her deep thread of knowing. Also, I think of Matthew Arnold. If he could have overheard our dialogue, how would it have felt to him, to know of Sue's experience, to realise that his words had found their way to her, 'pursuing with indiscernible flow' their way across centuries and continents?

Re-membering the Body's Song

Crisis

What Sue Tells Us about Her Depression

Of the six reading experiences presented this is the only one to originally have unfolded in a group setting. Moreover, the first time I learned of Sue's experience was in a similar group. Sue read an extract from the poem before telling us that the encounter with Arnold's poem had been a breakthrough moment for her. I think everyone there could directly sense the experiential truth of what she said; she was indeed 'full of feeling'. Therefore Sue's tone sounded more elegiac than apologetic when she initiated our dialogue by lamenting that 'it's a shame that the tape wasn't on then, really'; although she could not recall *what* she had said then, only *how* she had felt. In fact, she did not tell us much about her experience – only that it had been a major breakthrough for her and that she had been coming out of a depression. Her experience of the *Buried Life* being about a moment of shared feeling, I understood Sue to be concerned lest she no longer may speak from *within* the experience, but be restricted to talking *about* it. Not only did she feel that her experience was difficult to convey in words, but that she had already shared its truth with me beforehand. Furthermore, I took her to imply that successfully relating her experience to me would depend on a moment of meeting occurring between *us*, in our dialogue. So I invited her to read the poem for me again, in its entirety. I do believe that her fullness of feeling was revived in our meeting.

What does Sue tell us about the circumstances and experience of her crisis? Firstly, here is how she configures its trajectory:

> 'I had come here because I'd gotten into quite a severe depression. I almost needed to shock myself out of it, so I gave up my job and just, you know, came over.'

> 'I'll either finish my life now, or I will give this a go … because nothing can be worse than it is now.' 'But actually, the amount of energy it takes and effort it takes to create a life, it was like the shock I needed. It was a very helpful thing, to have to struggle so hard in a strange place … I would have sunk otherwise.'

> 'I think my life was already on a sort of upward trajectory by the time I read it.'

> 'I was still really in this depression, actually, and it took probably about a year of being here before it really lifted properly. Something about this poem connected in with that in some way. I'm not quite sure how, but it just felt so enlivening.' She goes on to state that 'it was like [the poem] broke through all of that'.

She points towards two distinct turns in her upward trajectory: the relocation process and the encounter with Arnold's poem. Moreover, she gives this account of the experience of being depressed:

> 'With a depression it's like everything is *dampened*, and there is this *weight* on you, and it's hard to have anything that really excites you, so I felt this excited me.'

> 'A lot of the time I did feel like I was *wading through treacle*, it was so *hard to have forward motion*."

This is a very rudimentary description of depression, although familiar from other phenomenological descriptions (in which terms such as numbness are prevalent).[2] It does tell us, however, that there is a strong somatic component, a visceral-kinetic dimension to

---

[2] Interestingly, Veronica in describing her depression also speaks of a weight on her chest.

the experience. Her description of the depression is concentrated around metaphors of heaviness, dullness and thick liquid. 'Dampening' means that something is dull and has lost its force. It also signifies something moistening – Sue additionally uses the metaphor of 'wading through treacle' – a dark and thick liquid which is hard to stir. The weight on her also signifies inertia. I get the sense that she is buried under something dense and heavy, and cannot move or breathe. It is pertinent that when relating the anecdote about the woman in prison, Sue says she was 'blocking' at first, contrasting this with her own experience where she 'didn't feel any inclination to block it'. 'Block' means an obstacle, made of solid material. Etymologically it is connected to the trunk of a tree. So in depression one is under the weight of a block, and one blocks out experiencing. Similarly, the verb 'to bury' may mean both 'interring' and 'protecting'. The poem breaks through this block, creating excitement and bringing new life; 'A lost pulse of feeling stirs again.'

Despair and Despondency

Sue does not expound on the reasons for her severe depression, nor elaborate its aspects. But she does say that the poem addresses 'problems', 'concerns', that she has had for most of her life. From what she does indicate, it can be surmised that these concerns are of how to communicate with loved ones, how to be authentic and how to access a deeper part of herself – and therefore that her depression is connected to perceived difficulties with these concerns. This inner conflict is symbolised as being set apart from her closest friends by not sharing their love of poetry. However, the depression may well be rooted in factors not to do with external circumstances, and not to be understood only in psychological terms.

Depression is now one of the principal causes of functional impairment worldwide and considered a major threat to public health.[3] However, there exists no precise definition or unitary conceptualisation of the condition, nor agreement on remission criteria. According to Nesse, there are different theories as to its function: 'Is depression an adaptation, an adaptation gone awry, or a pathological state unrelated to any function?'[4] But this question springs from a view of depression as primarily characterised by low mood and pessimism. If depression is defined as 'a significant lowering of mood, with or without feelings of guilt, hopelessness and helplessness, or a drop in self-esteem', then it may be overdiagnosed; for depression goes beyond misery and distress, argues Gordon Parker.[5] In their investigation of the taxonicity of depression, Beach and Amir found that

---

[3] Harvey A. Whiteford, Louisa Degenhardt, Jürgen Rehm, Amanda J. Baxter, Alice J. Ferrari, Holly E. Erskine, Fiona J. Charlson, Rosana E. Norman, Abraham D. Flaxman, Nicole Johns, Roy Burstein, Cristopher J. L. Murray and Theo Vos, 'Global Burden of Disease Attributable to Mental and Substance Use Disorders: Findings from the Global Burden of Disease Study 2010', *The Lancet* 382, no. 9904 (2013): 1575–86.

[4] Randolph M. Nesse, 'Is Depression an Adaptation?', *Archives of General Psychiatry* 57, no. 1 (2000): 14.

[5] Gordon Parker, 'Is Depression Overdiagnosed?', *British Medical Journal* 335, no. 7615 (2005): 328.

any test should also 'tap multiple vegetative signs', because of the prominence of somatic symptoms in diagnoses of depression (disturbance of sleep, appetite, sexuality, weight and other basic homeostatic processes). They argue that focus on somaticity 'dovetails with recent evolutionary theorizing about depression'.[6] Transcultural studies such as a major WHO comparison study show that the core syndrome of depression is not primarily emotional/psychological, but rather 'loss of vitality, appetite and drive, fatigue, sleep disturbances, and various somatic complaints such as feelings of pain, burning, tension, numbness, or heaviness are overall much more frequent than depressive mood'.[7] Thus, we see that depression comprises two aspects of lived experience: emotions and cognitions on the one hand, vegetative-somatic factors on the other. Sometimes one or other is prevalent and at other times both, as in a severe depression. These dimensional differences can already be found reflected in the affective terms of our language. Perhaps one could say that a minor depression is characterised by *despair*, the loss of hope, low mood and so on; a major depression by *despondency*, the loss of heart – understood as both vitality and meaning.

In their article 'Embodied Affectivity: On Moving and Being Moved', Thomas Fuchs and Sabine C. Koch elaborates a model of *interaffectivity*, which is 'regarded as an intertwinement of two cycles of embodied affectivity, thus continuously modifying each partner's affective affordances and bodily resonance'.[8] They emphasise that

> a lack or loss of bodily affectability is characteristic of severe *depression*. The constriction, rigidity and missing tension-flow modulation of the lived body in depression leads to a general emotional numbness and finally to affective depersonalization. [...] The deeper the depression, the more the affective qualities and atmospheres of the environment fade. The patients are no longer capable of being moved and affected by things, situations or other persons. They complain of a painful indifference, a 'feeling of not feeling' and of not being able to sympathise with their relatives anymore.[9]

Thus, the depressed person comes to feel disconnected from the world and lose their participation in the interaffective space that we normally share with others.[10]

Remission

Martin Baker argues that there is considerable variability in the specific characteristics that are accepted as indicators of remission. According to Whiteford et al., remission can be defined as 'rescinded diagnoses or below threshold scores on standardised symptom

---

[6] Stephen R. H. Beach and Nadir Amir, 'Is Depression Taxonic, Dimensional or Both?', *Journal of Abnormal Psychology* 112, no. 2 (2003): 228.
[7] See Thomas Fuchs, 'Depression, Intercorporeality, and Interaffectivity', *Journal of Consciousness Studies* 20, no. 7–8 (2013): 220.
[8] Thomas Fuchs and Sabine C. Cock, 'Embodied Affectivity: On Moving and Being Moved', *Frontiers in Psychology* 5, no. 508 (2014): 1.
[9] Ibid., 7.
[10] Fuchs, 'Depression, Intercorporeality, and Interaffectivity', 219–38.

messages',[11] concluding that there is a high rate of spontaneous recovery as 'just over half of those with a major depressive episode will remit within a year without intervention'.[12] Zimmerman et al. maintain the importance of taking the depressed person's perspective on what constitutes remission. Hence they found that a return to normal functioning and relief from symptoms was not deemed sufficient by the patients themselves, as they pointed to positive markers of new growth: "Patients indicated that the presence of positive features of mental health such as optimism, vigour and self-confidence was a better indicator of remission than the absence of the symptoms of depression.'[13]

Deciding to move, mustering energy and resources to find a new home and occupation, does this not constitute recovery from depression? Had remission not been achieved before the reading experience? What we may conjecture is that any functional impairment had been overcome prior to the reading experience. But affective impairment remains as a felt lack of vitality. In their research on embodiment experiences in depression, Danielsson and Rosberg found that at the core of participants' struggle was an 'ambivalent striving against fading': on the one hand resisting urges to withdraw from life, on the other yielding to the need for a pause. The body-feeling was marked by numbness and a sense of confinement, estrangement and heaviness.[14] The ambivalent striving is echoed in Sue's story. She managed to avoid such withdrawal; by uprooting she, in a sense, overrode the other need of delving into the feelings. In a study exploring lived experiences of basic body awareness therapy, Danielsson and Rosberg found that treatment resulted in an 'opening towards life' that was characterised by 'vitality springing forth, […] recognising patterns in one's body, and grasping the vagueness'.[15] Thus it seems that uprooting signalled the conquering of the fading pull, whereas the enlivening and energising reading brought about an opening where vitality could spring forth.

In her deeper wisdom Sue devises a radical cure for her depression: uprooting and relocating, thus having to deal with the bare necessities of subsistence. She leaves her whole life behind because it must somehow have become meaningless to her. And by struggling to establish herself in London, she is forced to deal with basic practicalities in order to get by, thus removing herself from the objects of rumination and preventing herself from opportunities for ruminating, allowing her to return to normal functioning. But if recovering from depression is regarded dialectically, then this is a necessary but

---

[11] Harvey A. Whiteford, M. G. Harris, G. McKeon, A. Baxter, C. Pennell, J. J. Barendregt and J. Want, 'Estimating Remission from Untreated Major Depression: A Systematic Review and Meta-Analysis', *Psychological Medicine*, 43 (2013): 1569.

[12] Ibid., 1582.

[13] Mark Zimmerman, Joseph B. McGlinchey, Michael A. Posternak, Michael Friedman, Naureen Attiullah and Daniela Boerescu, 'How Should Remission from Depression Be Defined? The Depressed Patient's Perspective', *American Journal of Psychiatry* 163, no .1 (2006): 150.

[14] Louise Danielsson and Susanne Rosberg, 'Depression Embodied: An Ambiguous Striving against Fading', *Scandinavian Journal of Caring Sciences* 29, no. 3 (2015): 501–509.

[15] Louise Danielsson and Susanne Rosberg, 'Opening toward Life: Experiences of Basic Body Awareness Therapy in Persons with Major Depression', *International Journal of Qualitative Studies on Health and Well-being* 10, no. 1 (2015): 1–13.

not sufficient step for her. For it is not just a question of *getting out of* a depression, but also of *getting into* the experience of vitality and the creation of meaning. Hence, when Sue in her appraisal regards these two steps, uprooting and relocating, as life-saving, she implies that they rescued her because they prevented her from sinking. They kept her afloat. But if there is a part of saving that is about *more* than being rescued, to do with experiencing the lived body 'singing with' meaning, then perhaps one could say that the poem saved her still. By taking care of what was necessary, she opens herself up to grace and possibility. Her *problem* is already solved by the time she encounters the poem. I think it is rather clear from Sue's response that her understanding of being saved is that it means being *rescued*, averting the existential danger. But salvation has an additional meaning of getting into contact with a source of vitality, nourishment and meaning, which, when one shares it with other people, only increases. A depression can be turned into a solvable problem: apply psychopharmaca to repair a neurochemical balance, counter-ruminative cognition and take proactive measures to remedy the situation. But a crisis is more than, other than, a problem to be solved. It calls not only for activity, but for passivity. 'I don't know, something about this poem connected in with that in some way. I'm not quite sure how. But it just felt so enlivening. […] I felt this excited me. It was like this broke through all of that.' She says that the reading of the poem not only coincided with the end of her depression, but it was also connected to it because it enlivened her. I understand her 'I don't know' to mean that she cannot objectively know that the poem caused the end of the depression; perhaps it would have lifted in time anyway, without it. However, what she does know is that after having read it, she has been uplifted and lifted up. We may regard her way out of depression as consisting of three phases: First, she *lifts herself* out of her depression by uprooting, and second, she struggles to find the job. Then, in the third and final phase her depression *is lifted* as the poem breaks through the dampening, the weight of the depression, and *lifts her up*. Will and grace both play their part.

Transaction with the Literary Work

Impact

After providing a brief orientation section, describing where and when she first read the poem, Sue says that from the moment the first part of the poem was read out loud, she had 'a strong, strong feeling for it'. She says she was immediately 'captivated'. Now, she probably only uses this word in the sense that the poem completely took hold of her attention, but the use of the word 'captivated' is noteworthy, in lieu of the importance of the anecdote of the Woman in Prison – through which much of Sue's reading experience is refracted. To be captivated also means to be held prisoner. The woman in prison refuses to be captivated by poetry, until finally 'The Bluebird' manages to hatch an opening in her block. By allowing herself to be captivated, she is released.

As Sue emphasises several times, the 'impact' has two principal components: She 'felt that I completely understood the experience that he was writing of', and she experienced a transvaluation of poetry itself: 'Suddenly I was awake to this possibility of what poetry might do.' Sue says: 'I did feel a bit shocked.' But does she mean shocked over her own reaction to the poem or over her discovery of poetry's value? It is fair to say that it was both, her response is a composite of the two. I will discuss each of these aspects in turn, beginning with the experience that Arnold writes about, before moving on to her discovery of the value of poetry.

Sue uses the word 'impact' several times. This may simply reflect the fact that she has been, and is, working in a context where the discourse of medicine and its emphasis on evidence-based treatments is prevalent. Here, 'impact' merely signifies the measurable effect that an intervention has on a given problematic state of affairs. The notion of impact comes from physics, where it designates the pressure exercised by one body upon another at the moment of collision. The forceful impression the poem makes is felt bodily; it is an affection. Eric Méchoulan, in an article critiquing the current discourse in which 'impact' is used to mean measurable effect, points out that it was Coleridge who first introduced this as a figurative term meaning 'forceful impression'. In his *Biographia Literaria*, Coleridge maintains that 'in any given perception there is a something which has been communicated to it [the mind] by an impact, or an impression *ab extra*'. According to Méchoulan, Coleridge intends to 'stress the unintelligibility of that 'something' that has been communicated to the mind by the senses'.[16] Thus, it is an affective figure, denoting the felt force of an influence that cannot be rationally comprehended, yet has significance, in its insistence on being suffered or experienced. Thus, something can have a significant effect without having much impact. For instance, I can take a medicine that is very effective, and within days I am much better and back to normal, without really reflecting on what happened to me. In this sense it did not have much impact, it did not leave a forceful impression and it is not incumbent on me to make meaning of the experience.

In her elaboration on the nature of this impact, Sue employs images grounded in physics and music. She introduces the anecdote of the Woman in Prison to illustrate a truth she has discovered: there is a poem for everyone – an encounter in which 'everything sort of fits'. When you encounter such a poem 'you can't hold yourself back' – it becomes impossible to 'block' the experience. The Woman in Prison serves a twofold function: it is a way of illustrating her own experience, and it also symbolises the essence of her purpose: to share this life-enhancing experience with other people. It is crucial to note that when describing the breaking through to the buried part of herself, Sue does so in reference to sharing the experience with others, and she uses the metaphors of resonance, attunement and striking a chord. In his phenomenological understanding of depression as a disturbance of intercorporeality and interaffectivity, Fuchs analyses 'depression as a *detunement* of the *resonant* body that mediates our participation in a *shared* affective space. Instead of expressing the self, the body is turned into a *barrier* to all impulses directed to the environment'[17] (my emphasis). The matching metaphors of Sue's description and

---

[16] Éric Méchoulan, 'Impacting the University: An Archeology of the Future', trans. Roxanne Lapidus, *SubStance* 42, no. 1 (2013): 8.
[17] Fuchs, 'Depression, Intercorporeality, and Interaffectivity', 219.

Fuch's intercorporeality theory also find their resonance in the themes, movements and images of the poem itself.

Let us look more closely at her metaphoric field of resonance – attunement – accordance. Attunement is an important theme in her story: elsewhere she speaks of poems being 'tuned in', 'they're the right tune for you'; she speaks of 'tuning into' another person; of being 'tuned into' poetry; of having 'tuned into' a deeper way of knowing. A frequently recurring verb is 'to resonate'. This is originally an acoustic term, meaning 'prolongation of sound by reverberation'. The literal sense of 'sound again' later took on the figurative sense of pertaining to feelings and emotions. The verb has entered common parlance and does not therefore seem to be a reflective choice, but when repeated so many times and occurring in conjuncture with several musical metaphors, itself begins to *resonate*. A resonator is an 'instrument or chamber formed to respond to a single tone'. In the field of affective neuroscience, the physics-derived concept of resonance has become a root metaphor: 'Physicists speak of resonance as a sympathetic vibration between two elements that allows these elements to suddenly synchronise signals and act in a new harmony'; resonance accordingly becomes a root metaphor for intersubjectivity: 'There is a correspondence, a flow that is beyond empathy and [is] the source of a deep intimacy' in which two persons are attuned to one another mentally and emotionally.[18]

When striving to articulate the kind of change that being moved by a poem creates, Sue says that 'it helps you access some part of yourself that [...] has been a bit buried'. Then, elaborating on what it is that has been buried, she finds that she is 'struggling to find the right kind of metaphor'. Implicitly, only metaphoric language can approach and illuminate this feeling, precisely because it has been buried outside verbal consciousness. She is searching for the right words that *resonate* with her felt sense:

Sue: You know, a bit that's unknown, or kind of … *un-resonated*. That hasn't been … the strings haven't been played, or something – like a sort of instrument that's not been used fully, so … Well, I don't know if that's the right metaphor – I am struggling to find the right metaphor, really. (Pause).
Thor: You said 'unresonated'?
Sue: Mmm, some sort of deeply – or, because what it feels like is that, when that happens, you – even if you don't tell anyone else, it's like you can't *not* experience it if you get a piece of writing that does that to you – you're just going to … you're whole being is going to … *sing* with it.

The first one she hits on is 'unresonated': 'a bit that's unknown, or kind of [...] unresonated'. The pauses are places where real thinking is going on, as if she is trying to *excavate* something buried deep. Then she digs further: 'That hasn't been [...] the strings haven't been played, or something – like a sort of instrument that's not been used fully.'

---

[18] Susan Johnson, 'Extravagant Emotion', in *The Healing Power of Emotion: Affective Neuroscience, Development and Clinical Practice*, ed. Diana Fosha, Daniel J. Siegel and Marion F. Solomon (New York: W. W. Norton., 2009), 273.

It is a string instrument, perhaps like a lyre. But she does not feel quite satisfied that this hits the mark. She goes back to 'resonating' again, eventually locating a more fitting metaphor: 'You're just going to, your whole being is going to [...] *sing* with it.' The emphasis placed on sing indicates two things: she has found the right word and she is now experiencing that feeling as she says it. She does not merely say 'sing', she says 'sing with'; does she mean sing along? She does not say that the body is going to sing along to the music of the poem. I think 'sing with' must be taken to mean that the body sings with the knowledge that something has opened up, and that it sings from and about this knowledge. She stays within the same metaphoric field, moving from resonance to accessing a string instrument to singing, not just with the voice but with the entire body. The way the poem creates resonance is that your whole body sings with it, and when this happens you uncover a hidden or forgotten instrument inside, whose strings you can now begin to play. Thus resonance is a sounding back and forth: she as reader must be attuned, tuned into, the poem. The lyric makes the body sing in response, and this singing puts her in contact with a buried part that is itself like an unplayed lyre.

In our shared reading of this poem, much of the reflection revolved around the two lines that Sue deemed to be of greatest importance to her, and which may be said to represent two crystallising moments in her reading experience:

1. But hardly have we, for one little hour,
   Been on our own line, have we been ourselves –
2. A bolt is shot back somewhere in our breast

To Be on One's Own Line and the Bolt Shot Back

Initially, it seems rather puzzling that Sue regards 'being on one's own line' as having 'even more impact' than 'the bolt shot back'. Why would she do so, when the sum of her statements point to the latter constituting the essence of her experience? As far as I understand her, the breakthrough moment happens at 'the bolt shot back'. 'But hardly have we [...] Been on our own line' is connected to 'Hardly had skill to utter one of all the nameless feelings'; they go to the core of our predicament: we cannot speak our hidden self and we cannot be our own true self. Why would the 'crisis formulation' – our inability to be our genuine, authentic self and to communicate the truth – be seen as more important than the moment of its resolution, when the hidden is opened up or let out?

Of the first line, Sue remarks: 'I mean he is quite hard on; I'm not entirely sure that's true for me, but there's something about the being authentic, you know, being who you really are. And I think that has been quite a big thing for me in my life.' She does not completely subscribe to his expression, finding perhaps that he exaggerates. Yet at the same time it is precisely this utterance that allows the full force of recognition of the supreme importance she has always attached to being authentic. In the poem's reiteration of this theme, Sue finds reflected her inner drama of struggling for authenticity and intimacy. This line validates both the reality of her depression and the deeper reason for it: being true to herself and at the same time true to the other is difficult for her. Sue reiterates her reservation: 'Unless I'm not understanding what he's meaning entirely, it's not like I entirely agree with it.' And still it was for her the most important *line* in the poem, the one 'that stuck out the most to me'. To stick out: easily noticed, but also going over the edge of something. If you are on your own line, you are bound to stick out. And you may get stuck there, unable to connect to other lines. The past form of 'to stick' is stuck. To be depressed is to be stuck: buried under a heavy load, or stuck in an immobile treacle. It is a peculiarity that Arnold uses the rhetorical 'we' here. This 'we' threatens to disintegrate, so that the reader may think: he is exaggerating, I am not part of that We. In order for the poem to succeed, the reader must participate in this we. It can be difficult to admit that we have not been ourselves. But Arnold manages to weave a We *into* the very fabric of these lines. When we look at the resonant prosody that runs through these lines: 'But hardly have we, for one little hour, / Been on our own line, have we been ourselves –', we find that there are several internal phonetic repetitions: ha-ha-ha, ly-we, been-line, one-on-own, hour-our as well as the repetition of clauses such as 'have we been on our own line' and 'have we been ourselves'. Thus the lines come to have suggestive force for the reader, who is as yet reluctant to *embody* Arnold's great claim. My interpretation is that this thought, which resonates so deeply with Sue – 'hardly have we been on our own line' – keeps reverberating through the rest of the reading, until, when the bolt is shot back, it unlocks her heart and she comes to know both the hills where her life rose, the connection with the source of vitality, and the sea where it goes, the sharing of the source of vitality with others.

What does Sue says about 'the bolt shot back'? The first time she quotes it is in reference to the truth she discovered in relation to the woman in prison. It has become a metaphor for the discovery of the person's greatest need, of how to get past someone's defenses and unlock their heart. This is how Sue proceeds to meditate upon the line:

> Yes. A bolt is shot back somewhere in our breast. *Bolt. Shot. Back.* I've never fully understood what a bolt shot back means, but it sounds so […] *right*. I think it's like […] I imagine it to be a shock, a shocking awakening. Like an aha-moment, a sitting up moment. Or a […] it was like a bolt was shot back somewhere in *my* breast.

She 'tastes' each word; three monosyllabic words that all may either be verbs or nouns. The [o] sound is carried over into the next word, and subsequently the [b] is repeated: b – o – o – b, creating almost a chiasmus, and a resonating, reverberating sound awaiting the end of the line's '*b*reast'. As if a lightning bolt is followed by shots of thunder. The bolted vault that was shut is now violently, suddenly, forced ajar. Sue is looking for the right figurative meaning, first alighting on shock, then elaborating on this by turning shock into adjective. Next she states that it is like an aha-moment, and sets off to nuance this before halting, pausing and eventually saying that it is what it is, and she experienced it in her own breast. She repeats by emphasising each word, as if they were three successive hammer blows, or a reverberating echo. When she says she doesn't fully understand it, she must mean that its figurative meaning is equivocal. She uses the present tense: it *is* almost like a shock – it is unclear here whether she is describing the figurative meaning of the phrase, or her own experience. But finally, she moves from working out what it may mean to saying that she experienced it literally, on her body, as impact. There are three stages to this movement: it is sounded, it is imagined, it is internalised. The bolt shooting back is the affective component, in the light of which she realises what 'hardly have we been on our own line' means for her. She has struggled all her life to be on her own line, to be authentic, to be herself, to be in contact with an inner source of meaning, and at the same time create authentic intimate relationships. The speaker spends the greater part of the time expounding on the cause, nature and consequences of our predicament, and only briefly touches on the event of becoming 'aware of one's life's flow'. For the realisation to *strike*, so that the bolt really *shoots* back and impacts deeply upon us, the ground must have been thoroughly prepared. We must come to deeply inhabit the diagnosis of our situation, we must feel the full force of the 'hardly', in order to feel fully the sudden transition from the 'buts' to the 'bolt', so that it does not only remain a claim, a proposition, but also becomes a fully embodied truth. And the truth works backwards, the bolt is shot *back*: the result of the lost pulse of feeling stirring again. Sue is made aware of her life's flow; she no longer needs to struggle, she *is* on her own line because this is the very same line that connects us deeply, the resonating chord, when we mutually attune to one another. For such a bolt to have *impact*, the reader must have been brought to a deep state of tranquil alertness. It is as if reading this long poem in a group has brought Sue into such a deep, contemplative rest where her 'eye sinks inward, and the heart lies plain'. This is a physiological process, where the heart rhythm slows down, and the mind quietens, and the eyes moisten.

Incidentally, the word 'hardly', used twice in the poem and contained within what constitutes for Sue the most important line – although paradoxically she also regards it as hyperbolic – etymologically has passed through a three-step-downward trajectory that seems to imitate that of depression itself. Initially, it meant 'in a hard manner, with great exertion and effort', then via the intermediate meaning of 'not easily, with trouble' has come to mean 'barely, just'.[19] It is worth bearing in mind that the word 'depression' literally means a pressing down on. As if the flow between *impressivity* (ability to open up towards the world, vitality) and *expressivity* (capacity to communicate to others what one is feeling) is restricted, thus signifying both de-impressivity and de-expressivity. And perhaps the poem describes both problems: the inability to express one's true feelings, and the incapacity to establish a channel where the stream of vitality can in-flux the psyche. For there are two principal threads or streams of metaphors coursing through the poem. We have one thread consisting of *constrictions*: *locked* (unlock the heart), *chained* (lips unchained), *bolted* (bolt shot back); another one that represents *movement*: *stream, eddying, flow, current, coursing, rolling, gliding*, as in the 'unregarded river of our life pursue with indiscernible flow its way'. Fate has buried this stream in order to protect us from ourselves, so that we are forced to obey our 'being's law'. In the 'din of strife' it seems that we

---

[19] See https://www.etymonline.com/: *c.*1200, 'in a hard manner, with great exertion or effort', from Old English *heardlice* 'sternly, severely, harshly; bravely; excessively' (see *hard* (adj.) + *-ly* (2)). Hence 'assuredly, certainly' (early 14c.). Main modern sense of 'barely, just' (1540s) reverses this, via the intermediate meaning 'not easily, with trouble' (early 15c.). Formerly with superficial negative (*not hardly*).

inevitably have to lock our hearts. We are cut off from a source, a stream, of vitality. That this life is *buried*, may signify two different things: That a part of us is dead and interred, or that it is being sheltered and protected, and thus recoverable.

How may we 'become aware of our life's flow'? How can we inquire in to the mystery of our heart? This is not possible through introspection, or by digging through layers of psychic material in self-analysis: 'And many a man in his own breast then delves, But deep enough, alas, none ever mines.' No action can bring us into contact with the buried life, nor can discursive communication do so: 'And long we try in vain to speak and act Our hidden self.' How, then? It seems to be that only after we have given up on this inward striving may we allow something to happen. Only when we realise that it is not through activity, but through passivity, that the 'lost pulse of feeling' may 'stir again' In the attentive togetherness, through the attunement attained of holding hands and looking deeply into each other's eyes, through the resonance created when we let ourselves be caressed by the tone of the other's voice, will the heart unlock. Only in this 'unwonted calm' can we sense the flow. Why is this deep resting such a 'flying and elusive shadow'?

Daniel Stern, in his research in developmental psychology on affect attunement, says that the affect that emerges in the course of joyous play between mother and infant may not be divided and collocated in one or the other.[20] Rather, it springs up from the 'in-between', or from the encompassing process in which the two are immersed – giving rise to what Stern terms 'vitality affects' or 'vitality contours'. These shared states are experienced through interbodily affection.[21] We gather that contemplation is not introspection, but rather a form of 'trans-spection': by looking through the other's eyes, resting in the presence of the other, may we read our own soul. The soul is not 'in there', but 'between' and 'around' us. Fuchs, in his discussion of intercorporeality, maintains that in other cultures there is less of a tendency to regard affective experiences as intrapsychic, 'but rather as bodily, expressive, interpersonal, or even atmospheric processes'.[22] He argues that mutual bodily resonance 'mediated by posture, facial, gestural, and vocal expression, engenders our attunement to others'.[23]

How are we to understand the poem's ending: 'And then he thinks he knows /The hills where his life rose, And the sea where it goes'? Does Arnold mean that this knowledge is an illusion – man only thinks that he knows, whereas in actual fact he does not? That would undercut the entire thrust of the poem's movement, however. It is not a knowledge that can be grasped, held on to, turned into propositions. It borders on the ineffable. What does 'think' mean here? We cannot truly know 'whence our lives come and where they go'. But the thinking one does in this state, in this intersubjective matrix,

---

[20] Daniel N. Stern, *The Interpersonal World of the Human Infant: A View from Psychoanalysis and Developmental Psychology* (New York: Basic Books, 1985), 132.
[21] Daniel N. Stern, *Forms of Vitality: Exploring Dynamic Experience in Psychology and the Arts* (Oxford: Oxford University Press, 2010).
[22] Fuchs, 'Depression, Intercorporeality and Interaffectivity', 221.
[23] Ibid., 222.

is different from the discursive, rational thinking and introspection one normally engages in; this is of course the central tenet of the whole poem. The poem lays claim to a deeper and different form of thinking, taking place in the imaginative space opened up by the emphasis on 'and *then*'. A thinking that happens beyond the verbal, in a moment of meeting: in this paradoxical still and resting flow imagination is opened up. He cannot know, and neither does he assume that he knows – and yet, it is *as if* he knows. In contemplation we may feel that although we are far from the Stream, it is near to us. It is quite clear that the experience of temporality changes in this attunement. In this restive silence, time slows down, becomes an elongated moment with (vitality) contours and shapes: hills, river.

In their research into how the attention to bodily sensations and the cultivation of interoceptive, proprioceptive and kinaesthetic awareness can be understood, Schmalzl et al. remark that 'dyadic contemplation is at the core of many Eastern movement-based systems'. In such dyadic contemplation, 'they enter a state of enhanced connectivity'.[24] This state corresponds to what Siegel refers to as 'resonance',[25] characterised by a sharing of affective and somatosensory experience that happens mainly automatically. This state involves a simultaneous activation of affective and sensory brain structures in both individuals. Social neuroscience research on empathy corroborates these findings.[26] Thus, in the contemplative dyad, through a process of attunement and mutual resonance the block or barrier, in relation to the environment and in relation to the deeper vitality affects of the body, is experienced as dissolved or broken through.

The knowledge of life's buried flow is ineffable, arising *between* two people in a moment of meeting. Neither you nor I have the skill to put into words these nameless feelings. These are neither *my* personal feelings, nor yours. To think so only leads to a divide between us, and a feeling of being inauthentic. It is only when you and I together, in dyadic contemplation, stay close to the source of these nameless feelings, that we, through mutual attunement, enter into contact with the stream. Now we have intimate communication, but beyond the discursive, rational. This seems to be the central tenet of the poem, and the core of Sue's realisation. Is there a conceptual term that encompasses the interpersonal understanding and the musicality of this dyadic attunement that brings us into contact with deeper truth and vitality?

Synesis: Knowing Together

In the *Odyssey*, 10.515, the word *synesis* can be found, denoting 'a union of two rivers'. In Plato's *Cratyllus* it means 'come together'. The received etymology is rendered as

---

[24] Laura Schmalzl, Mardi A. Crane-Godreau and Peter Payne, 'Movement-Based Embodied Contemplative Practices: Definitions and Paradigms', *Frontier in Human Neuroscience* 8, no. 205 (2014): 4.

[25] Daniel J. Siegel, *The Mindful Brain: Reflection and Attunement in the Cultivation of Well-Being* (New York: W.W. Norton, 2007).

[26] Tania Singer and Claus Lamm, 'The Social Neuroscience of Empathy', *Annals of the New York Academy of Sciences* 1156 (2009): 81–96.

'perceive', 'apprehend'. In Plato it means sagacity in respect to something, an inherent form of knowing. This is corroborated in the Septaguint, where synesis is listed as one of the seven gifts of the Holy Spirit. The confluence of these two meanings, *flowing together* and *intuitive understanding*, point us in the direction of an implicit form of knowing that can only be achieved when two subjectivities come together. In her analysis of instances of this word in a text by Aristoxenus, Flora Levin finds that this kind of understanding 'is more significant than the English words "understanding" and "comprehension" suggest'. She argues that Aristoxenus takes synesis to mean 'musical intuition': 'This implies more than mere recognition or superficial understanding of melodic lines; it suggests, rather, a total musical competence.'[27] Aristoxenus says that the activity of synesis 'is something hidden deep down in the soul, and is not palpable or apparent to the ordinary man'.[28] Thus, the concept of synesis brings together four principle aspects of the communication between the poem and Sue: a stream hidden deep down in the soul, a non-verbal, bodily attunement, the confluence of two rivers, knowing myself in and through the other. It is reflected in the intersubjective theories of Stern's developmental psychology, affective neuroscience and Fuch's phenomenological intercorporeality: a contemplative dyad where knowledge is not achieved by introspection, but happens between the two, when hearts and minds are brought to alert rest, requiring attunement and creating a resonance that reveals deeply hidden qualities of the soul. That this perception be likened to musical intuition makes sense. Synesis brings these notes into accordance, creating a chord that resonates. This deepening movement is reflected in the conceptual model of the three-stage process that unfolds in shared reading. First, there is a 'getting in', as the readers engage in the pendulum of immersion and reflection on what is read; second, a 'staying in' as this experience deepens, themes are reiterated and increasingly begin to resonate with the affective schemas of each participant; third, a possible 'breaking through', an experience of a shift, the acknowledging that something is different – one has been moved and what was stuck or inert has begun to move again.

Resolution

Remembrance

Sue says that 'if you have had that experience of being moved by something then I suppose you, well *I*, would like other people to have that experience, for sure'. What, in a moment of sharing, has moved you, you would like to share with others, so that they can be moved too. I find it interesting that she catches herself mid-utterance, shifting from the general second-person to first-person. She takes care, of course, not to impose her personal experience and value on others; this is *her* individual destiny, to facilitate that experience for others. Yet, the initial generalisation still echoes: If you have been moved like I have been moved, you cannot but want others to participate in this, 'you cannot

---

[27] Flora R. Levin, 'Synesis in Aristoxenian Theory', *Transactions and Proceedings of the American Philological Association* 103 (1972): 212.
[28] Ibid., 213.

help yourself.' That which has helped her to say I, to be on her own line, demands to be brought forth to others. It is a universal experience. And it is where I becomes you and you becomes I, not just rhetorically, but truly: the I-Thou. To be on one's own line is to be on a transpersonal line, to share and dare; 'a bold swinging – demanding the most intensive stirring of one's being – into the life of the other'.[29]

What the poem does for Sue, I think can best be described as an *anamnesis*. Sue says that the meeting is 'powerful because someone was speaking about this thing that I *always* felt' – it is 'something I'm already being aware of'. Towards the very end, she concludes that she loves the poem. It 'opened something up in me. Something that I will always carry with me.' What the meeting with Arnold has achieved is 'reminding me of something important, getting back to sort of excavating something "from the soul's subterranean depth"'. She concludes that the poem *has* changed her. 'And what I mean by change is, it does make you into a different person, it helps you access some part of yourself that you […] that has been buried.'

From Disdain to Wonder

Sue says that her initial reaction was so strong for two reasons: she recognised her own experience in the poem's first stanza. And she found it 'mind-blowing' that Matthew Arnold could communicate with her like that. Poetry had never come alive for her before. This is a common enough experience of poetry – high-flung phrases that are hard to understand; poetry is remote and 'says nothing to me about my life'. Thus, the first time she 'gets it', it is from an unlikely source – a 'Victorian' poem. She experiences a direct communication between herself and Arnold, across the historical and cultural divide. An old poem need not be 'dug up' by means of contextualisation, theoretical perspectives and historical documents; it is made new by carefully paying attention. What she assumed was *past*, has suddenly become *contemporaneous*; the speaker is here, now – demanding that she be present too. ('The fact that the poem has travelled such a great distance in time adds to its power. It makes it timeless, you know, these ideas are timeless […] I feel like I know this guy, that's the feeling.') Ironically, the communication between author and reader is about the inability to communicate even to one's nearest and dearest – what they share is this longing to share: 'can we not even, if we love each other enough, can we not break through this, whatever this thing is that wouldn't, can't, communicate with each other'. I find this absolutely *wonderful*: two concurrent events take place in her. Sue realises that someone is speaking to her about his deepest concerns, and these are also *her* deepest concerns – it is an experience they can share. And in the act of discovering this, she also realises that *this* is what a poem can do: as the poem comes alive in the present moment, she and Arnold come alive too, 'enlivened', and, so to speak, unburied.

In his treatment *Of the Affects*, Spinoza contrasts *wonder* and *disdain*. Of wonder Spinoza says that it is the imagination of something we have not encountered before. Normally, when we are faced with an object that we have seen before and which is familiar, 'we shall

---

[29] Martin Buber, *The Knowledge of Man* (New York: Harper and Row, 1965), 81.

immediately recollect the others'. We presume it to have 'nothing but what is common to many things' and 'we consider nothing in it but what we have seen before with others'; however, things are very different when we imagine that there is something singular in the object that we have never encountered before. Thus, says Spinoza, this affection of the mind, '*this imagination of a singular thing, insofar as it is alone in the mind*, is called *wonder*'.[30] And this is precisely Sue's affection upon encountering a poem that communicates intimately with her. This has never happened before. It is a singularity. She never expected anything from poetry, and here she is, discovering that a poem by a male Victorian can speak to and for her, across the centuries and continents, over and beyond gender issues, as she felt she 'completely understood this experience he is writing of'. 'It felt so current, even though I know he was writing in eighteen hundred something.' The poem is 'timeless', and 'true and authentic' because it comes from the 'heart, the innermost place of a person'. This is wonder-full; 'It was the most magical, amazing stuff.'

To wonder is opposed to *disdain*, Spinoza then says. He attributes the general cause of disdain to this: 'because we see that someone wonders at something', or 'something appears at first glance like things we admire, love', we are determined to wonder at the same thing. However, if 'from the thing's presence' or from 'considering it more accurately' we are forced to deny that it can be the cause of wonder, 'then the mind remains determined by the thing's presence to think more of the things which are not in the object than of those which are.'[31] In other words, we can only see what is missing. Therefore, whereas wonder is imagination of a thing which touches us deeply in its newness, 'disdain is an imagination of a thing which touches the mind so little.'[32] Such disdain is at the heart of Sue's anecdote about her group of poetry lovers. This group of friends is dearly important to her. She says she feels closer to them than to her own family and that 'it's the most home I feel'. And yet she was distanced from them in one respect: they would read poetry while Sue was 'bored, ignoring it, I was always resistant to it'. Still, 'if my friends valued something, then that would make me curious.' So she would try, but 'couldn't overcome the hurdle'; 'poetry just felt like a waste of time.'

Epiphany

In my understanding, Sue, through reading Arnold's poem, has experienced a sudden about-turn in which disdain is transformed into wonder. That which had been found to be wanting, to be of little value, all of a sudden embodies the greatest value, and becomes the key to reaching out to people and touching their hearts. In alchemical terms, this is tantamount to finding the gold in the dung-heap – to a king being born in a manger. This is an instance of a positive surprise. 'Suddenly I was awake to this possibility of what poetry might do. […] It did feel that big, actually.' She can no longer imagine her

---

[30] Benedict de Spinoza, 'Of the Origin and Nature of the Affects', in *Ethics*, trans. Edwin Curley (London: Penguin, 1996), 97.
[31] Ibid.
[32] Ibid., 105.

life without poetry. Whereas Jane experienced a negative surprise in that *Shikasta* did not conform to her expectations of Lessing's work, Sue has a positive surprise. She did not expect anything good, yet experiences an awakening. This *ekstasis* is one of being *lifted up* into *wonder*, what Kuiken et al. term 'sublime enthrallment'.

Is this turnaround what an epiphany is? For an objective epiphany to take place, argues Tigges, 'there must be a larger context to set off the triviality of the epiphanic image'.[33] He is here following Beja's Joycean conception, where epiphany occurs as the result of an encounter with a trivial or insignificant thing or event. But Bidney, in his definition of epiphany as 'a moment that is felt to be expansive, mysterious and intense' explicitly rejects the criteria of triviality.[34] Nichols defines it as 'momentary manifestations of significance in ordinary experience'.[35] Much of the disagreement revolves around the difference between the trivial and insignificant on the one hand, and the ordinary on the other. What this disagreement occludes, however, is that what was previously regarded as insignificant suddenly becomes of the greatest significance: the object itself shines forth. Upon hearing a shout in the street, Daedalus discovers that '*that* is God'. The previously trivial has been found to be of supreme value. This is the essence of the epiphany. This, and one other thing: the epiphany is the narrative not just of coming upon the king in the manger, *but also of setting out to find him*, guided by the iridescence of a star. Retrospectively, Sue feels as if there is a God: in starting a new life and finding the magic of sharing poetry she 'was following some kind of deep thread of knowing'.[36] This is part of Sue retroactively ascribing meaning to her life's journey:

> So it's more looking and at the time I wouldn't have said there is a God. Looking back I think how incredibly fortunate I've been. It feels like a whole lot of things were leading to this, a combination of things in my life made it all make a lot of sense.

So this, then, is epiphany: upon turning disdain into wonder, as loss of soul turns into anamnesis of the buried life through an intercorporeal moment of meeting, she discovers

---

[33] Wim Tigges, 'The Significance of Trivial Things: Towards a Typology of Literary Epiphanies', in *Moments of Moment: Aspects of the Literary Experience*, ed. Wim Tigges (Atalanta, GA: Rodopi BV, 1999), 21.

[34] Martin Bidney, *Patterns of Epiphany: From Wordsworth to Tolstoy, Pater and Barrett Browning* (Carbondale: Southern Illinois University Press. 1997).

[35] Ashton Nichols, *The Poetics of Epiphany* (Tuscaloosa: University of Alabama Press, 1987).

[36] Why does she employ this metaphor, rather than stay close to the imagery of the *Buried Life*? I make the following conjecture: After years of doing Shared Reading, Sue is likely to be familiar with the common stock of poetry used by the Reader. One fine poem that has proved popular in reading groups is *The Way It Is* by William Stafford, in which a central motive is the 'thread you follow'. See William Stafford, *The Way It Is: New and Selected Poems* (Minneapolis, MN: Graywolf, 1998). I imagine Sue coming across this poem and finding that it captures her journey: she can see now that she has followed the thread, and because she held it she couldn't get lost. Thus, the 'deep thread of knowing' is not just a metaphor for an integrated life story, but, being deployed by her after being saved, it performatively connects for her the three life-changing events into a coherent story. It is the experience of the *Buried Life* that has opened her up to this knowledge.

that all along she has followed a thread. 'The Thou meets me through grace – it is not found by seeking,' says Buber.[37] But when grace has been experienced, you also know that it sought you; it brought you to a place you had always known.

---

[37] Martin Buber, *I and Thou*, trans. Ronald Gregor Smith (London: Bloomsbury Academic, 2013), 8.

Chapter Eight

READING BY HEART: LEXITHYMIA AND TRANSFORMATIVE AFFECTIVE PATTERNS

When reflecting on these five idiographs, relating them to each other and against the background of previous research and theoretical horizons presented in the introduction, what meaning can be appropriated from them? If, as stated in the section on methodology, essences are 'the web of ideal possibilities and relationships that constitute a particular domain of experience',[1] then what metanarrative can be woven from the discernible web of empirical-conceptual configurations? That is the question I will address in this final chapter by tracing and connecting three deep threads running through and interlacing the particular domain of Life-Changing Reading Experiences.

The process of a transformative reading experience, from its inception prior to the act of reading until its ultimate integration into the self-narrative of the reader, crystallises around certain phenomena. It is not a case of self-help reading, in which the reader has identified a problem, and then looks for an apt source that will provide a solution. Instead, what transpires is that, over and beyond the initial motivation for picking up the book – whether it was by obligation or serendipity, through titillation, after recommendation or by association with a pleasurable state – at some point it turns into an I–Thou encounter; at some point these readers unreservedly give themselves over to, and surrender to, the experience, and become fully involved, body, heart and mind. Furthermore, in this evolving and deepening devotional transaction, these readers are deeply moved. The experience of a panoply of feelings that traditionally have straddled aesthetic and religious domains – such as wonder, awe, tenderness, jubilation and faith – come into full awareness. When this happens, the expanded affect-consciousness allows for an altered sense of self in which the crisis can be resolved. Thus, in being moved new movement is created: that which was stuck is loosened, that which was frozen melts, that which was in the dark is brought into light and so on. Such transformations of the subject's sense of self does not mean that life becomes easier or free from suffering, but rather that, as the muddled, restrictive, unclear or shallow self-experience is given greater depth, clarity, connectedness and openness, a renewed vitality and sense of direction becomes available to the subject.

Hence, the threads to be described in the following are these: (i) the characteristics of the *mode of engagement* of these readers, which brings about (ii) realisations that are affectively experienced as a process of *being moved*. Thus, (iii) when a life-crisis – consisting

---

[1] Dermot Moran, *Introduction to Phenomenology* (London: Routledge, 2000), 108.

of a complex affective cluster experienced as stuckness, restriction, despair, confusion or isolation – is resolved through such a realisation, a qualitative change in self-concept becomes possible. These qualitative alterations of self-organisation/-experience/-understanding I have conceptualised as *alloioses*.

Mode of Engagement

It is through a particular mode of engagement that the transformative affective experiences are brought to life and realised. The principal aspects identified in the idiographic interpretations can be summarised as follows:

Esther describes a mode of engagement I have called *readerese*, where she is talking to and with the characters. Veronica describes a similar way of engagement, in which she urges Connie ahead. This engagement involves not only voicing, but also an interoceptive activity: feeling what the character is going through, and acting as if able to influence these feelings. An essential element of Veronica's mode of engagement with the novel is the visceral and a bodily form of knowing, in which she is gradually brought to a felt sense of awareness. I have called this mode of embodied cognition *enkinaesthetic*. Several of these readers engage in meditatively reading significant passages as 'holding-grounds' that enable a process of affective mentalisation – in this engagement the reader '*feels felt*' – that is a feeling of being held or embraced, allowing one space to find words for one's own subjective feelings. Janes' mode of engagement I described in terms of *metabolism*, as she employs metaphors of nourishment to describe her reading experience. Jane talks about a *hunger* for reading, and for the need to *digest* the truth revealed through *Shikasta*. The metaphor of digestion is also essential in Nina's recurrent transaction with the work, which I termed *palilexia*: a *deepening attunement* to the work through repeated readings allows her to integrate the subjective realities of both Ken and Nell. Sue's mode of engagement may be understood as a form of *synesis*, an interaffective attunement that lets a deeper understanding resonate in dyadic contemplation.

Readerese and Bi-Directional Empathy

What we see emerging here are different aspects that partly overlap each other and that point towards a larger configuration. How can we circle in the essence of this many-faceted mode of engagement? We are not looking for the common denominator of these modes. Rather, they are all partial designations of a more comprehensive pattern. What is evident about the modes of engagement identified in the life-changing reading experiences is that they all converge on what we may call the *bodily-affective* aspects of reading. *Readerese, feeling felt, enkinaesthesia, palilexia, metabolic reading* and *synesis*, in pointing to physical, kinaesthetic, affective, physiological, interoceptive and metabolic aspects of reading, all relate to embodied cognition as well as embodied affect in the transaction with the literary work. We may see them as related to the mode of engagement that Kuiken et al. identified as 'expressive enactment'. As explicated in the introductory chapter, Kuiken et al. define self-modifying feelings as a distinct level of feeling in relation to the literary text. It is marked by a particular approach to the text characterised by a combination of an absorptive trait and a situation of crisis. They specify three features that set expressive enactment apart from other modes: explicit description of feeling, blurred boundaries and reiterative modification of emergent affective theme. There is in all these five cases description of feeling and reiteration of an affective theme, and there is a blurring of boundary. The engagement takes place in a transitional space in which distinctions between reader and the imaginary other are suspended. When talking about a character, the reader is also talking about herself, and vice versa. For instance, as Nina says: 'I read myself into it.' A possible distinction from expressive enactment is that Kuiken et al. point to the hybridity of this mode: such reading focuses both on formal features and the affective content of the text. To what extent do my readers attend to formal features? Several of them specifically remarks on the style of the writer, but there is no explicit discussion of formal features as such. Even so, we cannot conclude that these readers do not read hybridically. Their modes of engagement share the properties of expressive enactment. However, the reading experiences of these readers do not necessarily follow a hermeneutical arc. It is not required that the reader be aware of, and clarify or explicate, all the ambiguities and polysemic aspects of a text in order to create meaning.

What is necessary, however, is that there is a process of *einfühlung*, an empathy with the imagined other taking place in a transitional space where the relation is dialogic. This empathy also allows for absorption and aesthetic enjoyment. Interestingly, aesthetic appreciation becomes not only a matter of *taste,* but also a matter of *digestion*. What is highly significant is that there is a two-way transport taking place: by moving towards and into the character, it is as if the reader at the same time is at the receiving end of empathy and compassion from the other. Empathy emerges as a *bi-directional process*.

For instance, Veronica discovers that she can do for herself what she does for Connie: empathise. And she can empathise with herself through taking the perspective of the mother coming back to life. This is the result of a refracted form of two-way empathy, and ties in with Vessel et al.'s observation that

> intense aesthetic experience can sometimes be thrillingly bidirectional: not only does the perceiver feel as if they understand the artwork, but there is a sense that the artwork 'understands the perceiver, expressing one's innermost thoughts, feelings or values'. Therefore, in aesthetic experience, unlike in self-referential emotions, one is 'not focused on appraisal but on a sense of understanding, gained insight and meaning'.[2]

Thus, *readerese* may be understood to imply not only an active capacity for expressive enactment, but also a passive capacity for receiving compassion, nourishment and empathy. In transitional space there is a double movement: *enkinaesthetically* moving towards and into the imaginary other, and *being moved* in return.

---

[2] Edward A. Vessel, G. Gabrielle Starr and Nava Rubin. 'Art Reaches within: Aesthetic Experience, the Self and the Default Mode Network'. *Frontiers in Neuroscience* 7, no. 258 (2013), 7.

Reading as Necessity: Contact and Nourishment

In addition to this bidirectional empathy, the qualities of the mode of engagement converge upon three metaphoric fields: contact, nourishment and sacred space.

The enkinaesthetic-visceral aspect is apparent in all the narratives. Esther says: 'As you read you shout out inside yourself: "No, no, no!"; "Stop being so bloody self-destructive!" [...] You care about the characters, and you address them and talk to them.' There is a clear interoceptive quality to this 'readerese' description. Veronica likes to 'cradle and hold' the book when she engages with the work: 'And if there's a particularly good passage I'll almost like stroke the page, haha, and obviously connect with it. [...] And for me when I'm reading, just the act of, I guess, sitting a certain way, or physically picking it up, the way that I physically hold myself, the physical process of turning the pages, makes me physically feel that I'm in it. The way that I can touch the page if something good happens, the way that I can sort of close it and turn it away from me.' Nina uses the metaphor of dancing to express this internally felt movement: 'It is like dancing, in a way, a particular way of moving. You are permitted to draw threads to yourself, but at the same time you are allowed to let yourself go, to dissolve into it, to dance with what comes.' Sue also employs musical metaphors: 'your whole being is going to, *sing* with it.' Also, her reading was not only affective but had a physiological component: 'Yeah, I think I probably did have a weep actually.' Jane stresses that knowledge has an affective component: 'I think that we are here *to know*. I don't mean intellectually, a lot of our knowing is in our gut, in our heart. You've already got your feelings, sometimes you just haven't got any language for them.'

Moreover, the metaphoric field of nourishment is also connected to *enkinaesthesia* or the *visceral*. In three of the narratives, the metaphor of eating is used. Jane talks of her reading motivation in terms of hunger. Veronica talks of digesting the experience: 'So, yeah, afterwards, when I was digesting it.' Esther expands on this to include the entire process of eating as a metaphor of the reading experience: 'It really is a form of dialogue, where you taste it, chew on it, digest it.' This lends confirmation to the finding reported by Usherwood and Toyne that the reading experience was described in terms of nourishment: 'When talking about the nourishment on offer through imaginative literature, several participants developed the eating metaphor.'[3]

On the one hand, literary reading is regarded as *contact*. To read is to be in intimate contact with someone, across time and space and cultural differences. Through processes of attunement and resonance, we feel touched, held, moved – and thus understood by this other subjectivity. According to Fonagy et al., 'the biological need to feel understood [...] takes precedence over almost all other goals'.[4] Such contact is not a substitute for physical closeness or social relation, but it is a unique need. When we feel understood,

---

[3] Bob Usherwood and Jackie Toyne, 'The Value and impact of reading imaginative literature', *Journal of Librarianship and Information Science* 34, no. 1 (2002): 39.
[4] Quoted in Diane Fosha, *The Transforming Power of Affect. A Model for Accelerated Change* (New York: Basic Books, 2000), 57.

and we feel 'seen', 'heard', 'moved', 'touched' or 'held', it opens up interior space for new ways of relating to ourselves and our feelings.

On the other hand, we conceive of literary reading as *nourishment*. Literature affords sustenance and food for thought and feeling. The process of attending to the work and creating meaning involves not just *tasting* the work, but also *digesting* it. Through *metabolism* we process the work and we are changed by it. There are spiritual needs as well as material needs. The self is sustained by both. These findings represent an important addition to cognitive approaches to the purposes of literary reading. Within cognitive approaches, the focus of attention is predominantly on *action*: on what the reader does during the act of reading. Consequently, there is a tendency to valorise literature as *useful*. For instance, in his work *Thinking with Literature*, Terence Cave uses metaphors such as *tools*, *vehicles*, *instruments*.[5] Reading by heart, on the other hand, is predominantly directed towards *passion:* what happens to the reader during engagement with the literary work. What comes to light then is an intuitive conception of literature not in terms of *use*, but in terms of spiritual *necessity*.

Reading and the Importance of a Sacred Space

Several of the other 16 readers interviewed talk of reading as providing a sacred space that must be protected. For instance, Camilla says of this sacred space: 'I need to protect that space, and it did feel uncomfortable thinking that I was going to talk about them. I maybe have a need for this holiness, too. A great reading experience is sacred, the space in which you become absorbed in the book. I feel a peaceful stillness inside.' Nina talks of needing external space in order to access the inner space: 'I seldom read on trains, for instance, or in public places. It is too existential a thing for that, because something happens when I read. It's a way of working through my own inner stuff. I want to be by myself. I need to be able to let myself go, to weep or whatever. I'll read for a while, and then something will happen inside me. And if I am surrounded by people, then that movement will not have enough space. So I have a very intimate relationship to books.' Sue says she wanted to protect her experience: 'No, well, it just felt so personal, I actually didn't want anyone to see or notice. I did feel a bit shocked, and I think I didn't really want to talk about it, because there was nobody there that I knew very well. It just felt very, I felt like it was, oh, that it was touching a really tender place. I felt quite protective with myself at the time.' They are all talking about a place or space inside. This 'place' is described as *holy and tender*. The discourse of the numinous meets the visceral-affective in this intimate space. It must be *protected* from intrusion by others or by one's own thoughts. Reading is an intimate experience that puts you in contact with the sacred and tender place inside. This intimate relationship with the book is different both from social relationships and therapeutic relations. In several of the other interviews not presented in the previous chapters, the readers indicate that the book provides a unique relationship that social relations cannot offer. For instance, Camilla says:

---

[5] Terence Cave, *Thinking with Literature*. (Oxford: Oxford University Press, 2016).

And there are very few other situations where you don't need to give something back if you want to receive solace. So if I came to you and said: 'Oh I feel absolutely terrible!' I would have had to explain what had happened, or why I felt that way. And then we, then I would have wallowed and got lost in the maze of my own thoughts. I do of course think that sometimes it can be healthy to talk about matters, but there are times when that is just experienced as adding to the confusion. And also, the sense that once something has been said, once it is out there, it cannot be retracted. It has a finality, you have stated what things are like. Whereas here, in the meeting with the text, you are set free: your experience is not distorted, your experience remains intact – and at the same time your reading is your experience of it.

This is seconded by Nina, who finds that in reading 'it is up to us to regulate the distance. We can come and go, and that's vital. […] it has its own unique value. If I only had people to relate to, I would end up very confused and depleted, and if I only had books I would of course get lonely.' Veronica distinguishes reading from the therapeutic relation:

> When you're in therapy, you're either being asked questions, which you then have to consider and think about and process, and you're maybe trying to juggle, is this the right answer? Is this really what I think? Are they going to judge me, or what? […] You are aware, even if they say that you're not, you are aware that you're very vulnerable and kind of giving things up that you're maybe not sure if that's even what you really think. Whereas with reading *The Winter's Tale*, it's almost like the kind of realisations that you make about yourself or your feelings, they rise up unannounced.

This understanding of the relationship with the work as being unique is related to the sacred space. In social and therapeutic relationships there is the risk of being judged, of having to explain ourselves and the obligation to take turns. In reading there is an experiential process that is not interrupted by such concerns – the inner sanctuary is protected and enlarged. The relationship with the work is therefore felt to be a form of contemplation. The temple must be protected, and it allows an experience that is separate from that of social interactions.

The mode of engagement converges on the bodily-affective experiences of internal movement, contact and nourishment on the one hand and on the tender, vulnerable and sacred space of contemplation on the other. In my interpretation of Jane, in discussing the hunger for spiritual nourishment, I referred to the reading practice of *Lectio Divina*. This mode of engagement with sacred texts combine precisely the *enkinaesthesia* of eating and digestion, with contemplation in and of the *holy* relationship to the source and the living word. As Ferguson remarks of medieval writers on reading, they

> conceive the activity of reading in alimentary metaphors; the reader 'tastes' the words of Scripture on the 'palate' of the heart, or indeed literally in the mouth as he or she pronounces them; one has then to 'chew' the text thoroughly and 'digest' it, that is so to say, proceed towards interpretation and personal appropriation.[6]

---

[6] Duncan Robertson, *The Medieval Experience of Reading. Cistercian Studies Series*, vol. 238 (Collegeville, MN: Liturgical Press, 2011), 31.

Lectio Divina was originally a ruminative form of medieval reading practice linking study and textual interpretation, where the reader, in an encounter with 'the living word' would listen to the sacred text 'as though it were spoken to one directly and personally', according to Duncan Robertson. This was a subjective form in reading, in contrast to the objective aim of biblical exegesis.[7] Robertson argues that *Lectio Divina* was a standard of medieval literary culture, and that it should be rediscovered by modern readers to restore 'a fullness of active, affective, intellectual and creative literary participation'.[8] He links it to reader-response theory, arguing that it can bring even the most hermetic text to life for the reader. Robertson claims that theories of reader-response have completely bypassed medieval practices. He says that, for instance, Tomkins, in her essay 'The Reader in History: The Changing Shape of Literary Response', 'skips blithely from Plato to the Renaissance without pause for the Middle Ages and without considering religious approaches. In the context of a discussion of reading, these omissions constitute a serious oversight.'[9]

In *Lectio Divina*, the reader is 'called upon to "listen to" the sacred text' in order to develop 'a true mutuality of response between the reader and the text'.[10] This listening is closely akin to the *synesis* described in the interpretation of Sue's attunement to the poem. It has the nature of a 'progressively deepening dialogue', just like the *palilexia* of Nina's engagement. To meditate on a text is to interiorise it and learn it by heart, like Esther did with *Episode*. Says Robertson: '*meditatio* chiefly means repetition, memorization and recitation. The term refers to the process of learning texts by heart.'[11] This process 'requires the participation of the whole body and the whole mind'.[12] In communication with the author, the text becomes the 'living word', and the reader feels 'as if they were his own utterances; and will certainly take them as aimed at himself'. One reads the words 'as though they were directed on one personally; they become the expressions of one's own experience. [...] one becomes not only a reader but their true and final author'.[13]

Lexithymia: Reading the Heart, Reading by Heart

This reading practice, neglected by reader-response approaches, closely mirrors that of our five readers. It cannot properly be called a *lectio divina*, in as much as they are not reading Scripture. But they are reading with their hearts, and in realising the meaning of the text, learning by heart. I therefore propose that *at the heart* of their reading experience, the *essence* of their mode of engagement, is a *reading by heart*. The synesis is a mode of understanding that is far deeper than the intellectual, and requires attunement and mutual resonance. Sue's is a heart-to-heart relation with Arnold's poem. Jane speaks

---

[7] Ibid., xiii.
[8] Ibid., 233.
[9] Ibid., 31.
[10] Ibid., xiii.
[11] Ibid., xiv.
[12] Ibid., 7.
[13] Ibid., 85.

of the feeling way of knowing: this is a knowing in one's heart. Nina and Esther have re-membered their texts and learned them by heart. Veronica is enabled to listen to her heart.

Furthermore, a life-crisis may be understood to be a crisis of the heart: The crisis of loss is the crisis of a broken heart. The resolution of conflict is to move from dis*cord* to con*cord*. The healing of the bruise happens through *thumos*, another word for heart. The resolution of a crisis of identity comes with finding the *courage*. The resolution of a faith crisis may be said to lead to a *credo*, another word related to heart. And when the lost pulse of feeling stirs again, this is connected to the *cardio*, the beating of the heart.

To read by heart means then both to be in a crisis, and to engage one's whole heart and mind in the reading. I propose to name this mode of engagement *lexithymia*. In psychopathology, 'alexithymia' is the name of a disorder. It describes problems in affect regulations, such as difficulties with recognising, processing and regulating emotions. The literal meaning of alexithymia is 'no words for feelings'. Alexithymic persons are thought to have a paucity of internal psychic structures for the awareness of and elaboration of affect. The alexithymia construct has been examined with regard to various aspects of emotional processing.[14] According to Nemiah et al., it is comprised of four components: (i) a difficulty in identifying feeling and distinguishing between feelings and the bodily sensations of emotional arousal, (ii) difficulty describing feeling to others, (iii) externally oriented cognitive style and (iv) constricted imaginal processes.[15] Others have introduced a fifth component: an incapacity or reduced ability to experience emotional feelings. Lexithymia is in these theories the normal manifestation of affect regulation, in other words simply the absence of alexithymia.[16] I propose instead that *lexithymia* be given a positive definition. It marks the capacity to identify and describe feelings, experience them and suffer them; increased imaginative capacity and a metacognitive style. Moreover, lexithymia is the capacity to engage the heart in contemplation. Thus, lexithymia involves the capacity for readerese, entering and establishing a sacred, transitional space in which the reader empathises enkinaesthetically with the imagined other, and receives empathy in return, experienced as vital contact (touched, held, embraced) and nourishment – the process of being moved.

Realisation through the Experience of Being Moved

The verb 'to realise' runs with striking frequency through the five narratives. And each reader explicitly or implicitly testifies to being deeply moved by the encounter with the

---

[14] Graeme J. Taylor, R. Michael Bagby and James D. A. Parker, *Disorders of Affect Regulations: Alexithymia in Medical and Psychiatric Illness* (Cambridge: Cambridge University Press, 1997).
[15] J. C. Nemiah, H. Freyberger and P. E. Sifneos, 'Alexithymia: A view of the Psychosomatic Process', in *Modern Trends in Psychosomatic Medicine*, vol. 3, ed. O. W. Hill (London: Butterworths, 1976), 430–39.
[16] Peter Paul Moormann, Bob Bermond, Harrie C. M. Vorst and Lea Rood, 'New Avenues in Alexithymia Research: The Creation of Alexithymia Types', in *Emotion Regulation, Conceptual and Clinical Issues*, ed. Johan Denollet, Ivan Nyklicek and Ad Vingerhoerts (New York: Springer, 2008), 27–42.

literary work. The realisations experienced are instances of being moved: realisation *comes to* the reader in a particular phenomenal way, and may be divided into the two temporal categories of *sudden* or *gradual* realisation. However, the realisations each have different affective and phenomenal qualities that the following concepts are meant to encompass.

Esther's encounter with the poem is experienced as a sudden, unexpected *revelation* through attending to a detail that is sensual and kinetic. It leads to a realisation of profound affective importance. Therefore it feels important to learn the poem by heart. Accordingly, I suggest that to *realise* something is to learn with, and in, and through the heart in a synthesis of cognitive insight and affective depth.

Veronica experiences a gradual emerging of a *crystallised felt sense* that involves metacognition and affect. This crystallisation comes about through the bi-directional empathic transport and enables her to realise her lack of self-compassion. Nina experiences a gradual form of realisation that may be regarded as a *transmuting internalisation*. With each reading new aspects of feeling emerge, until the 'Nell gaze' comes into full view and can be grasped. Hereby, she has strengthened the psychic structure necessary to embrace her identity.

Jane is "shocked and affected". There is an element of consternation as the view from above is taken up, and she comes to view her life from a larger vantage-point. I have termed this special form of the sublime, a process which unsettles and takes a long time to integrate, *ekpleksis*. Sue experiences resonance with the poem through a process of attunement between the song of the lyric and the song of the body. Also, she is surprised that this is possible. This double realisation is one of *wonder*.

These experiences are not discrete categories. Instead, they are differing qualitative aspects of the larger phenomenon of arriving at a deeply felt personal truth. I suggest that to realise something of deep personal relevance, through being moved, is what opens up for transformation of self.

The Paradox of Fiction and Being Moved

In philosophical aesthetics there is a notorious debate regarding what is known as 'Radford's Puzzle': 'The Paradox of Fiction'.[17] The essence of the puzzle is this: how can we be moved by Anna Karenina when we know that she does not really exist?[18] There have been various attempts to solve the puzzle.[19] But it seems that no one has put forth the Paradox of Fact: how we can know that a real person is suffering, yet not be moved?

Neuroscientific research into the imagery neurons of the human brain has established that the emotional brain does not distinguish between imagined and perceived

---

[17] Colin Radford and Michael Weston, 'How Can We Be Moved by the Fate of Anna Karenina?' *Proceedings of the Aristotelian Society* 49 (1975): 67–80.

[18] See Eva Dadlez, 'Ideal Presence: How Kames Solved the Problem of Fiction and Emotion', *Journal of Scottish Philosophy* 9, no. 1 (2011): 115–33. Doi: 10.3366/jsp.2011.0009.

[19] The most well-known and debated response to Radford's Puzzle is that of Kendall Walton, 'Spelunking, Simulation and Slime: On Being Moved by Fiction', in *Emotion and the Arts*, ed. M. Hjort and S. Laver (Oxford: Oxford University Press, 1997), 37–49.

experiences: "The emotional brain responds in essentially the same ways to imaginal experiences as to externally perceived experiences, as was demonstrated by Kreiman, Koch and Fried. Thus, for the emotional brain, the imaginal experiences during reenactment are real."[20] The implication of this finding, propose Ecker et al., is that 'new experiences that are imaginal can be effective for creating new neural circuits and new responses, because the emotional centers in the subcortex hardly distinguish between perceptions arising externally versus internally'.[21]

Vessel et al. have investigated the neural underpinnings of aesthetically moving experience, to find out why we are so influenced and moved by works of art. As they say, art at its best 'can feel strikingly personal' and 'intense aesthetic experience often carries with it a sense of intimacy, "belonging" and closeness with the artwork'.[22] Their approach is to look at what happens in those cases where the recipient has been deeply moved by what they see, isolating 'the neural dimensions of aesthetic *responses* as opposed to reactions to particular features of a given work of art'.[23] They found that there were 'strikingly higher response of frontal regions for artworks rated as the most aesthetically moving.'"[24] During and after the most moving experiences, self-referential mentation is activated in a different way, encompassing affective response and personal relevance. The most moving artworks 'produce a clearly differentiable pattern of signal, going beyond mere liking, to something more intense and personally profound'.[25] Thus, the most moving aesthetic experiences are felt to be personally relevant.

This finding from neuroaesthetics corroborates both Ross's and Kuiken et al.'s emphasis on self-implication in transformative reading experience. Self-relevance emerges as an integral aspect of intensely moving aesthetic experience and transformative expressive reading. Thus, the the phenomena of being deeply moved and of self-implication are concomitants that enable the experience of being changed.

In the Introduction I stated that in Aristotle's view of change, there are two kinds of change, *metabole and kinesis*. The kinesthetic refers not only to physical movement in space (locomotion) but also to qualitative visceral internal movement, *being moved*. Fuchs and Kochs have developed a theory of embodied affectivity. They regard emotions as the outcome of circular interactions between affective qualities in the environment and the subject's bodily resonance, which takes on kinesthetic qualities. They argue that there are four basic emotional movements: moving towards the other, moving the other towards oneself, moving the other away from oneself and moving oneself away from the other. These movements are connected to a bodily felt sense. Thus they maintain that emotions

---

[20] Bruce Ecker, Robin Ticic and Laurel Hulley, *Unlocking the Emotional Brain: Eliminating Symptoms at Their Roots Using Memory Reconsolidation* (New York: Routledge, 2012), 86.
[21] Ibid., 31.
[22] Edward A. Vessel, G. Gabrielle Starr and Nava Rubin, 'Art Reaches within: Aesthetic Experience, the Self and the Default Mode Network', *Frontiers in Neuroscience* 7, no. 258 (2013): 7.
[23] Edward A. Vessel, G. Gabrielle Starr and Nava Rubin, 'The Brain on Art: Intense Aesthetic Experience Activates the Default Mode Network', *Frontiers in Human Neuroscience* 6 (2012): 1.
[24] Ibid., 6.
[25] Ibid.

can be 'experienced as the directionality of one's potential movement, although this movement need not necessarily be realised in physical space; they are phenomena of lived space.'[26] These are active *moves*, but what about *being moved*?

In my view, there are two different kinds of affections: emotions and being moved. Emotion of course comes from ex + movere, to 'move out'. Emotions have an action component. Emotion 'ends' in movement. But being moved is also a process, an en + movere, to 'be moved in'. An internal movement that has no action tendency, but rather a contemplation tendency. Interestingly, this finds its counterpart in rhetoric. In a discussion of Heidegger's understanding of Aristotle and rhetoric, Daniel Gross argues that pathos, one of the three *pisteis* (forms of appeal) in rhetoric, involves an account of how people are being moved. Gross emphasises that 'pathe are not merely psychological emotions […]. Rather, the pathe indicate possible ways of being-moved that tie humans in a unique way to their embodiment.'[27] Is there no word for this being in-moved? I believe there is, and it is a word that originated within aesthetics. The word *empathy* literally designates precisely this em + movement. Empathy is thus the process of being moved. In my view, emotion and empathy are therefore complementary affective terms that belong to different realms (participant vs. witness) and have different ends (action vs. contemplation). What is extremely important about empathy is that the *einfühlung* into the other (whether it be living person, animate object or artistic image) moves us, and being moved, we return to ourselves somehow altered, experiencing affects such as awe, wonder, tenderness, self-empathy or self-compassion.

The psychologist Diane Fosha, who has developed an experiential psychotherapy grounded in transformational theory, emphasises the centrality of affect in transformative processes: 'Affects develop in the transitional space between self and other. There, they gain meaning and texture through being reflected by the self's other and enriched by complementary response.'[28] They become internalised and reflected in the psychic structure in the form of 'an internal affective holding environment'. Experiences of core affect, which is both an intrapsychic and interpersonal phenomenon, may lead to realisations that alter the self-concept. When we experience the safety to feel, in the absence of defences, core affective experiences, marked by 'a subjective, personally elaborated experience; some change in bodily state; and the release of an adaptive tendency',[29] may unfold. It is important to note that these need not involve any of the categorical emotions. Instead, they involve self and relational affective experiences. Fosha distinguishes between these thus: 'categorical emotions are the self's reactions to events; *self affective experiences* however, are the self's reading of the self, and *relational affective*

---

[26] Thomas Fuchs and Sabine C. Cock, 'Embodied Affectivity: On Moving and Being Moved', *Frontiers in Psychology* 5, no. 508 (2014): 4.

[27] Daniel M. Gross, 'Introduction: Being-Moved. The Pathos of Heidegger's Rhetorical Ontology', in *Heidegger and Rhetoric*, ed. Daniel M. Gross and Ansgar Kemmann (Albany: State University of New York Press, 2005), 26.

[28] Diane Fosha, *The Transforming Power of Affect: A Model for Accelerated Change* (New York: Basic Books, 2000), 22.

[29] Ibid., 15.

experiences are the self's reading of the emotional status of the relationship.' Thus, the so-called aesthetic emotions, which take place in a context of personal safety or disinterestedness, may in my view be better understood in terms of self and relational affective experiences.

According to Fosha, the processing of affective experiences to completion ushers in a 'core state'. In *core state*, the persons have a subjective sense of 'truth' and a heightened sense of authenticity and vitality. Core state phenomena culminates in the realisation of personal truth and strengthening of the individual's core self. In core state, persons experience a sense of expansion and liberation of the self, as well as openness to and capacity for deep contact and interrelatedness:

> The core state [...] refers to an altered state of openness and contact, where the individual is deeply in touch with essential aspects of his own experience. The core state is the internal affective holding environment generated by the self. In this state, core affective experience is intense, deeply felt, unequivocal, and declarative.[30]

There is the subjective experience of newness, purity, depth and 'truth'. One of the phenomenological qualities of such an experience is the feeling of tenderness. Etymologically, *tenderness* is related to attention, entertainment and sustenance. Perhaps this tenderness is a component in all experiences of being moved by literature.

Alloiosis: Qualitative Change from Crisis to Resolution

My idiographic interpretations revealed five different kinds of crises, and five kinds of resolutions that constitute qualitative changes in self-experience, and seem to be intrinsically connected. The different kinds of resolutions can be rendered thus:

Anagnorisis is the term for reconciliation through the recognition of the true being of the other, and the bond that unites.
Listening to the Heart: escaping from old strictures and regaining inner freedom through the ability to listen to one's felt sense.
Nostos: achieving self-identity, the confluence of inner self and outer role.
Metanoia: Shifting from one philosophical framework/worldview to a more comprehensive one; thereby experiencing a conversion to conjunctive faith.
Anamnesis: Recovering from a loss of vitality to remember a dead or lost part of self.

Resolution can be conceptualised as the final stage of a process, the culmination of having integrated the realisation that was achieved through being moved as a result of the readerese mode of engagement. I have chosen the term resolution for this end-state because, in addition to the meaning 'solving or ending difficulty' it carries other important implications: it signifies the process of reducing things into simpler forms; a determination to hold firm to a conviction; and to show things clearly and with great

---

[30] Ibid., 20–21.

detail. It is only retroactively, after having lived through the experience, that the reader can clearly conceptualise the life-crisis and its resolution.

Crises

In comparing different crises, I found that we may operate with three broad kinds: developmental, situational and existential (inner conflicts related to things such as life purpose, direction and spirituality) crises. The crises described in the narratives correspond to this model. Esther's story represents a situational/relational crisis of conflict. Furthermore, there are two developmental/psychodynamic crises: Nina's represents an identity crisis, Veronica's a crisis of separation, related to the attachment system. And finally there are two kinds of spiritual crises: Jane's crisis of meaning/worldview and Sue's crisis of depression or loss of soul/vitality. If we complement this list with another prominent and inevitable life-crisis, as exemplified in Camilla's story, that of loss of a significant other, we arrive at the following structure of crises:

> *Interpersonal/situational*: conflict and loss/bereavement
>
> *Developmental/psychodynamic*: identity diffusion and attachment-related wounds
>
> *Spiritual/existential*: faith/life-philosophy and depression/loss of vitality

In each crisis there is a complex configuration of various affects and cognitions to be worked out and lived through.

Complex Affective Configurations

The neuropsychologist Panksepp regards emotions as evolutionary adaptive programmes. By researching the phylogenetic development of the brain, he has developed a model for how we can understand fundamental primary affective systems. These systems have a definite neurological substrate on which complex emotional processes are based. Panksepp has identified seven different affective systems, all related to how we act to solve problems in relation to our environment, and connected through complex forms of co-activation. The seeking system drives us to explore and master our surroundings. The fear system has developed to help the organism predict and handle dangers. The pleasure system is primarily tied to sexuality. The care system has evolved in order for humans and animals to look after their offspring and is the foundation of our social orientation. The grief system functions to restore contact with caregivers in situations of separation. It produces pain upon separation, well-being when there is contact. The play system has evolved to have two main functions: preparing the child for adult life, and to co-operate with other systems in creating social bonds. The rage system primarily serves to make other beings act in accordance with one's needs and desires. Whereas anger, according to Panksepp, is a secondary state, rage protects what is fundamentally important for the organism.[31] It ties emotions to action tendencies, and to

---

[31] Jaak Panksepp, *Affective Neuroscience: The Foundations of Human and Animal Emotions* (New York: Oxford University Press, 1998).

concrete challenges in the environment. Panksepp's systems are located in the brain. In the Darwinistic approaches to literature, these evolutionary adaptive programmes are related to the function of literature as adaptivity. However, this approach tends to privilege realistic fiction, which comes closest to representing the problems and situations these programmes are designed to solve. Like Ekman's theory of basic emotions, there is a finite number to the systems. They both converge on the number seven. Both theories posit that the basic emotions are universal. As Panksepp says, 'these emotions appear to be universal and to be associated with specific neuroendocrine patterns and brain sites [...]'.[32] And Daniel Siegel, with reference to Ekman's theory, says that each of the seven 'categorical emotions' reveals 'the way in which we create common pathways of neural firing that link together states of activation into a functional whole we call an emotional state of mind'.[33] Ekman's theory pertains to the communication aspect of emotions: what we convey to other people. We thus have two systems which have radically different *loci*, the human brain and the human (inter-) face. But they both regard emotions as discrete entities. The view of evolutionary theorists that emotions are universal, hardwired psycho-affective programmes that solve ancient and recurrent threats to our survival[34] is criticised by social constructionists, who view emotions as socially learned responses constructed in culturally embedded discourses governed by social concerns.[35] In their view, cultures over time create new kinds of responses to new kinds of situations. Although these contrasting biological and social approaches conceive of the source of emotions in markedly different ways, both ascribe important relational functions to emotion. And both assume that emotions help us solve many of the basic problems of social life. A view of emotions as discrete and as constructive responses to specific causes is too simple, however. Greenberg argues that we rarely encounter emotions in pure form, 'but rather observe combinations or sequences such as fear of anger or a blend of sadness and shame. The nature of the combinations of emotions is complex, as all emotions have, to varying degrees, components of other emotions within them.'[36] I believe that starting out from the emotions, or the neuropsychological programmes, occludes the lived experiences of the complex situations in which people find themselves embedded. Human beings do not always solve problems or adapt to situations by acting. We also suffer. Thus, the conceptualisation of emotion as adaptation to a problematic situation does not address the complexities of the life-crises. A different approach to understanding emotion is provided by Cochran and Claspell, an approach which they call 'dramaturgical':

---

[32] Ibid., 260.
[33] Daniel J. Siegel, 'Emotion as Integration: A Possible Answer to the Question, What Is Emotion?', in *The Healing Power of Emotion: Affective Neuroscience, Development and Clinical Practice*, ed. Diana Fosha, Daniel J. Siegel and Marion Solomon (New York: W.W. Norton, 2009), 161.
[34] John Tooby and Leda Cosmides, 'The Past Explains the Present: Emotional Adaptations and the Structure of Ancestral Environments', *Ethology and Sociobiology* 11, no. 4–5 (1990): 375–424.
[35] See, for instance, Catherine Lutz and Geoffrey M. White, 'The Anthropology of Emotions', *Annual Review of Anthropology* 15 (1986): 405–36; Lisa Feldman Barrett. *How Emotions Are Made: The Secret Life of the Brain.* (New York: Pan Books, 2017).
[36] Leslie S. Greenberg and René H. Rhodes, 'Emotion in the Change Process', in *How People Change: Inside and Outside Therapy,* ed. Rebecca C. Curtis and George Stricker (New York: Plenum, 1991), 50.

> It seems clear that what endures over time is not arousal. [...] What seems capable of enduring are meanings. For example, beliefs and judgments endure, but not any kind of belief or judgment will do, for emotions are nothing if not dramatic. If it is meaning that endures, it must be a particular kind of meaning, what is meaningful rather than, for instance, just referential. ... The underlying thesis of this book is that meanings are organized into a dramatic structure, a story. To experience a certain emotion is to be involved in a particular type of life drama.[37]

They are interested in states and processes that are played out over long time periods. They argue that certain emotions are dramatic and that therefore they are processual and involve meanings which are structured like dramas. They are interested not just in emotions as transient states in response to concrete incidents. There are experiences which we undergo or suffer, and which involve meaning-making and a complex pattern of interaction of emotions, or that leave us stuck. Thus, we appear to have two kinds of 'programmes': the simple configuration of episode-emotion-adaptation, and the complex one of crisis-poeisis-resolution. To understand our affective responses to works of literature is therefore not so much about concrete emotions being aroused, as about seeing the reader as already immersed in a complex of feelings and affects that may sometimes constitute a crisis, other times more simply a 'mood'. Although I do not concur with Cochran and Caspell in describing such long-term affectively coloured states as emotions, I find it interesting that they use the term 'dramatic'. Whereas emotions are brought about through specific events that we may regard as *episodes*; there are long-lasting affects that have the structure of a drama. In thematising such experiences they fall back on fundamental aesthetic-poetic categories. Are there, then, perhaps other long-lasting affective situations that unfold more like epic or lyric plots?

A crisis is a forking path: it may lead to resolution and the creation of meaning, or it may lead to self-fragmentation, regression, denial or loss of meaning. A crisis is not a *problem*, a 'throwing-before-me', that I can solve strategically. To get through a crisis, I depend on an encounter with grace or mercy, taking place in a sacred, transitional space – for which a catalyst is needed. Living through such crises depends less on activity than passivity. It is through being moved that one finds the capacity to suffer the crisis. A theory of the complex patterns of crisis-catalyst-resolution would therefore, like Panksepp's and Ekman's theories, attempt to determine fundamental affective responses, but unlike theirs start out from the crises in which people are embedded and the dramatically patterned affective processes which they undergo in resolving these crises. My investigation, in identifying a set of crises and their resolutions, point to the possibility of the transformation of affects being related to genres such as the dramatic, the epic and the lyric, and to aesthetic categories such as catharsis and the sublime. Is it possible that each crisis corresponds not only to a particular kind of change, but also to a particular kind of genre and a particular kind of affective category, and that each of these may be said to constitute fundamental *transformative affective patterns*?

---

[37] Larry Cochran and Emily Claspell, *The Meaning of Grief: A Dramaturgical Approach to Understanding Emotion* (New York: Greenwood, 1987), 14.

Pathemata and Transformative Affective Patterns

Two of the foundational concepts of literary history and philosophical aesthetics, Aristotle's *katharsis* and Longinus's *hypsos,* are both connected to *the experience of being moved.* Aristotle's definition of tragedy in his *Poetics* is famous:

> Tragedy, then, is imitation (*mimesis*) of a serious and complete action (*praxis*) possessing magnitude […] accomplishing through (*dia*) pity and fear the purification (*katharsis*) of such passions (*pathemata*).[38]

Much of the critical discussion of this passage has revolved around *mimesis* and *katharsis*, two of the foundational concepts of Western literary history. Less attention has been granted to the term *pathemata*, and its meanings. Some translations render it 'emotions'. According to the Aristotelian scholar Else, it can also mean ' "distressing experiences" or "incidents"', and Aristotle reputedly used it as synonymous with *pathos*.[39] However, it also means 'that which befalls one', 'undergoing an experience' and 'the capacity to experience strong emotions'.[40] Moreover, rendering *praxis* as 'action' is also problematic, as *praxis* involves 'passion' just as much as action. And the preposition *dia*, usually rendered 'through', is ambiguous as it could mean 'in the course of' as well as 'by means of'. I suggest that the complex affective configurations, consisting of conflicting feelings, defences, beliefs and wishes, correspond to the term *pathemata*. If so, then the process of catharsis would be one possible means of creating resolution of a life-crisis. Through connecting pathemata to resolutions via such aesthetic categories and poetic genres, a theory of transformative affective patterns would emerge.

A noteworthy fact is that in the relation of philosophy to rhetoric, two of the three forms of *pisteis*, ethos and logos, have foundational status with regard to ethics, logic and epistemology. But in relation to *pathos*, we have no such fundamental philosophy, as pathos is partly reduced to the study of illness – pathology – and partly subsumed under ethics (where it is subordinated to rationality). The later emergence of aesthetics and of psychology treats emotion as a primary affective term. There is as yet no proper science of that dimension of affection which encompasses experiences of being moved, and of different pathemata, in relation to poetics and aesthetics. A systematic consideration of the relationships between experiences of being moved in relation to life-crises, realisations and resolutions would have to encompass literary archegenres and affective processes other than just *catharsis* and *ekstasis*.

Gerard Genette, in his mapping of the historical trajectory of originary genres and their relationships, seems to indicate an opening for this. In concluding that 'the major imaginable parametres of the generic system come down to three kinds of "constants"

---

[38] Aristotle, *Poetics*, trans. Malcolm Heath (London: Penguin), 10.
[39] Gerald F. Else, *Aristotle's Poetics: The Argument* (Cambridge, MA: Harvard University Press, 1963), 229.
[40] See http://biblehub.com/str/greek/3804.htm. Accessed 7 January 2018.

(thematic, modal and formal)'[41] he still holds the possibility open for another foundation. As Genette himself points out, in Aristotle's definition of tragedy he finds it insufficient to use the parametres of theme, mode and form. Accordingly, he also includes the affective category of catharsis. Interestingly, Genette asserts,

> I by no means intend to deny to literary genres any sort of 'natural' and transhistorical foundation. On the contrary, to me another obvious (albeit vague) fact is the presence of an existential attitude, of an 'anthropological structure' [...], of a 'mental disposition' [...], of an 'imaginative design' or of a 'feeling' that is properly epical, lyrical, dramatic – but also tragic, comic, elegiac, fantastic, romantic etc. – whose nature, origin, continued existence [...] are still to be studied.[42]

If one started from the premise that literature is mankind's responses to universal life-crises, then a poetics could be grounded in patterns of affective experiences rather than in a study of the sign. That would require further empirical investigations in order to map universal life-crises and develop phenomenological descriptions of the corresponding *pathemata* and their resolutions, as well as theoretical elaborations of genres and aesthetic affective categories. In a time of crisis for literary studies and the humanities, such a transdisciplinary explorative endeavour could prove worth undertaking, bringing together affective studies, aesthetics, poetics and phenomenology in an attempt to listen to ordinary readers' experiences.

Art for Heart's Sake

The aim of this investigation has been to *listen carefully* to those who have experienced, profoundly, a transformative engagement with a work of imaginative literature. Accordingly, the principal thrust and main part of this dissertation is devoted to the full presentation of the individual narratives of life-changing reading experiences, and to interpreting these ideographically to preserve the unique nature of the encounter and to understand and appropriate their meaning. The transformative reading experiences of the participants in this study have themselves undergone many turns: the reading experience is transformed in memory, the remembrance in the interview, the dialogue in the recording, the record in the transcription, the transcript in the textual editing, the text in being interpreted and, finally, the interpretation in the act of comparison and appropriation. Each of the transformations can be regarded as part of a distillation process: at journey's end is the essence of the life-changing fiction-reading experience (LCFRE). Hence, the knowledge arrived at is not a reconstruction of what *really* happened, but the carrying forth of *ideal* meaning.

Essentially, such *intimate reading* is a dialogic process where different understandings, vocabularies and traditions interpenetrate and serve to intermediate between the horizon of the researcher and the participants' voices. To bring out the emerging properties of these intimations, I have attempted to sustain a dialogue between the readers' own

---

[41] Ibid., 78.
[42] Ibid., 67–68.

narratives and modern psychological research on the one hand, and classical concepts belonging to a (cloudy) horizon of transformation and affect on the other. There is no one discourse, theory or conceptual field that 'covers' these readers' experiences. The interpretations are 'dialogic' also in the sense that not only do the classical and psychological terms throw light on the readers' experiential accounts, but, importantly, the readers' accounts also enable a deeper, concrete and specific understanding of the classical tradition's affective language. This hermeneutic approach may thus lead to a renewed engagement with the classical literary tradition's language of affection.

This inquiry has sprung out of a quest for the restoration of art for heart's sake, a return of literature to its home in the feeling life of human beings. This is its *nostos*: that imaginative literature is the language of the heart. To engage with this language is to be moved, deeply. Reading by heart follows its own arc from readerese, via being moved by *someone* in the work, to the core state of deepened affect consciousness: through subjecting oneself to the imaginative world, and, as Philip Davis writes of the experience of reading, 'taking books personally to such a depth inside, that you no longer have a merely secure idea of self and relevance to self, but a deeper exploratory sense of a reality somehow finding unexpected relations and echoes in you'.[43] From such deep impressions new configurations of self may be created, as the crisis can be resolved and given meaning within an enlarged self-understanding. In a sacred, transitional space, I as reader experience empathy and compassion for an imagined other, which in turn reflexively allows me to experience compassion for myself. And from this place of self-compassion I may experience genuine compassion for other people.

- To sum up, then, literature has saved your life?
- Yes, it has, in a way. I would say so. In a way. Because I think that if I hadn't read so much, my foundation would have been smaller and less solid. I would have had a poorer understanding of life. I am forever in debt to libraries, for giving me access to all these books.

---

[43] Philip Davis, *The Experience of Reading* (London: Routledge, 1992), xvi, as quoted in the Introduction to this dissertation.

BIBLIOGRAPHY

Allport, Gordon W. *Personality: A Psychological Interpretation*. New York: Holt, 1937.
Angus, Lynne E., and Leslie S. Greenberg. *Working with Narrative in Emotion-Focused Therapy. Changing Stories, Healing Lives*. Washington, DC: American Psychological Association, 2011.
Appleyard, J. A. *Becoming a Reader. The Experience of Fiction from Childhood to Adulthood*. Cambridge: Cambridge University Press, 1991.
Aristotle, *Poetics*, translated by Malcolm Heath. London: Penguin, 1996.
Arnold, Matthew. *Complete Poetical Works*. Hastings: Delphi Classics, 2013.
Baldwin, Matthew, and Mark J. Landau. 'Exploring Nostalgia's Influence on Psychological Growth'. *Self and Identity* 13, no. 2 (2014): 162–77.
Banai, Erez, Mario Mikulincer and Phillip R. Shaver. '"Selfobject" Needs in Kohut's Self Psychology. Links with Attachment, Self-Cohesion, Affect Regulation, and Adjustment'. *Psychoanalytic Psychology* 22, no. 2 (2005): 224–60.
Bandura, Albert. 'Self-Efficacy: Toward a Unifying Theory of Behavioral Change'. *Psychological Review* 84, no. 2 (1977): 191–215.
Barrett, Lisa Feldman. *How Emotions Are Made: The Secret Life of the Brain*. New York: Pan Books, 2017.
Batcho, Krystine. 'Nostalgia: The Bittersweet History of a Psychological Concept'. *History of Psychology* 16, no. 3 (2013): 165–76.
Beach, Stephen R. H., and Nadir Amir. 'Is Depression Taxonic, Dimensional or Both?'. *Journal of Abnormal Psychology* 112, no. 2 (2003): 228–36.
Berman, Steven L., and Marilyn J. Montgomery. 'Problematic Identity Processes: The Role of Identity Distress'. *Identity. An International Journey of Theory and Research* 14, no. 4 (2014): 241–45.
Beyers, Wim, and Koen Luyckx. 'Ruminative Exploration and Reconsideration of Commitment as Risk Factors for Suboptimal Identity Development in Adolescence and Emerging Adulthood'. *Journal of Adolescence* 47 (2016): 169–78.
Bidney, Martin. *Patterns of Epiphany: From Wordsworth to Tolstoy, Pater and Barrett Browning*. Carbondale: Southern Illinois University Press. 1997.
Billington, Josie. *Is Literature Healthy?* Oxford: Oxford University Press, 2016.
Bishop, Sue Marquis, and Gary M. Ingersoll. 'Effects of Marital Conflict and Family Structure on the Self-Concepts of Pre- and Early Adolescents'. *Journal of Youth and Adolescence* 18, no. 1 (1989): 25–38.
Bjørneboe, Jens. *The Silence*, translated by Esther Greenleaf Mürer. Chester Springs, PA: Dufour Editions, 2000.
Blyton, Enid. *Adventures of the Wishing-Chair*. London: Hodder, 2015.
Bonifazi, Anna. 'Inquiring into Nostos and Its Cognates'. *American Journal of Philology* 130, no. 4 (2009): 481–510.
Booker, Christopher. *The Seven Basic Plots: Why We Tell Stories*. London: Bloomsbury Press, 2004.
Boym, Svetlana. *The Future of Nostalgia*. New York: Basic Books, 2001.
Bryman, Alan. *Social Research Methods*. 3rd edn. Oxford: Oxford University Press, 2008.
Buber, Martin. *The Knowledge of Man*. New York: Harper and Row, 1965.
Buber, Martin. *I and Thou*, translated by Ronald Gregor Smith. London: Bloomsbury Academic, 2013.

Bukowski, Charles. *The Last Night of the Earth Poems*. New York: Ecco, 1992.
Caplan, Gerald. *Prevention of Mental Health Disorders in Children*. New York: Basic Books, 1961.
Caplan, Gerald. *An Approach to Community Mental Health*. London: Tavistock, 1961.
Carlsson, Johanna, Maria Wängquist and Ann Frisén. 'Life on Hold: Staying in Identity Diffusion in the Late Twenties'. *Journal of Adolescence* 47 (2016): 220–29.
Carroll, William C. *The Metamorphoses of Shakespearean Comedy*. Princeton, NJ: Princeton University Press, 1985.
Caswell, Caroline P. *A Study of Thumos in Early Greek Epic*. Leiden: E.J. Brill, 1990.
Cave, Terence. *Thinking with Literature*. Oxford: Oxford University Press, 2016.
Clandinin, D. Jean. *Handbook of Narrative Inquiry: Mapping a Methodology*. London: Sage, 2007.
Clark, Raymond T. *Catabasis: Vergil and the Wisdom Tradition*. Amsterdam: Grüner, 1981.
Cochran, Larry, and Emily Claspell. *The Meaning of Grief: A Dramaturgical Approach to Understanding Emotion*. New York: Greenwood Press, 1987.
Cohen, Laura J. 'Phenomenology of Therapeutic Reading with Implications for Research and Practice of Bibliotherapy'. *Arts in Psychotherapy* 21, no. 1 (1994): 37–44.
Colaizzi, Paul F. 'Psychological Research as the Phenomenologist Views It'. In *Existential-Phenomenological Alternatives for Psychology*, edited by Ronald S. Valle and Mark King, 48–71. Oxford: Oxford University Press, 1978.
Cooper, Robin P., Jane Abraham, Sheryl Berman and Margaret Staska. 'The Development of Infant's Preference for Motherese'. *Infant Behavior and Development* 20, no. 4 (1997): 477–88.
Cova, Florian, and Julien A. Deonna. 'Being Moved'. *Philosophical Studies* 169, no. 3 (2013): 447–66.
Cummings, E. Mark, and Patrick T. Davies. *Children and Marital Conflict*. New York: Guilford Press, 1994.
Czarniawska, Barbara. *Narratives in Social Science Research*. London: Sage, 2006.
Dadlez, Eva. 'Ideal Presence: How Kames Solved the Problem of Fiction and Emotion'. *Journal of Scottish Philosophy* 9, no. 1 (2011): 115–33.
Danielsson, Louise, and Susanne Rosberg. 'Depression Embodied: An Ambiguous Striving against Fading'. *Scandinavian Journal of Caring Sciences* 29, no. 3 (2015): 501–509.
Danielsson, Louise, and Susanne Rosberg. 'Opening toward Life: Experiences of Basic Body Awareness Therapy in Persons with Major Depression'. *International Journal of Qualitative Studies on Health and Well-Being* 10, no. 1 (2015): 1–13.
Davis, Philip. *The Experience of Reading*. London: Routledge, 1992.
Davis, Philip. *Reading and the Reader*. Oxford: Oxford University Press, 2013.
Dempsey, Nicholas P. 'Stimulated Recall Interviews in Ethnography'. *Qualitative Sociology* 33 (2010): 349–67.
de Spinoza, Benedict. *Ethics*, translated by Edwin Curley. London: Penguin, 1996.
Dixon, Thomas. *From Passions to Emotions: The Creation of a Secular Psychological Category*. Cambridge: Cambridge University Press, 2009.
Duras, Marguerite. *The Lover*, translated by Barbara Bray. London: Harper Perennial, 2006.
Ecker, Bruce, Robin Ticic and Laurel Hulley. *Unlocking the Emotional Brain: Eliminating Symptoms at Their Roots Using Memory Reconsolidation*. New York: Routledge, 2012.
Ekman, Paul. *Emotions Revealed*. London: Phoenix, 2003.
Eliot, George. *The George Eliot Letters*, vol. 5, edited by Gordon S. Haight. New Haven: Yale University Press, 1955.
Ellroy, James. *The Black Dahlia*. London: Windmill Books, 2011.
Else, Gerald F. *Aristotle's Poetics: The Argument*. Cambridge, MA: Harvard University Press, 1963.
Erikson, Erik H. *Identity: Youth and Crisis*. New York: Norton, 1968.
Falconer, Rachel. *Hell in Contemporary Literature: Western Descent Narratives since 1945*. Edinburgh: Edinburgh University Press, 2005.
Felski, Rita. "'Context Stinks!'" *New Literary History* 42, no. 4 (2011): 573–91.
Felski, Rita. *Uses of Literature*. Malden, MA: Blackwell, 2009.

Fernald, Anne. 'Four-Month-Old Infants Prefer to Listen to Motherese'. *Infant Behavior and Development* 8, no. 2 (1985): 181–95.
Feuerbach, Ludwig. *The Essence of Christianity*, translated by Marian Evans (George Eliot). Project Gutenberg. London: Kegan Paul, 1890.
Findlay, Edward F. *Caring for the Soul in the Postmodern Age: Politics and Phenomenology in the Thought of Jan Patocka*. Albany: State University of New York Press, 2002.
Fletcher, Judith. 'The Catabasis of Mattie Ross in the Coen's True Grit'. *Classical World* 107, no. 2 (2014): 237–54.
Flett, Gordon L., and Paul L. Hewitt. *Perfectionism: Theory, Research and Treatment*. Washington, DC: American Psychological Association, 2002.
Fosha, Diane. *The Transforming Power of Affect: A Model for Accelerated Change*. New York: Basic Books, 2000.
Fowler, James W. *Stages of Faith: The Psychology of Human Development and the Quest for Meaning*. San Francisco, CA: Harper & Row, 1981.
Frye, Northrop. *The Anatomy of Criticism: Four Essays*. Princeton, NJ: Princeton University Press, 2000.
Fuchs, Thomas. 'Depression, Intercorporeality, and Interaffectivity'. *Journal of Consciousness Studies* 20, no. 7–8 (2013): 219–38.
Fuchs, Thomas, and Sabine C. Cock. 'Embodied Affectivity: On Moving and Being Moved'. *Frontiers in Psychology* 5, no. 508 (2014): 1–12.
Gadamer, Hans-Georg. 'The Hermeneutics of Suspicion'. *Man and World* 17 (1984): 313–23.
Gadamer, Hans-Georg. *Truth and Method*, 2nd edn, translated by Joel Weinsheimer and Donald G. Marshall. New York: Continuum, 2003.
Gallese, Vittorio, Morris N. Eagle and Paolo Migone. 'Intentional Attunement: Mirror Neurons and the Neural Underpinnings of Interpersonal Relations'. *Journal of the American Psychoanalytic Association* 55, no. 1 (2007): 131–76.
Gendlin, Eugene T. 'The Client's Client: The Edge of Awareness'. In *Client-Centered Therapy and the Person-Centered Approach: New Directions in Theory, Research and Practice*, edited by R. L. Levan and J. M. Shlien, 76–107. New York: Praeger, 1984.
Gendlin, Eugene T. 'The Primacy of the Body, not the Primacy of Perception'. *Man and World* 25, no. 3–4 (1992): 341–55.
Gendlin, Eugene T. *Focusing*. London: Rider, 2003.
Genette, Gerard. *Narrative Discourse: An Essay in Method*, translated by Jane E. Lewin. Ithaca, NY: Cornell University Press, 1980.
Genette, Gerard. *The Architext: An Introduction*, translated by Jane E. Lewin. Berkeley: University of California Press, 1992.
Gottman, John. 'An Agenda for Marital Therapy'. In *The Heart of the Matter: Perspectives on Emotion in Marital Therapy*, edited by Susan M. Johnson and Leslie S. Greenberg, 259–96. New York: Brunner/Mazel, 1994.
Greenberg, Leslie S. *Emotion-Focused Therapy*. Theories of Psychotherapy Series. Washington, DC: American Psychological Association, 2011.
Greenberg, Leslie S., and René H. Rhodes. 'Emotion in the Change Process'. In *How People Change: Inside and Outside Therapy*, edited by Rebecca C. Curtis and George Stricker, 39–58. New York: Plenum Press, 1991.
Greenberg, Leslie S., and Rhonda N. Goldman. *Emotion-Focused Couples Therapy: The Dynamics of Emotion, Love and Power*. Washington, DC: American Psychological Association, 2008.
Gross, Daniel M. 'Introduction: Being-Moved. The Pathos of Heidegger's Rhetorical Ontology'. In *Heidegger and Rhetoric*, edited by Daniel M. Gross and Ansgar Kemmann, 1–46. Albany: State University of New York Press, 2005.
Grych, John H., and Frank D. Fincham. 'Marital Conflict and Children's Adjustment: A Cognitive-Contextual Framework'. *Psychological Bulletin* 108, no. 2 (1990): 267–90.
Gubrium, Jaber F., and James A. Holstein. *Analysing Narrative Reality*. London: Sage, 2009.

Hadot, Pierre. *Philosophy as a Way of Life: Spiritual Exercises from Socrates to Foucault*, translated by Michael Chase. Oxford: Blackwell, 1995.
Hadot, Pierre. *What Is Ancient Philosophy?*, translated by Michael Chase. Cambridge, MA: Harvard University Press, 2002.
Hagerup, Inger. *Samlede dikt*. Oslo: Aschehoug, 2015.
Haidt, Jonathan. *The Happiness Hypothesis: Finding Modern Truth in Ancient Wisdom*. New York: Basic Books, 2006.
Harris, Russ. *ACT Made Simple*. Oakland, CA: New Harbinger, 2009.
Heidegger, Martin. *The Fundamental Concepts of Metaphysics: World, Finitude, Solitude*, translated by William McNeill and Nicholas Walker. Bloomington: Indiana University Press, 1995.
Hendry, Irene. 'Joyce's Epiphanies'. *Sewanee Review* 54, no. 3 (1946): 449–67.
Hepper, Erika G., Timothy D. Ritchie, Constantine Sedikides and Tim Wildschut. 'Odyssey's End: Lay Conceptions of Nostalgia Reflect Its Original Homeric Meaning'. *Emotion* 12 (2012): 102–19.
Holdaway, Gervase. *The Oblate Life*. Norwich: Canterbury Press, 2008.
Holland, Norman N. *5 Readers Reading*. New Haven, CT: Yale University Press, 1975.
James, Richard K., and Burl E. Gilliland. *Crisis Intervention Strategies*. Pacific Grove, PA: Brook/Cole, 2001.
James, William. *The Varieties of Religious Experience: A Study in Human Nature*, edited by Martin E. Marty. London: Penguin, 1982.
Jauss, Hans Robert. *Aesthetic Experience and Literary Hermeneutics: Theory and History of Literature*, vol. 3, translated by Michael Shaw. Minneapolis: University of Minnesota Press, 1982.
Johnson, Susan. 'Extravagant Emotion. Understanding and Transforming Love Relationships in Emotionally Focused Therapy'. In *The Healing Power of Emotion: Affective Neuroscience, Development and Clinical Practice*, edited by Diana Fosha, Daniel J. Siegel and Marion F. Solomon, 257–79. New York: W.W. Norton, 2009.
Kelly, Rachel. *Black Rainbow: How Words Healed Me – My Journey through Depression*. London: Yellow Kite Books, 2014.
Kilbourne, Brock, and James T. Richardson. 'Paradigm Conflict, Types of Conversion, and Conversion Theories'. *Sociological Analysis* 50, no. 1 (1989): 1–22.
Kneisl, Carol R., and E. Riley. 'Crisis Intervention'. In *Psychiatric Nursing*, edited by H. Wilson and Carol R. Kneisl, 5th edn, 711–31. Menlo Park, CA: Addison and Wesley, 1996.
Kohut, Heinz. *The Restoration of the Self*. Madison, CT: International Universities Press, 1977.
Kohut, Heinz. *Self Psychology and the Humanities: Reflections on a New Psychoanalytic Approach*. New York: W.W. Norton, 1985.
Koziak, Barbara. 'Homeric Thumos: The Early History of Gender, Emotion, and Politics'. *Journal of Politics* 61, no. 4 (1999): 1068–91.
Kroger, Jane, Monica Martinussen and James E. Marcia. 'Identity Status Change during Adolescence and Young Adulthood: A Meta-Analysis'. *Journal of Adolescence* 33, no. 5 (2010): 683–98.
Kuiken, Don, David S. Miall and Shelley Sikora. 'Forms of Self-Implication in Literary Reading'. *Poetics Today* 25, no. 2 (2004): 171–203.
Kuiken, Don, Leah Phillips, Michelle Gregus, David S. Miall, Mark Verbitsky and Anna Tonkonogy. 'Locating Self-Modifying Feelings within Literary Reading'. *Discourse Processes* 38, no. 2 (2004): 267–86.
Kuiken, Don, Paul Campbell and Paul Sopcak. 'The Experiencing Questionnaire: Locating Exceptional Reading Moments'. *Scientific Study of Literature* 2, no. 2 (2012): 243–72.
Kvale, Steinar. 'The Psychoanalytic Interview as Qualitative Research'. *Qualitative Inquiry* 5, no. 1 (1999): 87–113.
Laertius, Diogenes. *The Lives and Opinions of Eminent Philosophers*, vol. 1, books 1–5. Loeb Classical Library No. 184, translated by R. D. Hicks. Cambridge, MA: Harvard University Press, 1925.

Langbaum, Robert. 'The Epiphanic Moment in Wordsworth and Modern Literature'. In *Moments of Moment: Aspects of the Literary Experience*, edited by Wim Tigges, 37–85. Atalanta, GA: Rodopi BV, 1999.
Lawrence, D. H. *The Letters of DH Lawrence*, vol. 2, June 1913–Oct. 1916, edited by George J. Zytaruk and James T. Boulton. Cambridge: Cambridge University Press, 1981.
Lawrence, D. H. *The Letters of D.H. Lawrence*, vol. 6, March 1927–Nov. 1928, edited by James T. Boulton and Margaret Boulton. Cambridge: Cambridge University Press, 1993.
Lawrence, D. H. *The Selected Letters of D.H. Lawrence*, edited by James T. Boulton. Cambridge: Cambridge University Press, 1996.
Lawrence, D. H. *Lady Chatterley's Lover*. Richmond: Alma Classics, 2015.
Lessing, Doris. *Shikasta*. London: HarperCollins, 2002.
Levin, Flora R. 'Synesis in Aristoxenian Theory'. *Transactions and Proceedings of the American Philological Association* 103 (1972): 211–34.
Long, Theodore E., and Jeffrey K. Hadden. 'Religious Conversion and the Concept of Socialization: Integrating the Brainwashing and Drift Models'. *Journal for the Scientific Study of Religion* 22, no. 1 (1983): 1–14.
Lutz, Catherine, and Geoffrey M. White. 'The Anthropology of Emotions'. *Annual Review of Anthropology* 15 (1986): 405–36.
Luyckx, Koen, Seth J. Schwartz, Michael D. Berzonsky, Bart Soenens, Maarten Vansteenkiste, Ilse Smits and Luc Goossens. 'Capturing Ruminative Exploration: Extending the Four-Dimensional Model of Identity Formation in Late Adolescence'. *Journal of Research in Personality* 42, no. 1. (2008): 58–82.
MacIntyre, Alasdair. *Whose Justice? Whose Rationality?* South Bend, IN: University of Notre Dame Press, 1988.
Mar, Raymond A., Keith Oatley, Maja Djikic and Justin Mullin. 'Emotion and Narrative Fiction: Interactive Influences before, during and after Reading'. *Cognition and Emotion* 25, no. 5 (2011): 818–33.
Marcel, Gabriel. *Creative Fidelity*, translated by Robert Rosthal. New York: Fordham University Press, 2002.
Marcel, Gabriel. *Homo Viator: An Introduction to a Metaphysics of Hope*. South Bend, IN: St Augustine Press, 2010.
Marcia, James E. 'Development and Validation of Ego Identity Status'. *Journal of Personality and Social Psychology* 3, no. 5 (1996): 551–58.
McAdams, Dan P. *The Art and Science of Personality Development*. New York: Guildford Press, 2016.
McAdams, Dan P. *The Redemptive Self: Stories Americans Live By*. Oxford: Oxford University Press, 2013.McAdams, Dan P., and Philip J. Bowman. 'Narrating Life's Turning Points: Redemption and Contamination'. In *Turns in the Road: Narrative Studies of Lives in Transition*, edited by Dan McAdams, Ruthellen Josselson and Amia Lieblich, xv. Washington, DC: American Psychological Association, 2001.
McAdams, Dan P., Ruthellen Josselson and Amia Lieblich, eds. *Turns in the Road: Narrative Studies of Lives in Transition*. Washington, DC: American Psychological Association, 2001.
McDonald, Matthew G. 'The Nature of Epiphanic Experience'. *Journal of Humanistic Psychology* 48, no. 1 (January 2008): 89–115. Doi: 10.1177/0022167807311878.
Méchoulan, Éric. 'Impacting the University: An Archeology of the Future', translated by Roxanne Lapidus. *SubStance* 42, no. 1 (2013): 7–27.
Menninghaus, Winfried, Valentin Wagner, Julian Hanich, Eugen Wassiliwizky, Milena Kuehnast and Thomas Jacobsen. 'Towards a Psychological Construct of Being Moved'. *PLOS One* 10, no. 6 (2015): e0128451.
Miall, David S. 'Beyond the Schema Given: Affective Comprehension of Literary Narratives'. *Cognition and Emotion* 3, no. 1 (1988): 55–78.

Miall, David S. 'Empirical Approaches to Studying Literary Readers'. *Book History* 9, no. 1 (2006): 291–311.
Miall, David S., and Don Kuiken. 'A Feeling for Fiction: Becoming What We Behold'. *Poetics* 30, no. 4 (2002): 221–41.
Miller, William R., and Janet C'de Baca. *Quantum Change: When Epiphanies and Sudden Insights Transform Ordinary Lives*. New York: Guilford Press, 2001.
Moos, Rudolf H., and Jeanne A. Schaefer. 'Life Transitions and Crises: A Conceptual Overview'. In *Coping with Life Crises: An Integrated Approach*, edited by Rudolf H. Moos, 3–28. New York: Plenum Press, 1986.
Moormann, Peter Paul, Bob Bermond, Harrie C. M. Vorst and Lea Rood. 'New Avenues in Alexithymia Research: The Creation of Alexithymia Types'. In *Emotion Regulation, Conceptual and Clinical Issues*, edited by Johan Denollet, Ivan Nyklicek and Ad Vingerhoerts, 27–42. New York: Springer, 2008.
Moran, Dermot. *Introduction to Phenomenology*. London: Routledge, 2000.
Moretti, Franco. 'Conjectures on World Literature'. *New Left Review* 1 (2000): 54–68.
Mukarovsky, Jan. *Structure, Sign and Function*, translated and edited by John Burbank and Peter Steiner. New Haven, CT: Yale University Press, 1977.
Myers, Kelly A. '*Metanoia* and the Transformation of Opportunity'. *Rhetoric Society Quarterly* 41, no. 1 (2011): 1–18.
Nagy, Gregory. *The Ancient Greek Hero in 24 Hours*. Cambridge, MA: Belknap Press of Harvard University Press, 2013.
Nell, Victor. *Lost in a Book: The Psychology of Reading for Pleasure*. New Haven, CT: Yale University Press, 1988.
Nemiah, J. C., H. Freyberger and P. E. Sifneos. 'Alexithymia: A View of the Psychosomatic Process'. In *Modern Trends in Psychosomatic Medicine*, vol. 3, edited by O. W. Hill, 430–39. London: Butterworths, 1976.
Nesse, Randolph M. 'Is Depression an Adaptation?'. *Archives of General Psychiatry* 57, no. 1 (2000): 14–20.
Nichols, Ashton. *The Poetics of Epiphany*. Tuscaloosa: University of Alabama Press, 1987.
Nichols, Stephen G. 'Introduction: Philology in a Manuscript Culture'. *Speculum* 65, no. 1 (1990): 1–10.
Nock, A. D. *Conversion: The Old and the New in Religion from Alexander the Great to Augustine of Hippo*. Baltimore, MD: Johns Hopkins University Press, 1998.
Nussbaum, Martha. *The Therapy of Desire: Theory and Practice in Hellenistic Ethics*. Princeton, NJ: Princeton University Press, 1994.
Nyborg, Karine. *Ikke rart det kommer kråker*. Oslo: Aschehoug, 2010.
O'Hara, Mary. *My Friend Flicka*. London: Eyre and Spottiswoode, 1972.
Oliphant, Mrs. *The Days of My Life*. New York: Jefferson, 2015.
Ovid. *Metamorphoses*, translated by David Raeburn. London: Penguin, 2004.
Paloutzian, Raymond F., James T. Richardson and Lewis R. Rambo. 'Religious Conversion and Personality Change'. *Journal of Personality* 67, no. 6 (1999): 1047–79.
Panksepp, Jaak. *Affective Neuroscience: The Foundations of Human and Animal Emotions*. New York: Oxford University Press, 1998.
Panksepp, Jaak, and Lucy Biven. *The Archeology of Mind: Neuroevolutionary Origins of Human Emotions*. New York: W.W. Norton, 2012.
Parker, Gordon. 'Is Depression Overdiagnosed?'. *British Medical Journal* 335, no. 7615 (2005): 328.
Peters, Gerald. *The Mutilating God: Authorship and Authority in the Narrative of Conversion*. Amherst: University of Massachusetts Press, 1993.
Petitmengin, Claire. 'Describing One's Subjective Experience in the Second Person: An Interview Method for the Science of Consciousness'. *Phenomenology and the Cognitive Sciences* 5, no. 3–4 (2006): 229–69. Doi: 10.1007/s11097-006-9022-2.

Pirsig, Robert. *Lila: An Inquiry into Morals*. Richmond, VA: Alma, 2011.
Plath, Sylvia. *The Bell Jar*. London: Faber and Faber, 2005.
Plato. *Phaedrus*, translated by Robin Waterfield. Oxford: Oxford University Press, 2002.
Plato. *The Republic*, translated by Tom Griffith. Cambridge: Cambridge University Press, 2000.
Polkinghorne, Donald E. 'Narrative Configuration in Qualitative Analysis'. *Qualitative Studies in Education* 8, no. 1 (1995): 5–23.
Pope, Alexander. *The Major Works*, edited by Pat Rogers. Oxford: Oxford University Press, 2006.
Prochaska, James O., and Carlo Di Clemente. 'Trans-Theoretical Therapy: Toward a More Integrative Model of Change'. *Psychotherapy Research & Practice* 19, no. 3 (1982): 276–88. Doi: 10.1037/hoD88437.
Radford, Colin, and Michael Weston. 'How Can We Be Moved by the Fate of Anna Karenina?'. *Proceedings of the Aristotelian Society* 49 (1975): 67–80.
Richards, I. A. *Practical Criticism: A Study of Literary Judgment*. London: Routledge & Kegan Paul, 1954.
Ricoeur, Paul: *Philosophical Anthropology*, translated by David Pellauer. Malden, MA: Polity Press, 2016.
Ricoeur, Paul. *Hermeneutics and the Human Sciences*, translated by John B. Thompson. Cambridge: Cambridge University Press, 1995.
Riessman, Catherine Kohler. *Narrative Methods for the Human Sciences*. Los Angeles, CA: Sage, 2008.
Robbins, Steven B., and Michael J. Patton. 'Self-Psychology and Career Development: Construction of the Superiority and Goal Instability Scales'. *Journal of Counseling Psychology* 32, no. 2 (1985): 221–31.
Robertson, Donald. *Stoicism and the Art of Happiness*. London: Hodder and Stoughton, 2013.
Robertson, Duncan. *The Medieval Experience of Reading*. Cistercian Studies Series, vol. 238. Collegeville, MN: Liturgical Press, 2011.
Robinson, Jenefer. *Deeper Than Reason: Emotion and Its Role in Literature, Music and Art*. Oxford: Clarendon Press, 2005.
Robinson, Oliver C. 'Sampling in Interview-Based Qualitative Research: A Theoretical and Practical Guide'. *Qualitative Research in Psychology* 11, no. 1 (2014): 25–41.
Rogers, Carl R. *A Way of Being*. Boston, MA: Houghton Mifflin, 1980.
Rogers, Mary Jo, and Grayson N. Holmbeck. 'Effects of Interparental Aggression on Children's Adjustment: The Moderating Role of Cognitive Appraisal and Coping'. *Journal of Family Psychology* 11, no. 1 (1997): 125–30.
Rosenblatt, Louise M. 'The Literary Transaction: Evocation and Response'. *Theory into Practice* 21, no. 1 (1982): 268–77.
Rosenblatt, Louise M. *Literature as Exploration*, 5th edn. New York: Modern Language Association of America, 1995.
Ross, Catherine Sheldrick. 'Finding without Seeking: The Information Encounter in the Context of Reading for Pleasure'. *Information Processing and Management* 35, no. 6 (1999): 783–99.
Samuel, Steven, and Salman Akhtar. 'The Identity Consolidation Inventory (ICI): Development and Application of a Questionnaire for Assessing the Structuralization of Individual Identity'. *American Journal of Psychoanalysis* 69, no. 1 (2009): 53–61.
Scherer, Klaus R. 'Which Emotions Can Be Induced by Music? What Are the Underlying Mechanisms? And How Can We Measure Them?'. *Journal of New Music Research* 33, no. 3 (2004): 239–51.
Schmalzl, Laura, Mardi A. Crane-Godreau and Peter Payne. 'Movement-Based Embodied Contemplative Practices: Definitions and Paradigms'. *Frontier in Human Neuroscience* 8, no. 205 (2014): 1–6.
Schulman, James L. 'Introduction'. In *The Travels and Adventures of Serendipity: A Study in Sociological Semantics and the Sociology of Science*, edited by Robert K. Merton and Elinor Barber. Princeton, NJ: Princeton University Press, 2004.

Schwartz, Seth J. 'The Evolution of Eriksonian and Neo-Eriksonian Identity Theory and Research: A Review and Integration'. *Identity* 1, no. 1 (2009): 7–58.
Sedikides, Constantine, Tim Wildschut, Jamie Arndt and Clay Routledge. 'Nostalgia: Past, Present and Future'. *Current Directions in Psychological Science* 17, no. 5 (2008): 304–307.
Shaver, Philip R., and Mario Mikulincer. 'Adult Attachment Strategies and the Regulation of Emotion'. In *Handbook of Emotion Regulation*, edited by J. J. Gross, 446–65. New York: Guilford Press, 2007.
Shields, David. *How Literature Saved My Life*. New York: Alfred A. Knopf, 2013.
Shiota, Michelle N., Dacher Keltner and Amanda Mossman. 'The Nature of Awe: Elicitors, Appraisals, and Effects on Self-Concept'. *Cognition and Emotion* 21, no. 5 (2007): 944–63.
Siegel, Daniel J. 'Emotion as Integration: A Possible Answer to the Question, What Is Emotion?' In *The Healing Power of Emotion: Affective Neuroscience, Development and Clinical Practice*, edited by Diana Fosha, Daniel J. Siegel and Marion Solomon, 145–71. New York: W.W. Norton, 2009.
Siegel, Daniel J. *The Mindful Brain: Reflection and Attunement in the Cultivation of Well-Being*. New York: W.W. Norton, 2007.
Sikora, Shelley, Don Kuiken and David S. Miall. 'Expressive Reading: A Phenomenological Study of Readers' Experience of Coleridge's *The Rime of the Ancient Mariner*'. *Psychology of Aesthetics, Creativity, and the Arts* 5, no. 3 (2011): 258–68.
Silvia, Paul J. 'Emotional Responses to Art: From Collation and Arousal to Cognition and Emotion'. *Review of General Psychology* 9, no. 4 (2005): 342–57.
Singer, Tania, and Claus Lamm. 'The Social Neuroscience of Empathy'. *Annals of the New York Academy of Sciences* 1156 (2009): 81–96.
Sipiora, Phillip. 'Introduction: The Ancient Concept of Kairos'. In *Rhetoric and Kairos: Essays in History, Theory and Praxis*, edited by Philip Sipiora and James S. Baumlin, 1–22. Albany: State University of New York Press, 2002.
Skalski, Jon E., and Sam A. Hardy. 'Disintegration, New Consciousness, and Discontinuous Transformation: A Qualitative Investigation of Quantum Change'. *Humanistic Psychologist* 41, no. 2 (2013): 159–77.
Smith, John E. 'Time and Qualitative Time'. In *Rhetoric and Kairos: Essays in History, Theory and Praxis*, edited by Philip Sipiora and James S. Baumlin, 46–57. Albany: State University of New York Press, 2002.
Snow, David A., and Richard Machalek. 'The Sociology of Conversion'. *Annual Review of Sociology* 10 (1984): 167–90.
Solomon, Marion F. 'Emotions in Romantic Partners'. In *The Healing Power of Emotion: Affective Neuroscience, Development and Clinical Practice*, edited by Diana Fosha, Daniel J. Siegel and Marion F. Solomon, 232–56. New York: W.W. Norton, 2009.
Solomon, Robert C. *Passions: Emotions and the Meaning of Life*, 2nd edn. Indianapolis, IN: Hackett, 1993.
Stafford, William. *The Way It Is: New and Selected Poems*. Minneapolis, MN: Graywolf Press, 1998.
Stern, Daniel N. *The Interpersonal World of the Human Infant: A View from Psychoanalysis and Developmental Psychology*. New York: Basic Books, 1985.
Stern, Daniel N. *The First Relationship: Infant and Mother*. Cambridge, MA: Harvard University Press, 2002.
Stern, Daniel N. *The Present Moment in Psychotherapy and Everyday Life*. New York: W.W. Norton, 2004.
Stern, Daniel N. *Forms of Vitality: Exploring Dynamic Experience in Psychology and the Arts*. Oxford: Oxford University Press, 2010.
Stuart, Susan. 'Enkinaesthesia: The Essential Sensuous Background for Co-Agency'. In *Knowing without Thinking: Mind, Action, Cognition and the Phenomenon of the Background*, edited by Zdravko Radman, 167–86. Basingstoke: Palgrave Macmillan, 2012.
Sullivan, Shirley Darcus. *Psychological Activity in Homer: A Study of Phren*. Ottawa: Carleton University Press, 1988.
Swatton, Susan, and Jean O'Callaghan. 'The Experience of "Healing Stories" in the Life Narrative: A Grounded Theory'. *Counselling Psychology Quarterly* 12, no. 4 (1997): 413–29.

Sweeney, Terence. 'Against Ideology: Gabriel Marcel's Philosophy of Vocation'. *Logos: A Journal of Catholic Thought and Culture* 16, no. 4 (2013): 179–203.
Taylor, Graeme J., R. Michael Bagby and James D. A. Parker. *Disorders of Affect Regulations: Alexithymia in Medical and Psychiatric Illness*. Cambridge: Cambridge University Press, 1997.
Thomae, Hans. 'The Nomothetic-Idiographic Issue: Some Roots and Rrecent Trends'. *International Journal of Group Tensions* 28, no. 1 (1999): 187–215.
Tigges, Wim. 'The Significance of Trivial Things: Towards a Typology of Literary Epiphanies'. In *Moments of Moment: Aspects of the Literary Experience*, edited by Wim Tigges, 11–35. Atalanta, GA: Rodopi BV, 1999.
Todd, Robert T. 'Introduction'. In *Themistius: On Aristotle's Physics 5–8. Ancient Commentators on Aristotle*, edited by Richard Sorabji, translated by Robert T. Todd, 1–10. Bloomsbury: London, 2008.
Tooby, John, and Leda Cosmides. 'The Past Explains the Present: Emotional Adaptations and the Structure of Ancestral Environments'. *Ethology and Sociobiology* 11, no. 4–5 (1990): 375–424.
Torrance, Alan J. 'Auditus Fidei: Where and How Does God Speak? Faith, Reason and the Question of Criteria'. In *Reason and the Reasons of Faith*, edited by Paul J. Griffiths and Reinhard Hütter, 27–52. New York: T &T Clark, 2005.
Trevarthen, Colwyn, and Kenneth J. Aitken. 'Infant Intersubjectivity: Research, Theory, and Clinical Applications'. *Journal of Child Psychology and Psychiatry* 42, no. 1 (2001): 3–48.
Tyson, Lois. *Critical Theory Today: A User Friendly Guide*. New York: Routledge, 2006.
Usherwood, Bob, and Jackie Toyne. 'The Value and Impact of Reading Imaginative Literature'. *Journal of Librarianship and Information Science* 34, no. 1 (2002): 33–41.
Van Deurzen, Emmy. 'Existential Therapy'. In *Handbook of Individual Therapy*, edited by Windy Dryden, 179–208. London: Sage, 2002.
Vattimo, Gianni. *Art's Claim to Truth*, translated by Luca D'Isanto. New York: Columbia University Press, 2008.
Vessel, Edward A., G. Gabrielle Starr and Nava Rubin. 'The Brain on Art: Intense Aesthetic Experience Activates the Default Mode Network'. *Frontiers in Human Neuroscience* 6 (2012): 1–17. Doi: 10.3389/fnhum.2012.00066.
Vessel, Edward A., G. Gabrielle Starr and Nava Rubin. 'Art Reaches within: Aesthetic Experience, the Self and the Default Mode Network'. *Frontiers in Neuroscience* 7, no. 258 (2013): 1–9. Doi: 10.3389/fnins.2013.00258.
Vischer Bruns, Christina. *Why Literature? The Value of Literary Reading and What It Means for Teaching*. London: Continuum, 2011.
Walton, Kendall. 'Spelunking, Simulation and Slime: On Being Moved by Fiction'. In *Emotion and the Arts*, edited by M. Hjort and S. Laver, 37–49. Oxford: Oxford University Press, 1997.
Waterman, Alan S. 'Personal Expressiveness: Philosophical and Psychological Foundations'. *Journal of Mind and Behavior* 11, no. 1 (1990): 47–74.
Wells, Adrian. *Metacognitive Therapy for Anxiety and Depression*. New York: Guilford Press, 2009.
Wengraff, Tom. *Qualitative Research Interviewing: Biographic Narrative and Semi-Structured Methods*. London: Sage, 2001.
White, William L. 'Transformational Change: A Historical Review'. *Journal of Clinical Psychology/In Session* 60, no. 5 (2004): 461–70.
Whiteford, Harvey A., Louisa Degenhardt, Jürgen Rehm, Amanda J. Baxter, Alice J. Ferrari, Holly E. Erskine, Fiona J. Charlson, Rosana E. Norman, Abraham D. Flaxman, Nicole Johns, Roy Burstein, Cristopher J. L. Murray and Theo Vos. 'Global Burden of Disease Attributable to Mental and Substance Use Disorders: Findings from the Global Burden of Disease Study 2010'. *Lancet* 382, no. 9904 (2013): 1575–86.
Whiteford, Harvey A., M. G. Harris, G. McKeon, A. Baxter, C. Pennell, J. J. Barendregt and J. Want. 'Estimating Remission from Untreated Major Depression: A Systematic Review and Meta-Analysis'. *Psychological Medicine*, 43 (2013): 1569–85.
Wild, T. Cameron, Don Kuiken and Don Schopflocher. 'The Role of Absorption in Experiential Involvement'. *Journal of Personality and Social Psychology* 65, no. 3 (1995): 569–79.

Winterson, Jeanette. *Why Be Happy When You Could Be Normal?* London: Vintage, 2011.
Zhou, Xinyue, Constantine Sedikides, Tim Wildschut and Ding-Guo Gao. 'Counteracting Loneliness. On the Restorative Function of Nostalgia'. *Psychological Science* 19, no. 10 (2008): 1023–29.
Zimmerman, Mark, Joseph B. McGlinchey, Michael A. Posternak, Michael Friedman, Naureen Attiullah and Daniela Boerescu. 'How Should Remission from Depression Be Defined? The Depressed Patient's Perspective'. *American Journal of Psychiatry* 163, no .1 (2006): 148–50.

INDEX

absorption trait 6
accommodation 154–55, 158
active listening 26
adaptive appraisal 116
admiration 4, 155
Aemilianus, Scipio 154
Aesop's fable 129
aesthetic emotions 15, 201
aesthetic mode of engagement in reading 3
affect attunement 184
affect-consciousness 191, 208
affections 201, *See also* being moved; emotions
affective configurations 203–5
  and pathemata 206–7
affective neuroscience 180, 185
affective schemas 51
afterthought 147, 158
Aitken, Kenneth J. 126
Akhtar, Salman 84
alexithymia 198
algos 97–99
alloiosis 11, 202
  crises 203
Allport, Gordon 35, 149
Amir, Nadir 175
anabasis 158
anagnorisis 120–23, 202
anamnesis 158, 187, 202
anamorphosis 65
anger 62, 203
  and compassion 119, 123
Angus, Lynne E. 32
De Anima (Aristotle) 11
anteroductive logic of inquiry 17–19
apex moments 7
archaic needs 90, 94
Aristotle 7, 11, 200, 206
Aristoxenus 185
art
  and emotions 15
  for heart's sake 207–8

ontological legitimation of 2
truth of 2
"as if" experience 151–52, 157
ascription variation 33
Ashbery, John 151
attachment theory 51, 125, 203
attunement ix, 180, 194
authenticity 84
autobiographical reasoning 32
awareness 60–62
awe emotion 154–55, 201

Baker, Martin 176
Baldwin, Matthew 96
Balint, Michael 25
basic emotions theory 203, 205
Batcho, Krystine 97
Beach, Stephen R.H. 175
being changed 11
being moved 11, 13–15, 180, 191, 193, 198–99, 206, 208
  and paradox of fiction 199–202
Bennett, Arnold 121
Berman, Steven L. 86
Beyers, Wim 86
bibliotherapy 1
bi-directional empathy 193, 199
Bidney, Martin 189
Biographia Literaria 179
biographic-narrative interview method 27–29
Bishop, Sue M. 116
Bjørneboe, Jens 115n2
bodily-affects 120, 126, 150, 192, 196
bodily-aspects 59
body awareness therapy 177
Bonifazi, Anna 97
Booker, Cristopher 124
Bowman, Philip J. 17
Boym, Svetlana 96
brainwashing model 88
Bryman, Alan 36

Buber, Martin 189
Buried Life, The 161, 174, 189n36, *See also* Sue's story

Caplan, Gerald 12, 13n66
care system 203
Carlsson, Johanna 86
Carroll, William 124
Caswell, Caroline P. 62, 63
catabasis. *See* katabasis
categorical emotions 203
catharsis 4, 7, 205, 206
causal relationship 127
Cavanaugh 96
Cave, Terence 195
change 10–11, 200
   conceptualisations of process 11
   dispositional traits 10–11
   and meaning 11, 18
   and motivation 11
   meaning, and change 11
Chapman, George 62
characteristic adaptations 11
Chaucer 128
children's coping 116
Cicero 154
Clark, Raymond J. 92
Claspell, Emily 203–5
Cochran, Larry 203–5
coercion model 88
coherence variation 33
Colaizzi, Paul F. 9, 34
Coleridge 179
Colwyn, Trevarthe 126
comedy 4, 124–26, 129
comic katharsis 124–26
commitment 85, 86
   reconsideration of 86
commitment to action 51
compassion 4, 55, 193, 208, *See also* self-compassion
   and anger 119, 123
concentration variation 33
confusion 116
conjunctive faith 148, 149, 156
connectedness 90
connection 55–56
conscious knowledge 145
consistent attitudes and behaviour 84
contact field, of engagement mode 194–95
contemplative dyad 185
coping strategy 116

core affective schemas 51
core state 202
courage 198
Cova, Florian 13
Cratyllus 185
credo 198
crises 12–13, 191, 198, 202, 203, 205
crisis-catalyst-resolution 205
crisis-poeisis-resolution 205
crisis-surrender-redemption 10
critical angry blaming 117
critical selection of the narratives 17
crystallised felt sense 199
crystallising moment 61, 65
cultural crisis 13
cultures 203

Danielsson, Louise 177
data production, reliability of 19–20
Davis, Philip 5, 147, 208
Deonna, Julien A. 13
depression 173–74, 175
developmental crisis 13
developmental psychology 185
Di Clemente, James O. 51
digestion of truth 192
disdain and wonder 187–88
disequilibrium 85
disorganisation 85
dispositional traits 10–11
Dixon, Thomas 14
Djikic, Maja 11
double metamorphosis 119
dramaturgical approach 203–5
dyadic contemplation 185

Ecker, Bruce 199
efferent mode of engagement in reading 3
EFT. *See* emotion-focused therapy (EFT)
einfühlung 193, 201
Ekman, Paul 203, 205
ekpleksis 154–55, 199
ekplektic 155
elevation 155
Eliot, George 13, 150, 152, 156, 158
emotion
   and being moved 14
emotional brain 199
emotional movements 200
emotion-focused therapy 129
emotion-focused therapy (EFT) 125, 127, 129
emotions 201, 203, 206

INDEX

aesthetic emotions 15
  and art 15
  fear 51
  pure form of 203
  universality 203
empathy 25, 26, 58, 126, 185, 201, 208
  bi-directional 193, 199
  einfühlung 193, 201
empty stories 32
engagement, mode of 192
  bi-directional empathy 193, 199
  contact and nourishment 194–95
  lexithymia 197–98
  readerese 192–93
  reading as necessity 194–95
  sacred space 195–97
enkinaesthesia 61–62, 192, 194, 196
epiphany 120, 188–89
Episode 101, 118, 119, 121, 122, 124, 128, 130, 197, *See also* Esther's story
episode-emotion-adaptation 205
episodes 205
epistrophe 160
Erikson, Erik H. 84, 85
essence(s) 18
  of religious experience 10
Esther's story 101–14
  crisis
    Bjørneboe versus Børlie 114–15
    consequences of inter-parental conflict 116–18
  resolution
    language of emotions, quest for 129–30
  transaction
    comic katharsis 124–26
    metamorphosis 118–19
    readerese 126
    reading experience 127–28
    revelation (anagnorisis) 120–23
ethos 206
existential crisis 13
exploration 85
expressive enactment 5–9, 192

faith 148–49
  and belief, distinction between 156
Falconer, Rachel 92
false self 84, 91, 94
fear 116
fear system 203
feeling and knowing 150
feeling felt 192

feelings felt 192
Felski, Rita 4n15
felt sense of awareness 7, 60–62, 192, 200
Ferguson 196
fertility tradition, katabasis narratives 92
Feuerbach 158
fiction 2
  paradox of 199–202
  virtue of 2
Finlay, Edward J. 158
Fitzgerald 62
Fletcher, Judith 92
Fonagy, Peter 194
forsakenness 118, 123
Fosha, Diane 201–2
Fowler, James W. 148, 156
Frye, Northrop 54, 124, 129
Fuchs, Thomas 176, 179, 184, 185, 200

Gadamer, Hans-Georg 2, 18
Gallese, Vittorio 126
Gendlin, E. T. 7, 60
genesis 11
Genette, Gerard 206–7
Gilliland, Burl E. 13n66
Goleman 51
Gottman, John 117
Greenberg, Leslie S. 32, 51, 129, 203
grief system 203
Gross, Daniel 201
Guardian, The 2
guilt 116

Hadden, Jeffery K. 88
Hadden, Jeffrey K. 88
Hadot, Pierre 154, 158
Haidt, Jonathan 154–55
Heidegger, Martin 21, 201
Hendry, Irene 120
Hepper, Erika G. 96
hermeneutic arc 18–19, 192
hermeneutic-phenomenological approach 18
hermeneutics 18
  and logic of inquiry 18
  double filiation 18
hero, identification with 4
hiemenos 99
Holdaway, Gervase 149
Holmbeck, Grayson N. 116
homecoming 99
hora 64
huh! expression 150

human soul 62–63
hunger for reading 192
Husserl 18
hybrid engagement 7
hypsos 206

ideal reader 3
idealisation 90
idealist ontology 18
identity
  achievement ix, 84, 85, 92
  confusion 124
  consolidation 84
  development 84, 85
  diffusion ix, 84, 85, 86, 87–88
  distress 86
  foreclosure ix, 85, 86, 99
    and diffusion 87–88
  formation 85
  statuses 85, 86
idiographic interpretations 17, 34, 35–36
imagination, faith as a form of 148
individuative-reflective faith 148, 149
infant-elicited social behaviour 126
infants
  attachment system 51
  self-organisation system 51
Ingersoll, Gary M. 116
inner dreamer 84
inner self 158
inquiry, anteroductive logic of 17–19
integrated memory variation 33
intellectual and emotional belief, distinction between 152
interaction modes 4
interaction patterns 55
interaffectivity 176, 179
intercorporeality 179
interestedness 14
interoceptive activity 192
inter-parental conflict 116–18
intersubjectivity 180
intimate reading 207
  critical selection of narratives for interpretation 31–32
  idiographic interpretations 35–36
  interview method 25–29
    biographic-narrative interview 27–29
    shared reading of significant passages 29
  life-changing fiction reading experience, construct of 33–34
  narrative structure analysis 34–35

narratives presentation 30
philology 30
recruitment strategy 22–25
reliability 19–20
sampling 21–22
validity 20–21
intimation 25
ironic mode of identification with hero 4
irony comedy 124

James, Richard K. 13n66
James, William 10, 152, 157
Jane's story 131–45
  crisis
    framework metaphor 147–49
    hunger metaphor 147–49
    kairos and *metanoid* 145–47
  resolution
    purpose of life 157–60
    spiritual transformation 156–57
  transaction
    "as if" experience 151–52
    ekpleksis and awe 154–55
    feeling and knowing 150
    hunger for reading 149–50
    metaphorical thinking 151–52
    shocking recognition of frightening truth 153–54
Jauss, Hans Robert 4, 55, 56
Johnson, Susan 117–18, 125

kairos 145–47
kalypsis 99
Kant, Immanuel 155
katabasis 92, 158
katharsis 206
Keating, Thomas 149
Keltner, Dacher 154–55
kinesis 200
Kneisl, Carol R. 13
knowing together 185, 192
Koch, Sabine C. 176
Kochs 200
Kohlberg 148
Kohut, Heinz 90, 94
Koziak, Barbara 62
Kroger, Jane 85
Kuiken, Don 5, 6, 7, 15, 56, 155, 188, 192, 200

Lady Chatterley's Lover 37, 40, 54, 58, 65, *See also* Veronica's story
Laertius, Diogenes 57

INDEX

Landau, Mark J. 96
Langhof, Wolfgang 115n2
Laws 145
Lazarus 15
Lectio Divina 149, 196, 197
Levi, Doro 146
Levin, Flora 185
life-changing reading experiences 3, 6, 17, 21, 22, 31, 34, 191
  construct of 33–34
  series of transformation 17
listening to the heart 202
lived experiences 203
logos 206
Logos 1
Long, Theodore E. 88
Longbaum, Robert 120
love of the book, variation 34
Luyckx, Koyen 86

Machalek, Richard 88
Mansfield, Katherine 7
manuscript 30
Mar, Raymond 8
Marcel, Gabriel 159–60
Marcia, James E. 85
marital relationships, negative future trajectories of 117
Marxist-feminism 145
McAdams, Dan 10, 11, 17
McDonald, Matthew G. 120
McIntyre, Alasdair 62
meaning, and change 18
Méchoulan, Eric 179
megalopsychia 154
Menninghaus, Winfried 13–14
Merton, Robert 65
metaballein 155, 156
metabole 12, 200
metabolic reading 154, 192, 195
metacognition 58, 61
Metamorphoses 119
metamorphosis 118–19, 124, 126, 130
metanoia 158, 160, 202
metaphoric self-implication 7, 56
metaphorical thinking 151–52
Miall, David 4, 5, 6, 7, 15
Midsummer Night's Dream, A 124
Mikulincer, Mario 118
Miller, Carolyn R. 146
mimesis 206
mmm expression 150

model reader 3
Moos, Rudolf H. 12–13
moratorium ix, 85, 86, 91–94
Mossman, Amanda 155
motherese 126, 126n28
motivation 11
Mukarovsky, Jan 2–3
My Friend Flicka 67, 91, 95, *See also* Nina's story
Myers, Kelly R. 146, 158, 159
mythos 54

Nagy, Gregory 63, 64
narrative analysis 34–35
narratives presentation 30
necessity, rule of 157
Nemiah, J. C. 198
neologism 'intimant' 25
Nesse, Randolph M. 175
Nichols, Stephen 30, 189
Nina's story 67–83
  crisis
    conversion and apostasy 87–88
    source of strength, sacrifice of 89–90
    struggle 83–86
  MySpace (homecoming) 99
  resolution
    nostos and *algos* 96–99
  transformation
    moratorium 91–94
    transmuting internalisation 94–96
Nock, A. D. 157
nostalgia 96–99
nostos 97–99, 202
nourishment field, of engagement mode 194–95
Nussbaum, Martha 1–2

O'Callaghan, Jean 9
Odyssey, The 93, 97, 122, 185
Of the Affects 187
oikalgia 99
onomatopoetica 152
Ovid 119

palilexia ix, 95, 96, 192, 197
palilogia 95
palintropos 95
Paloutzian, Raymond F. 90
Panksepp, Jaak 51, 203, 205
parental conflict 115, 116–18
Parker, Gordon 175

particular incident narratives (PINs),
    pushing for 27
passion 195
pathemata 206–7
pathos 206
Patten, Michael J. 90
Peat Bog Soldiers, The 115n2
pendulum movement 56, 58
perfectionism 94
peripeteia 123, 129
personal crisis impact 6
Peters, Gerald 157
Petitmengin, Claire 26, 27
Phaedrus 62n24
phenomenological intercorporeality 185
phenomenology 18
philology 18, 30
Philosophy of As If 152
phthora 12
Piaget, Jean 148, 158
pisteis 206
Plato 62–63, 62n24, 145, 185
play system 203
pleasure-readers 8
Poetics 206
poetry, as a medicine for the soul 1
Polkinghorne, Donald E. 30
Pope, Alexander 62
Practical Criticism 152
praxis 206
presuppositions 10
    being moved 13–15
    change 10–11
    crisis 12–13
problematic beliefs 116, 128
Prochaska, Carlo 51
progressive modes of reading 5
progressive movement of interaction 61
progressive versus regressive encounters 4
proximity variation 33
psychological coercion 89
psychological crisis 13
psychosocial development
    model 84, 85

Radford's Puzzle 199
Radway, Janice 3
rage system 203
Reader Organisation, The 1
reader response theory 3
readerese 126, 192–93, 208
reader-response criticism 3

reading 58
    by heart x, 195, 197–98
    of heart 197–98
    as an intimate experience 195
    as necessity 194–95
    for pleasure 64
reception studies 4
reconciliation 123
redemption 10
redemption sequence 17
regressive development 85
regressive movement patterns 86
regressive versus progressive encounters 4
reliability 19–20
remembrance 186–87
remission 176–77
Republic, the 62n24
Republic, The 154
research design overview 21
resolution variation 33
resolutions 202
resonance 185, 194, 199
revelation 120–23, 199
Richards, I. A. 152
Ricoeur, Paul 2, 18
Riessman, Catherine Kohler 26, 35
rigidification 85
Riley, E. 13
Robbins, Steven B. 90
Robertson, Duncan 197
Robinson, Jenefer 15, 15n77
Robinson, Oliver C. 21
Rogers, Carl 27
Rogers, Mary Jo 116
romantic comedy 124
Rosberg, Susanne 177
Rosenblatt, Louise 3
Ross, Catherine 8–9, 200
rumination 86, 88

sacred space, and engagement mode 194, 195–97
sampling in interview-based qualitative
    research 21–22
Samuel, Steven 84
satire 124
Schaefer, Jeanne A. 12–13
Scherer, Klaus R. 15
Schleiermacher 18
Schmalzl, Laura 185
Schulmann, James L. 64
Schwartz, Seth J. 86
second transformation 119

Sedikides, Constantine 96
seekers 90
seeking system 203
self 32
  as a mental-affective system 90
self-analysis 184
self-cohesion 90
self-compassion 58, 59, 65, 201, 208
  through discovery of compassion for fictional character 56–59
self-efficacy 51, 53
self-empathy 57, 201
self-implication 7, 200
self-modifying feelings 5–9
self-relevance 200
self-surrender 10
self-understanding 2
serendipity 64
sexuality 54
Shakespeare, William 124
shared reading ix, 1, 25, 29, 34, 158, 181
Shaver, Philip R. 118
Shikasta 131, 145, 147, 149, 150, 151, 155, 158, 160, 189, 192, *See also* Jane's story
Shiota, Michelle N. 155
Siegel, Daniel 185, 203
Sikora, Shelley 5, 7
Silence, The 115n2
Silvia, Paul J. 15
simile self-implication 7
single question aimed at inducing narrative (SQUIN) 27, 29
Sipiora, Philip 146
situational crisis 13
Smith, John E. 145
Snow, David A. 88
social drift model 88
social support 116
Solomon, Marion 119
Solomon, Robert 14
Spinoza, Benedict de 155, 187–88
spiritual crisis 147
spiritual help 10
spiritual transformation 156–57
stable body image 84
Stafford, William 189n36
Stern, Daniel x, 51, 126, 184, 185
stoics 154
Stuart, Susan 61–62
Study of Thumos in Early Greek Epic, A 62
subjective self-sameness 84
sublime 205

sublime disquietude 155
sublime enthrallment 188
sublime feeling 7
subordination 153
subservation 17, 25
Sue's story 161–73
  crisis
    depression 173–74
    despair and despondency 175–76
    remission 176–77
  resolution
    disdain to wonder transition 187–88
    epiphany 188–89
    remembrance 186–87
  transaction
    breakthrough moment 181–85
    impact 178–81
    synthesis, knowing together 185
Sullivan, Shirley 63
Swatton, Susan 9
Sweeney, Terence 159
symballein 55
sympathetic mode of identification with hero 4
synesis 192, 197
synthesis 185
synthetic-conventional faith 148

tacit knowing 145
temporal continuity 84
tenderness 201, 202
text production 17
text-interpretation and self-interpretation, reciprocity of 4
Therapy of Desire, The 1–2
Thinking with Literature 195
thumos 62–63, 66, 198
Tigges, Wim 189
Todd, Robert 11
Tolstoy, Leo 149
Tomkins 197
Torrance, Alan J. 158
tragedy 206
transformation versus conversion 10
transformative reading 2
  potential for 3
transmuting internalisation 94–96, 199
Troilus and Criseyde 128
Truth and Method 2

Unbearable Lightness of Being, The 37
unconventional religious groups, reasons for people joining 88

unfinished story 32
universal life-crises 207
University of Liverpool 2
untold story 32

Vaihinger 152
validity 20–21
  external validity 20
Varieties of Religious Experience 10
vastness 154–55
Veronica's story 37–51
  bodily aspects of reading 59
  crisis
    admitting and solving problem 51–53
    the bruise 53–54
  resolution
    mother perspective 65–66
    thumos 62–63
    timing 64
  transaction
    connection 55–56
    felt sense 60–62
    self-compassion through discovery of compassion for fictional character 56–59
Vessel, Edward A. 193, 200

"view from above" 154, 199
visceral 194
Vischer Bruns, Christina 56
visionary realism 152, 158
vocation 159–60
vulnerability 123

Walpole, Horace 64, 65n36
Waterman, Alan S. 85, 86
Way It Is, The 189n36
Wells, Adrian 88
Wengraffm Tom 27–28
Whiteford, Harvey A. 176
Why be Happy When You Could Be Normal? 1
Will to Believe 152
Windelband, Wilhelm 35
Winter's Tale, The 58, 65, 66
Winterson, Jeanette 1
wisdom tradition, katabasis narratives 92
wonder 199, 201
wonder and disdain 187–88
Wordsworth, William 147
worldview conflict, and parental conflict 115
wow expression 150

Zimmerman, Mark 176